BODY

BODY

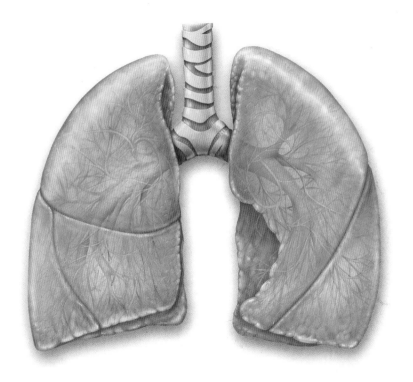

Authors
John Farndon
Nicki Lampon (Tiger Media)

First published in 2010 by Miles Kelly Publishing Ltd
Harding's Barn, Bardfield End Green, Thaxted, Essex, CM6 3PX, UK

2 4 6 8 10 9 7 5 3 1

Editorial Director Belinda Gallagher
Art Director Jo Brewer
Managing Editor Rosie McGuire
Assistant Editor Claire Philip
Cover Designer Simon Lee
Volume Designer Martin Lampon (Tiger Media)
Junior Designer Kayleigh Allen
Image Manager Liberty Newton
Indexer Indexing Specialists (UK) Ltd
Production Manager Elizabeth Collins
Reprographics Anthony Cambray, Stephan Davis,
Jennifer Hunt, Ian Paulyn

ISBN 978-1-84810-301-6

Printed in China

British Library Cataloguing-in-Publication Data
A catalogue record for this book is available from the British Library

Made with paper from a sustainable forest

www.mileskelly.net
info@mileskelly.net

www.factsforprojects.com

Self-publish your
children's book

buddingpress.co.uk

Contents

Body structure

Musculoskeletal system

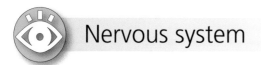

Nervous system

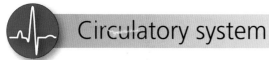

Circulatory system

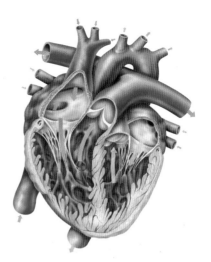

Immune system

Respiratory system

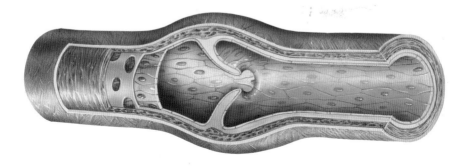

Digestive and urinary systems

Hormones and metabolism

Health and disease

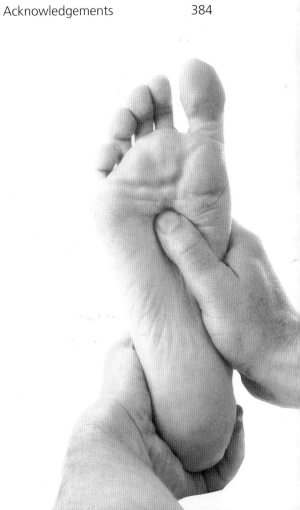

Body structure

The human body

There are nearly seven billion people in the world and we are all different.

The human body is a fascinating and complicated structure made up of millions of cells that all work together.

These cells combine to make tissues. Two or more tissues combine to make organs and several organs combine to make body systems.

These systems are all controlled by complicated interactions of signals and chemicals passing around the body.

Hair colour can vary dramatically

Some people need glasses to see clearly

Just over 50 percent of the population is female

Humans are different from all other animals and have adapted to live all around the world.

We are the only animals to walk upright, allowing us to use our hands for many things.

We have very developed brains and can work out problems, communicate in many ways and enjoy cultural activities, such as music and art.

We love and hate, laugh and cry. We are capable of many emotions and are constantly exploring the world around us.

Our bodies come in all shapes and sizes. One of the world's tallest men is 2.36 m tall, while one contender for the title of world's shortest man is currently only 50.8 cm tall.

We all have an individual skin colour

We can be tall or short, fat or thin

◄ *Human beings are all individual. Apart from identical twins, no two people are alike.*

13

Body systems

- **Your body systems** are interlinked – each has its own task, but they are all dependent on one another.

- **The skeleton** supports the body, protects major organs, and provides an anchor for the muscles.

- **The nervous system** is the brain and the nerves – the body's control and communications network.

- **The digestive system** breaks down food into chemicals that the body can use to its advantage.

- **The immune system** is the body's defence against germs. It includes white blood cells, antibodies and the lymphatic system.

- **Water balance** inside the body is controlled by the urinary system. This removes extra water as urine and gets rid of impurities in the blood.

- **The respiratory system** takes air into the lungs to supply oxygen, and lets out waste carbon dioxide.

- **The reproductive system** is the smallest of all the systems. It is basically the sexual organs that enable people to have children. It is the only system that is different in men and women.

- **Other body systems** include the hormonal system (controls growth and internal co-ordination by chemical hormones), integumentary system (skin, hair and nails), and the sensory system (eyes, ears, nose, tongue, skin, balance).

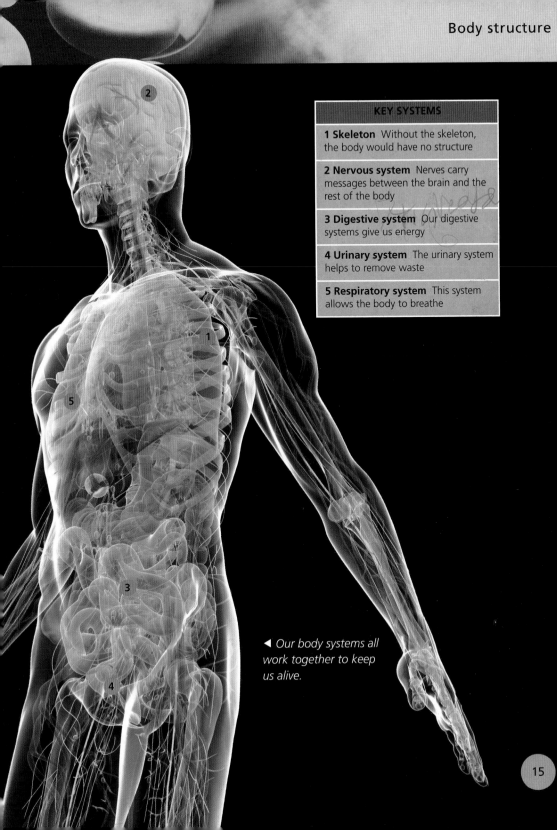

KEY SYSTEMS

1 Skeleton Without the skeleton, the body would have no structure

2 Nervous system Nerves carry messages between the brain and the rest of the body

3 Digestive system Our digestive systems give us energy

4 Urinary system The urinary system helps to remove waste

5 Respiratory system This system allows the body to breathe

◀ *Our body systems all work together to keep us alive.*

Anatomy

- **Anatomy is the study** of the structure of the human body.

- **Comparative anatomy** compares the structure of our bodies to those of animals' bodies.

- **The first great anatomist** was the ancient Roman physician, Galen (AD 129–199).

- **The first great book** of anatomy was written in 1543 by the Flemish scientist Andreas Vesalius (1514–1564). It is called *De Humani Corporis Fabrica* ('On the Fabric of the Human Body.')

- **In order to describe** the location of body parts, anatomists divide the body into quarters.

▶ *Much of our basic knowledge of human anatomy comes from the anatomists of the 16th and 17th centuries, who meticulously cut up corpses and then accurately drew what they saw.*

Fig. 20

- 🤚 **The anatomical position** is the way the body is positioned to describe anatomical terms – upright, with the arms hanging down by the sides, and the eyes, palms and toes facing forwards.

- 🤚 **The central coronal plane** divides the body into front and back halves. Coronal planes are any slice across the body from side to side, parallel to the central coronal plane.

- 🤚 **The ventral** or anterior is the front half of the body.

- 🤚 **The dorsal** or posterior is the back half of the body.

- 🤚 **Every part** of the body has a Latin name, but anatomists use a simple English name if there is one.

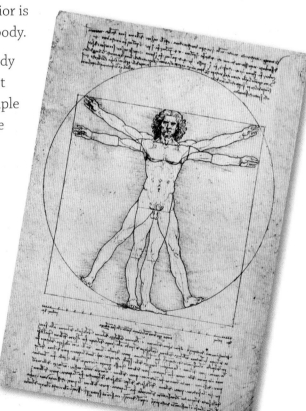

▶ *This drawing by Leonardo da Vinci is called* Vitruvian Man *and shows a man of perfect proportions.*

17

Tissues

A tissue is a body substance made from many of the same type of cell. Muscle cells make muscle tissue, nerve cells form nerve tissue, and so on.

As well as cells, some tissues include other materials.

Connective tissues are made from particular cells (such as fibroblasts), plus two other materials – long fibres of protein (such as collagen) and a matrix. Matrix is a material in which the cells and fibres are set like the currants in a bun.

Connective tissue holds all the other kinds of tissue together in various ways. The adipose tissue that makes fat, tendons and cartilage is connective tissue.

Bone and blood are both connective tissues.

▼ *Lungs are largely made from special lung tissues, but the mucous membrane that lines the airways is epithelial tissue.*

Lungs

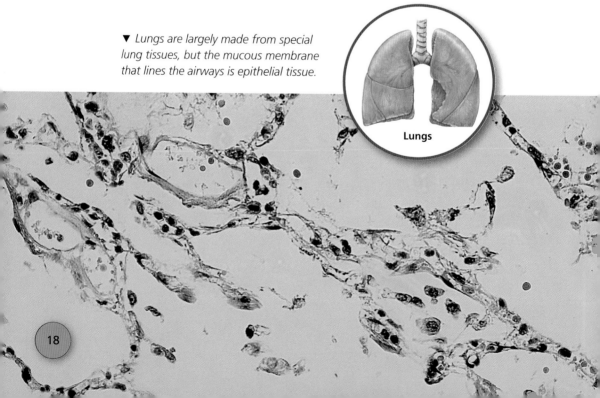

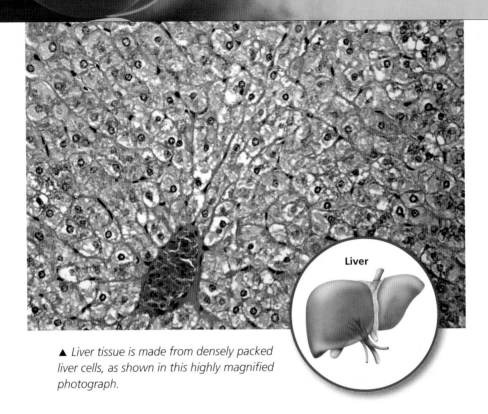

Liver

▲ *Liver tissue is made from densely packed liver cells, as shown in this highly magnified photograph.*

- **Epithelial tissue** is good lining or covering material, making skin and other parts of the body.

- **Epithelial tissue** may combine three kinds of cell to make a thin waterproof layer – squamous (flat), cuboid (box-like) and columnar (pillar-like) cells.

- **Nerve tissue** is made mostly from neurons (nerve cells), plus the Schwann cells that coat them.

- **The heart** is made mostly of muscle tissue, but also includes epithelial and connective tissue.

DID YOU KNOW?

Your body is entirely made up of tissues and fluid.

19

Organs

- **Organs are made** from combinations of tissues.

- **A collection** of related organs form a body system.

- **Body organs** include the brain, heart, lungs, kidneys and digestive organs. These all work together to keep the body functioning.

- **The largest organ** is the skin, which covers the whole body.

- **The smallest organ** is the pineal gland, a tiny organ in the brain that produces a substance that affects sleep.

- **The brain** controls the functions of many of the other body organs, making sure we keep breathing and our hearts keep beating.

- **We can survive** without some organs.

- **Some people** only have one kidney or lung or have had their appendix or spleen removed because of damage or disease.

- **Some organs**, such as the heart or liver, can be replaced by transplant surgery if they are damaged or diseased.

DID YOU KNOW?

The word 'organ' means instrument or tool in Greek.

ORGAN	WHAT IT DOES
BRAIN	Controls the nervous system
HEART	Keeps blood flowing round the body
LUNGS	Enable us to get oxygen from the air we breathe
VOICE BOX	Produces sounds that we turn into speech
STOMACH	Starts to break down food
LIVER	Produces chemicals essential for survival and digestion
GALL BLADDER	Helps digestion of food
PANCREAS	Helps to control sugar levels in the body
SPLEEN	Produces cells that help fight infections
SMALL INTESTINE	Processes food and absorbs useful substances
APPENDIX	Has no known use in humans
LARGE INTESTINE	Absorbs water from food and gets rid of unwanted material
KIDNEYS	Help control the body's fluid balance
BLADDER	Stores urine
SKIN	A protective covering over the body

Cells

- **Cells are** the basic building blocks of your body. Most are so tiny you would need 10,000 to cover a pinhead.

- **There are** over 200 different kinds of cell in your body, including nerve cells, skin cells, blood cells, bone cells, fat cells, muscle cells and many more.

- **A cell** is basically a little parcel of organic (life) chemicals with a thin membrane (casing) of protein and fat. The membrane holds the cell together, but lets nutrients in and waste out.

- **Inside the cell** is a liquid called cytoplasm, and floating in this are various minute structures called organelles.

- **At the centre** of the cell is the nucleus – this is the cell's control centre and it contains the amazing molecule DNA. This molecule not only has all the instructions the cell needs to function, but also has the pattern for new human life.

- **Each cell** is a dynamic chemical factory, and the cell's team of organelles is continually busy – ferrying chemicals to and fro, breaking up unwanted chemicals, and putting together new ones.

- **The biggest cells** in the body are nerve cells. Although the main nucleus of a nerve cell is microscopic, the tails of some cells can extend for a metre or more through the body, and be seen even without a microscope.

- **Among the smallest** cells in the body are red blood cells. These are just 0.0075 mm across and have no nucleus, since nearly their only task is ferrying oxygen.

Most body cells live for a very short time and are continually being replaced by new ones. The main exceptions are nerve cells – these are long-lived, and rarely replaced.

Mitochondria are the cell's power stations, turning chemical fuel supplied by the blood as glucose into energy packs of the chemical ATP

The endoplasmic reticulum is the cell's main chemical factory, where proteins are built under instruction from the nucleus

The ribosomes are the individual chemical assembly lines, where proteins are put together from basic chemicals called amino acids

The nucleus is the cell's control centre, sending out instructions via a chemical called messenger RNA whenever a new chemical is needed

The lysosomes are the cell's dustbins, breaking up any unwanted material

The Golgi bodies are the cell's despatch centre, where chemicals are bagged up inside tiny membranes to send where they are needed

▲ This illustration shows a typical cell, and some of the different organelles (special parts of a cell) that keep it working properly. The instructions come from the nucleus in the cell's control centre, but every kind of organelle has its own task.

Cell division

- **Cells in the body** are constantly dividing. Cells divide to replace ones that have become worn out, and during growth.

- **When a cell divides** it normally copies itself exactly.

- **The genetic material** that is in the centre of the cell splits apart and is duplicated so that the cell contains two copies.

- **The genetic material** then separates so that one copy sits in each half of the cell.

- **The cell** then gradually splits into two cells, each containing one set of the copied genetic material. This process is called mitosis.

- **Sperm and egg cells** are made by a slightly different type of cell division called meiosis. Each sperm and egg cell only has half the genetic material of other cells.

- **Occasionally** the genetic material does not copy properly and one of the new cells contains more or less genetic material than normal. This is called a mutation.

- **Mutations can be good**. Evolution takes place when good mutations give a better chance of survival and so are passed on.

- **Mutations can also** cause diseases such as cancer.

◄ *Identical twins occur when one fertilized cell splits into two.*

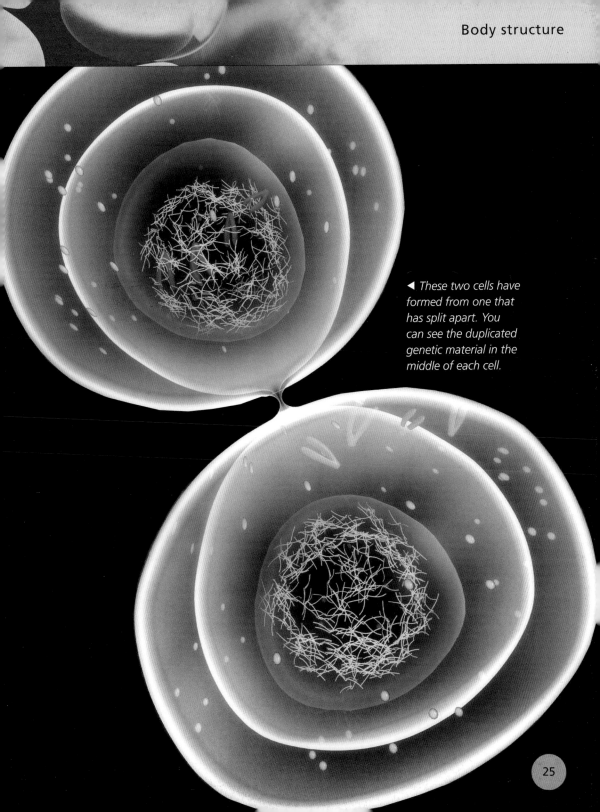

◄ These two cells have formed from one that has split apart. You can see the duplicated genetic material in the middle of each cell.

Cancer

Cancer is a disease in which cells multiply abnormally, creating growths called tumours.

The word 'cancer' comes from the Greek word for crab, as it spreads a bit like a crab's claw.

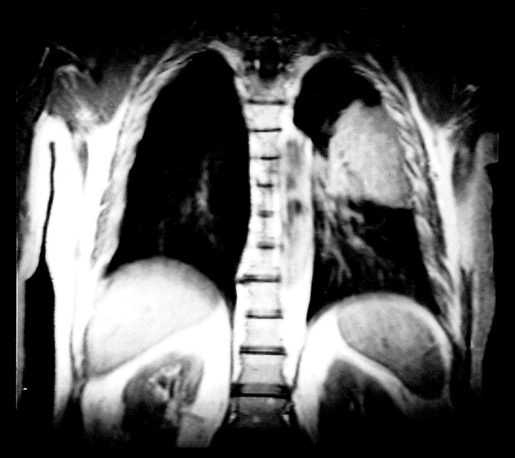

▲ *This coloured scan of a chest shows a large lung tumour (seen here as a pink area).*

DID YOU KNOW?
Cancer that has spread to another part of the body is said to have 'metastasised'.

- **Cancer can** start anywhere in the body. Once you have cancer it may spread around the body.

- **The most common** type of cancer is skin cancer. However, most skin cancers do not spread and are easily treated by removing the tumour.

- **You are much more** likely to get skin cancer if you sunbathe or use sunbeds.

- **More people** die of lung cancer than of any other type of cancer. Lung cancer is far more common in people who smoke.

- **Some types** of cancer run in families but others are caused by our lifestyle. A healthy diet with lots of vegetables and fibre can help to prevent cancer of the large intestine.

- **Infection** with some viruses increases the risk of getting certain types of cancer.

- **Cancer is usually treated** by removing the tumour. Some people also need drugs and radiation treatment to make sure all the cancer cells have been destroyed.

- **Six million people** around the world die of cancer every year. The risk increases as you get older.

▶ *Some substances, such as the chemicals in cigarettes, are known to increase the risk of getting cancer.*

Chromosomes

- **Chromosomes are** the microscopically tiny, twisted threads inside every cell that carry your body's life instructions in chemical form.

- **There are 46 chromosomes** in each of your body cells, divided into 23 pairs.

- **One of each** chromosome pair came from your mother and the other from your father.

- **In a girl's** 23 chromosome pairs, each half exactly matches the other (the set from the mother is equivalent to the set from the father).

- **Boys have** 22 matching chromosome pairs, but the 23rd pair is made up of two odd chromosomes.

- **The 23rd chromosome pair** decides what sex you are, and the sex chromosomes are called X and Y.

- **Girls have two** X chromosomes, but boys have an X and a Y chromosome.

- **In every** matching pair, both chromosomes give your body life instructions for the same thing.

◀▶ *A girl turns out to be a girl because she gets an X chromosome from her father. A boy gets a Y chromosome from his father.*

A normal body cell has 46 chromosomes, divided into 23 pairs

▼ *Two sets of chromosomes, one each from the mother and the father, combine at fertilization.*

The male sperm cell has 23 chromosomes

Male

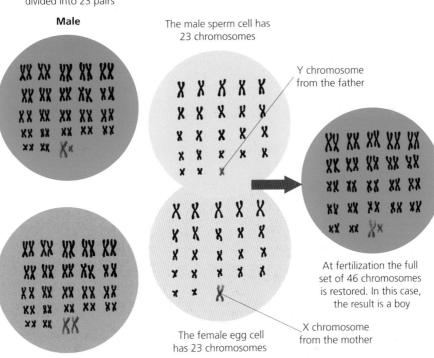

Y chromosome from the father

At fertilization the full set of 46 chromosomes is restored. In this case, the result is a boy

The female egg cell has 23 chromosomes

X chromosome from the mother

Female

The chemical instructions on each chromosome come in thousands of different units called genes.

Genes for the same feature appear in the same locus (place) on each matching pair of chromosomes in every human body cell.

DNA

Cells are the basic building blocks of your body. Most are so tiny you would need 10,000 to cover a pinhead.

DNA (Deoxyribonucleic Acid) is the molecule inside every cell that carries all your genes. Most of the time, DNA is coiled up inside the chromosomes, but when needed, it unravels.

The structure of DNA was first identified in 1953 by James Watson and Francis Crick, who announced they had 'found the secret of life'.

DNA is shaped in a double helix with linking bars, like a twisted rope ladder.

The bars of DNA are four special chemicals called bases – guanine, adenine, cytosine and thymine.

The base adenine always pairs with thymine, and the base guanine always pairs with cytosine.

The bases in DNA are arranged in groups of three called codons, and the order of the bases in each codon varies to provide a chemical code for the cell to make a particular amino acid.

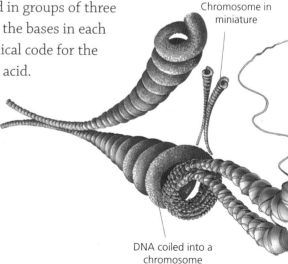

Chromosome in miniature

▶ *The sequence of bases along one strand of the DNA is a perfect mirror image of the sequence on the other side. When the strand divides down the middle, each can be used like a template to make a copy. This is how instructions are issued.*

DNA coiled into a chromosome

🖐 **When the cell** needs to make a new protein, the DNA 'unzips' and the codons are matched by free bases, which make a copy of that part of the DNA.

🖐 **The DNA copy** is then matched by amino acids floating in the cell, which join together in the right order to make a specific protein.

🖐 **Because DNA** is responsible for making proteins, it is essential for growth, development and body function.

🖐 **Each cell** contains about 2 m of DNA and if you unravelled all the DNA in your body it would stretch about 199 billion km.

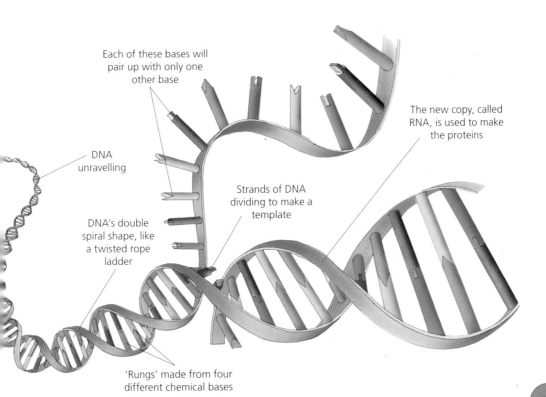

Each of these bases will pair up with only one other base

The new copy, called RNA, is used to make the proteins

DNA unravelling

Strands of DNA dividing to make a template

DNA's double spiral shape, like a twisted rope ladder

'Rungs' made from four different chemical bases

Genes

- **Genes are** the body's chemical instructions for your entire life. They hold information for growth, survival, having children and, perhaps, even for dying.

- **Individual genes** are instructions to make particular proteins – the body's building-block molecules.

- **Small sets of genes** control features such as the colour of your hair or your eyes, or create a particular body process such as digesting fat from food.

- **Each of your body cells** (except egg and sperm cells) carries identical sets of genes. This is because all your cells were made by other cells splitting in two, starting with the original egg cell in your mother.

- **Your genes** are a mixture – half come from your mother and half from your father. But none of your brothers or sisters will get the same mix, unless you are identical twins.

- **Genes make us unique** – making us tall or short, fair or dark, brilliant dancers or speakers, healthy or likely to get particular illnesses, and so on.

- **Genes are sections** of DNA – a microscopically tiny molecule inside each cell.

- **Occasionally**, genes are faulty. Some faulty genes can cause diseases and these are called genetic disorders.

> **DID YOU KNOW?**
> Each cell in your body has about 90,000 pairs of genes.

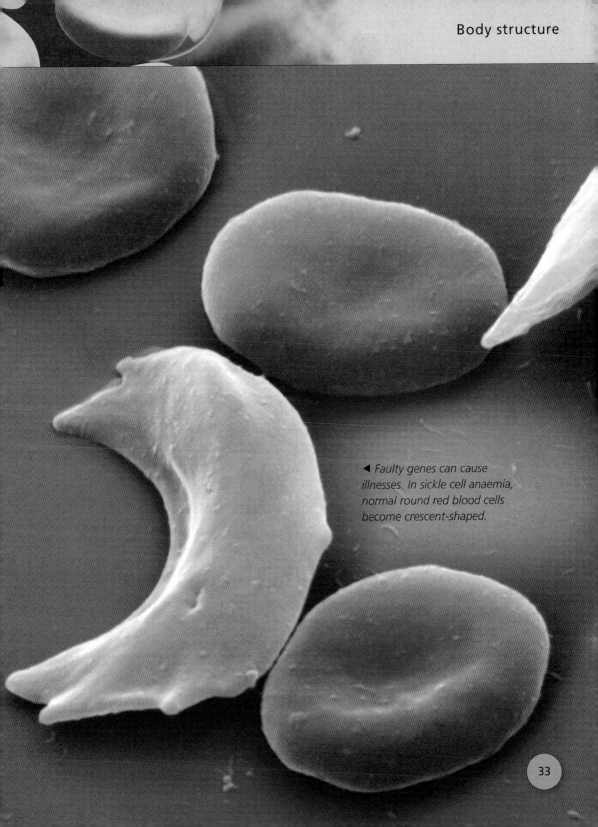

◄ Faulty genes can cause illnesses. In sickle cell anaemia, normal round red blood cells become crescent-shaped.

The human genome

- **The human genome** is all the genes found in the 23 pairs of chromosomes that a normal human being carries.

- **Humans have** about 20,000–25,000 genes, separated by 'junk' pieces of DNA that have no function.

- **About 97 percent** of the human genome is 'junk' and does not code for a gene.

- **The Human Genome Project** was started in 1990 and aimed to find the precise code of all the genes in the human genome. It was completed in 2003.

- **Many diseases** have a genetic component, and tests that look for a tendency to develop certain diseases, such as some types of cancer, are being developed.

▼ *Just like DNA, fingerprints are unique and can be used to identify criminals.*

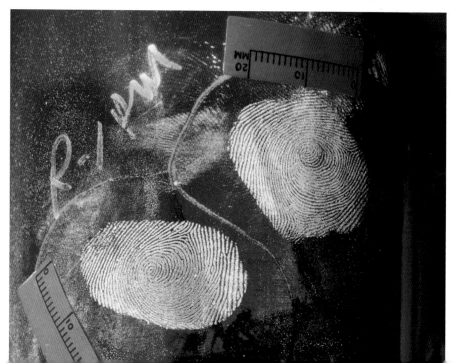

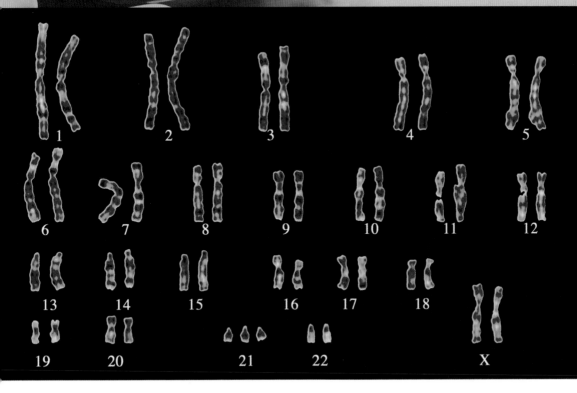

▲ *Normally, humans have two copies of every chromosome. Down's syndrome is caused by the presence of three copies of chromosome 21, as shown above.*

Now that scientists know which genes cause some diseases, and where on the genome they are located, one day they may be able to replace damaged genes and cure these diseases.

All human beings have 99.9 percent of the same genes. It is the 0.1 percent difference that makes us all different.

Scientists can use this 0.1 percent difference to compare samples of DNA and identify criminals.

It is thought that one day we may all carry identity cards that are encoded with our genome.

Heredity

- **Your heredity** is all the body characteristics you inherit from your parents, whether it is your mother's black hair or your father's knobbly knees.

- **Characteristics** are passed on by the genes carried on your chromosomes.

▼ *We look the way we do because we inherit characteristics, such as the colour of our eyes, from our parents.*

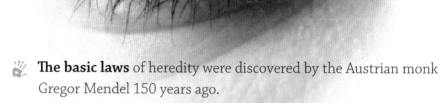

- **The basic laws** of heredity were discovered by the Austrian monk Gregor Mendel 150 years ago.

- **Your body characteristics** are a mix of two sets of instructions – one from your mother's chromosomes and the other from your father's.

- **Each characteristic** is the work of only one gene – either your mother's or your father's. This gene is said to be 'expressed'.

- **A gene** that is not expressed does not vanish. Instead, it stays dormant (asleep) in your chromosomes, possibly to pass on to your children.

- **A dominant gene** is one that is always expressed.

- **A recessive gene** is one that loses out to a dominant gene and stays dormant.

- **When there is** no competition, a recessive gene may be expressed – that is, when the genes from both of your parents are recessive.

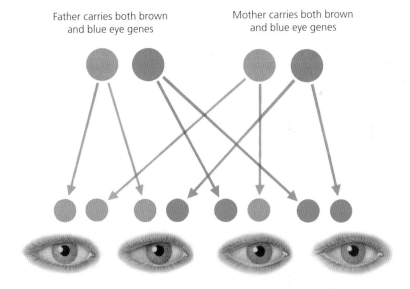

Father carries both brown
and blue eye genes

Mother carries both brown
and blue eye genes

2 brown eye genes = offspring with brown eyes
1 brown eye gene + 1 blue eye gene = offspring with brown eyes
1 blue eye gene + 1 brown eye gene = offspring with brown eyes
2 blue eye genes = offspring with blue eyes

▲ *In this example, both parents have genes for brown and blue eyes. Brown eye genes are dominant, so offspring are more likely to have brown eyes.*

Skin

- **Skin is** your protective coat, shielding your body from the weather and from infection, and helping to keep it at just the right temperature.

- **It is also** your largest sense receptor, responding to touch, pressure, heat and cold.

- **Skin makes** vitamin D for your body from sunlight.

- **The epidermis** (the thin outer layer) is just dead cells.

- **It is made** mainly of a tough protein called keratin – the remains of skin cells that die off.

- **Below the epidermis** is a thick layer of living cells called the dermis, which contains the sweat glands.

▲ The skin on the sole of your foot is hairless and thicker than anywhere else on your body.

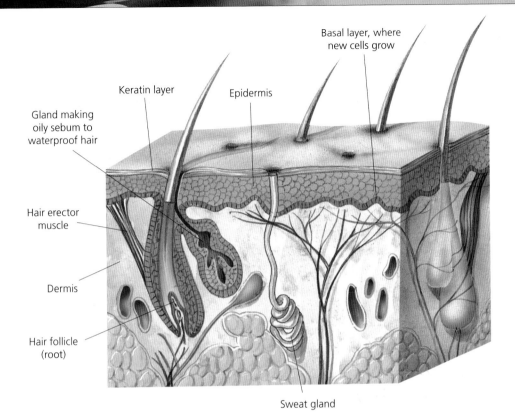

Basal layer, where
new cells grow

Keratin layer

Epidermis

Gland making
oily sebum to
waterproof hair

Hair erector
muscle

Dermis

Hair follicle
(root)

Sweat gland

▲ *This is a cross-section of skin, hugely magnified, showing its key components.*

Skin is 6 mm thick on the soles of your feet, while the skin on your eyelids is just 0.5 mm thick.

Hair roots have tiny muscles that pull the hair upright when you are cold, giving you goose bumps.

The epidermis contains cells that make the dark pigment melanin – this gives dark-skinned people their colour and fair-skinned people a tan.

DID YOU KNOW?

Even though its thickness averages just 2 mm, your skin gets an eighth of all your blood supply.

Hair

Humans are one of very few land mammals to have almost bare skin. But even humans have soft, downy hair all over, with thicker hair in places.

Lanugo is the very fine hair babies are covered in when they are inside the womb, from the fourth month of pregnancy onwards.

> **DID YOU KNOW?**
> Many people think that hair continues to grow after death, but this is a myth.

▼ *A microscopic view of a hair. It is only alive and growing at its root, in the base of the follicle. The shaft that sticks out of the skin is dead, and is made of flat cells stuck firmly together.*

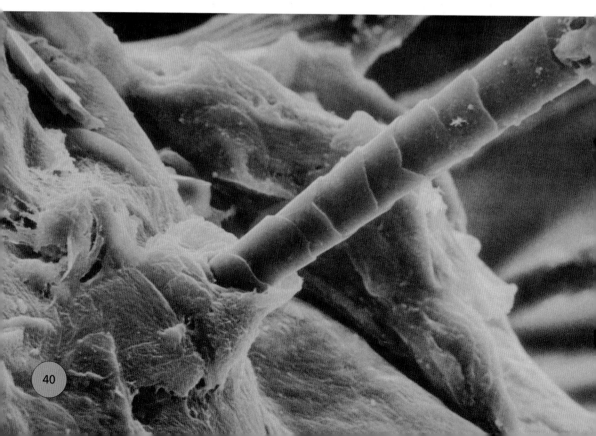

Brown hair

▶ *The colour of your hair depends upon melanin made in melanocytes at the root.*

Vellus hair is fine, downy hair that grows all over your body until you reach puberty.

Terminal hair is the coarser hair on your head, as well as the hair that grows on a man's chin and around an adult's genitals.

The colour of your hair depends on how much there are of pigments called melanin and carotene in the hairs.

Blonde hair

Hair is red or auburn if it contains carotene.

Black, brown and blonde hair get its colour from black melanin.

Red hair

Each hair is rooted in a pit called the hair follicle. The hair is held in place by its club-shaped tip, the bulb.

Hair grows as cells fill with a material called keratin and die, and pile up inside the follicle.

The average person has 120,000 head hairs and each grows about 3 mm per week.

Nails

- **Nails protect** the ends of our fingers and toes. They are formed of dead cells, strengthened by a protein called keratin.

- **Without nails**, we would not be able to scratch. They also help us judge pressure when picking up objects.

- **Nails grow** from a nail root, which is hidden by a fold of skin at the base of the nail called a cuticle.

- **The pale half moon** at the base of the nail is called the lunula after the Latin word for the moon.

▼ *White spots on nails are very common. Many people think they are caused by a lack of calcium but they are usually due to a minor injury.*

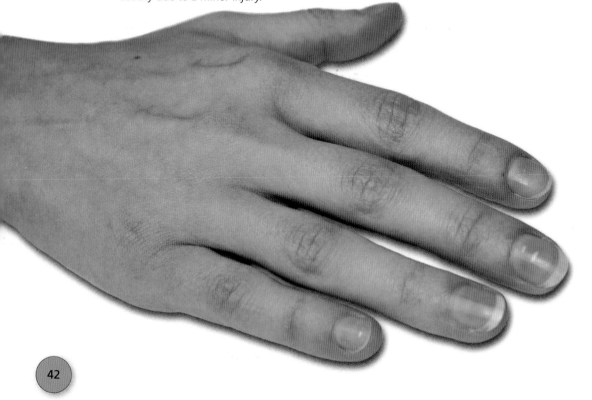

- **Most nails** only grow by about 0.5 mm a month. Fingernails grow faster than toenails.

- **Nails grow faster** in summer than in winter.

- **The nails** on your right hand will grow faster than the nails on your left hand if you are right handed. If you are left handed, the nails on your left hand will grow faster.

- **The record** for the longest nails in the world is held by a woman in the USA, who grew her nails to a total length of 8.65 m.

- **It is believed** that people have been painting their nails with nail polish or varnish since around 3000 BC.

- **Contrary to popular belief**, nails do not continue to grow after death.

DID YOU KNOW?

It can take up to six months for a lost fingernail and 18 months for a toenail to regrow completely.

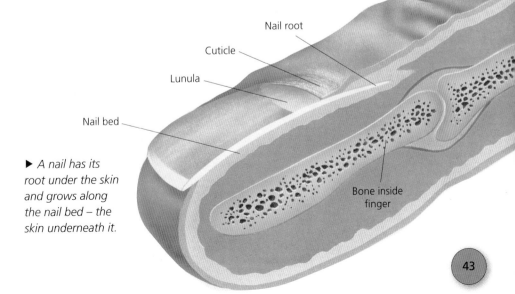

Nail root

Cuticle

Lunula

Nail bed

Bone inside finger

▶ A nail has its root under the skin and grows along the nail bed – the skin underneath it.

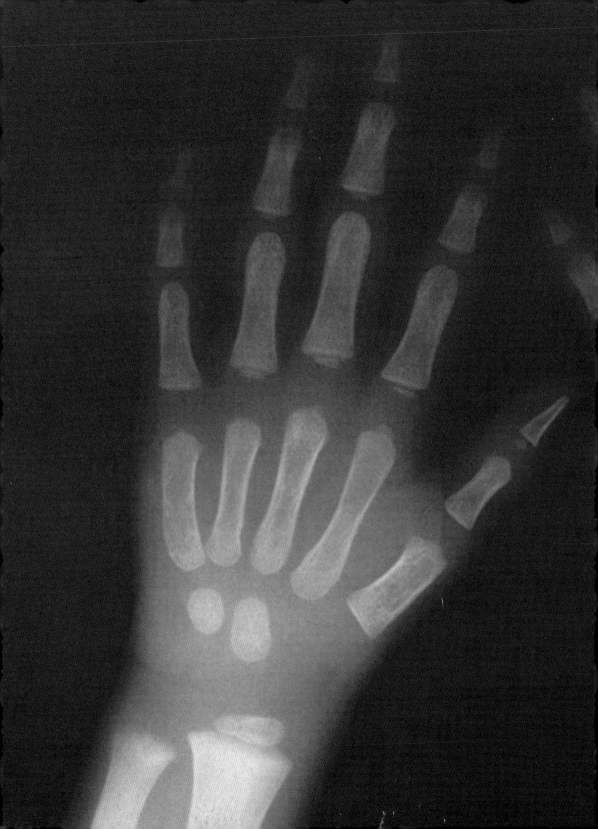

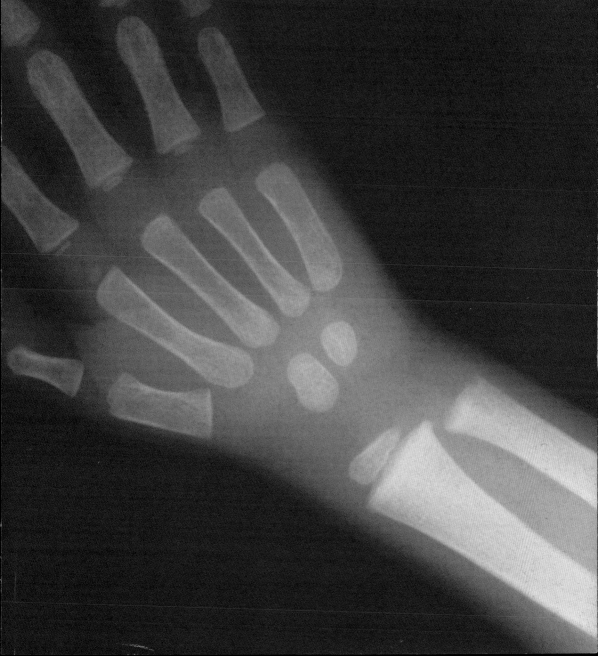

Musculoskeletal system

The skeleton

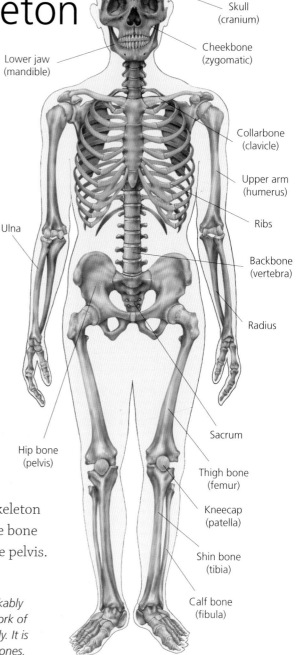

Your skeleton is a rigid framework of bones, which provides an anchor for your muscles, supports your skin and other organs, and protects vital organs.

An adult's skeleton has 206 bones, joined together by rubbery cartilage. Some people have extra vertebrae (the bones of the backbone, or spine).

A baby's skeleton has 300 or more bones, but some of these fuse (join) together as the baby grows.

The parts of an adult skeleton that have fused into one bone include the skull and the pelvis.

▶ *Your skeleton is the remarkably light, but very tough framework of bones that supports your body. It is made up of more than 200 bones.*

Skull (cranium)

Cheekbone (zygomatic)

Lower jaw (mandible)

Collarbone (clavicle)

Upper arm (humerus)

Ribs

Ulna

Backbone (vertebra)

Radius

Hip bone (pelvis)

Sacrum

Thigh bone (femur)

Kneecap (patella)

Shin bone (tibia)

Calf bone (fibula)

- **The skeleton** has two main parts – the axial and the appendicular skeleton.

- **The axial skeleton** is the 80 bones of the upper body. It includes the skull, the vertebrae of the backbone, the ribs and the breastbone. The arm and shoulder bones are suspended from it.

- **The appendicular skeleton** is the other 126 bones – the arm and shoulder bones, and the leg and hip bones.

- **The word 'skeleton'** comes from the ancient Greek word for dry.

- **Most women and girls** have smaller and lighter skeletons than men and boys.

▼ *Muscles pull and push against the bones on the skeleton to enable us to run and walk.*

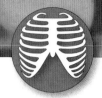

Bone

- **Bones are so strong** that they can cope with twice the squeezing pressure that granite can, or four times the stretching tension that concrete can.

- **Weight for weight**, bone is at least five times as strong as steel.

- **Bones are so light** they only make up 14 percent of your body's total weight.

- **Bones get their rigidity** from hard deposits of minerals such as calcium and phosphate.

▼ Bones are strong but very light because, on the inside, they have many holes.

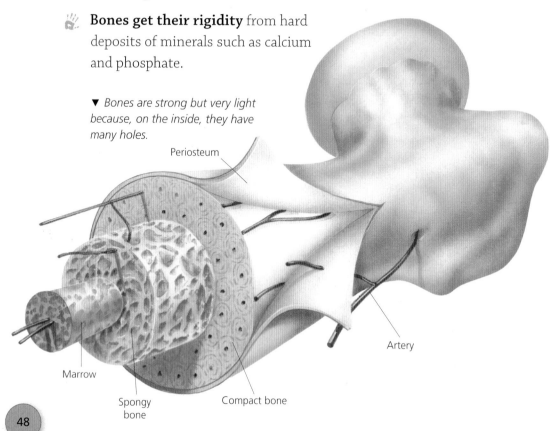

Periosteum

Artery

Marrow

Spongy bone

Compact bone

48

- **Bones get their flexibility** from tough, elastic, rope-like fibres of collagen.

- **The hard outside** of bones (called compact bone) is reinforced by strong rods called osteons.

- **The inside of bones** (called spongy bone) is a light honeycomb, made of thin struts or trabeculae, perfectly angled to take stress.

- **The core** of some bones, such as the long bones in an arm or leg, is called bone marrow. It is soft and jelly-like.

- **In some parts** of each bone, there are special cells called osteoblasts that make new bone. In other parts, cells called osteoclasts break up old bone.

- **Bones grow** by getting longer near the end, at a region called the epiphyseal plate.

▶ Milk contains a mineral called calcium, which is essential for building strong bones. Babies and children need plenty of calcium to help their bones develop properly.

Fractures

- **A fracture** is a broken bone.

- **Most fractures** are caused by an injury, such as a fall. Bones weakened by disease may sometimes fracture by themselves. This is called a pathological fracture.

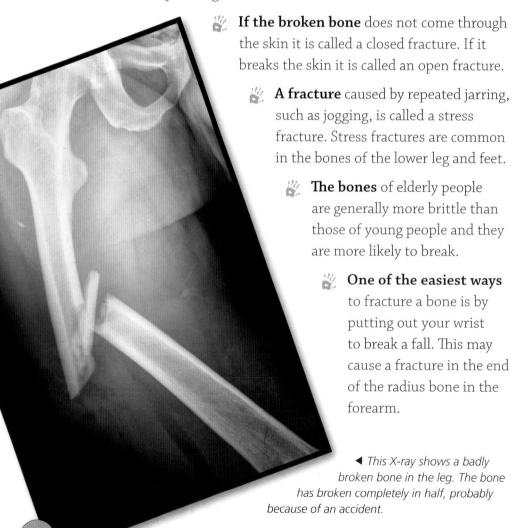

- **If the broken bone** does not come through the skin it is called a closed fracture. If it breaks the skin it is called an open fracture.

- **A fracture** caused by repeated jarring, such as jogging, is called a stress fracture. Stress fractures are common in the bones of the lower leg and feet.

- **The bones** of elderly people are generally more brittle than those of young people and they are more likely to break.

- **One of the easiest ways** to fracture a bone is by putting out your wrist to break a fall. This may cause a fracture in the end of the radius bone in the forearm.

◄ *This X-ray shows a badly broken bone in the leg. The bone has broken completely in half, probably because of an accident.*

The clavicle, or collarbone, is the bone that is broken most often, usually because of a fall.

▼ Modern casts are light and waterproof but still keep broken bones still and allow them to heal.

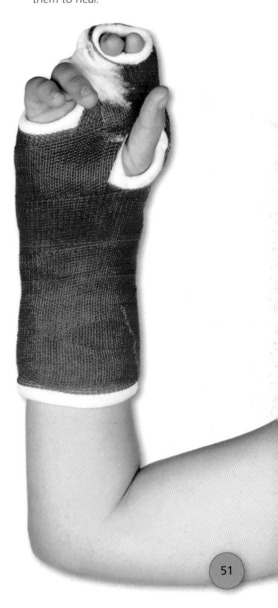

- **Fractures are treated** by lining up the broken ends of the bone and keeping them still in a plaster or plastic cast.

- **If a fracture** is complicated, surgery may be needed to put the bone back together properly or to hold it together with metal pins or plates.

- **Osteoblasts** (bone-making cells) heal broken bones by gradually converting tissue into bone.

- **Bones usually** take about six weeks to heal, although they may be weak for several months. Children heal faster than adults.

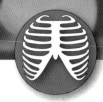

Marrow

- **Marrow** is the soft, jelly-like tissue in the middle of certain bones.

- **Bone marrow** can be red or yellow, depending on whether it has more blood tissue or fat tissue.

- **Red bone marrow** is the body's blood factory. This is where all blood cells, apart from some white cells, are made.

- **All bone marrow** is red when you are a baby, but as you grow older, more and more turns yellow.

- **In adults**, red marrow is only found in the ends of the limbs' long bones, breastbone, backbone, ribs, shoulder blades, pelvis and the skull.

- **Yellow bone marrow** is a store for fat, but it may turn to red marrow when you are ill.

- **All the different kinds** of blood cell start life in red marrow as one type of cell called a stem cell. Different blood cells then develop as the stem cells divide and re-divide.

- **Some stem cells** divide to form red blood cells and platelets.

- **Other stem cells** divide to form lymphoblasts. These divide in turn to form various different kinds of white cells, such as monocytes and lymphocytes.

- **The white cells** made in bone marrow play a key part in the body's immune system. This is why bone-marrow transplants can help people with illnesses that affect their immune system.

> **DID YOU KNOW?**
> Animal bone marrow is an important food in many cultures.

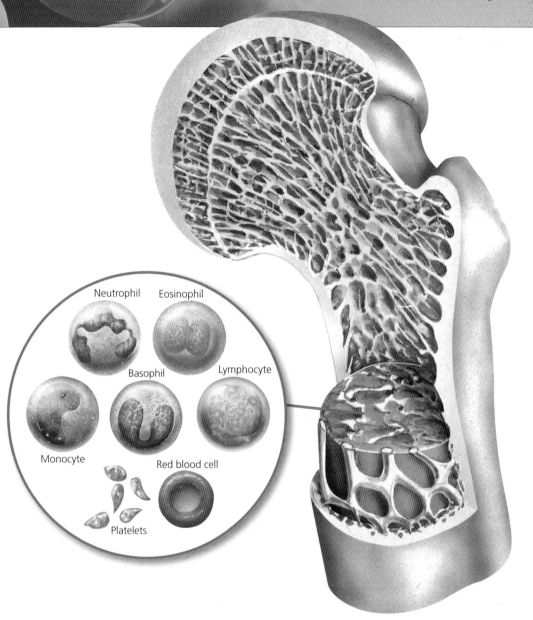

Neutrophil Eosinophil

Basophil

Lymphocyte

Monocyte

Red blood cell

Platelets

▲ *Inside the tough casing of most bones is a soft, jelly-like core called the marrow, which can be either red or yellow. The red marrow in certain bones is the body's blood-cell factory, making five million new cells a day. Some varieties of blood cells are shown above.*

The skull

- **The skull** or cranium is the hard bone case that contains and protects the brain.

- **Although it looks** as though the skull is a single bone, it is actually made up of 22 separate bones, cemented together along rigid joints called sutures.

- **The dome** on top is called the cranial vault and it is made from eight curved pieces of bone fused (joined) together.

- **As well as the sinuses** of the nose, the skull has four large cavities – the cranial cavity for the brain, the nasal cavity (the nose) and two orbits for the eyes.

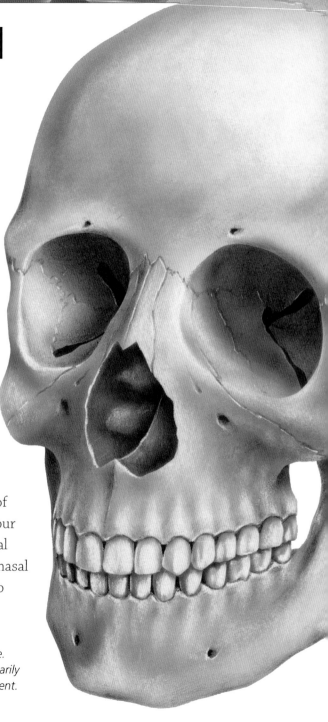

▶ *Skulls vary in size and shape. A bigger skull does not necessarily mean a person is more intelligent.*

▶ *A child's skull, shown here in this X-ray photo, is quite large in relation to the rest of the child's body. As our bodies grow, our skull starts to look smaller in proportion.*

There are holes in the skull to allow blood vessels and nerves through, including the optic nerves to the eyes and the olfactory tracts to the nose.

The biggest hole is in the base. It is called the foramen magnum, and the brain stem goes through it to meet the spinal cord.

In the 19th century, people called phrenologists thought they could work out people's characters from little bumps on their skulls.

Archaeologists can reconstruct faces from the past using computer analysis of ancient skulls.

55

Sinuses

- **The sinuses** are air-filled holes in the skull around the eyes and the nose.

- **Sinuses develop** gradually as you grow and help make the skull lighter.

- **The sinuses** also make the voice resonate and may help to protect the face against blows by acting a little like an air bag.

- **Most sinuses** lie in pairs – one on each side of the face.

- **There are two sinuses** in the forehead (frontal sinuses), several by the sides of the nose (ethmoid sinuses), one in each of the cheekbones (maxillary sinuses) and two deep in the skull (sphenoid sinuses).

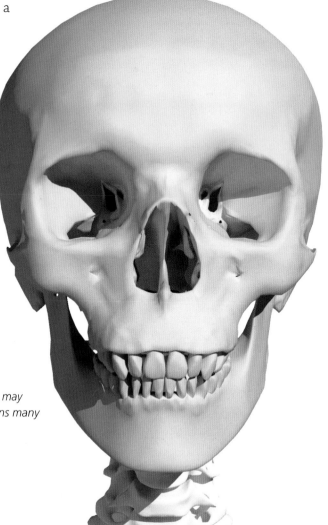

▶ Although the human skull may look like solid bone, it contains many spaces called sinuses.

▲ *Most of the sinuses lie in the bones around the nose and cheeks.*

- **The sinuses** are lined with glands that produce mucus, which passes through small holes in the bones of the skull and into the back of the nose.

- **The mucus** traps dust and tiny particles and helps to keep the air in your airways moist and warm.

- **The linings** of the sinuses may become swollen when you have a cold or if you have an allergy. This causes a headache and is called sinusitis.

- **Sinusitis** is very common and most people will get it at some point in their lifetime.

- **The word 'sinus'** is Latin and means a fold or pocket.

The backbone

- **The backbone**, otherwise known as the spine, extends from the base of the skull down to the hips.

- **It is not a single bone**, but a column of drum-shaped bones called vertebrae (singular, vertebra).

- **There are 33 vertebrae** in total, although some of these fuse or join as the body grows.

- **Each vertebra** is linked to the next by small facet joints, which give limited movement.

- **The vertebrae** are separated by discs of rubbery material called cartilage. These cushion the bones when you run and jump.

▶ The joint between the top two bones of the spine allows us to turn our heads.

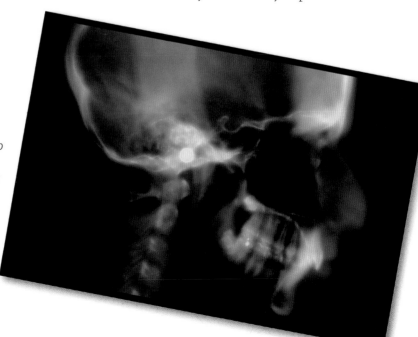

■ **The bones** of the spine are divided into five groups from top to bottom. These are the cervical (7 bones), the thoracic (12 bones), the lumbar (5 bones), the sacrum (5 bones fused together), and the coccyx (4 bones fused together).

■ **The cervical spine** is the vertebrae of the neck. The thoracic spine is the back of the chest, and each bone has a pair of ribs attached to it. The lumbar spine is the small of the back.

▶ *The backbone is not straight – instead, its 33 vertebrae curve into an S-shape.*

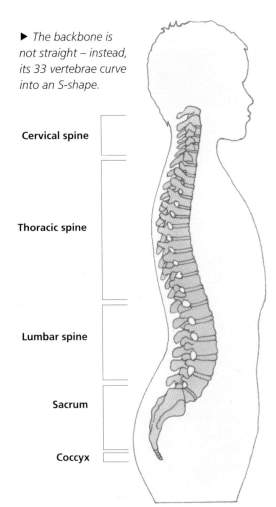

■ **A normal spine** curves in an S-shape, with the cervical spine curving forwards, the thoracic section curving backwards, the lumbar forwards, and the sacrum curving backwards.

■ **On the back** of each vertebra is a bridge called the spinal process. The bridges on each bone link together to form a tube that holds the spinal cord, the body's central bundle of nerves.

Cervical spine

Thoracic spine

Lumbar spine

Sacrum

Coccyx

Ribs

▼ The ribs provide a framework for the chest and form a protective cage around the heart, lungs and other organs.

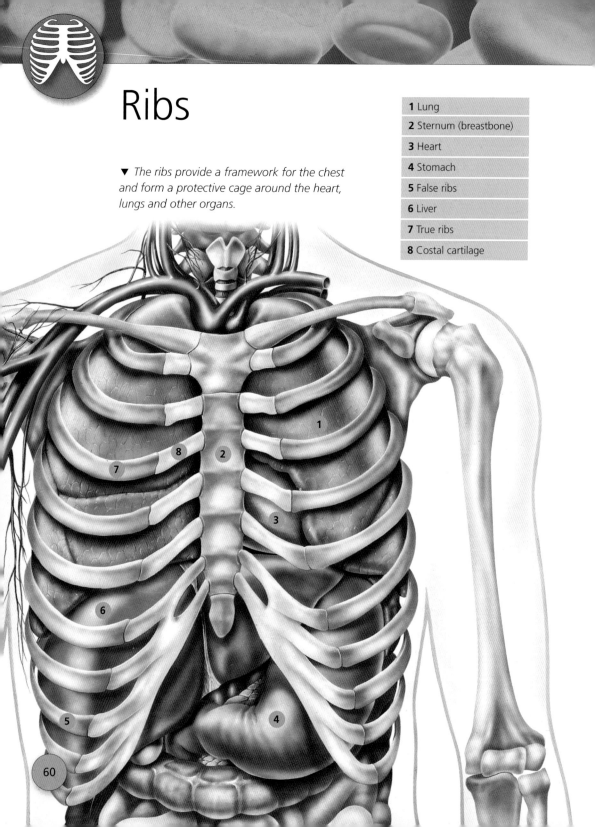

- **The ribs** are the thin, flattish bones that curve around your chest.

- **Together**, the rib bones make up the rib cage.

- **The rib cage** protects the backbone and breastbone, as well as your vital organs – heart, lungs, liver, kidneys, stomach, spleen and so on.

- **You have 12 pairs** of ribs altogether.

- **Seven pairs** are called true ribs. Each rib is attached to the breastbone in front and curves around to join on to one of the vertebrae that make up the backbone via a strip of costal cartilage.

- **There are three pairs** of false ribs. These are attached to vertebrae but are not linked to the breastbone. Instead, each rib is attached to the rib above it by cartilage.

- **There are two pairs** of floating ribs. These are attached only to the vertebrae of the backbone.

- **The gaps** between the ribs are called intercostal spaces, and they contain thin sheets of muscle that expand and relax the chest during breathing.

- **Flail chest** is when many ribs are broken (often in a car accident) and the lungs heave the chest in and out.

The pelvis

The pelvis is made up of two hip bones, each of which is made up of three bones that fuse together at puberty – the ilium, the pubis and the ischium.

The pelvic bones join the sacrum (part of the backbone) at the back and are fused together by cartilage at the front.

Organs in the lower part of the abdomen, such as the bladder and female reproductive organs, are protected by the pelvis.

The pelvis also supports the weight of the upper body and helps transfer weight to and from the legs when standing and walking.

Strong muscles in the thigh and buttocks enable us to walk and sit. These are attached to the pelvis.

The human pelvis is shaped differently to every other animal's to allow us to walk upright easily.

▼ *The pelvic bones support and protect the organs of the pelvis. This illustration shows a female pelvis containing the reproductive organs (1) and the bladder (2).*

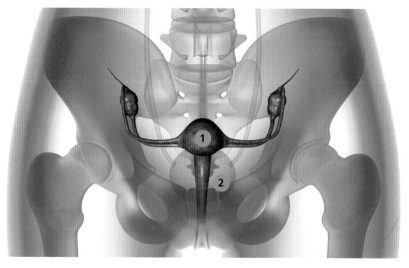

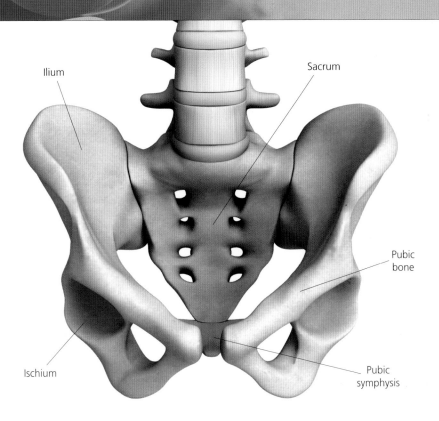

Ilium

Sacrum

Pubic bone

Ischium

Pubic symphysis

▲ *The two pelvic bones are connected to the lower back of the backbone.*

In women and girls, the pelvis is much wider than in men and boys. This is because the opening has to be wide enough for a baby to pass through when it is born.

Forensic scientists are able to use this difference in pelvis shape to tell whether a skeleton belonged to a man or a woman.

During labour, hormones cause the cartilage at the front of the pelvis to loosen, allowing the baby to pass through the pelvis more easily.

Joints

- **Body joints** are places where bones meet. There are about 400 joints in the human body.

- **Every time** you sit down, walk, play a sport or move at all you are using your joints.

- **Joints provide flexibility** by allowing movement and create stability by holding bones together.

- **Most body joints** let bones move, but some kinds of joint only let them move in certain ways.

- **Only fixed joints**, such as those in the skull, allow no movement.

- **All other joints** contain cartilage to cushion the ends of the bones. Some joints also contain fluid to lubricate the bones.

▶ *Gymnasts must have supple, flexible joints in order to perform complicated exercises such as this.*

- **Semi-movable joints**, such as those in the pelvis and backbone, allow a little movement.

- **Synovial joints** are flexible joints, lubricated with oily 'synovial fluid' and cushioned by cartilage.

- **A dislocated joint** occurs when bones are forced out of place, often by playing sport.

- **The cartilage** in joints may wear out through age or overuse through sport. In some cases surgery may be needed to replace the joint with an artificial one.

DID YOU KNOW?
You have about 30 small joints in each hand and wrist.

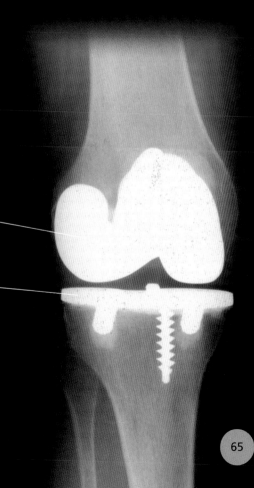

Cap on base of thigh bone

Plate screwed into top of shin bone

▶ This X-ray shows an artificial knee joint. The ends of the two bones have been replaced with metal surfaces.

Fixed and semi-movable joints

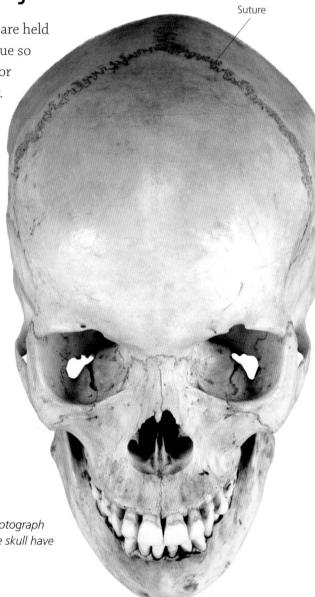

Suture

- **In a fixed joint**, bones are held together by fibrous tissue so that they do not move or only move very slightly.

- **The skull** is not one bone, but 22 separate bones bound tightly together with fibres so that they cannot move.

- **These fixed joints** in the skull are called sutures.

- **The skull bones** are not fused together at birth. The soft spots where the bones are not joined are called fontanelles and usually disappear by about 18 months.

▶ *The jagged lines in this photograph show where the bones of the skull have fused together.*

- **In a semi-movable joint**, the bones are held together by cartilage that only allows a little movement.

- **The pubic symphysis** is a semi-movable joint that holds the two pelvic bones together at the front of the pelvis.

DID YOU KNOW?

The cartilage in the joints in your spine is stronger than in other joints.

- **In women**, the pubic symphysis loosens during labour to allow the baby to be born more easily.

- **There are semi-movable joints** between each of the bones (vertebrae) of the backbone. Although each only moves slightly, together they provide flexibility.

- **These relatively inflexible joints** in the spine are cushioned by pads of cartilage.

- **The cartilage** acts as shock absorbers for the spine when we run or jog.

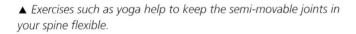

▲ Exercises such as yoga help to keep the semi-movable joints in your spine flexible.

Synovial joints

- **Synovial joints** are freely movable joints and are the most common type of joint in the body.

- **In a synovial joint** the bones are cushioned with cartilage and the joint space is filled with a lubricating fluid called synovial fluid. The joint is encased by a capsule that is often reinforced by ligaments that hold it all together.

- **There are six types** of synovial joint.

- **In ball-and-socket joints**, such as the shoulder and hip, the rounded end of one bone sits in the cup-shaped socket of the other, and can move in almost any direction.

- **Hinge joints**, such as the elbow, knees, fingers and toes, let the bones swing to and fro in two directions like door hinges.

- **Swivel joints** turn like a wheel on an axle. Your head can swivel to the left or to the right on your spine.

- **Saddle joints** such as those in the thumb have the bones interlocking like two saddles. These joints allow great mobility with considerable strength.

- **Plane joints** in the wrist and the foot allow almost flat bone surfaces to slide over each other but only in short distances.

- **In ellipsoidal joints** the domed end of one bone fits into a cavity on the other bone allowing a limited rotation. These types are joints are found at the base of the fingers and in the wrist.

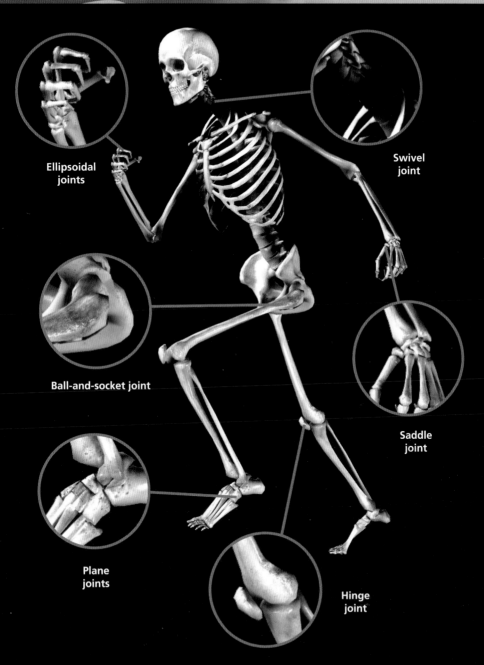

Ellipsoidal
joints

Swivel
joint

Ball-and-socket joint

Saddle
joint

Plane
joints

Hinge
joint

▲ *Synovial joints allow the body to move in many ways so we can walk,
run, play and work.*

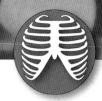

Knee joint

- **The knee** is a synovial joint and the biggest joint in the body.

- **It acts as a hinge** between the femur (thighbone) and the two bones in the lower leg.

- **The knee joint** doesn't just straighten or bend, it also rotates slightly.

- **Cartilage in the knee** makes two dish shapes called menisci (singular, meniscus) between the thigh and lower leg bones.

- **These cartilages** are often damaged when playing sport such as football or rugby, especially if the leg twists suddenly with the knee bent.

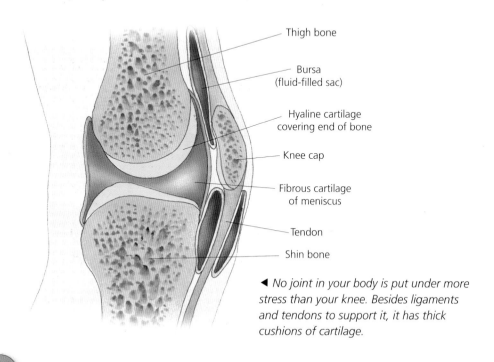

Thigh bone

Bursa
(fluid-filled sac)

Hyaline cartilage
covering end of bone

Knee cap

Fibrous cartilage
of meniscus

Tendon

Shin bone

◄ *No joint in your body is put under more stress than your knee. Besides ligaments and tendons to support it, it has thick cushions of cartilage.*

▲ *Falling at an awkward angle, which can happen during sports such as rugby, may cause a knee injury.*

🖐 **Cartilage can also** become damaged with age or through overuse, especially in people who do a lot of squatting or lifting, which puts extra pressure on the knee.

🖐 **The knee** is constantly under stress when getting up or sitting down, walking or running.

🖐 **For the knee joint** to work well, the joint needs to be in good condition and the muscles around the knee need to be strong.

🖐 **The knee** is one of the joints in the body that can be replaced by an artificial joint if it becomes too damaged or diseased to work properly.

🖐 **The knee cap** is a small bone that sits outside the joint and is held in place by tendons that attach to the muscles of the upper and lower legs.

71

Cartilage

Cartilage is a rubbery substance used in various places around the body. You can feel cartilage in your ear if you move it back and forward.

▼ *A single blow to the nose can easily damage the nasal cartilage, as often happens to boxers.*

DID YOU KNOW?

Cartilage is an old English word and comes from the Latin 'cartilago', which means gristle.

Cartilage is made from cells called chondrocytes embedded in a jelly-like substance with fibres of collagen, all wrapped in an envelope of tough fibres.

There are three types of cartilage: hyaline, fibrous and elastic.

Hyaline cartilage is the most widespread in your body. It is almost clear, pearly white and quite stiff. Hyaline cartilage is used in many of the joints between bones to cushion them against impacts.

Fibrous cartilage is really tough cartilage used in between the bones of the spine and in the knee.

Elastic cartilage is very flexible and used in your airways, nose and ears.

Cartilage grows quicker than bone, and the skeletons of babies in the womb are mostly cartilage, which gradually ossifies (hardens to bone).

Osteoarthritis is when joint cartilage breaks down, making certain movements painful.

Scientists can now make artificial cartilage that can be used to help repair damaged joints.

Tendons and ligaments

Tendons are cords that tie a muscle to a bone or tie a muscle to another muscle.

Most tendons are round, rope-like bundles of fibre. A few, such as the ones in the abdomen wall, are flat sheets called aponeuroses.

Tendon fibres are made from a rubbery substance called collagen.

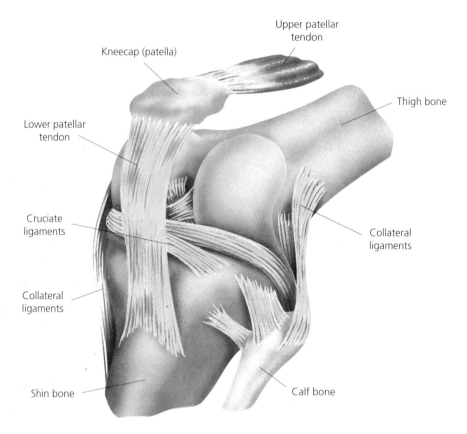

Upper patellar tendon

Kneecap (patella)

Thigh bone

Lower patellar tendon

Cruciate ligaments

Collateral ligaments

Collateral ligaments

Shin bone

Calf bone

▲ Collateral (side) ligaments stop the knee wobbling from side to side. Cruciate (crossing) ligaments tie the knee across the middle to stop it bending or straightening too much. Tendons hold the kneecap in place.

Your fingers are moved mainly by muscles in the forearm, which are connected to the fingers by long tendons.

The Achilles tendon pulls up your heel at the back.

Ligaments are cords attached to bones on either side of a joint. They strengthen the joint.

Ligaments also support various organs, including the liver, bladder and uterus (womb).

Women's breasts are held in place by bundles of ligaments.

Ligaments are made up of bundles of tough collagen and a stretchy substance called elastin.

▶ Tendons provide a link between muscle and bone. They prevent muscles tearing when they are put under strain.

75

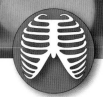

Muscles

- **Muscles are special fibres** that contract (tighten) and relax to move parts of the body.

- **Muscles give our bodies** their different shapes and help to hold the body upright.

- **Most muscles** attach to bones using tendons and most muscles cross over a joint so they can move the joint.

- **Muscles are usually** arranged in pairs, because although muscles can shorten themselves, they cannot forcibly make themselves longer. So the flexor muscle that bends a joint is paired with an extensor muscle to straighten it out again.

- **There are three types** of muscle – skeletal, smooth and heart muscle.

- **Most of the muscle** in the body is skeletal muscle. There are around 640 skeletal muscles and they make up about half the weight of your body.

- **Your body's longest muscle** is the sartorius, on the inner thigh.

- **The widest muscle** is the external oblique, which runs around the side of the upper body.

- **Your body's biggest muscle** is the gluteus maximus in your buttock (bottom).

- **The shortest muscle** is the stapedius, which attaches to one of the tiny bones in the ear.

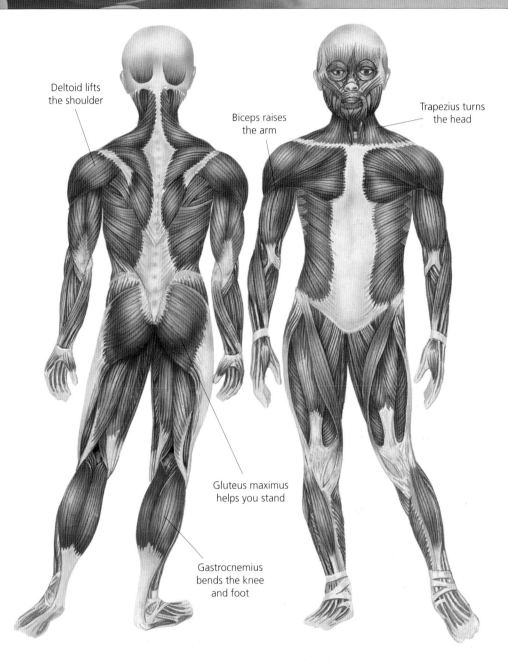

Deltoid lifts
the shoulder

Biceps raises
the arm

Trapezius turns
the head

Gluteus maximus
helps you stand

Gastrocnemius
bends the knee
and foot

▲ *Your body has several layers of muscle. Most are attached to bones using tough fibres called tendons.*

77

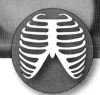

Muscle types

- **Voluntary muscles** are all the muscles you can control by will (conscious thought), such as your arm muscles.

- **Involuntary muscles** are the muscles you cannot control at will, but which work automatically, such as the muscles that move food through your intestine.

- **Most voluntary muscles** cover the skeleton and are therefore called skeletal muscles.

- **Skeletal muscles** are made of special cells called myofibrils.

  Body of muscle

- **Hundreds or thousands** of these fibres bind together like fibres in string to form each muscle.

- **Each myofibril** is marked with dark bands, giving the muscle its name of stripy or 'striated' muscle.

- **Skeletal muscle** is strong but cannot keep working for long periods of time like other types of muscle. Athletes have to train so that their skeletal muscles will work for longer.

- **Most involuntary muscles** form sacs or tubes such as the intestine or the blood vessels. They are called smooth muscle because they lack the bands or stripes of voluntary muscles.

- **Heart muscle** is a unique combination of skeletal and smooth muscle. It has its own built-in contraction rhythm of 70 beats a minute, and special muscle cells that work like nerve cells for transmitting the signals for waves of muscle contraction to sweep through the heart.

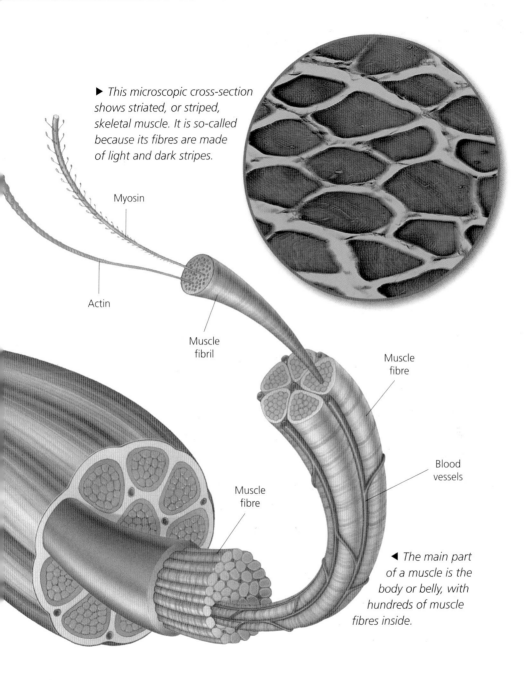

▶ This microscopic cross-section shows striated, or striped, skeletal muscle. It is so-called because its fibres are made of light and dark stripes.

Myosin

Actin

Muscle fibril

Muscle fibre

Blood vessels

Muscle fibre

◀ The main part of a muscle is the body or belly, with hundreds of muscle fibres inside.

Muscle movement

- **Most muscles** are long and thin and they work by pulling themselves shorter – sometimes contracting by up to half their length in response to signals from the brain.

- **The stripes** in skeletal muscle are alternate bands of filaments of two substances: actin and myosin.

- **The actin and myosin** interlock, like teeth on a zip.

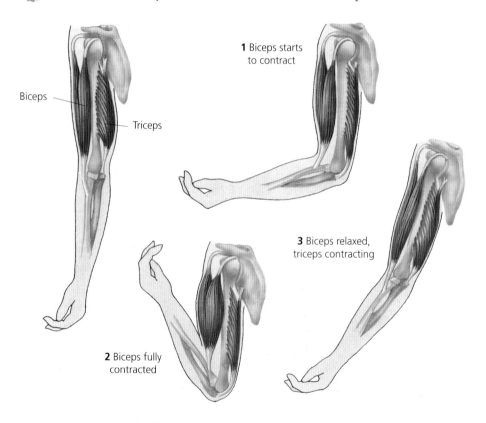

Biceps

Triceps

1 Biceps starts to contract

3 Biceps relaxed, triceps contracting

2 Biceps fully contracted

▲ Muscles, such as the biceps and triceps in the upper arm, work in pairs, pulling in opposite directions to one another.

- **When a nerve signal** comes from the brain, chemical 'hooks' on the myosin twist, yanking the actin filaments along, and shortening the muscle.

- **The chemical hooks** on myosin are made from a stem called a cross-bridge and a head made of a chemical called adenosine triphosphate or ATP.

- **ATP** is sensitive to calcium, and the nerve signal from the brain that tells the muscle to contract does its work by releasing a flood of calcium to trigger the ATP.

- **Muscles can only pull** and not push and are usually paired across joints.

- **When one muscle** contracts it pulls on the joint, causing movement. The muscle on the other side of the joint will be relaxed.

- **To move** the joint back to its original position the contracted muscle relaxes and the opposing muscle contracts.

▶ *Training with weights strengthens individual muscles, such as the biceps in the arm.*

The arm

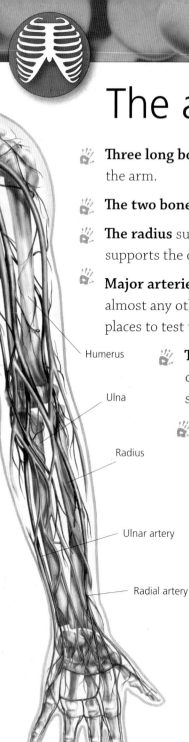

Humerus

Ulna

Radius

Ulnar artery

Radial artery

- **Three long bones**, linked by a hinge joint at the elbow, make up the arm.

- **The two bones** of the lower arm are the radius and the ulna.

- **The radius** supports the thumb side of the wrist; the ulnar supports the outside of the wrist.

- **Major arteries** come nearer the surface at the wrist than at almost any other place in the body, so the wrist is one of the best places to test the pulse.

- **The bone** of the upper arm is the humerus. It connects to the shoulder blade (the scapula) at the shoulder joint, which is a ball-and-socket joint.

- **There are two major muscles** of the upper arm – the biceps (which bends the elbow), and the triceps (which straightens it).

- **The muscles** in the lower arm help to turn and move the wrist, hand and fingers.

- **The shoulder** is one of the most flexible but least stable joints of the skeleton, since it is set in a very shallow socket. Dislocated shoulders, in which the bone is dislodged from the joint, are common in contact sports such as rugby.

◄ *Look at the inside of your wrist on a warm day and you may be able to see the radial artery beneath the skin.*

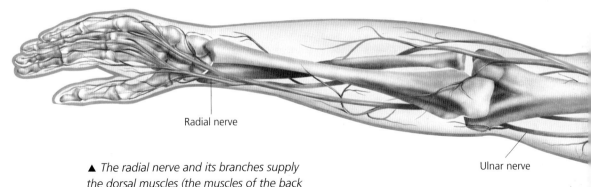

Radial nerve

Ulnar nerve

▲ *The radial nerve and its branches supply the dorsal muscles (the muscles of the back and shoulder).*

Shoulder joints are supported by six major muscle groups, including the powerful deltoid (shoulder) muscles.

Because of the wide range of movement of the shoulder and the ability to rotate the forearm and wrist, we can use our arms to do many different activities.

DID YOU KNOW?

The term 'funny bone' refers to the upper arm bone or humerus – a pun on the word 'humorous'.

▼ *A complicated network of muscles and nerves allow you to move your arm in many directions.*

Extensor muscles straighten fingers

Triceps straightens arm

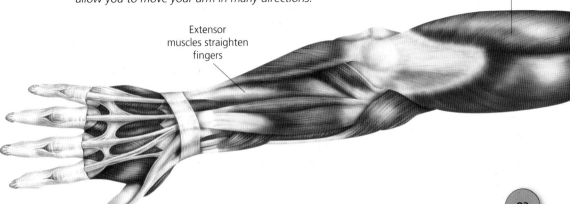

The hand

🖐️ **The hand** is made from 26 bones, including the carpals (wrist bones), the metacarpals (hand bones) and the phalanges (finger bones).

🖐️ **The wrist** contains eight small bones called the carpals.

🖐️ **There are no** strong muscles in the hand. When you grip firmly, most of the power comes from muscles in the lower arm, linked to the bones of the hand by long tendons.

🖐️ **Humans and other primates**, such as moneys, are different to all other animals as we have opposable thumbs. This means our thumbs can touch the tips of the fingers on the same hand.

🖐️ **There are more** nerve endings in the hand than anywhere else in the body. The fingertips are especially sensitive to touch.

◄ *The intricate network of bones in your hands enables you to perform delicate and complex movements such as writing or playing a musical instrument.*

▲ *Muscles and nerves in your hand and lower arm all act together with your brain so you can use equipment like mobile phones.*

Between 70 and 80 percent of people are right-handed, which means that they have more co-ordination in their right hand than in their left.

In the past, children who were left-handed were forced to write with their right hand. Even today, most tools, instruments and devices are made for right-handed people.

Some people have more than the usual numbers of fingers on one or both hands. This is called polydactyly.

We use our hands all the time. They are capable of delicate gestures, such as stroking a cat, or tough activities such as digging the garden. We can play instruments or make beautiful objects and even use them to communicate through sign language.

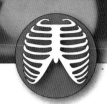

The leg

- **The leg** is made from three long bones, linked by a hinge joint at the knee.

- **The femur** (thigh bone) is the body's longest bone.

- **It connects** to the pelvis at the hip joint, which is a ball-and-socket joint.

- **The hip** is one of the strongest joints in the body. The ball at the end of the femur sits in a very deep cup in the pelvis, making it almost impossible to dislocate.

- **The two bones** of the lower leg are the tibia and fibula.

- **The tibia** is the main shinbone at the front of the leg; the fibula lies to the outer side and slightly behind.

DID YOU KNOW?
In anatomy, the word 'leg' is just used for the part of the leg between the knee and ankle.

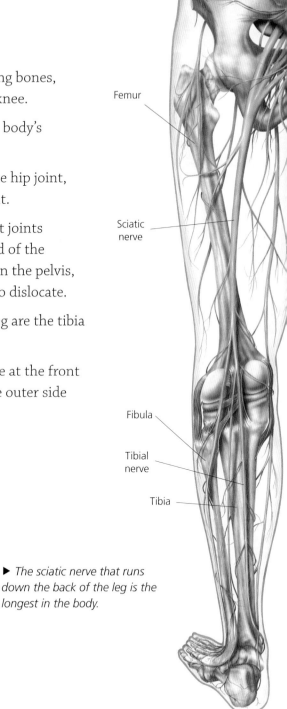

Femur

Sciatic nerve

Fibula

Tibial nerve

Tibia

▶ The sciatic nerve that runs down the back of the leg is the longest in the body.

The muscles of the leg are especially strong to enable us to sit, stand, walk and run. The largest muscle in the body, the gluteus maximus, is used for stepping or standing up.

Muscles in the lower leg help to turn and move the ankle, foot and toes.

Human legs are longer in proportion to their bodies than those of most other animals. This is because we have adapted to walk upright on two legs.

Since the start of the 1900s, women in Western cultures have been removing hair from their legs as a sign of beauty.

▲ Our legs contain large bones, muscles and nerves so they can take the weight and strain of our bodies.

The foot

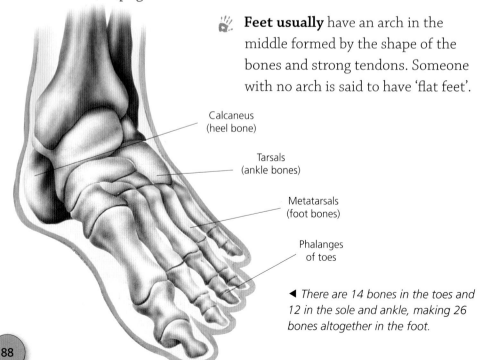

- **The foot** is made from 24 bones, including the tarsus (ankle bones), the metatarsus (foot bones) and the phalanges (toe bones).

- **The ankle** and part of the foot nearest the ankle contains eight bones called the tarsus bones.

- **Movement of the ankle**, foot and toes mostly comes from muscles in the lower leg, linked to the bones of the foot by long tendons.

- **We use our feet** and toes for balance. Our big toes are especially important; without them it would be much harder to walk and stand upright.

- **Feet usually** have an arch in the middle formed by the shape of the bones and strong tendons. Someone with no arch is said to have 'flat feet'.

DID YOU KNOW?

The foot contains dozens of muscles, tendons and ligaments.

Calcaneus
(heel bone)

Tarsals
(ankle bones)

Metatarsals
(foot bones)

Phalanges
of toes

◄ *There are 14 bones in the toes and 12 in the sole and ankle, making 26 bones altogether in the foot.*

88

◀ *Ballerinas who dance en pointe (on their toes) have to wear special shoes to help support their feet.*

There are many customs associated with feet around the world. In some countries it is considered offensive to expose the soles of your feet to another person. It is also thought rude to touch with your feet or point your feet towards someone else.

In many countries it is thought polite to remove your shoes when you enter someone else's home.

In China, young girls used to have their feet bound to make them very small. This was thought to be attractive but was very painful and is now no longer done.

The world record for the most fingers and toes in one person is 25, with 12 fingers and 13 toes.

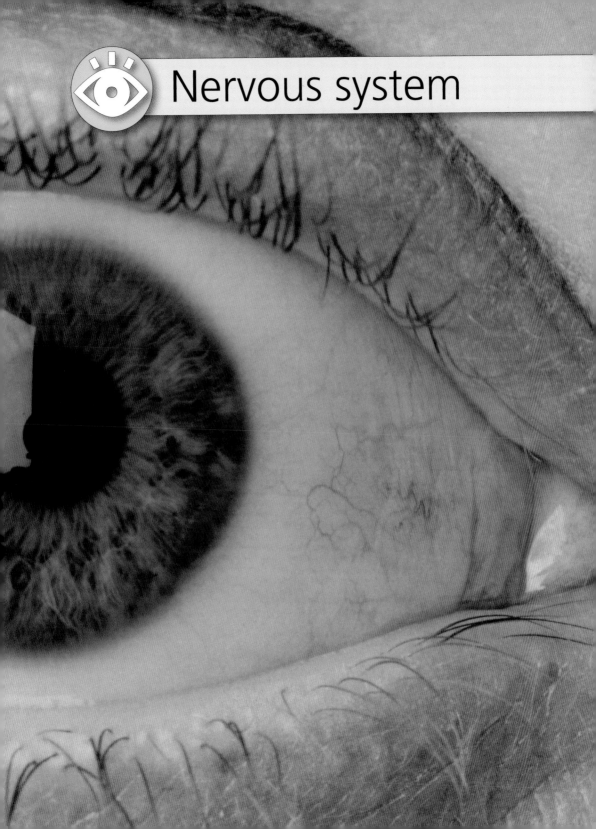

The nervous system

The nervous system is your body's control and communication system, made up of nerves and the brain.

Nerves are your body's hot lines, carrying instant messages from the brain to every organ and muscle – and sending back an endless stream of data to the brain about what is going on both inside and outside your body. The nervous system is divided into two parts – the central nervous system and the peripheral nervous system.

The central nervous system (CNS) consists of the brain and spinal cord.

The peripheral nervous system (PNS) is made up of the nerves that branch out from the CNS to the rest of the body.

Some PNS nerves are as wide as your thumb. The longest is the sciatic nerve, which runs from the base of the spine to the knee.

The PNS can be divided into nerves that control voluntary actions, such as walking or throwing a ball, and autonomic nerves that control all the body's functions.

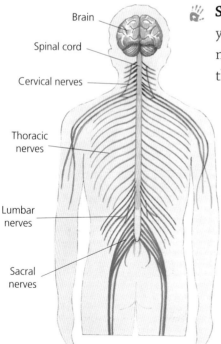

Brain

Spinal cord

Cervical nerves

Thoracic nerves

Lumbar nerves

Sacral nerves

◄ *Spinal nerves branch off the spinal cord in pairs, with one nerve on either side. They are arranged in four groups, and there is one pair between each of the 32 vertebrae.*

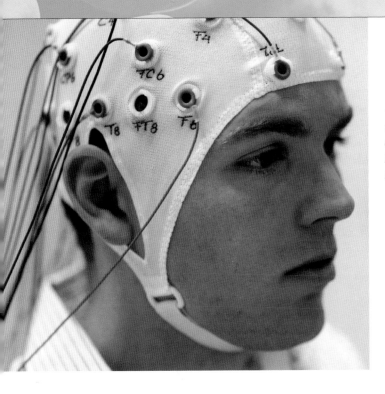

◄ *The process of having brain waves measured is called electroencephalography. It is used to help diagnose nervous system disorders.*

The autonomic nervous system (ANS) is part of the PNS. It controls all internal body processes such as breathing automatically, without you even being aware of it.

The ANS is split into two complementary (balancing) parts – the sympathetic and the parasympathetic. The sympathetic system speeds up body processes when they need to be more active, such as when the body is exercising or under stress. The parasympathetic slows them down.

Nerves can be divided into motor nerves, which carry messages from the brain to muscles to control movement, and sensory nerves, which carry messages from sensory receptors in the body to the brain.

In many places, sensory nerves run alongside motor nerves.

Central nervous system

- **The central nervous system** (CNS) is made up of the brain and the spinal cord (the nerves of the spine).

- **It is responsible** for collecting information from all the other nerves in the body, processing data and sending out appropriate responses.

- **The CNS** contains billions of densely packed interneurons – nerve cells with very short connecting axons (tails).

- **A surrounding bath of liquid** called cerebrospinal fluid cushions the CNS from damage.

- **There are 86 main nerves** branching off the CNS.

- **There are 12 pairs** of cranial nerves and 31 pairs of spinal nerves.

- **Cranial nerves** are the 12 pairs of nerves that branch off the CNS out of the brain.

- **Spinal nerves** are the 31 pairs of nerves that branch off the spinal cord.

- **The spinal nerves** are made up of eight cervical nerve pairs, 12 thoracic pairs, five lumbar pairs, five sacral pairs and one coccyx pair.

- **Many spinal nerves** join up just outside the spine in five 'spaghetti junctions' called plexuses.

DID YOU KNOW?

The CNS sends out messages to more than 640 muscles around the body.

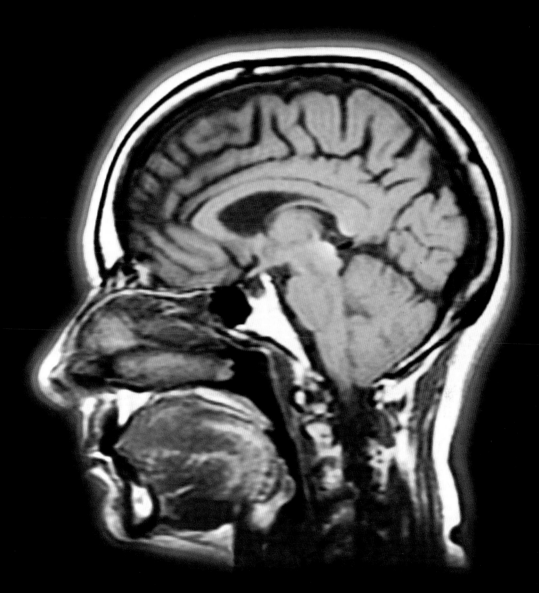

▲ *The brain's cortex (outer layer) is only 5 mm thick, but flattened out would cover an area almost as big as an office desk, and contains at least 50 billion nerve cells.*

The brain

The human brain is made up of more than 100 billion nerve cells called neurons.

Each neuron is connected to as many as 25,000 other neurons – so the brain has trillions and trillions of different pathways for nerve signals.

As well as controlling our day-to-day actions and responses, the brain enables us to think, learn, understand and create.

The main part of the brain is called the cerebrum and is divided into two halves. The left half controls the right side of the body, while the right half controls the left side of the body.

The cerebellum at the base of the brain controls co-ordination and fine movement.

Girls' brains weigh 2.5 percent of their body weight, on average, while boys' brains weigh 2 percent.

◄ *Taking the top off the skull shows the brain to be a soggy, pinky-grey mass, which looks rather like a giant walnut.*

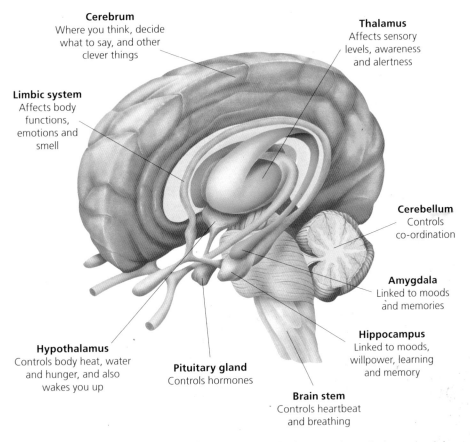

Cerebrum
Where you think, decide
what to say, and other
clever things

Thalamus
Affects sensory
levels, awareness
and alertness

Limbic system
Affects body
functions,
emotions and
smell

Cerebellum
Controls
co-ordination

Amygdala
Linked to moods
and memories

Hippocampus
Linked to moods,
willpower, learning
and memory

Hypothalamus
Controls body heat, water
and hunger, and also
wakes you up

Pituitary gland
Controls hormones

Brain stem
Controls heartbeat
and breathing

▲ In this illustration, the right hemisphere (half) of the cerebrum is shown in pink,
surrounding the regions that control basic drives such as hunger, thirst and anger.

About 0.85 litres of blood shoots through your brain every
minute. The brain may be as little as 2 percent of your body
weight, but it demands 12–15 percent of your blood supply.

An elephant's brain weighs four times as much as the human
brain. Some apes, monkeys and dolphins have a brain-body ratio
quite similar to that of humans.

The cerebral cortex

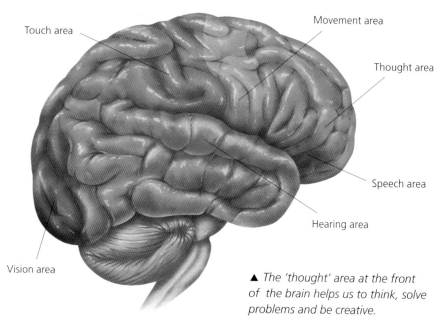

Touch area

Movement area

Thought area

Speech area

Hearing area

Vision area

▲ *The 'thought' area at the front of the brain helps us to think, solve problems and be creative.*

A cortex is the outer layer of any organ, such as the brain or the kidney.

The cerebral cortex is a layer of interconnected nerve cells around the outside of the brain, called 'grey matter'.

Conscious thoughts and actions happen in the cerebral cortex.

Many signals from the senses are registered in the brain in the cerebral cortex.

The visual cortex is around the lower back of the brain. It is the place where all the things you see are registered in the brain.

The somatosensory cortex is a band running over the top of the brain like a headband. This is where a touch on any part of the body is registered.

- **Just in front** of the sensory cortex lies the motor cortex. It sends out signals to body muscles to make them move.

- **The more nerve endings** there are in a particular part of the body, the more of the sensory cortex it occupies.

- **A huge proportion** of the sensory cortex is taken up by the lips and face.

- **The hands** take up almost as much of the sensory cortex as the face.

- **A human brain** has a cerebral cortex four times as big as a chimpanzee, about 20 times as big as a monkey's, and about 300 times as big as a rat's.

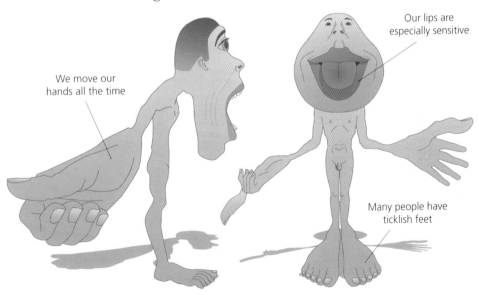

We move our hands all the time

Our lips are especially sensitive

Many people have ticklish feet

▲ These cartoons show the body in proportion to how much of the brain is needed to control movement (on the left) or process senses (on the right).

The spinal cord

- **The spinal cord** is the bundle of nerves running down the middle of the backbone.

- **It is the route** for all nerve signals travelling between the brain and the body.

- **The spinal cord** can actually work independently of the brain, sending out responses to the muscles directly.

- **The outside** of the spinal cord is made of the long tails or axons of nerve cells and is called white matter; the inside is made of the main nerve bodies and is called grey matter.

- **Your spinal cord** is about 43 cm long and one centimetre thick. It stops growing when you are about five years old.

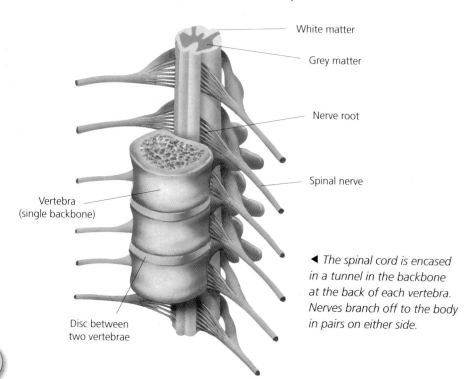

White matter

Grey matter

Nerve root

Spinal nerve

Vertebra
(single backbone)

Disc between
two vertebrae

◄ *The spinal cord is encased in a tunnel in the backbone at the back of each vertebra. Nerves branch off to the body in pairs on either side.*

▲ *If the spinal cord is damaged, nerves cannot carry messages to and from the brain and muscles. This may mean the person cannot walk and has to use a wheelchair.*

DID YOU KNOW?
The most common cause of a spinal cord injury is a traffic accident.

Damage to the spinal cord can cause paralysis.

Injuries below the neck can cause paraplegia – paralysis below the waist.

Injuries to the neck can cause quadriplegia – paralysis below the neck.

Descending pathways are groups of nerves that carry nerve signals down the spinal cord – typically signals from the brain for muscles to move.

Ascending pathways are groups of nerves that carry nerve signals up the spinal cord – typically signals from the skin and internal body sensors going to the brain.

Peripheral nervous system

- **The peripheral nervous system** (PNS) consists of the 12 cranial nerves in the head and the 31 pairs of spinal nerves that branch off the spinal cord.

- **Spinal nerves** can be divided into groups: there are eight pairs of cervical nerves in the neck, 12 pairs of thoracic nerves in the chest, five pairs of lumbar nerves in the abdomen, five pairs of sacral nerves in the lower back and one pair of coccygeal nerves at the base of the spine.

- **Several of the spinal nerves** combine to form collections of nerves called nerve plexuses.

- **Located in the head**, the cervical plexus provides the nerves that supply the neck and shoulders.

- **The plexus** in the neck and upper arm is called the brachial plexus and supplies the arm and the upper back.

- **Nerves in the abdomen** are provided by the solar plexus. The lumbar plexus contains nerves that supply the abdomen and the leg muscles.

- **Long bundles** of nerve fibres make up the nerves of the PNS. These are in turn made from the long axons (tails) of nerve cells, bound together like the wires in a telephone cable.

- **The sciatic nerve** to each leg is the longest nerve in the body. Its name is from the Latin for 'pain in the thigh'.

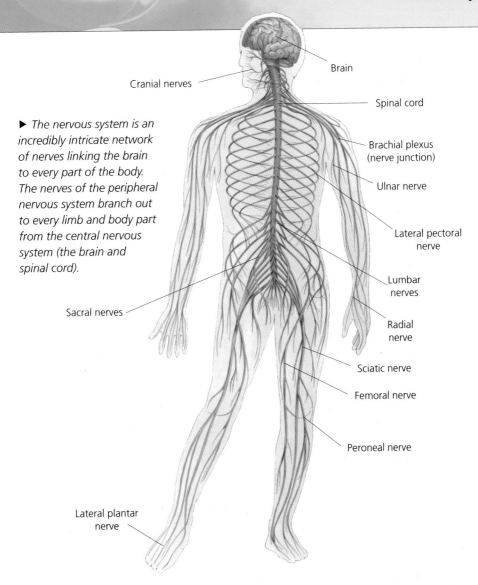

Brain

Cranial nerves

Spinal cord

▶ *The nervous system is an incredibly intricate network of nerves linking the brain to every part of the body. The nerves of the peripheral nervous system branch out to every limb and body part from the central nervous system (the brain and spinal cord).*

Brachial plexus (nerve junction)

Ulnar nerve

Lateral pectoral nerve

Lumbar nerves

Sacral nerves

Radial nerve

Sciatic nerve

Femoral nerve

Peroneal nerve

Lateral plantar nerve

The ulnar nerve controls the muscles in the forearm, hand and fingers. When you hit your 'funny bone' you are actually bruising this nerve.

Pins and needles occur when you pinch one of your peripheral nerves by sitting awkwardly or holding an arm or leg in a funny position for a long time.

Cranial nerves

- **There are 12 pairs** of cranial nerves that emerge directly from the brain.

- **The nose** is linked to the brain by the olfactory nerves.

- **The eyes** are linked to the brain by the optic nerves, which carry visual information, and the oculomotor, trochlear and abducens nerves, which move the eyeballs in their sockets.

- **The trigeminal nerves** control chewing and receive sensation from the face.

- **The facial nerves** control your facial expression and carry information about your sense of taste to the brain.

- **Balance and movement** are aided by the vestibulocochlear nerves.

- **The glossopharyngeal nerves** also carry information about your sense of taste to the brain.

- **The vagus nerves** perform many functions, including controlling your heart rate and speech.

- **Some of the movements** of your neck and shoulders, such as shrugging, are controlled by the accessory nerves.

- **The last nerve**, the hypoglossal nerve, helps you to swallow and talk by controlling the tongue.

DID YOU KNOW?

Cranial means something to do with the skull. However, not all cranial nerves go to the head.

▶ *Cranial nerves come from the underside of the brain and connect the brain with the face, including the eyes, nose and mouth.*

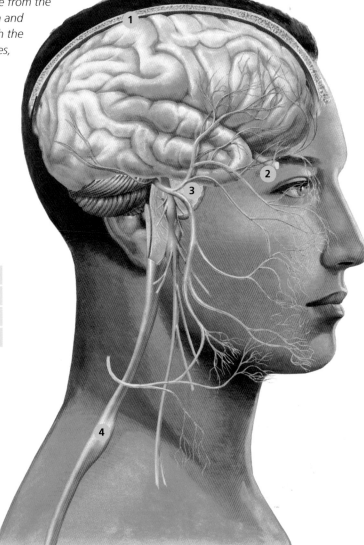

1 Skull

2 Optic nerve

3 Brain stem

4 Spinal cord

Nerve cells

- **Nerves are made** of very specialized cells called neurons.

- **Neurons are spider-shaped** with a nucleus at the centre, lots of branching threads called dendrites, and a winding tail called an axon, which can be up to one metre long.

- **Axon terminals** on the axons of one neuron link either to the dendrites or body of another neuron.

- **Neurons link up** like beads on a string to make your nervous system.

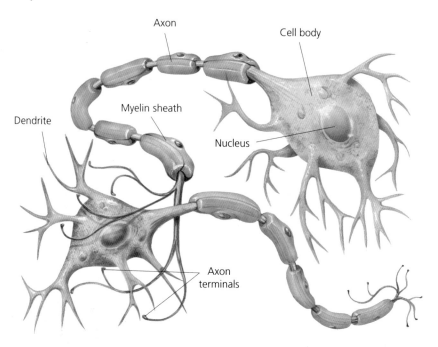

Axon

Cell body

Myelin sheath

Dendrite

Nucleus

Axon terminals

▲ Nerve cells, or neurons, are the 'wires' of the body's nervous system. They carry messages within, to and from the central nervous system along fine branches called dendrites and long tails called axons.

- **Most cells** are short-lived and are constantly being replaced by new ones. Neurons, however, are very long-lived – some are never actually replaced once you are born.

- **Nerve signals** travel as electrical pulses, each pulse lasting about 0.001 seconds.

- **When nerves are resting** there are extra sodium ions with a positive electrical charge on the outside of the nerve cell, and extra negative ions inside.

- **When a nerve fires**, little gates open in the cell wall all along the nerve, and positive ions rush in to join the negative ions. This makes an electrical pulse.

- **Long-distance nerves** are insulated (covered) by a sheath of a fatty substance called myelin, to keep the signal strong.

- **Myelinated (myelin-sheathed) nerves** shoot signals very fast – at more than 100 m/sec.

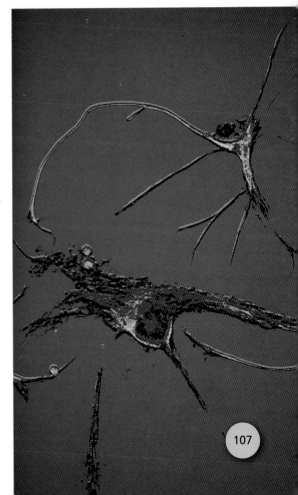

▶ *Microscopically tiny nerve cells were first seen when stained with silver nitrate by the Italian scientist Camillo Golgi in the 1870s.*

Synapses

- **Synapses** are the very tiny gaps between nerve cells.

- **When a nerve signal** goes from one nerve cell to another, it must be transmitted (sent) across the synapse by special chemicals called neurotransmitters.

DID YOU KNOW?

It is thought that an adult human might have as many as 500 trillion synapses in his or her brain.

- **Droplets of neurotransmitter** are released into the synapse whenever a nerve signal arrives.

- **As the droplets** of neurotransmitter lock on to the receiving nerve's receptors, they fire the signal onwards.

- **Each receptor site** on a nerve ending only reacts to certain neurotransmitters.

- **Sometimes several signals** must arrive before enough neurotransmitter is released to fire the receiving nerve.

- **More than 40** neurotransmitter chemicals have been identified.

- **Dopamine** is a neurotransmitter that works in the parts of the brain that control movement and learning. Parkinson's disease may develop when the nerves that produce dopamine break down.

- **Serotonin** is a neurotransmitter that is linked to sleeping and waking up, and also to your mood.

- **Acetylcholine** is a neurotransmitter that may be involved in memory, and also in the nerves that control muscle movement.

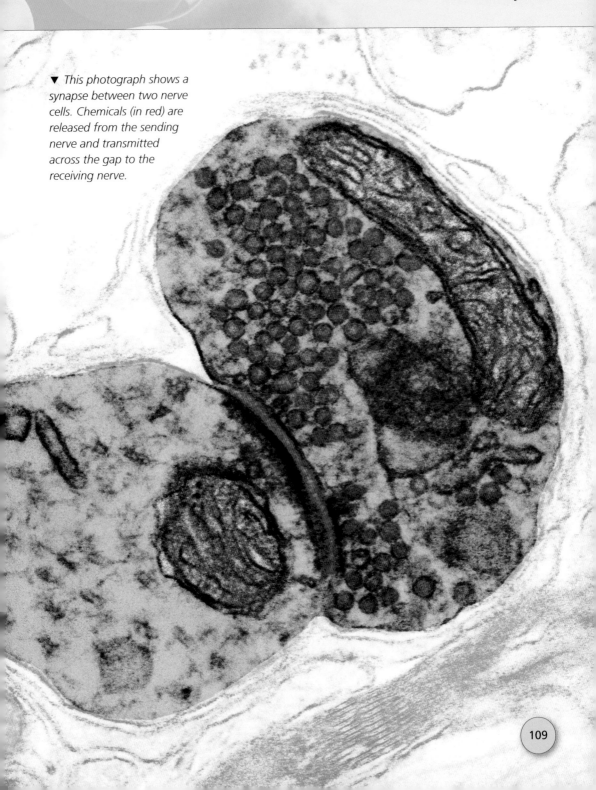

▼ *This photograph shows a synapse between two nerve cells. Chemicals (in red) are released from the sending nerve and transmitted across the gap to the receiving nerve.*

Sensory nerves

Sensory nerves are the nerves that carry information to your brain from sense receptors all over your body.

Sense receptors include the sense organs, such as the eyes, and receptors in the skin.

They are also located in the mouth, throat and in the lining of the internal organs.

▼ *We rely on sight more than our other senses, but to fully enjoy a firework display we need sight and sound.*

Each sense receptor in the body is linked to the brain by a sensory nerve.

Most sensory nerves feed their signals to the somatosensory cortex, which is the strip situated around the top of the brain where sensations are registered.

Massive bundles of sensory nerve cells form the nerves that link major senses such as the eyes, ears and nose, to the brain.

Sense receptors are everywhere in your skin, but places such as your face have more than your back.

▲ Some of our most pleasant feelings, such as being hugged or stroked, are sent to the brain by sensory nerves.

In the skin, many sense receptors are simply 'free' – meaning they are exposed sensory nerve-endings.

Free nerve-endings are rather like the bare end of a wire. They respond to all kinds of skin sensation and are almost everywhere in your skin.

We can tell how strong a sensation is by how fast the sensory nerve fires signals to the brain. But no matter how strong the sensation is, the nerve does not go on firing at the same rate and soon slows down.

111

Touch

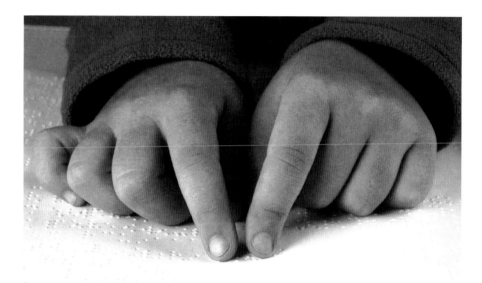

▲ *Our fingertips are most sensitive to touch, which can even compensate for lack of sight by allowing people to read Braille.*

Touch, or physical contact, is just one of the five senses.

Touch sensors in our skin help to relay information to the brain, enabling us to feel.

There are several aspects to touch – we feel light and deep pressure, hot, cold and pain.

We use touch to learn about our surroundings and carry out everyday activities such as holding things.

Without our sense of touch we would not know how much pressure to use when picking something up. We would drop things or squeeze them so tight they would break.

Touch also warns us of danger. We feel pain if we touch something too hot or too cold and we know to move away.

- **For blind and partially sighted people**, touch is particularly important in helping them to recognize their environment. Many blind people learn to read Braille so that they can still read books.

- **Touch is also important** for our well being. We all need to touch and be touched to grow up happy and healthy.

- **Anaesthetics** temporarily reduce or remove our sense of touch so that we don't feel pain.

- **If a nerve is damaged**, we may lose our sense of touch in the area that nerve supplies. People with diabetes sometimes lose their sense of touch in the fingertips or toes.

▶ *We can identify many things by touch alone.*

Touch sensors

- **Touch receptors** are spread all over the body in the skin. They respond to light and deep pressure, pain, hot and cold.

- **There are 200,000** hot and cold receptors in your skin, plus 500,000 touch and pressure receptors and nearly three million pain receptors.

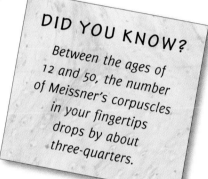

- **There are specialized receptors** in certain places, each named after their discoverer.

- **Merkel's discs** and Meissner's corpuscles are found near the surface of the skin and react instantly to light pressure.

- **Meissner's corpuscles** are particularly numerous in sensitive hairless skin areas such as the fingers and the palms of the hands.

- **Pacinian corpuscles** lie deeper in the skin and respond to deeper pressure and vibration.

- **Ruffini's endings** also lie deeper in the skin and respond to deep and steady pressure.

- **Free nerve endings** react to pressure, pain, heat and cold.

- **When we touch something**, pressure on the skin causes the receptors to move, sending signals to the brain, which interprets the signals as light or deep pressure, pain, heat or cold.

114

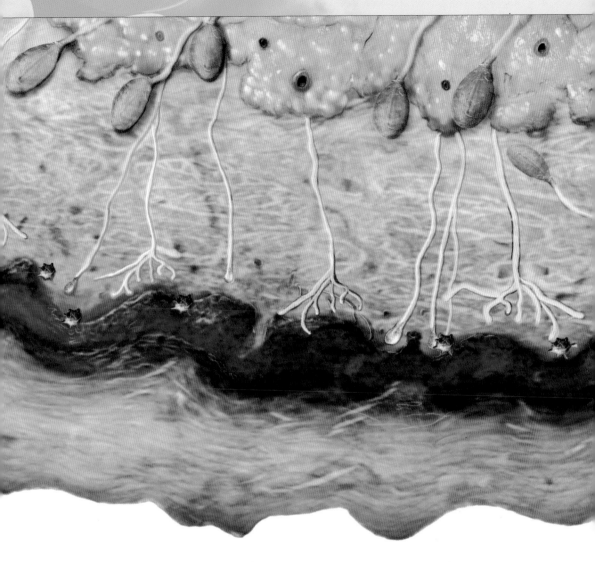

▲ *Beneath the top layer of the skin are many sensory receptors that help us to feel pain, pressure and temperature.*

It is the combination of all these receptors working together that enables us to do so many things, from hugging each other to drawing or painting.

The eye

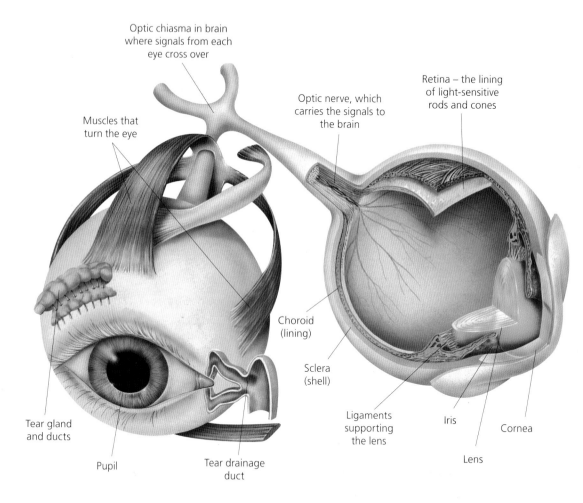

Optic chiasma in brain where signals from each eye cross over

Muscles that turn the eye

Optic nerve, which carries the signals to the brain

Retina – the lining of light-sensitive rods and cones

Choroid (lining)

Sclera (shell)

Tear gland and ducts

Pupil

Tear drainage duct

Ligaments supporting the lens

Iris

Cornea

Lens

▲ *This illustration shows the two eyeballs, with a cutaway to reveal the cornea and lens (which projects light rays through the pupil) and the light-sensitive retina (which registers it).*

- **Your eyes** are tough balls that are filled with a jelly-like substance called vitreous humour.

- **The eyes** are protected by bony sockets in the skull and from dust and dirt by our eyelids and eyelashes.

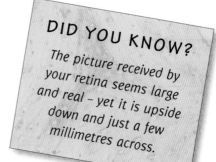

DID YOU KNOW?

The picture received by your retina seems large and real – yet it is upside down and just a few millimetres across.

- **The outer layer** of the eye, or the white of the eye, is called the sclera and helps keep the shape of the eye.

- **The cornea** is a thin, glassy dish across the front of your eye. It allows light rays through the eye's window, the pupil, and into the lens.

- **The iris** is the coloured, muscular ring around the pupil. The iris narrows in bright light and widens when light is dim.

- **The lens** is just behind the pupil. It focuses the picture of the world on to the back of the eye.

- **The back of the eye** is lined with millions of light-sensitive cells. This lining is called the retina, and it registers the picture and sends signals to the brain via the optic nerve.

- **Strong muscles** that surround each eye enable us to move our eyeballs in different directions.

- **Our eyes are kept moist** by tears, which are continuously produced by glands that lie just above each eye. Excess tears drain away from the corners of the eyes into the nose. They also help to wash away any dust from the eye.

Sight

- **When you look** at an object, light from the object hits the cornea at the front of your eye and is bent by the cornea on to the lens.

- **The lens** in the eye focuses the light onto the retina at the back of the eye. The most sensitive part of the retina is called the fovea.

- **The cells** in the retina collect the information and send signals to the brain, which interprets the signals as images.

- **There are two kinds** of light-sensitive cell in the retina – rods and cones. Rods are very sensitive and work in even dim light, but they cannot detect colours. Cones respond to colour.

- **Some kinds of cone** are very sensitive to red light, some to green and some to blue. One theory says that the colours we see depend on how strongly they affect each of these three kinds of cone.

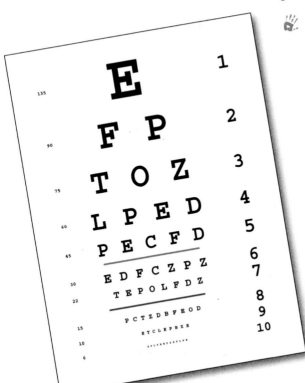

◄ An optician tests vision using a chart on a wall. The further down the chart you can read, the better your vision.

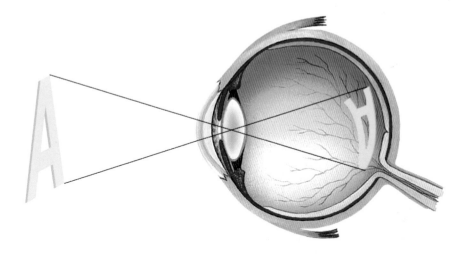

▲ *The eye produces upside-down images on the retina. Signals then travel to the brain, which interprets the image as the right way up.*

- **Each of your two eyes** gives you a slightly different view of the world. The brain combines these views to give an impression of depth and 3D solidity.

- **Although each eye** gives a slightly different view of the world, we see things largely as just one eye sees it. This dominant eye is usually the right eye.

- **Many people** do not have perfect vision. People who have difficulty seeing objects that are a long way away are called short-sighted. People who have difficulty seeing objects that are very close are called long-sighted.

- **Short and long sight** occurs when the light from the object you are looking at is not focused on the retina by the lens in the eye.

- **Glasses or contact lenses** are used to adjust the way the light enters the eye so that the lens will focus the light on the right place in the retina.

Colour vision

- **Seeing in colour** depends on eye cells called cones.

- **Cones do not work well** in low light, which is why things seem grey at dusk.

- **Some cones** are more sensitive to red light, some are more sensitive to green and some to blue.

- **The old trichromatic theory** said that you see colours by comparing the strength of the signals from each of the three kinds of cone – red, green and blue.

- **The trichromatic theory** does not explain colours such as gold, silver and brown.

- **The opponent-process theory** said that you see colours in opposing pairs – blue and yellow, red and green.

- **In opponent-process theory**, lots of blue light is thought to cut your awareness of yellow, and vice versa. Lots of green cuts your awareness of red, and vice versa.

◄ Seeing all the colours of the world around you depends on the colour-sensitive cone cells inside your eyes.

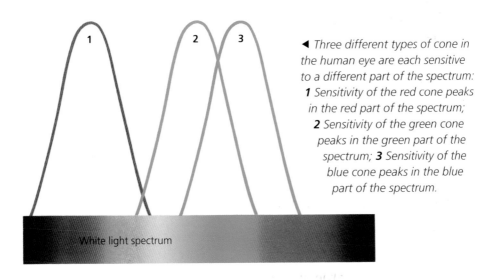

◄ Three different types of cone in the human eye are each sensitive to a different part of the spectrum: **1** Sensitivity of the red cone peaks in the red part of the spectrum; **2** Sensitivity of the green cone peaks in the green part of the spectrum; **3** Sensitivity of the blue cone peaks in the blue part of the spectrum.

White light spectrum

Now scientists combine these theories and think that colour signals from the three kinds of cone are further processed in the brain in terms of the opposing pairs.

Ultraviolet light is light in waves too short for you to see, although some birds and insects can see it.

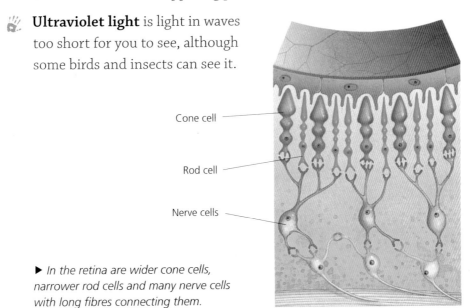

Cone cell

Rod cell

Nerve cells

▶ In the retina are wider cone cells, narrower rod cells and many nerve cells with long fibres connecting them.

The ear

- **Ears aren't just for hearing**; they also enable us to balance and keep our posture.

- **There are three parts** to the ear – the outer ear, which is the part you can see and the canal that leads to the eardrum, the middle ear and the inner ear.

- **Pinnae** (singular, pinna) are the ear flaps you can see on the side of your head. They are simply collecting funnels for sounds.

- **The canal** from the pinna is called the ear canal. Glands in the ear canal produce ear wax that helps to keep the ear clean.

- **The ear canal** leads to the eardrum – a thin membrane that separates the outer and middle ear.

- **Three bones** are found in the middle ear. These are the malleus (hammer), the incus (anvil) and the stapes (stirrup).

- **The stapes** is the smallest bone in the body and attaches to another membrane called the oval window, which separates the middle and inner ear.

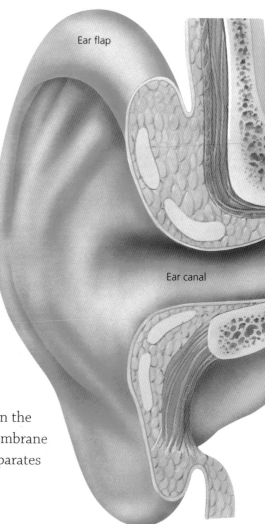

Ear flap

Ear canal

The oval window is 30 times smaller in area than the eardrum.

Beyond the oval window is the cochlea – a winding collection of three liquid-filled tubes, which looks a bit like a snail shell.

In the middle tube of the cochlea there is a flap that covers row upon row of tiny hairs. This is called the organ of Corti.

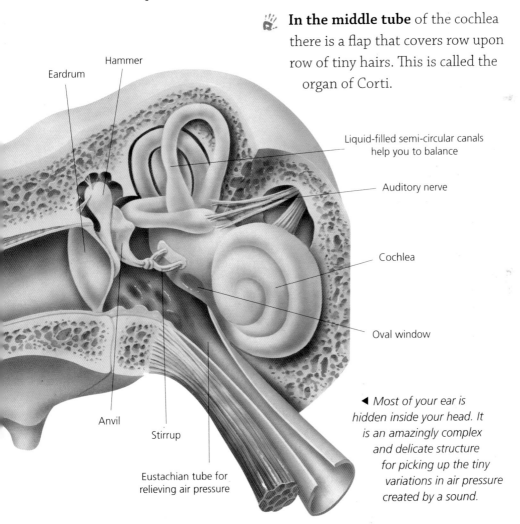

Eardrum

Hammer

Liquid-filled semi-circular canals help you to balance

Auditory nerve

Cochlea

Oval window

Anvil

Stirrup

Eustachian tube for relieving air pressure

◀ *Most of your ear is hidden inside your head. It is an amazingly complex and delicate structure for picking up the tiny variations in air pressure created by a sound.*

Hearing

The ears provide us with our sense of hearing. The outer part of the ear acts as a funnel for sounds, which travel down the eardrum.

A little way inside your head, the sounds hit a thin, tight wall of skin, called the eardrum, making it vibrate.

When the eardrum vibrates, it shakes the three little bones called ossicles in the middle ear.

When the ossicles vibrate, they rattle the tiny membrane called the oval window, intensifying the vibration.

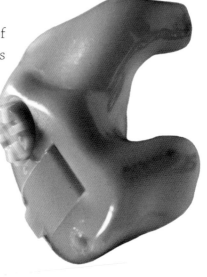

▲ *Modern hearing aids are small enough to fit inside the ear.*

The vibration of the oval window makes waves shoot through the liquid in the cochlea in the inner ear and wash over the flap of the organ of Corti, waving it up and down.

When the organ of Corti waves, it tugs on the many tiny hairs under the flap. These send signals to the brain via the auditory nerve, and you hear a sound.

DID YOU KNOW?

If your hearing is normal, you can hear sounds as deep as 20 hertz (Hz) – vibrations per second – and as high as 20,000 Hz.

There are up to 15,000 hair cells in the Organ of Corti.

The **average human adult** can hear frequencies between 20 and 20,000 hertz, but a bat can hear between 1000 and 120,000 hertz.

As we get older we have more difficulty hearing high-pitched sounds. Hearing aids help people who cannot hear well by amplifying sounds.

Hearing loss may also occur as a result of being exposed to loud noises over long periods of time, such as regularly listening to music from an MP3 player at high volumes.

▼ *Vibrations in the fluid in the inner ear are transmitted through nerves (shown in green), which run through bone (yellow) to hair cells in the organ of Corti, which send signals to the brain.*

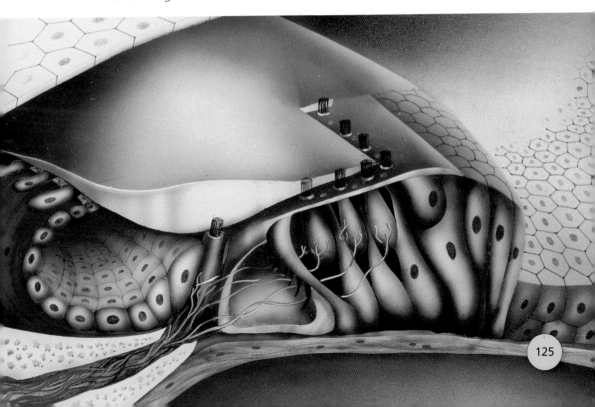

Balance

- **To stay upright**, your body must send a continual stream of data about its position to your brain – and your brain must continually tell your body how to move to keep its balance.

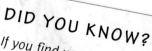
- **Balance is controlled** in many parts of the brain, including the brain's cerebellum.

- **Your brain** finds out about your body position from many sources, including your eyes, proprioceptors around the body, and the semicircular canals and other chambers in the inner ear.

- **Proprioceptors** are sense receptors in your skin, muscles and joints.

- **The semicircular canals** are three, tiny, fluid-filled loops in your inner ear.

- **Two chambers** (holes) called the utricle and saccule are linked to the semicircular canals.

- **When you move** your head, the fluid in the canals and cavities lags a little, pulling on hair detectors that tell your brain what is going on.

- **The canals** tell you whether you are nodding or shaking your head, and which way you are moving.

- **The utricle** and saccule tell you if you tilt your head or if its movement speeds up or slows down.

▼ *A rollercoaster ride can make you feel dizzy because the liquid inside your inner ear keeps spinning after you have stopped moving.*

The nose

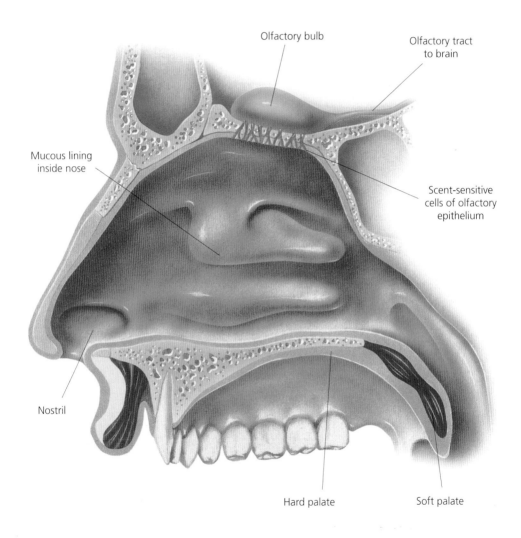

Olfactory bulb

Olfactory tract
to brain

Mucous lining
inside nose

Scent-sensitive
cells of olfactory
epithelium

Nostril

Hard palate

Soft palate

▲ *Scent particles dissolve in the mucous lining. The cells at the top of the nose
then send signals along the olfactory nerve to a special part of the brain.*

- **We use our noses** to smell and to breathe in air.

- **The nose** is made of skin and cartilage attached to the ethmoid bone of the skull. The two nostrils are separated by a piece of cartilage called the nasal septum.

DID YOU KNOW?
When two people rub noses together it is called an Eskimo kiss.

- **We breathe in** through our nostrils, which open up into the nasal cavity – a large space between the mouth and the brain.

- **The nasal cavity** is lined with cells that can detect different scents and smells.

- **The human nose** can tell the difference between more than 10,000 different chemicals.

- **The nose also warms** the air that we breathe in and makes it more humid.

- **Hairs within the nose** trap dust and other particles, preventing them from entering our airways.

- **Sneezing occurs** when dust enters and irritates the lining within the nose. Sneezing may also be caused by an allergy or an infection such as a cold.

- **In some people**, sudden exposure to bright light causes sneezing.

- **In New Zealand**, pressing two noses together (called a hongi) is a traditional greeting between Maori people.

Smell

Smells are scent molecules that are taken into your nose by breathed-in air. A particular smell may be noticeable even when just a single scent molecule is mixed in with millions of air molecules.

Dogs can pick up smells that are 10,000 times fainter than the ones humans can detect.

Inside the nose, scent molecules are picked up by a patch of scent-sensitive cells called the olfactory epithelium.

Olfactory means 'to do with the sense of smell'.

The olfactory epithelium contains over 25 million receptor cells.

▼ Dogs have a very keen sense of smell and are used for rescue, to sniff out drugs and for hunting.

Each of the receptor cells in the olfactory epithelium has up to 20 or so scent-detecting hairs called cilia.

When they are triggered by scent molecules, the cilia send signals to a cluster of nerves called the olfactory bulb, which then sends messages to the part of the brain that recognizes smell.

The part of the brain that deals with smell is closely linked to the parts that deal with memories and emotions. This may be why smells can often evoke vivid memories.

By the age of 20, you will have lost 20 percent of your sense of smell. By the age of 60, you will have lost 60 percent of it.

Smell is closely related to taste. If you have a cold and lose your sense of smell you will probably notice that food tastes odd or has no taste at all.

▶ *Manufacturers often use plant oils to make scented products such as soaps. Different smells are thought to create different moods. For example, the smell of lavender is thought to create a calm mood.*

Taste

- **The sense of taste** is the crudest of our five senses, giving us less information about the world than any other sense.

- **Taste is triggered by** certain chemicals in food, which dissolve in the saliva in your mouth and then send information to a particular part of the brain via sensory nerve cells on the tongue.

- **Taste buds** are receptor cells found around tiny bumps called papillae on the surface of your tongue.

- **They are sensitive** to four basic flavours: sweet, sour, bitter and salty.

- **The back of the tongue** contains big round papaillae shaped like an upside-down V. This is where bitter flavours are sensed.

- **The front of the tongue** is where fungiform (mushroom-like) papillae and filiform (hairlike) papillae carry taste buds that detect sweet, sour and salty flavours.

◀ *The tongue is sensitive to flavours, texture and temperature.*

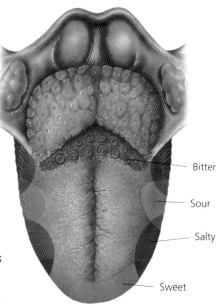

▶ Certain parts of the tongue are more sensitive to one flavour than to others.

Bitter

Sour

Salty

Sweet

- **As well as taste**, the tongue can also feel the texture and temperature of food.

- **Your sense of taste** works closely together with your sense of smell to make the flavour of food more interesting.

- **Strong tastes**, such as spicy food, rely less on the sense of smell than on pain-sensitive nerve endings in the tongue.

- **People can learn** to distinguish more flavours and tastes than normal, as is the case with tea- or wine-tasters.

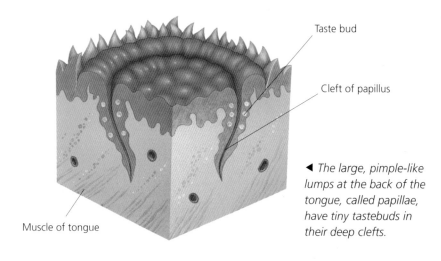

Taste bud

Cleft of papillus

Muscle of tongue

◀ The large, pimple-like lumps at the back of the tongue, called papillae, have tiny tastebuds in their deep clefts.

133

Motor nerves

- **Motor nerves** are connected to your muscles and tell your muscles to move.

- **Each major muscle** has many motor nerve endings that instruct it to contract (tighten).

- **Motor nerves** cross over from one side of the body to the other at the top of the spinal cord. This means that signals from the right side of your brain go to the left side of your body, and vice versa.

- **Each motor nerve** is paired to a proprioceptor on the muscle and its tendons. This sends signals to the brain to say whether the muscle is tensed or relaxed.

- **If the strain** on a tendon increases, the proprioceptor sends a signal to the brain. The brain adjusts the motor signals to the muscle so it contracts more or less.

- **Motor nerve signals** originate in a part of the brain called the motor cortex.

◄ When we need to act, motor nerves fire signals from the brain to the muscles to make them move.

▲ *Signals from the brain (shown as a flash of green light) travel down nerve cells to a muscle, telling the muscle to contract.*

- **All the motor nerves** (apart from those in the head) branch out from the spinal cord.

- **The gut** has no motor nerve endings but plenty of sense endings, so you can feel it but cannot move it consciously.

- **The throat** has motor nerve endings but few sense endings, so you can move it but not feel it.

- **Motor neuron disease** is a disease that attacks motor nerves within the central nervous system.

Reflexes

Reflexes are muscle movements that are automatic (they happen without you thinking about them).

Inborn reflexes are reflexes you were born with, such as urinating, or shivering when you are cold.

The knee-jerk is an inborn reflex that makes your leg jerk up when the tendon below your knee is tapped.

Primitive reflexes are reflexes that babies have for a few months after they are born.

One primitive reflex is when you put something in a baby's hand and it automatically grips it.

Reflex reactions make you pull your hand from hot things before you have had time to think about it.

▶ Even babies have reflexes – automatically grasping anything put into the palms of their hands.

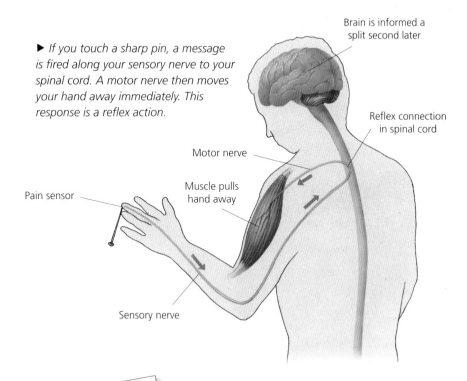

Brain is informed a
split second later

▶ *If you touch a sharp pin, a message
is fired along your sensory nerve to your
spinal cord. A motor nerve then moves
your hand away immediately. This
response is a reflex action.*

Reflex connection
in spinal cord

Motor nerve

Muscle pulls
hand away

Pain sensor

Sensory nerve

DID YOU KNOW?
Athletes often have
lightning reflexes – their
bodies react faster than
their brains can process.

Reflex reactions work by short-
circuiting the brain. The alarm signal
from your hand sets off motor signals
in the spinal cord to move the hand.

A reflex arc is the nerve circuit
from sense to muscle via the spinal
cord.

Conditioned reflexes are those you learn through habit, as
certain pathways in the nervous system are used again and again.

They can help you do anything, from holding a cup to playing
football, without thinking.

Co-ordination

◀ Dance of any kind tests the body's balance and co-ordination to its limits.

- **Co-ordination** means balanced or skilful movement.

- **To make you move**, your brain has to send signals out along nerves telling all the muscles involved exactly what to do.

- **Co-ordination of the muscles** is handled by the cerebellum at the back of your brain.

▲ *Any sport requires high degrees of muscle co-ordination. Team sports also need you to co-ordinate your movements exactly with other team members.*

- **The cerebellum** is given instructions by the brain's motor cortex.

- **The cerebellum's commands** are sent via the basal ganglia in the middle of the brain.

- **Proprioceptors are nerve cells** that are sensitive to movement, pressure or stretching. Proprioceptor means 'one's own sensors'.

- **They are all over your body** – in muscles, tendons and joints – and they all send signals to your brain telling it the position or posture of every part of your body.

- **The hair cells** in the balance organs of your ear are also proprioceptors.

139

Thinking

Some scientists claim that we humans are the only living things that are conscious, meaning that we alone are actually aware that we are thinking.

No one knows how consciousness works – it is one of science's last great mysteries.

Most of your thoughts seem to take place in the cerebrum (at the top of your brain), and different kinds of thought are linked to different areas, called association areas.

Each half of the cerebrum has four rounded ends called lobes – two at the front, called frontal and temporal lobes, and two at the back, called occipital and parietal lobes.

The frontal lobe is linked to your personality and it is where you have your bright ideas.

The temporal lobe is where you hear and understand what people are saying to you.

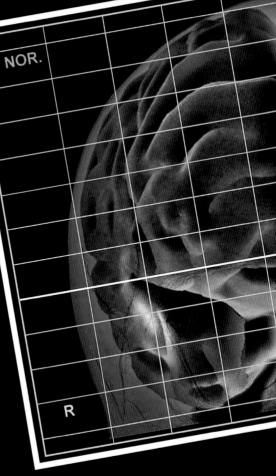

NOR.

R

The occipital lobe is where you work out what your eyes see.

DID YOU KNOW?

It is impossible to use all of your brain all of the time – different areas of the brain help us do different things.

 The parietal lobe is where you register touch, heat and cold, and pain.

 The left half of the brain (left hemisphere) controls the right side of the body. The right half (right hemisphere) controls the left side.

 One half of the brain is always dominant (in charge). Usually, the left brain is dominant, which is why up to 90 percent of people are right-handed.

L

▲ *This scan shows brain activity in someone reading aloud. The coloured active area on the right is the part of the brain that processes language.*

141

Memory

When you remember something, your brain probably stores it by creating new nerve connections.

You have three types of memory – sensory, short-term and long-term.

Sensory memory is when you go on feeling a sensation for a moment after it stops.

Short-term memory is when the brain stores things for a few seconds, like a phone number you remember long enough to press the buttons.

Long-term memory is memory that can last for months or maybe even your whole life.

Your brain seems to have two ways of remembering things for the long term. Scientists call these two different ways declarative and non-declarative memories.

Non-declarative memories are skills you teach yourself by practising, such as playing badminton or the flute. Repetition establishes nerve pathways.

Declarative memories are either episodic or semantic. Each may be sent by the hippocampus region of the brain to the correct place in the cortex, the brain's wrinkly outer layer, where you do most of your thinking.

HOW TO IMPROVE YOUR MEMORY

CHUNKING	To remember a long string of numbers, break it down into smaller chunks
SPACING IT OUT	Don't cram – space out your learning rather than trying to remember everything at once
CUES	Use something you do every day to help you remember other things
IMAGERY	Visualising images as you are learning can help you to remember items or names
SELF-REFERENCE	It is easier to remember something if you can link it with something personal
PLACE THINGS	To remember a collection of things, try imagining them in specific places in your home

Episodic memories are memories of striking events in your life, such as breaking your leg or your first day at a new school. You not only recall facts, but sensations.

Semantic memories are facts such as dates. The brain seems to store these in the left temporal lobe, at the front left-hand side of the brain.

Mood

Mood is your state of mind – whether you are happy or sad, angry or afraid, overjoyed or depressed.

Moods and emotions seem to be strongly linked to the structures in the centre of the brain, where unconscious activities are controlled.

Moods have three elements – how you feel, what happens to your body, and what moods make you do.

Some scientists think the way you feel causes changes in the body – you are happy so you smile, for example.

Other scientists think changes in the body alter the way you feel – smiling makes you happy.

▲ *Scientists are only just beginning to discover how moods and emotions are linked to particular*

Yet other scientists think moods start automatically – before you even know it – when something triggers off a reaction in the thalamus in the centre of the brain.

DID YOU KNOW?
Every mood is a combination of how much energy you have and how stressed you are.

The thalamus then sends mood signals to the brain's cortex and you become aware of the mood.

It also sets off automatic changes in the body through the nerves and hormones.

Certain memories or experiences are so strongly linked in your mind that they can often automatically trigger a certain mood.

▶ Why we react the way we do is unclear, but it is emotions such as happiness or frustration that make us unique as human beings.

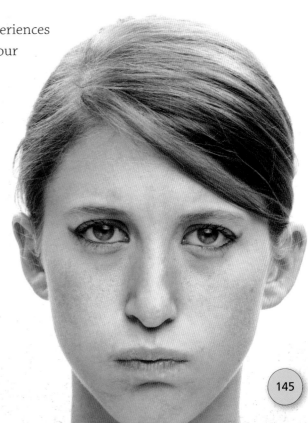

145

Fear and phobias

▶ *Some people have an intense fear or phobia of spiders.*

Fear is an emotion that occurs in response to danger. It can vary from mild fear, such as worry over an exam, to panic.

Fear is a normal reaction to a difficult situation and may help us avoid danger or cope with a threat.

A phobia is an intense fear of a particular situation or thing. Phobias are extreme reactions and often irrational.

Someone with a phobia will have a persistent fear of something that other people will not be afraid of, such as water or flying in an aeroplane.

Some phobias may develop after a traumatic experience. For example, someone who is bitten by a dog may then develop a phobia of dogs.

- **Between 10 and 20 percent** of people have a phobia. Most phobias do not interfere with everyday lives.

- **Social phobia** is the fear of meeting new people and of social situations.

- **Claustrophobia** is the fear of small spaces; agoraphobia is the fear of leaving home or of wide, open, unfamiliar spaces.

- **A fear of spiders** is called arachnophobia. The fear of snakes is called ophidiophobia.

- **Trypanophobia** is the fear of needles and injections. People who faint at the sight of blood may have this type of phobia.

▼ Fear can be exciting –
bungee jumping gives us an
adrenaline rush because
it is dangerous.

147

Communication

- **We communicate** in many different ways, not just through speech but also through our facial expressions, tone of voice and our body language.

- **Although we are the only animals** to use a complicated spoken language, all animals use sounds and body language to communicate.

- **We use our vocal cords** to speak, and we interpret other people's speech using our brains. However, it is not just what we say that is important. Our brains also interpret the tones of people's voices to help us understand what is meant.

- **Your expression,** posture and pose all contribute to your body language. It is thought that up to 70 percent of human communication is through body language.

- **Body language** can reveal whether you are telling the truth. Poker players use body language to tell if a person is bluffing or not.

▼ *A crowd at a sports event reveal their excitement and anticipation through their body language.*

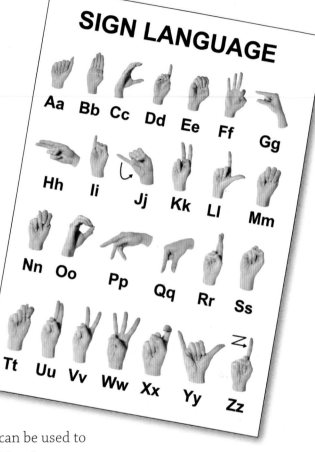

SIGN LANGUAGE

Aa Bb Cc Dd Ee Ff Gg

Hh Ii Jj Kk Ll Mm

Nn Oo Pp Qq Rr Ss

Tt Uu Vv Ww Xx Yy Zz

▶ *In its simplest form, sign language can spell out any word just using the hands. Hundreds of different sign languages are used around the world.*

Body language can also reveal whether you are bored, confident, anxious or interested in someone.

It is often easy to tell someone's mood just by looking at their face. We have over 30 muscles in our face – all of which can be used to make a huge variety of facial expressions.

Sign language is an important form of communication for people who cannot hear. A combination of hand, body and facial gestures is used to express words and phrases.

Sign language is not just for deaf people – divers use sign language to communicate with each other under water and soldiers use sign language when it is important to be quiet.

149

Sleeping

When you are asleep, many of your body functions go on as normal – even your brain goes on receiving sense signals. But your body may save energy and do routine repairs.

Lack of sleep can be dangerous. A newborn baby needs 18–20 hours of sleep a day. An adult needs around seven to eight hours.

Sleep is controlled in the brain stem. Dreaming is stimulated by signals fired from a part of the brain stem called the pons.

When you are awake, there is little pattern to the electricity created by the firing of the brain's nerve cells. But as you sleep, more regular waves appear.

While you are asleep, alpha waves sweep across the brain every 0.1 seconds. Theta waves are slower.

For the first 90 minutes of sleep, your sleep gets deeper and the brain waves become stronger.

After about 90 minutes of sleep, your brain suddenly starts to buzz with activity, yet you are hard to wake up.

- **After 90 minutes of sleep**, your eyes begin to flicker from side to side under their lids. This is called Rapid Eye Movement (REM) sleep.

- **REM sleep** is thought to show that you are dreaming.

DID YOU KNOW?
When you sleep is partly controlled by your body's internal clock – the circadian clock.

- **While you sleep**, ordinary deeper sleep alternates with spells of REM lasting up to half an hour.

▼ As we grow, we need less sleep. Toddlers and young children need around 11–15 hours a day.

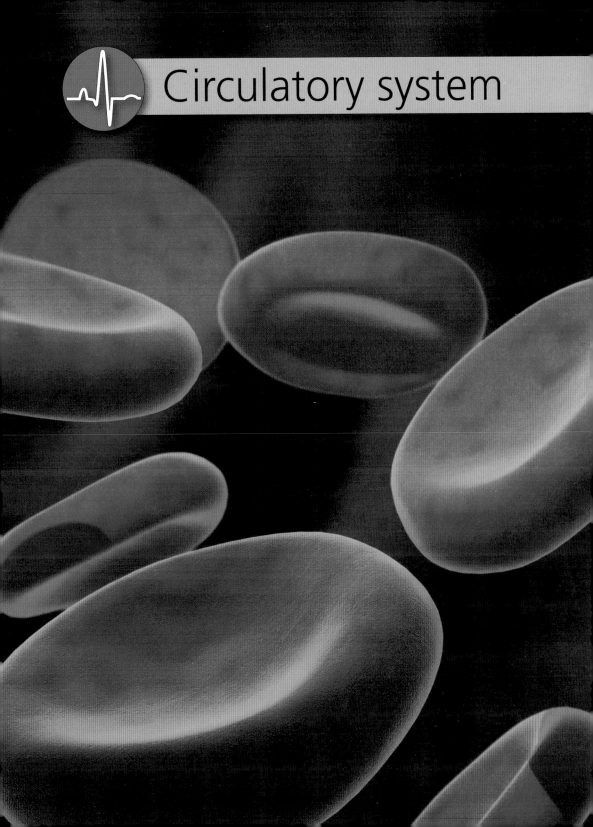

Circulatory system

Circulation

Your circulation is the system of tubes called blood vessels that carries blood out from your heart to all your body cells and back again.

Blood circulation was discovered in 1628 by the English physician William Harvey (1578–1657), who built on the ideas of the Italian anatomist Matteo Colombo (*c.* 1516–1559).

Each of the body's 600 billion cells gets fresh blood continuously, although the blood flow is pulsating.

On the way out from the heart, blood is pumped through vessels called arteries and arterioles.

On the way back to the heart, blood flows through venules and veins. For each outward-going artery there is usually an equivalent returning vein.

Blood flows from the arterioles to the venules through the tiniest tubes called capillaries.

The blood circulation has two parts – the pulmonary and the systemic.

The pulmonary circulation is the short section that carries blood low in oxygen from the right side of the heart to the lungs for 'refuelling'. It then returns oxygen-rich blood to the left side of the heart.

The systemic circulation carries oxygen-rich blood from the left side of the heart all around the body. It returns blood that is low in oxygen to the right side of the heart.

Inside the blood, oxygen is carried by the haemoglobin in red blood cells.

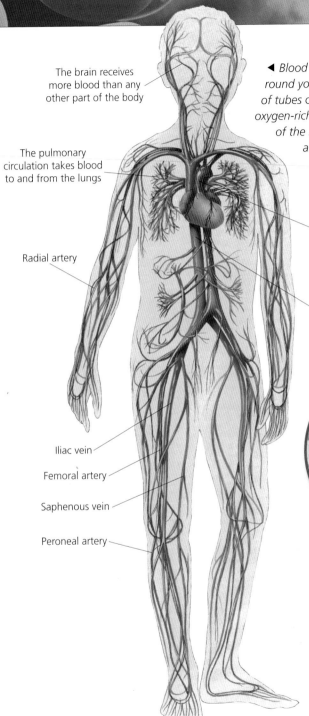

The brain receives more blood than any other part of the body

The pulmonary circulation takes blood to and from the lungs

Radial artery

Iliac vein

Femoral artery

Saphenous vein

Peroneal artery

◀ *Blood circulates continuously round and round your body, through an intricate series of tubes called blood vessels. Bright red, oxygen-rich blood is pumped from the left side of the heart through vessels called arteries and arterioles. Purplish-blue, low-in-oxygen blood returns to the right of the heart through veins and venules.*

Blood leaves the left side of the heart through a giant artery called the aorta

Blood returns to the heart through main veins called the vena cavae

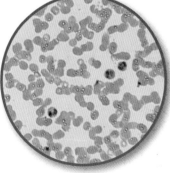

▲ *Red blood cells can actually be brown in colour, but they turn bright scarlet when their haemoglobin is carrying oxygen. After the haemoglobin passes its oxygen to a cell, it fades to dull purple.*

155

The heart

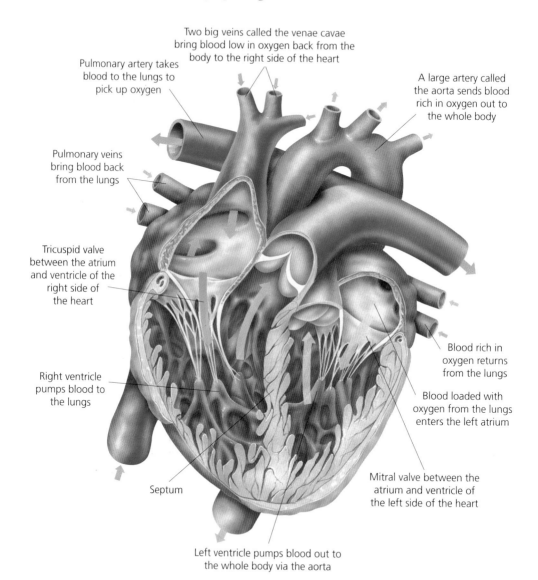

Two big veins called the venae cavae
bring blood low in oxygen back from the
body to the right side of the heart

Pulmonary artery takes
blood to the lungs to
pick up oxygen

A large artery called
the aorta sends blood
rich in oxygen out to
the whole body

Pulmonary veins
bring blood back
from the lungs

Tricuspid valve
between the atrium
and ventricle of the
right side of
the heart

Blood rich in
oxygen returns
from the lungs

Right ventricle
pumps blood to
the lungs

Blood loaded with
oxygen from the lungs
enters the left atrium

Septum

Mitral valve between the
atrium and ventricle of
the left side of the heart

Left ventricle pumps blood out to
the whole body via the aorta

▲ *The heart is a remarkable double pump, with two pumping chambers, the left
and the right ventricles. It contracts automatically to squeeze jets of blood out of
the ventricles and through the arteries.*

- **Your heart** is the size of your fist. It is inside the middle of your chest, slightly to the left.

- **The heart** is a powerful pump made almost entirely of muscle.

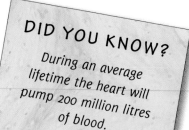

DID YOU KNOW?

During an average lifetime the heart will pump 200 million litres of blood.

- **The heart contracts** (tightens) and relaxes automatically about 70 times a minute to pump blood out through your arteries.

- **The heart** has two sides separated by a muscle wall called the septum.

- **The right side** is smaller and weaker, and it pumps blood only to the lungs.

- **The stronger left side** pumps blood around the body.

- **Each side of the heart** has two chambers. There is an atrium (plural atria) at the top where blood accumulates (builds up) from the veins, and a ventricle below that contracts to pump blood out into the arteries.

- **The ventricles** have much thicker muscular walls and are much stronger than the atria as they have to pump blood further around the body.

- **Each side of the heart** (left and right) ejects about 70 ml of blood every beat.

- **The coronary arteries** supply the heart. If they become clogged, the heart muscle may be short of blood and stop working. This is what happens in a heart attack.

157

Heart valves

- **There are two valves** in each side of the heart to make sure that blood flows only one way.

- **The mitral valve** between the left atrium and left ventricle is also known as the bicuspid valve as it has two flaps.

- **The valve** between the right atrium and the right ventricle is called the tricuspid valve as it has three flaps.

- **When the ventricles contract**, the blood in the chamber pushes back against the flaps of the valves, closing them and preventing blood from flowing back into the atria.

- **The aortic valve** guards the exit from the left ventricle into the aorta.

- **The pulmonary valve** guards the exit from the right ventricle, which leads into the pulmonary artery.

- **Known together** as semilunar valves, the aortic and pulmonary valves prevent blood flowing back into the two ventricles.

- **The closing** of the heart valves creates the 'lub-dup' sound of the heartbeat. The mitral and tricuspid valves close first to make the 'lub' sound; the semilunar valves close next to make the 'dup' sound.

- **Heart valves** are put under a lot of stress and strain and may become damaged or diseased. Occasionally a valve may not form properly and not work correctly from birth.

DID YOU KNOW?
When a doctor listens to your heart it is actually the sound of the heart valves closing that he or she hears.

Damaged valves can be replaced. Replacement valves may come from donors or pigs or a mechanical heart valve may be implanted.

▼ *This coloured scan shows an artificial heart valve (white, at the centre) where the main artery in the body, the aorta, enters the heart. The stitches used to close the chest can be seen at upper left.*

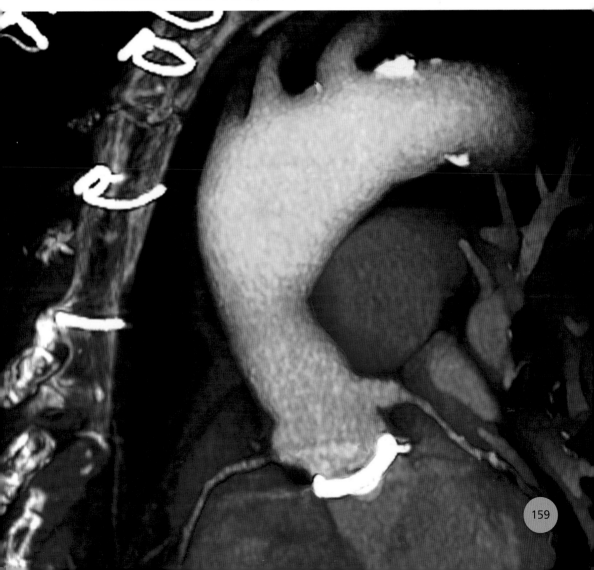

Heartbeat

- **The heartbeat** is the regular squeezing of the heart muscle to pump blood around the body.

- **It is also the term** given to the 'lub-dup' sound that the heart makes when it beats. This sound can be heard through a stethoscope.

- **The heartbeat sequence** is called the cardiac cycle and it has two phases – systole and diastole.

- **Systole is when** the heart muscle contracts (tightens). Diastole is the resting phase between contractions.

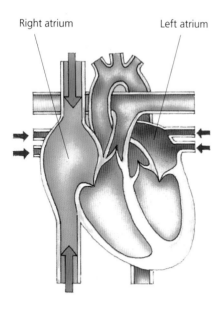

Right atrium   Left atrium

1 *Blood floods into the relaxed atria.*

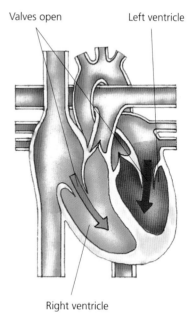

Valves open   Left ventricle

Right ventricle

2 *The wave of contraction squeezes blood into the ventricles.*

- **Systole begins** when a wave of muscle contraction sweeps across the heart and squeezes blood from each of the atria into the two ventricles.

- **When the contraction** reaches the ventricles, they squeeze blood out into the arteries.

- **In diastole**, the heart muscle relaxes and the atria fill with blood again.

- **Heart muscle** on its own would contract automatically.

- **Nerve signals** make the heart beat faster or slower.

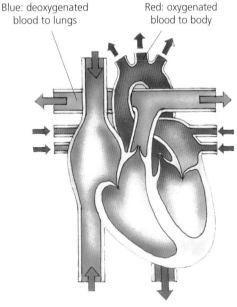
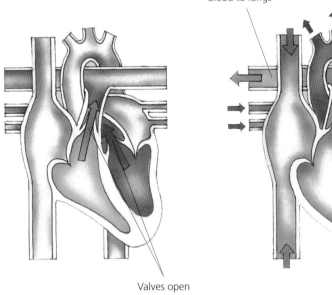

Blue: deoxygenated blood to lungs

Red: oxygenated blood to body

Valves open

3 *Blood is squeezed out of the ventricles into the arteries.*

4 *Blood starts to fill up the now relaxed atria again.*

161

Pulse

Your pulse is the powerful high-pressure surge or wave that runs through your blood and vessels as the heart contracts strongly with each beat.

You can feel your pulse by pressing two fingertips on the inside of your wrist where the radial artery nears the surface.

Other pulse points include the carotid artery in the neck and the brachial artery inside the elbow.

Checking the pulse is a good way of finding out how healthy someone is, which is why doctors do it.

Normal pulse rates vary between 50 and 100 beats a minute. The average for a man is about 71, for a woman it is 80, and for children it is about 85.

Tachycardia is the medical word for an abnormally fast heartbeat.

▼ *An ECG can show how healthy a person's heart is by monitoring how much the heart rate goes up and down during exercise.*

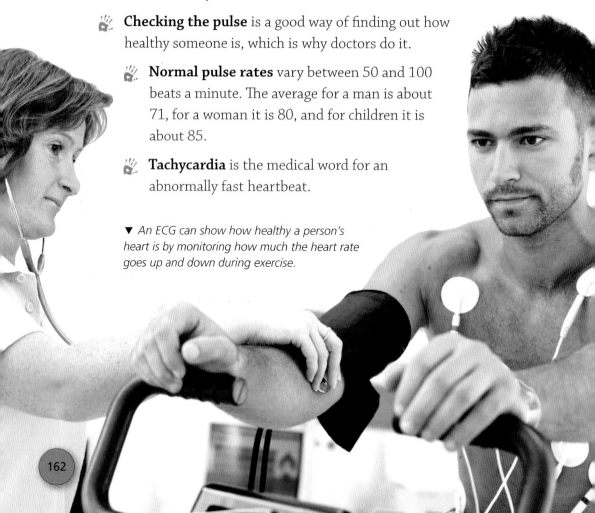

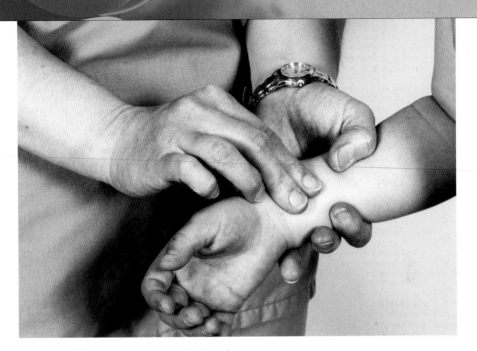

▲ *A doctor measures a patient's pulse by timing how many beats there are in a minute.*

Someone who has tachycardia when sitting down may have drunk too much coffee or tea, or taken drugs, or be suffering from anxiety or a fever, or have heart disease.

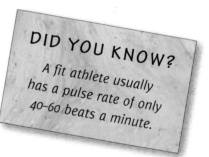

DID YOU KNOW?
A fit athlete usually has a pulse rate of only 40–60 beats a minute.

Bradycardia is an abnormally slow heartbeat rate.

Arrhythmia is any abnormality in a person's heartbeat rate.

Anyone with a heart problem may be connected to a machine called an electrocardiogram (ECG) to monitor (observe) their heartbeat.

Heart disease

- **Your heart beats** on average 70 times a minute and an average of 2.5 billion times in a lifetime.

- **Heart disease** is the main cause of death in many Western countries, including the UK and USA.

- **For the heart** to keep beating steadily, it needs a good supply of oxygen from its own blood supply. The arteries that supply the heart are called coronary arteries.

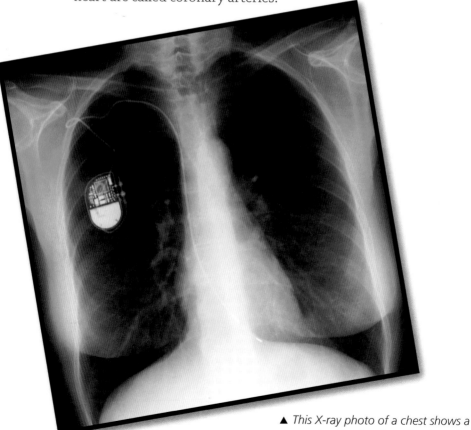

▲ *This X-ray photo of a chest shows a pacemaker that has been implanted to control an irregular heartbeat.*

- **Fatty deposits** in the coronary arteries can block the blood supply to the heart, causing chest pain or a heart attack.

- **In some cases**, surgery to widen the arteries will be successful in restoring the blood supply to the heart.

- **In other cases** surgery will be needed to provide the heart with new coronary arteries.

- **The rate** at which the heart beats is controlled by a small area in the heart, which sends out electrical impulses. If this area becomes damaged, the heart may start to beat irregularly, or even occasionally stop beating.

▲ *Eating fatty foods, such as cheeseburgers, can cause fat to build up in blood vessels, which may lead to a heart attack.*

- **Pacemakers** can be implanted to correct the heartbeat so that it is regular again.

- **Occasionally the heart muscle** may not work effectively. These people may need a heart transplant.

Arteries

- **An artery** is a tube-like blood vessel that carries blood away from the heart.

- **Systemic arteries** deliver oxygenated blood around the body. Pulmonary arteries deliver deoxygenated blood to the lungs.

- **An arteriole** is a smaller branch off an artery. Arterioles branch into microscopic capillaries.

- **Blood flows** through arteries at 30 cm per second in the main artery, down to 2 cm or less per second in the arterioles.

- **Arteries run alongside** most of the veins that return blood to the heart.

- **The walls of arteries** are muscular and can expand or relax to control the blood flow.

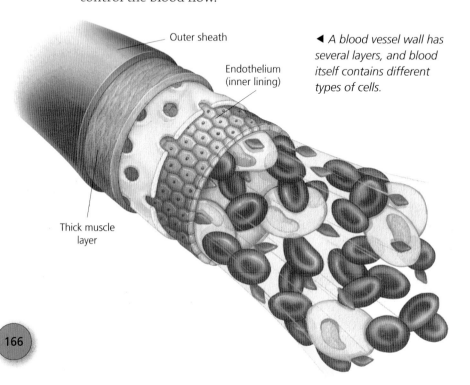

Outer sheath

Endothelium (inner lining)

Thick muscle layer

◄ A blood vessel wall has several layers, and blood itself contains different types of cells.

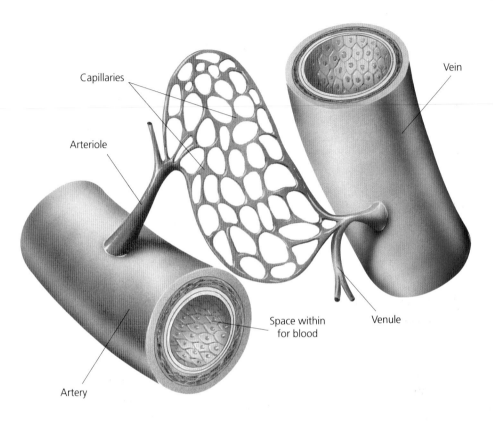

Capillaries

Arteriole

Vein

Artery

Space within
for blood

Venule

▲ *The two main kinds of blood vessel are arteries (red) and veins (blue). An artery branches into tiny capillaries, which join up to supply the vein.*

- **Arteries have thicker**, stronger walls than veins, and the pressure of the blood in them is a lot higher.

- **Over-thickening** of the artery walls may be one of the causes of hypertension (high blood pressure).

- **In old age** the artery walls can become very stiff. This hardening of the arteries (arteriosclerosis) can cut blood flow to the brain.

167

Capillaries

- **Capillaries** are the smallest of all your blood vessels, only visible under a microscope. They link the arterioles to the venules.

- **Capillaries were discovered** by Marcello Malphigi in 1661.

- **There are ten billion** capillaries in your body.

- **The largest capillary** is just 0.2 mm wide – thinner than a hair.

- **Each capillary** is about 0.5 mm to 1 mm long.

- **Capillary walls** are just one cell thick, so it is easy for chemicals to pass through them.

DID YOU KNOW?

The average capillary is 0.001 mm in diameter – just wide enough for red blood cells to pass through one at a time.

▶ You generate heat when exercising, which the body tries to lose by opening up capillaries in the skin, turning it red.

It is through the capillary walls that your blood passes oxygen, food and waste to and from each one of your body cells.

There are many more capillaries in active tissues such as muscles, liver and kidneys than there are in tendons and ligaments.

Capillaries carry less or more blood according to need. They carry more to let more blood reach the surface when you are warm. They carry less to keep blood away from the surface and save heat when you are cold.

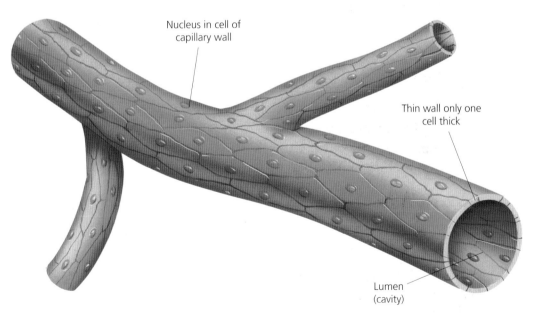

Nucleus in cell of capillary wall

Thin wall only one cell thick

Lumen (cavity)

▲ Capillaries are tiny tubes, barely wider than the blood cells they carry. They form an extensive network that twists and turns through the body's tissues.

Veins

- **Veins are pipes** in the body for carrying blood back to the heart.

- **Unlike arteries**, most veins carry 'used' blood back to the heart – the body cells have taken the oxygen they need from the blood, so it is low in oxygen.

- **When blood is low** in oxygen, it is a dark, purplish blue colour – unlike the bright red of the oxygenated blood carried by the arteries.

- **The only veins** that carry oxygenated blood are the four pulmonary veins, which carry blood from the lungs the short distance to the heart.

- **The two largest** veins in the body are the vena cavae, which flow into the heart from above and below.

KEY VEINS
1 Jugular vein
2 Brachial vein
3 Pulmonary vein
4 Vena cava

◄ *Veins carry blood from all around the body back to the heart.*

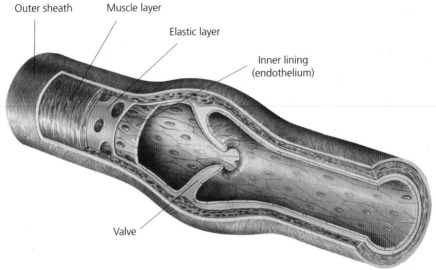

Outer sheath   Muscle layer

Elastic layer

Inner lining
(endothelium)

Valve

▲ *This shows a greatly enlarged cutaway of a small
vein. The valve prevents the blood from flowing
backwards away from the heart.*

Inside most veins are flaps that act as valves to make sure that the blood only flows one way.

The blood in veins is pumped by the heart, but the blood pressure is much lower than in arteries, and vein walls do not need to be as strong as those of arteries.

Unlike arteries, veins collapse when empty.

Blood is helped through the veins by pressure that is placed on the vein walls by the surrounding muscles.

> **DID YOU KNOW?**
>
> At any moment, 75 percent of the body's blood is in the veins.

Blood

DID YOU KNOW?

Oxygen in the air turns blood bright red when you bleed. In your veins it can be almost brown.

Blood is the reddish liquid that circulates around your body. It carries oxygen and food to body cells, and takes carbon dioxide and other waste away. It fights infection, keeps you warm, and distributes chemicals that control body processes.

Blood is made up of red cells, white cells and platelets, all carried in a liquid called plasma.

▼ *A centrifuge is used to separate the different components of blood. The spinning action of the machine separates the heavier blood cells from the lighter plasma.*

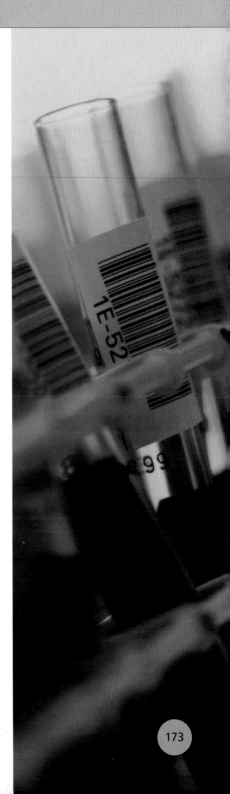

▶ *Blood contains millions of cells, carried in a clear, straw-coloured liquid called plasma.*

- **Plasma is 90 percent water**, plus hundreds of other substances, including nutrients, hormones and special proteins for fighting infection.

- **Blood plasma** turns milky immediately after a meal high in fats.

- **Platelets are tiny** pieces of cell that make blood clots start to form in order to stop bleeding.

- **The amount of blood** in your body depends on your size. An adult who weighs 80 kg has about 5 litres of blood. A child who is half as heavy has half as much blood.

- **A drop of blood** the same size as the dot on this 'i' contains around five million red cells.

- **If a blood donor** gives 0.5 litres of blood, the body replaces the plasma in a few hours, but it takes a few weeks to replace the red cells.

- **It takes about one minute** for your blood to circulate around your body. If you are exercising and your heart is beating fast, blood can circulate right round your body in about 20 seconds.

173

Blood cells

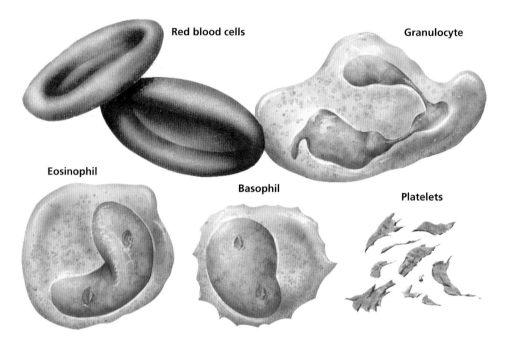

Red blood cells

Granulocyte

Eosinophil

Basophil

Platelets

▲ *These are some important kinds of cell in the blood – red cells, three kinds of white cells, and platelets.*

Your blood has two main kinds of cell – red cells and white cells – plus pieces of cell called platelets.

Red cells are button-shaped and they contain mainly a red protein called haemoglobin.

Haemoglobin is what allows red blood cells to ferry oxygen around your body.

Red cells also contain enzymes, which the body uses to make certain chemical processes happen.

White blood cells are big cells called leucocytes and most types are involved in fighting infections.

Most white cells contain tiny little grains and are called granulocytes.

Most granulocytes are giant white cells called neutrophils. They are the blood's cleaners, and their task is to eat up invaders.

Eosinophils and basophils are granulocytes that are involved in fighting disease. Some release antibodies that help fight infection.

Lymphocytes are also types of white cells.

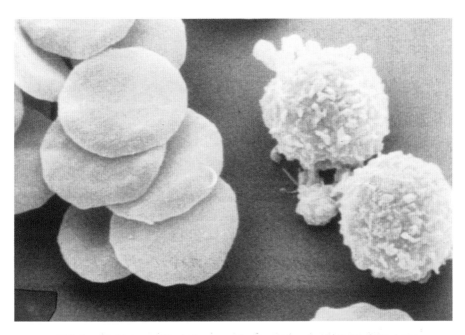

▲ This is a highly magnified photograph of red blood cells (left) and white blood cells.

Blood groups

- **Most people's blood** belongs to one of four different groups or types – A, O, B and AB.

- **Blood type O** is the most common, followed by blood group A.

- **Blood is also** either Rhesus positive (Rh+) or Rhesus negative (Rh-).

  - **Around 85 percent** of people are Rh+. The remaining 15 percent are Rh-.

    - **If your blood** is Rh+ and your group is A, your blood group is said to be A positive. If your blood is Rh- and your group is O, you are O negative, and so on.

      - **The Rhesus factors** got their name because they were first identified in Rhesus monkeys. (The Rhesus macaque is a species of monkey used extensively in medical research.)

◀ *Blood donors usually donate about 500 ml of blood at a time and are able to give blood about every two months.*

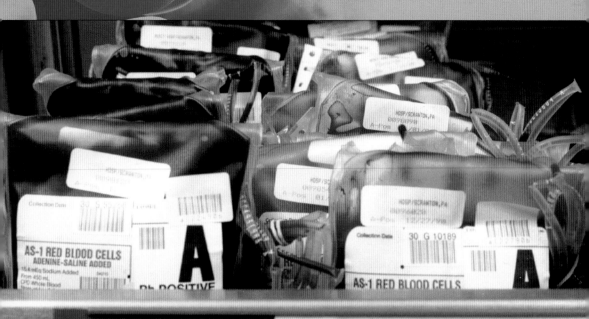

A Positive

▲ Donated blood is always tested to determine its blood group. Patients who have a blood transfusion must receive blood that matches their own group.

DID YOU KNOW?

People with O negative blood are called universal donors because their blood can be given to anyone else without causing a reaction.

A transfusion is when you are given blood from another person's body. Your blood is 'matched' with other blood considered safe for transfusion.

Blood transfusions are given when someone has lost too much blood due to an injury or operation. They are also given to replace diseased blood.

Wound healing

- **When we injure ourselves**, the damage causes a series of chemical reactions.

- **White blood cells** appear at the scene of the wound to fight infection.

- **Platelets** start to stick to each other and to the walls of the damaged blood vessels.

- **The sticky platelets** attract more platelets, forming a plug to stop you losing blood.

- **The platelets release** a sequence of chemicals called clotting factors (factors 1 through to 8).

- **At the final stage** of the clotting sequence a lacy, fibrous network is formed from a protein called fibrin.

- **The fibrin traps** red blood cells to form a blood clot that seals the damaged vessel.

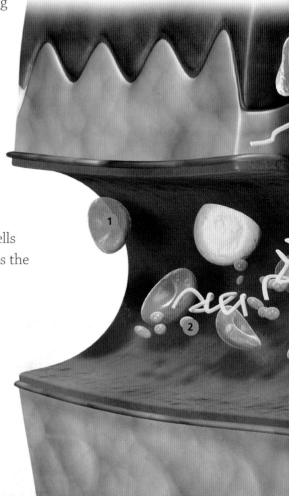

▶ *When you are injured, red blood cells (1) and platelets (2) leak out into the surrounding tissues and a sticky substance called fibrin (3) is produced to help heal the wound.*

- **The damaged vessel** slowly repairs itself and the clot gradually dissolves. Any clots on the surface of the skin turn into scabs, which dry up and fall off.

- **Some people** are not able to produce all the clotting factors. These people will bleed easily unless they receive injections of the missing clotting factor.

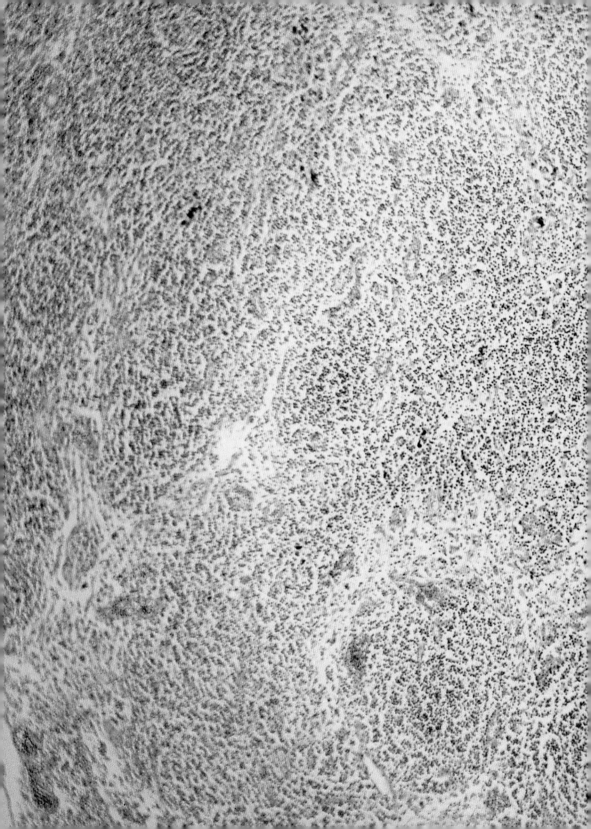

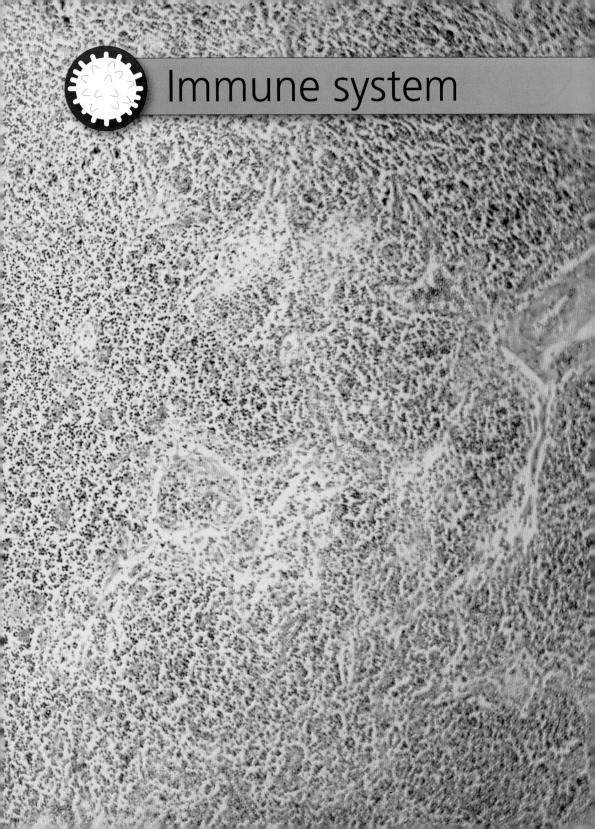

The immune system

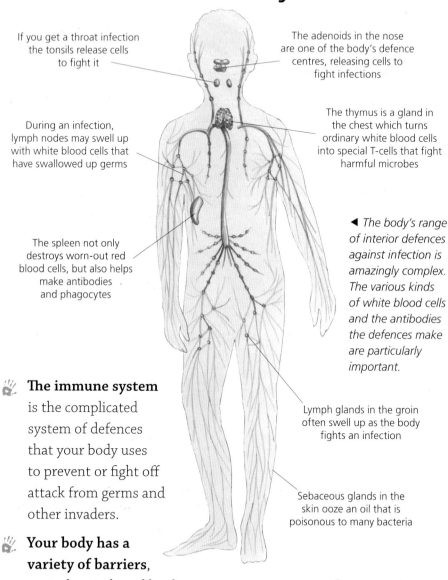

If you get a throat infection the tonsils release cells to fight it

The adenoids in the nose are one of the body's defence centres, releasing cells to fight infections

The thymus is a gland in the chest which turns ordinary white blood cells into special T-cells that fight harmful microbes

During an infection, lymph nodes may swell up with white blood cells that have swallowed up germs

◄ The body's range of interior defences against infection is amazingly complex. The various kinds of white blood cells and the antibodies the defences make are particularly important.

The spleen not only destroys worn-out red blood cells, but also helps make antibodies and phagocytes

Lymph glands in the groin often swell up as the body fights an infection

Sebaceous glands in the skin ooze an oil that is poisonous to many bacteria

The immune system is the complicated system of defences that your body uses to prevent or fight off attack from germs and other invaders.

Your body has a variety of barriers, toxic chemicals and booby traps to prevent germs from entering it. The skin is a barrier that stops many germs getting in, as long as it is not broken.

Mucus is a thick, slimy fluid that coats vulnerable, internal parts of your body such as your stomach and nose. It also acts as a lubricant (oil), making swallowing easier.

Mucus lines your airways and lungs to protect them from smoke particles as well as from germs. Your airways may fill up with mucus when you have a cold, as your body tries to minimize the invasion of airborne germs.

Itching, sneezing, coughing and vomiting are your body's ways of getting rid of unwelcome invaders. Small particles that get trapped in the mucous lining of your airways are wafted out by tiny hairs called cilia.

The body has many specialized cells and chemicals that fight germs that get inside you.

Complement is a mixture of liquid proteins found in the blood that attacks bacteria.

Interferons are proteins that help the body's cells to attack viruses and also stimulate killer cells.

Certain white blood cells are cytotoxic, which means that they are poisonous to invaders.

Phagocytes are big white blood cells that swallow up invaders and then use an enzyme to dissolve them. They are drawn to the site of an infection whenever there is inflammation.

Lymphocytes

- **Lymphocytes** are white blood cells that play a key role in the body's immune system, which targets invading germs.

- **There are two kinds** of lymphocyte – B lymphocytes (B-cells) and T lymphocytes (T-cells).

- **B-cells** develop into plasma cells that make antibodies to attack bacteria such as those that cause cholera, as well as some viruses.

- **T-cells** work against viruses and other micro-organisms that hide inside body cells. T-cells help identify and destroy these invaded cells or their products. They also attack certain bacteria.

- **There are two kinds** of T-cell – killers and helpers.

▼ A lymph node packed with lymphocytes fighting infection.

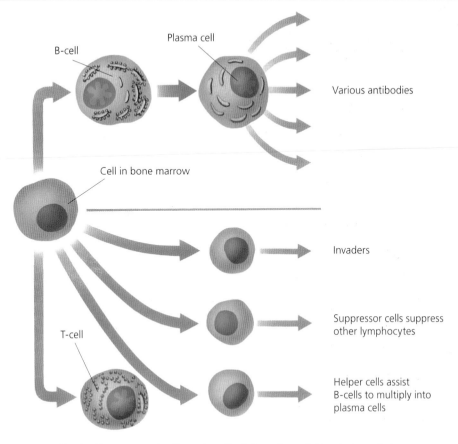

B-cell

Plasma cell

Various antibodies

Cell in bone marrow

Invaders

Suppressor cells suppress
other lymphocytes

T-cell

Helper cells assist
B-cells to multiply into
plasma cells

▲ *Our bodies are constantly under attack from harmful bacteria and viruses.*
Lymphocytes are key defenders, producing special cells to either identify, alert,
suppress or kill.

Helper T-cells identify invaded cells and send out chemicals called
lymphokines as an alarm, telling killer T-cells to multiply.

Invaded cells give themselves away by abnormal proteins on their
surface.

Killer T-cells lock on to the cells that have been identified by the
helpers, then move in and destroy them.

Some B-cells, called memory B-cells, stay around for a long time,
ready for a further attack by the same organism.

185

Antibodies

Antibodies are tiny proteins that make germs vulnerable to attack by white blood cells called phagocytes.

They are produced by white blood cells derived from B lymphocyctes.

There are thousands of different kinds of B-cell in the blood, each of which produces antibodies against a particular germ.

Normally, only a few B-cells carry a particular antibody. But when an invading germ is detected, the correct B-cell multiplies rapidly to cause the release of antibodies.

Invaders are identified when your body's immune system recognizes proteins on their surface as foreign. Any foreign protein is called an antigen.

Your body was armed from birth with antibodies for germs it had never met. This is called innate immunity.

DID YOU KNOW?
Human beings each generate around ten billion different antibodies.

If your body comes across a germ it has no antibodies for, it quickly makes some. It then leaves memory cells ready to be activated if the germ invades again. This is called acquired immunity.

Acquired immunity means you only suffer once from some infections, such as chickenpox. This is also how vaccination works.

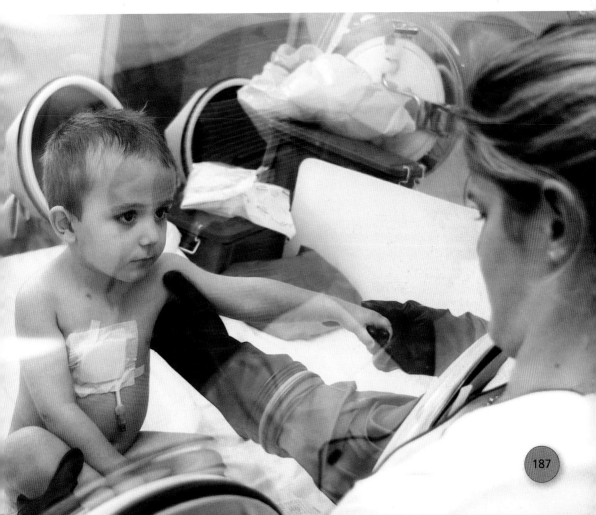

Allergies are sensitive reactions that happen in your body when too many antibodies are produced, or when they are produced to attack harmless antigens.

Autoimmune diseases are ones in which the body forms antibodies against its own tissue cells.

▼ *Some people's bodies cannot produce antibodies. As a result, they are vulnerable to infections and need special care in a sterile environment.*

Inflammation

* **Inflammation** is the redness, swelling, heat and pain that occurs as the result of an injury or infection.

* **When the body** is damaged, nearby cells release histamines and other chemicals.

▶ During an inflammatory response, blood vessels widen, causing swelling and redness, while special white blood cells (in purple and green) destroy any infection.

These chemicals increase blood flow to the area, widening local blood vessels and causing redness and heat.

The chemicals also attract white blood cells called leucocytes, which destroy any infection.

The leucocytes also release chemicals that control the inflammation.

Additional fluid at the injury causes swelling.

The area may also become painful if nerve endings in the skin are affected.

In some people, inflammation may occur when there has been no injury. In this case the body will start attacking its own tissues. This is called an autoimmune disease.

Arthritis, in which joints become swollen, painful and stiff, is an autoimmune disease.

DID YOU KNOW?
Acute inflammation means a sudden reaction that lasts a few days; chronic inflammation means a slower reaction lasting weeks or months.

189

Allergies

Allergies occur when your body produces too many antibodies or produces antibodies against normally harmless antigens. They cause inflammation.

It is not known why some people get allergies and some do not but they often occur in families. You are more likely to get an allergy if your parents, brothers or sisters have an allergy.

DID YOU KNOW?
Hay fever got its name because it was first noticed in farm workers harvesting hay.

Hay fever is an allergy to pollen and causes sneezing, watery and itchy eyes and a runny nose.

Trees, flowers and grasses all produce pollen, and people with hay fever may be allergic to one or several types of pollen.

Some people are allergic to dust. This can cause hay fever-like symptoms such as sneezing all year round.

◄ Flowers are not the only plants that produce pollen – trees, grasses and weeds produce large amounts of pollen too.

- **Pet fur**, nickel in jewellery, chemicals in soaps or perfumes and some foods are all common causes of allergic reactions.

- **Most allergies** are minor but some are life threatening. A severe allergic reaction may cause the mouth and throat to swell up, causing problems with breathing. This is called an anaphylactic reaction.

▶ *During a scratch test, substances that might cause allergies are scratched onto the skin. If a reaction occurs the patient is allergic to that substance.*

- **An anaphylactic reaction** may be caused by any substance if someone is allergic to it. Insect stings, some antibiotics and some foods such as peanuts are common antigens.

- **Someone with a severe allergy** usually carries drugs that prevent or treat an anaphylactic reaction.

191

Vaccination

- **Vaccination helps to protect you** against an infectious disease by exposing you to a mild or dead version of the germ in order to make your body build up protection in the form of antibodies.

- **Vaccination is also called immunization**, because it builds up your resistance or immunity to a disease.

- **In passive immunization** you are injected with substances such as antibodies that have already been exposed to the germ. This gives instant but short-lived protection.

- **In active immunization** you are given a killed or otherwise harmless version of the germ. Your body makes the antibodies itself for long-term protection.

▼ Vaccinations are crucial in many tropical regions where diseases are more widespread.

- **Children in many countries** are given a series of vaccinations as they grow up, to protect them against diseases such as diphtheria, tetanus and polio.

- **In cholera**, typhoid, rabies and flu vaccines, the germ in the vaccine is killed to make it harmless.

- **In measles**, mumps, polio and rubella vaccines, the germ is live attenuated – this means that its genes or other parts have been altered in order to make it harmless.

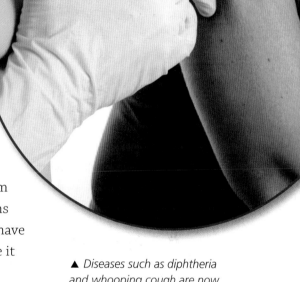

▲ *Diseases such as diphtheria and whooping cough are now rare in many countries thanks to vaccination.*

- **In diphtheria** and tetanus vaccines, the germ's toxins (poisons) are removed to make them harmless.

- **The hepatitis B vaccine** can be prepared by genetic engineering.

- **A new flu vaccine** is developed every year to protect against the current strain of the disease.

193

The lymphatic system

▶ *The lymphatic system is a branching network of little tubes that reaches throughout the body. It drains back to the centre of the body, running into the branches of the superior vena cava, the body's main vein to the heart.*

Drainage back into the blood system

Lymphatics (lymph vessels)

Concentrations of lymph nodes

Lymphatics (lymph vessels)

- **The lymphatic system** is your body's sewer, the network of pipes that drains waste from the cells.

- **It helps** to protect the body against infection by filtering out infectious organisms and helps to keep the amount of fluid in the body stable.

- **The 'pipes'** of the lymphatic system are called lymphatics or lymph vessels.

- **The lymphatics** are filled by a watery liquid called lymph fluid that, along with bacteria and waste chemicals, drains from body tissues such as muscles.

- **The lymphatic system** has no pump, such as the heart, to make it circulate. Instead, lymphatic fluid is circulated as a side effect of the heartbeat and muscle movement.

- **Lymph fluid** drains back into the blood via the body's main vein, the superior vena cava.

- **Valves within the lymphatics** prevent flow backwards along the vessels.

- **The lymphatic system** also consists of clumps of lymph nodes that help filter out infections.

- **The lymphatic system** is not only the lymphatics and lymph nodes, but includes the spleen, the thymus, the tonsils and the adenoids.

- **There are also collections** of lymphatic tissue in the intestines, called Peyer's patches.

- **On average**, at any time about 1–2 litres of lymph fluid circulate in the lymphatics and body tissues.

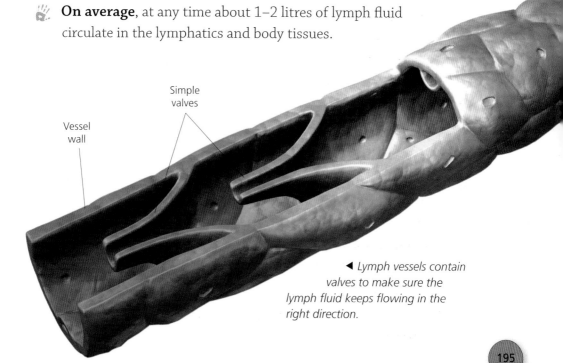

Simple
valves

Vessel
wall

◀ *Lymph vessels contain valves to make sure the lymph fluid keeps flowing in the right direction.*

Lymph nodes

At places in the lymphatic system there are tiny lumps called nodes. These are filters that trap germs that have got into the lymph fluid.

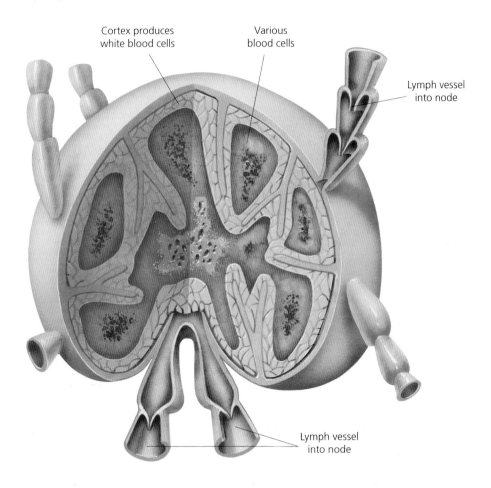

Cortex produces white blood cells

Various blood cells

Lymph vessel into node

Lymph vessel into node

▲ *This shows a cross-section of a lymph node. White blood cells are produced and stored here, and are released through the lymph vessels into the bloodstream.*

- **We have collections** of lymph nodes in our neck, armpits, groin and within our chest and abdomen.

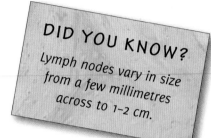

- **Lymph from particular areas** of the body filters into the nearest collection of nodes before passing on through the lymphatic system.

- **Lymph nodes** are covered with fibrous tissue. Inside the node is a network containing white blood cells.

- **As the lymph fluid** passes through the nodes it slows down so that armies of white blood cells called lymphocytes neutralize or destroy germs.

- **When you have a cold** or any other infection, the lymph nodes in your neck or groin, or under your arm, may swell as the lymphocytes fight germs. This is sometimes called 'swollen glands'.

- **Lymphocytes** also destroy cancer cells, which spread through the lymph fluid.

- **The tonsils** and the adenoids are bunches of lymph nodes that swell to help fight ear, nose and throat infections, especially in young children.

- **The adenoids** are at the back of the nose, and the tonsils are at the back of the upper throat.

- **If tonsils or adenoids** swell too much, they are sometimes taken out.

197

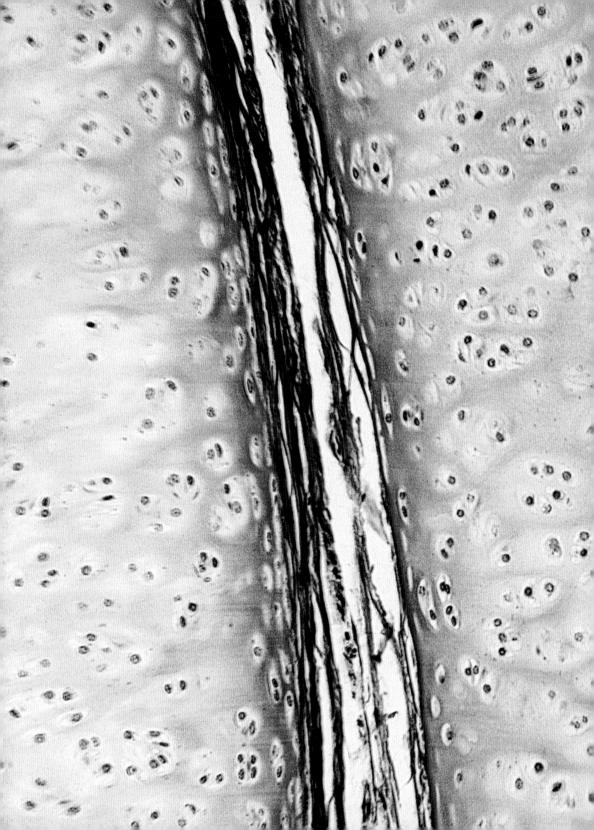

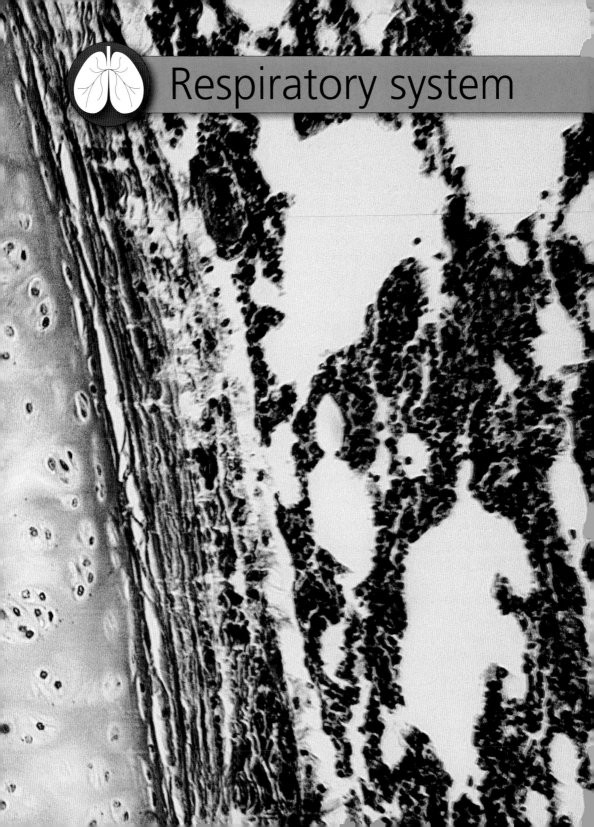

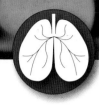

Respiratory system

- **The respiratory system** consists of the airways and the lungs.

- **It is necessary** for gas exchange – exchanging oxygen in the air that we breathe in for carbon dioxide in the air that we breathe out.

- **As air is breathed in** it passes through the nose, down the airways and into the lungs. Breathed out air passes in the opposite direction.

- **The respiratory system** works in partnership with the circulatory system to make sure every cell in the body receives oxygen and is able to get rid of its waste carbon dioxide.

- **The respiratory system** is controlled by the respiratory centre in part of the brain.

- **The respiratory system** takes up most of the space in the chest.

- **The lungs** and the lower part of the airways are enclosed and protected by the ribs.

- **Muscles in the rib cage** contract and relax as we breathe in and out.

- **A large muscle** under the lungs called the diaphragm also contracts and relaxes as we breathe.

DID YOU KNOW?

If you could open up your lungs and lay them out flat, they would cover half a football field.

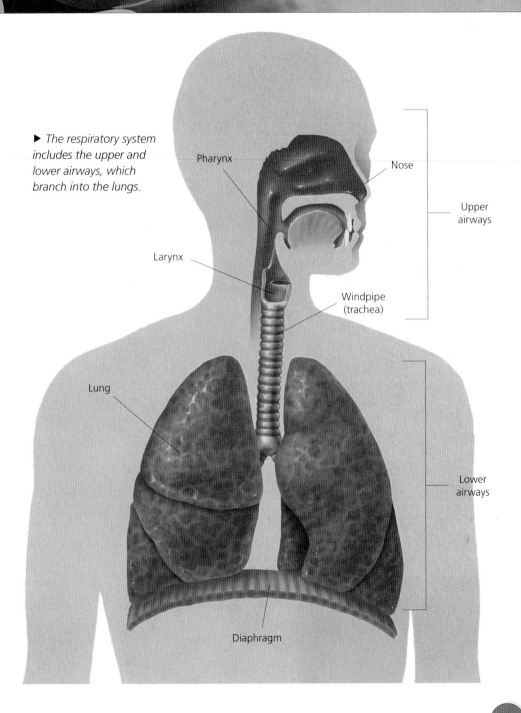

▶ *The respiratory system includes the upper and lower airways, which branch into the lungs.*

Pharynx

Nose

Upper airways

Larynx

Windpipe (trachea)

Lung

Lower airways

Diaphragm

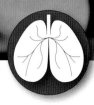

Airways

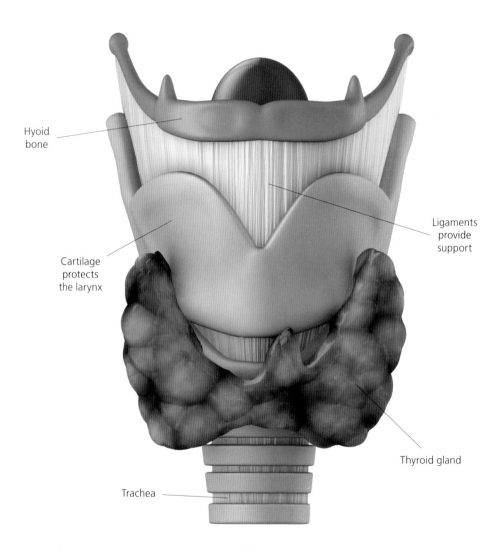

Hyoid
bone

Ligaments
provide
support

Cartilage
protects
the larynx

Thyroid gland

Trachea

▲ *Air travels in through your nose, down the throat and past the larynx, before entering the trachea and travelling on to the lungs.*

- **The upper airways** include the nose, the pharynx (throat) the larynx and the trachea (windpipe).

- **The lower airways** include the two main branches into the two lungs (the bronchi) and the small airways of the lungs (bronchioles).

- **Your throat** is the tube that runs down through your neck from the back of your nose and mouth.

- **The throat** is lined by rings of cartilage that keep it open while you breathe in and out.

- **Your throat** branches in two at the bottom. One branch, the oesophagus, takes food to the stomach. The other, the larynx, takes air to the lungs.

- **The two biggest airways** are called bronchi (singular bronchus), and they both branch into smaller airways called bronchioles.

- **The lining** of your airways is protected by a slimy film of mucus that traps dust and other particles to prevent them from getting into the lungs.

- **When you have a cold** your airways produce extra mucus to protect against infection.

- **There are also tiny hairs** called cilia in the lining of the airways. These help clear the lungs of dust and foreign particles.

DID YOU KNOW?
Your throat is linked to your ears by tubes that open when you swallow to balance air pressure.

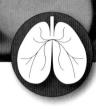

The lungs

- **Your lungs** are a pair of soft, spongy bags inside your chest.

- **The lungs** consist of bunches of minute air sacs called alveoli (singular alveolus).

- **Each bunch** of alveoli is found at the end of a bronchiole – small airways that eventually connect to larger airways and to the throat.

- **Alveoli are surrounded** by a network of tiny blood vessels, and alveoli walls are just one cell thick – thin enough to let oxygen and carbon dioxide seep through them.

- **There are around 300 million** alveoli in your lungs.

▶ Taken through a powerful microscope, this photo of a slice of lung tissue shows a blood vessel and the very thin walls of an alveolus next to it.

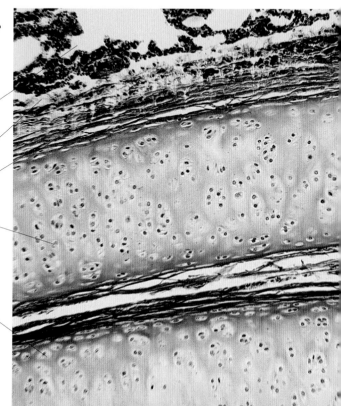

Alveoli

Alveolar walls

Capillary walls

Inside capillary

Another capillary

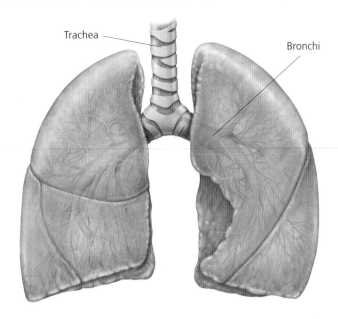

Trachea

Bronchi

▲ *Your trachea divides into two tubes called bronchi. One enters each lung.*

The large surface area of all these alveoli makes it possible for huge quantities of oxygen to seep through into the blood. Equally large amounts of carbon dioxide can seep back into the airways for removal when you breathe out.

If your lungs could be opened up and all the alveoli laid out flat they would cover one half of a tennis court.

People who live at high altitude have a bigger lung capacity than people who live at lower altitudes. This is because the air is thinner at high altitudes.

The alveoli can be damaged by substances such as tar in cigarettes. This makes it harder for oxygen to pass into the blood and causes breathing problems.

It is possible to survive with just one lung if one is damaged or diseased.

205

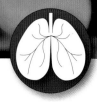

Breathing

Breathing in   **Breathing out**

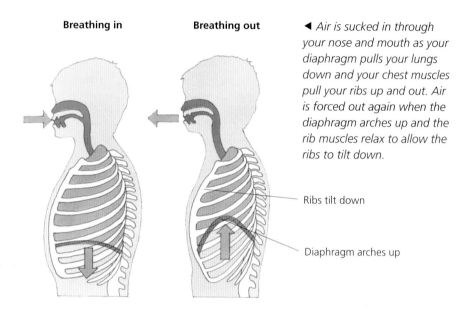

◄ *Air is sucked in through your nose and mouth as your diaphragm pulls your lungs down and your chest muscles pull your ribs up and out. Air is forced out again when the diaphragm arches up and the rib muscles relax to allow the ribs to tilt down.*

Ribs tilt down

Diaphragm arches up

You breathe because every single cell in your body needs a continuous supply of oxygen to burn glucose, the high-energy substance from digested food that cells get from blood.

Scientists call breathing 'respiration'. Cellular respiration is the way that cells use oxygen to burn glucose.

When you breathe in, air rushes in through your nose or mouth, down your windpipe and into the millions of branching airways in your lungs.

On average you breathe in about 15 times a minute. If you run hard, the rate soars to around 80 times a minute.

Newborn babies breathe about 40 times a minute.

- **If you live** to the age of 80, you will have taken well over 600 million breaths.

- **A normal breath** takes in about 0.4 litres of air. A deep breath can take in ten times as much.

- **Your diaphragm** is a dome-shaped sheet of muscle between your chest and stomach, which works with your chest muscles to make you breathe in and out.

- **Scientists call breathing in** 'inhalation' and breathing out 'exhalation'.

- **Breathing is automatic** and controlled by the brain. Although we can make ourselves breathe faster or hold our breath, normally we are not aware of our breathing.

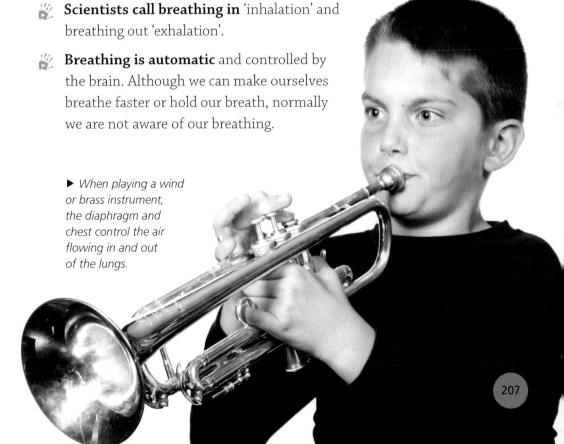

▶ *When playing a wind or brass instrument, the diaphragm and chest control the air flowing in and out of the lungs.*

207

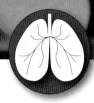

Gas exchange

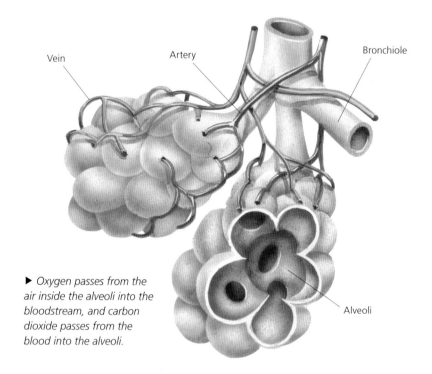

Vein

Artery

Bronchiole

Alveoli

▶ Oxygen passes from the air inside the alveoli into the bloodstream, and carbon dioxide passes from the blood into the alveoli.

Gas exchange is the exchange of oxygen and carbon dioxide and takes place throughout the body. All cells need oxygen to survive and need to get rid of waste carbon dioxide.

When you breathe in, air that contains oxygen is taken into your lungs.

In your lungs, the oxygen passes across the thin walls of the alveoli into the capillaries that surround the alveoli.

Once in the capillaries, the oxygen binds with haemoglobin in the red blood cells.

- **The oxygen** is then carried in your blood to your body cells.

- **In the body cells**, oxygen is released from the red blood cells and passes across the capillary walls to be used by the body.

- **At the same time**, waste carbon dioxide from the body cells passes across the capillary walls and dissolves in the plasma in the blood.

- **The carbon dioxide** is then returned by the blood to the lungs.

- **In the lungs**, the carbon dioxide leaves the plasma, crossing through the capillary walls and into the alveoli.

- **The carbon dioxide** is then breathed out.

▼ Scuba divers have to carry tanks of air to allow them to breathe underwater.

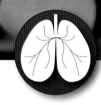

Coughing and hiccups

Coughing is the body's way of removing foreign particles and irritants in the airways and lungs.

Irritation of the airways causes a reflex reaction by stimulating nerves in the airways. These send a signal to the brain that triggers a cough.

The irritants are expelled from the airways, making the distinctive coughing sound.

Although a cough is normally a reflex action, we can also cough voluntarily if we want to.

Coughs are usually caused by an infection, such as a cold. Pollution, cigarette smoke and dust can also cause coughing.

Hiccups are caused when the muscle under the lungs (the diaphragm) contracts suddenly.

This sudden contraction forces air into the lungs. At the same time your throat closes, making the 'hiccup' sound.

Some people get hiccups after eating spicy food or drinking fizzy drinks. Other people get them for no specific reason.

Many people think that a shock, holding their breath or drinking water out of the wrong side of a glass will cure hiccups.

The longest recorded attack of hiccups is thought to be 69 years and five months.

DID YOU KNOW?

When you cough, you expel about 2.5 litres of air from your lungs.

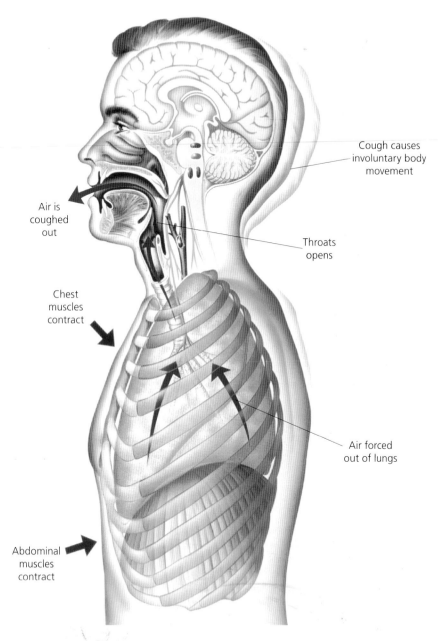

Cough causes
involuntary body
movement

Air is
coughed
out

Throats
opens

Chest
muscles
contract

Air forced
out of lungs

Abdominal
muscles
contract

▲ During a cough, irritation in your airways stimulates a reflex action,
forcing air out of your lungs.

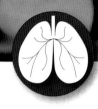

The vocal cords

- **Speaking and singing** depend on the larynx (voice box) in your neck.

- **The larynx** has bands of stretchy fibrous tissue called the vocal cords, which vibrate (shake) as you breathe air out over them.

- **When you are silent**, the vocal cords are relaxed and apart, and air passes freely.

- **When you speak or sing**, the vocal cords tighten across the airway and vibrate to make sounds.

- **The tighter** the vocal cords are stretched, the less air can pass through them, so the higher pitched the sounds you make.

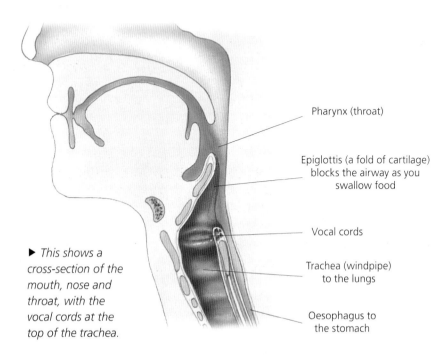

Pharynx (throat)

Epiglottis (a fold of cartilage) blocks the airway as you swallow food

Vocal cords

Trachea (windpipe) to the lungs

Oesophagus to the stomach

▶ *This shows a cross-section of the mouth, nose and throat, with the vocal cords at the top of the trachea.*

▼ *The vocal cords are soft flaps in the larynx, situated at the base of the throat. Our voices make sounds by vibrating these cords, as shown in the diagram.*

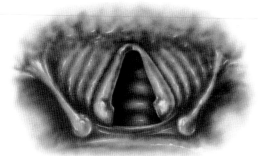 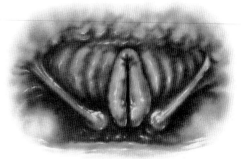

When the cords are apart no sound is made, as air can move freely past them

When the cords are pulled together by tiny muscles, air is forced through a small gap and the cords vibrate to create a sound

The basic sound produced by the vocal cords is a simple 'aah'. But by changing the shape of your mouth, lips and especially your tongue, you can change this simple sound into letters and words.

Babies' vocal cords are just 6 mm long.

Women's vocal cords are about 20 mm long.

Men's vocal cords are about 30 mm long. Because men's cords are longer than women's, they vibrate more slowly and give men deeper voices.

Boys' vocal cords are the same length as girls' until they are teenagers – when they grow longer, making a boy's voice 'break' and get deeper.

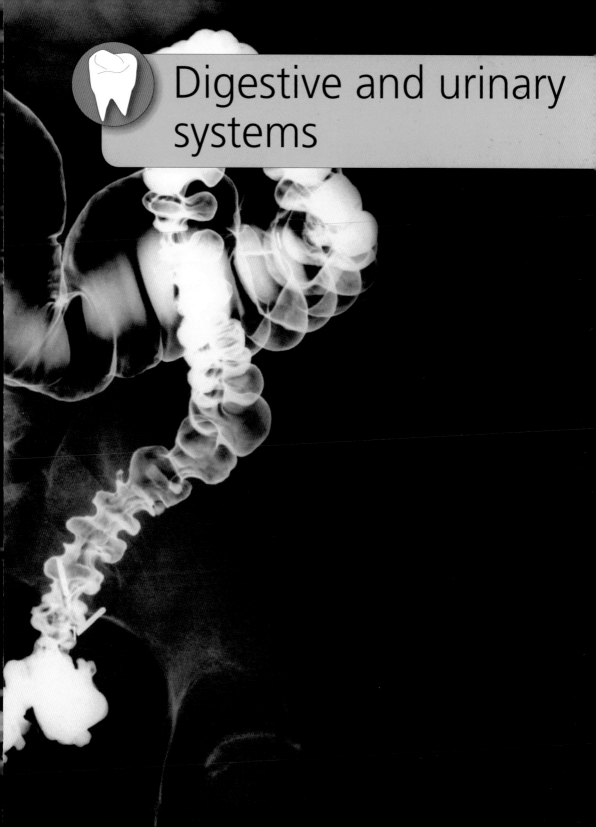

Digestive and urinary systems

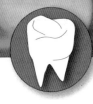

Teeth and gums

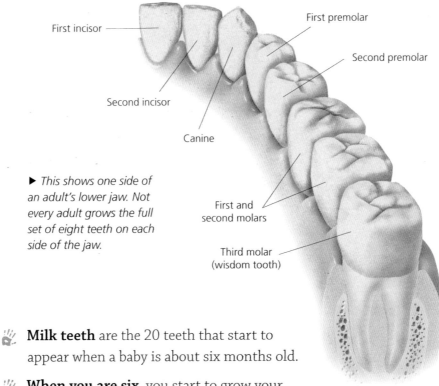

First incisor

First premolar

Second premolar

Second incisor

Canine

▶ *This shows one side of an adult's lower jaw. Not every adult grows the full set of eight teeth on each side of the jaw.*

First and second molars

Third molar (wisdom tooth)

Milk teeth are the 20 teeth that start to appear when a baby is about six months old.

When you are six, you start to grow your 32 adult teeth – 16 in the top row and 16 in the bottom.

Molars are big, strong teeth at the back of the mouth. There are usually six pairs. Their flattish tops are shaped for grinding food.

The four rearmost molars, one in each back corner of each jaw, are the wisdom teeth. These are the last to grow and sometimes they never appear.

Premolars are four pairs of teeth in front of the molars.

Incisors are the four pairs of teeth at the front of your mouth. They have sharp edges for cutting food.

- **Canines** are the two pairs of big, pointed teeth behind the incisors. Their shape is good for tearing food.

- **The enamel** on teeth is the body's hardest substance; dentine inside teeth is softer but still as hard as bone.

- **Teeth sit in sockets** in the jawbones and are held in place by the gums.

- **The gums** are layers of connective tissue that surround each tooth and help to prevent it from damage by infection.

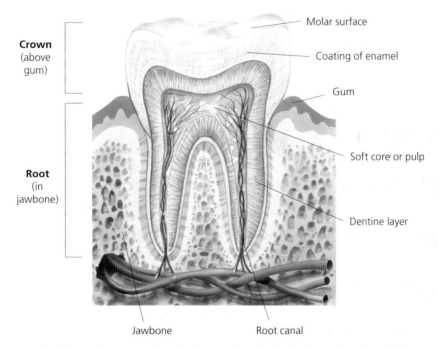

Crown (above gum)

Root (in jawbone)

Molar surface

Coating of enamel

Gum

Soft core or pulp

Dentine layer

Jawbone

Root canal

▲ *Teeth have long roots that slot into sockets in the jawbones, but they sit in a fleshy ridge called the gums. In the centre of each tooth is a living pulp of blood and nerves. Around this is a layer of dentine, then on top of that a tough shield of enamel.*

Tooth decay

Although teeth are covered in enamel – the hardest substance in the body – they can still be affected by disease.

If teeth are not cleaned regularly, an invisible layer of food and bacteria starts to build up on the surface of the teeth.

This mixture of food and bacteria is called plaque.

Plaque sticks to the teeth and the bacteria feed on the food within the plaque.

As the bacteria feed they produce an acid that starts to erode the enamel.

▶ *Teeth need brushing for several minutes at least twice a day to remove plaque and keep them healthy.*

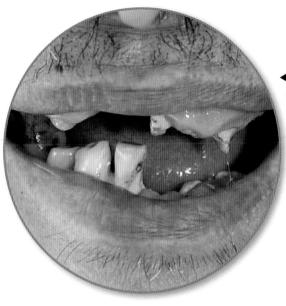

◀ If not treated, tooth decay can damage teeth so badly that they have to be removed.

If the plaque is not removed, eventually it will wear away the enamel and treatment will be needed to fill the hole in the tooth.

Toothache occurs when the acid wears away both the enamel and the dentine underneath and reaches the sensitive nerves in the centre of the tooth.

Fillings are usually used to repair holes in teeth caused by tooth decay. If a tooth is very badly affected it may need to be removed.

Plaque is hard to remove but regular brushing of your teeth and flossing can prevent it building up in the first place.

DID YOU KNOW?

Many countries add fluoride to the water supply to help harden teeth.

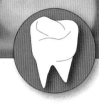

Digestive system

The digestive system uses the food that we eat and breaks it down into material that body cells can use for energy. It then eliminates what is left over as waste (faeces).

The digestive system consists of the digestive tract and the digestive organs.

Your digestive tract is basically a long, winding tube. It is also called the alimentary canal (gut). It starts at your mouth and ends at your anus.

If you could lay your gut out straight, it would be nearly six times as long as you are tall.

Muscular contractions in the gut move the food that you eat from one end to the other.

The digestive system also consists of several separate organs, including the salivary glands, liver, gall bladder and pancreas.

These organs produce enzymes and chemicals that help in the digestion of food.

It takes several days for food to pass right through the digestive tract.

On average, we digest 30,000 kg of food in a lifetime.

> **DID YOU KNOW?**
>
> In a fully grown adult, the digestive tract is about 7 m long.

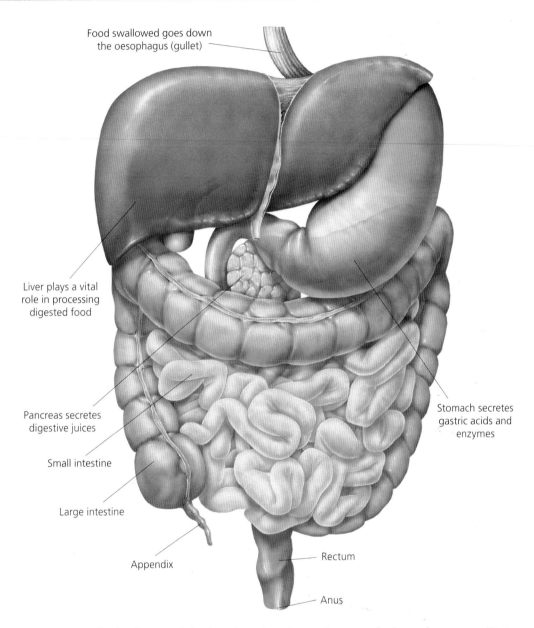

Food swallowed goes down
the oesophagus (gullet)

Liver plays a vital
role in processing
digested food

Pancreas secretes
digestive juices

Small intestine

Large intestine

Appendix

Stomach secretes
gastric acids and
enzymes

Rectum

Anus

▲ The food you eat is broken down into the nutrients your body needs as
it passes down through your oesophagus into your stomach and your small
intestine. Undigested food travels through your large intestine and leaves your
body via your anus.

221

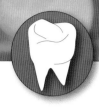

Hunger and appetite

- **Hunger occurs** when the body needs food; appetite is the desire to eat.

- **When the stomach is empty** or the sugar levels in our blood become lower than normal we start to feel hungry.

- **The feeling of hunger** comes from the hypothalamus – a gland in our brain.

- **Hunger often** gives us 'stomach pangs' or makes our stomachs rumble. This is the stomach contracting.

- **The feeling of hunger** usually begins a few hours after we last ate. Stomach pangs usually start around 12 hours after we last ate.

- **The smell and sight** of food may give us an appetite, making us look forward to eating and want to eat.

- **You can be hungry** without having an appetite or a desire to eat, and you can have an appetite or fancy eating something without being hungry.

LESS FILLING	MORE FILLING
Bowl of cornflakes or chocolate cereal	Bowl of porridge
Biscuit	Apple
Packet of crisps	Small bag of popcorn
Cheese on white toasted bread	Beans on brown toasted bread
Can of cola	Glass of milk
Bag of sweets	Pot of yoghurt
Doughnut	Small packet of roasted peanuts
Packet of pretzels	Chocolate and nut bar
Portion of mashed potato	Portion of wholemeal pasta

People who eat when they are not feeling hungry may eat more than they need and become overweight.

Some people prefer not to eat, even when they feel hungry. In extreme cases this can cause illness or be life threatening.

There are many people in the world who do not have enough to eat and go hungry every day.

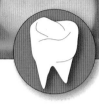

Digestion

- **Digestion is the process** by which your body breaks down the food you eat into substances that it can absorb (take in) and use.

- **Digestion mainly takes place** in the stomach and the small intestine.

- **Food is partly broken down by** mechanical processes, such as chewing and movements in the gut, and partly by enzymes.

- **The food you eat** is softened in your mouth by chewing and by chemicals in your saliva (spit).

- **When you swallow**, food travels down your oesophagus (gullet) into your stomach.

- **The stomach partly digests** the food, turning it into a liquid called chyme. This passes into your small intestine.

- **The chyme** is broken down even more in the small intestine and absorbed through the gut wall into the blood.

- **Food that cannot be digested** in your small intestine passes on into your large intestine. It is then pushed out through your anus as faeces when you go to the toilet.

- **Digestive enzymes** play a vital part in breaking food down so it can be absorbed by the body.

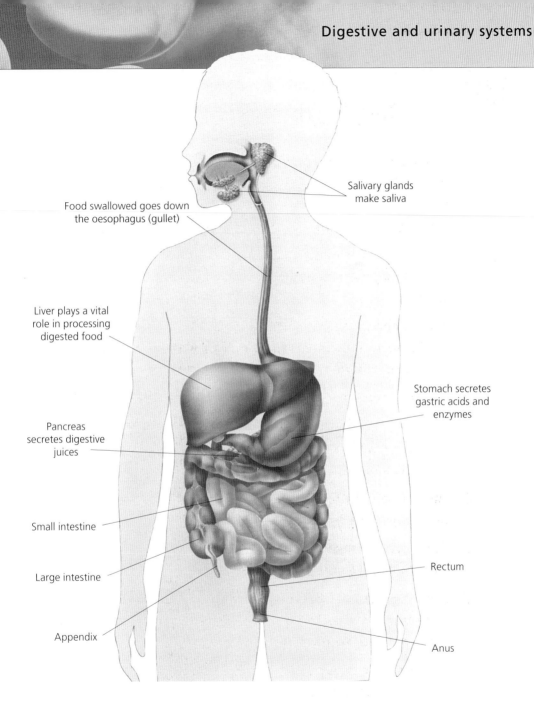

Salivary glands
make saliva

Food swallowed goes down
the oesophagus (gullet)

Liver plays a vital
role in processing
digested food

Stomach secretes
gastric acids and
enzymes

Pancreas
secretes digestive
juices

Small intestine

Large intestine

Rectum

Appendix

Anus

▲ *The digestive organs almost fill the lower part of the main body,
called the abdomen.*

Food processing

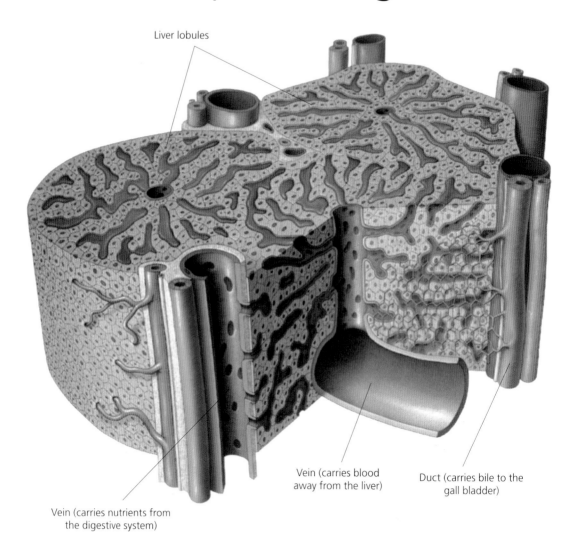

Liver lobules

Vein (carries nutrients from
the digestive system)

Vein (carries blood
away from the liver)

Duct (carries bile to the
gall bladder)

▲ *The liver is the body's main food processing centre. It processes food as we
need it and either stores the results or transfers them into the blood to be sent
around the body.*

- **The food we eat** consists of complex substances. During digestion, these molecules are broken down into simple nutrients that can be absorbed into the blood.

DID YOU KNOW?

You need some fat in your body – it is used to cushion and insulate your body and is a great energy store.

- **Carbohydrates** are broken down into glucose.

- **Proteins** are broken down into amino acids.

- **Fats** are broken down into fatty acids.

- **The liver** is the main processing centre of the body and also stores many substances for when they are needed.

- **Glucose** is the body's main source of energy and is use for growth and repair. Excess glucose is kept in the liver and muscles as a substance called glycogen.

- **Glycogen** can be turned back into glucose at once if the body suddenly needs energy.

- **Amino acids** are used to make new proteins, which the body uses to repair damage.

- **Fatty acids** are mainly used to make cell walls. Excess fatty acids are stored in fat cells.

- **Excess amino acids** can be converted into fatty acids and also stored in fat cells.

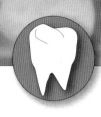

Enzymes

Enzymes are molecules that are mostly protein, and that alter the speed of chemical reactions in living things.

There are thousands of enzymes inside your body – it would not be able to function without them.

Some enzymes need an extra substance, called a coenzyme, to work. Many coenzymes are vitamins.

Most enzymes have names ending in 'ase', such as lygase, protease and lipase.

Pacemaker enzymes play a vital role in controlling your metabolism – the rate at which your body uses energy.

One of the most important enzyme groups is that of the messenger RNAs, which are used as communicators by the nuclei of body cells.

Many enzymes are essential for the digestion of food, including lipase, protease, amylase, and the peptidases. Many of these enzymes are made in the pancreas.

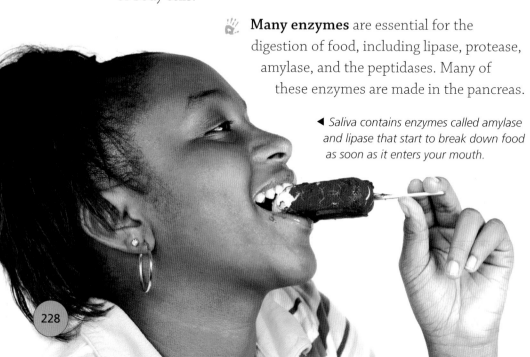

◀ *Saliva contains enzymes called amylase and lipase that start to break down food as soon as it enters your mouth.*

▲ *After you eat a meal, a complex series of enzymes gets to work, breaking food down into simple molecules that can be absorbed into your blood.*

- **Lipase** is released mainly from the pancreas into the alimentary canal (gut) to help break down fat.

- **Amylase** breaks down starches such as those in bread and fruit into simple sugars. There is amylase in saliva and in the stomach.

- **In the gut**, the sugars maltose, sucrose and lactose are broken down by maltase, sucrase and lactase.

Swallowing

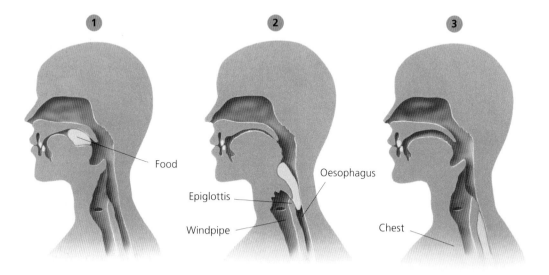

① ② ③

Food

Oesophagus

Epiglottis

Windpipe

Chest

▲ *After chewing (1), food is swallowed into the gullet, or oesophagus (2). This pushes the food powerfully down through the chest (3), past the heart and lungs, into the stomach.*

- **For digestion to start** we need to chew food to make it soft and easy to swallow and digest.

- **As we chew**, the salivary glands around the mouth produce saliva that helps to soften the food so that it is easier to swallow.

- **Saliva also contains** enzymes that start to break down and digest the food.

- **Swallowing occurs** when you push some chewed food towards the back of your mouth.

- **As you swallow**, two involuntary events occur.

- **The soft palate**, which is a flap of tissue at the back of the mouth, is pressed upwards to stop food getting into your nose.

- **The epiglottis**, which is a flap of cartilage at the top of the windpipe, tilts down over the larynx to stop food entering the airways.

- **The swallowed food** passes the closed off airways and enters the top of the digestive tract – the oesophagus.

- **Once in the oesophagus** the food is pushed towards the stomach by the muscles in the lining of the oesophagus.

- **This muscle contraction** is called peristalsis and occurs all along the digestive tract.

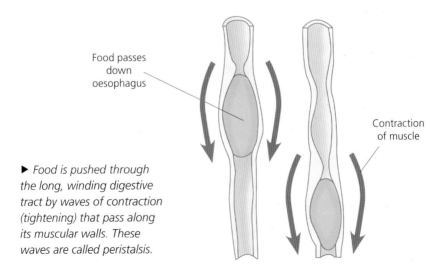

DID YOU KNOW?

Snakes swallow food whole and can swallow prey much larger than themselves.

Food passes down oesophagus

Contraction of muscle

▶ *Food is pushed through the long, winding digestive tract by waves of contraction (tightening) that pass along its muscular walls. These waves are called peristalsis.*

231

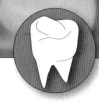

The stomach

Your stomach is a muscular-walled bag that mashes food into a pulp, helped by chemicals called gastric juices.

The word 'gastric' means to do with the stomach.

When empty, your stomach holds barely 0.5 litres, but after a big meal it can stretch to more than 4 litres.

The sight, smell and taste of food all start the production of gastric juices so that by the time the food reaches the stomach it is ready to start digestion.

The stomach lining is protected by mucus so that it does not digest itself.

The gastric juices produced by the stomach contain acid and enzymes that break down proteins.

The stomach also produces a substance called intrinsic factor that is necessary for us to absorb vitamin B12.

The stomach takes up to five hours to mix and digest solid food.

Once the food has been reduced to a liquid, the muscular ring at the exit of the stomach relaxes and the liquid enters the small intestine.

The mixture of churned food and gastric juices that leaves the stomach is called chyme.

Gall bladder

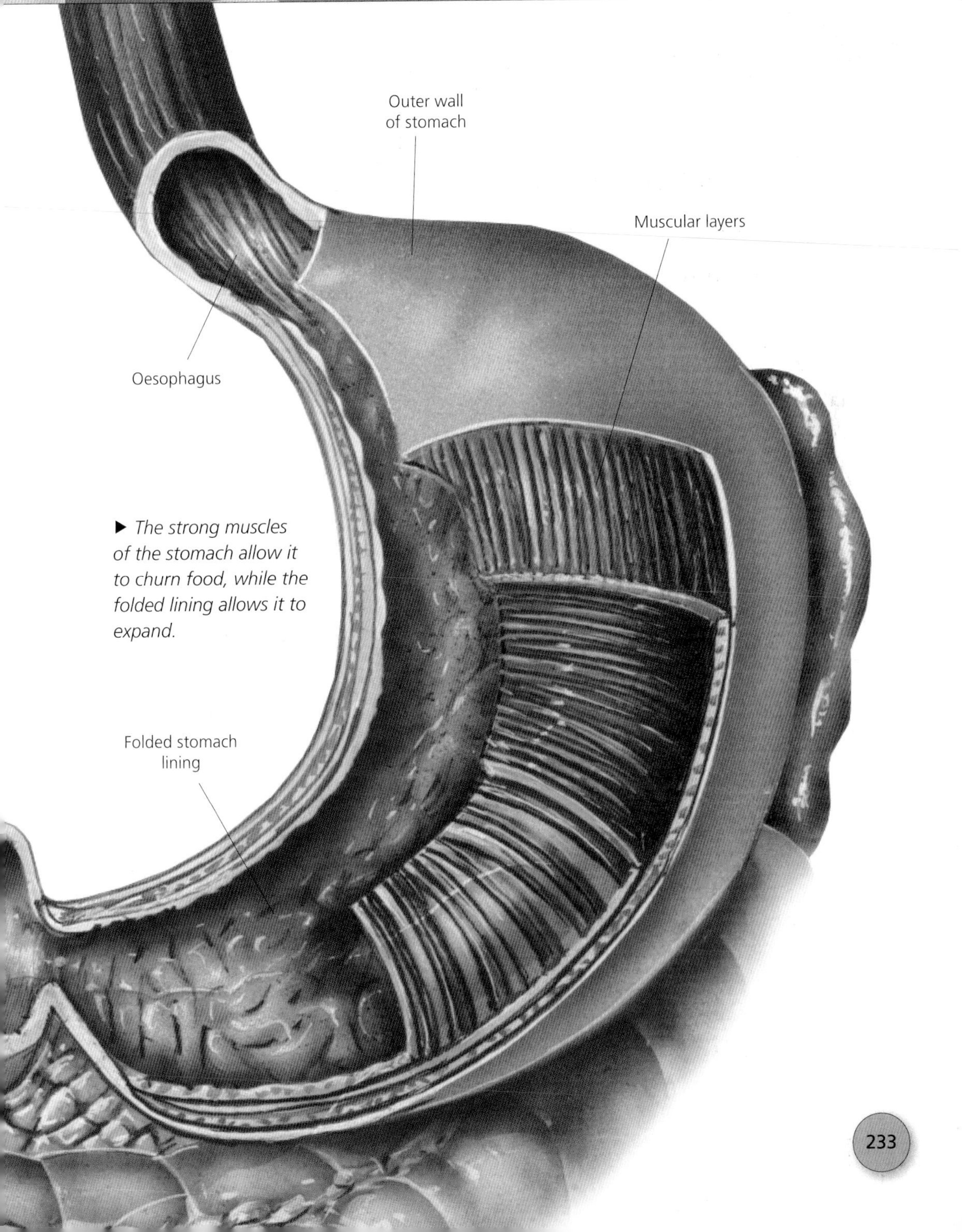

Outer wall
of stomach

Muscular layers

Oesophagus

▶ The strong muscles
of the stomach allow it
to churn food, while the
folded lining allows it to
expand.

Folded stomach
lining

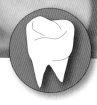

The liver

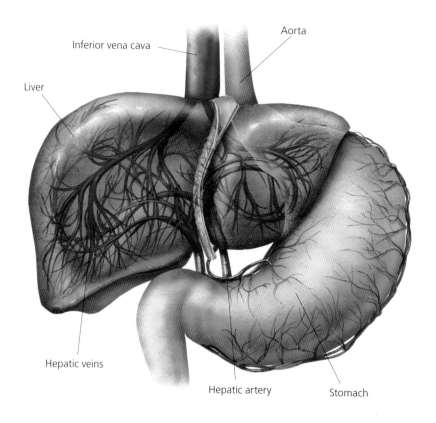

Inferior vena cava

Aorta

Liver

Hepatic veins

Hepatic artery

Stomach

▲ *Located under the ribs and next to the stomach, the liver is well supplied with blood vessels.*

The liver is the body's chemical processing centre.

It is the biggest internal organ, and the word hepatic means 'to do with the liver'.

The prime task of the liver is handling all the nutrients and substances digested from the food you eat and sending them out to your body cells when needed.

- **The liver turns** carbohydrates into glucose, the main energy-giving chemical for body cells.

- **Levels of glucose** in the blood are kept steady by the liver. It does this by releasing more when levels drop, and by storing it as glycogen, a type of starch, when levels rise.

- **The liver** packs off excess food energy to be stored as fat around the body.

- **It also breaks** down proteins and stores vitamins and minerals.

- **Bile** is a yellowish or greenish bitter liquid produced by the liver. It helps dissolve fat as food is digested in the intestines.

- **The liver clears** the blood of old red cells and harmful substances such as alcohol, and makes new plasma.

- **Lobules** are the liver's chemical processing units. They take in unprocessed blood on the outside and dispatch it through a collecting vein.

▶ *Harmful substances such as alcohol, which is found in alcoholic drinks such as wine, are filtered by the liver to help keep the body healthy.*

235

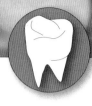

The pancreas

- **The pancreas** is a large, carrot-shaped gland that lies just below your stomach.

- **Two main types** of tissue are contained within the pancreas – one that releases hormones and one that releases pancreatic enzymes.

▼ *The pancreas lies on the right side of the body, tucked into the gut. The microscopic view shows the islets of Langerhans (in purple).*

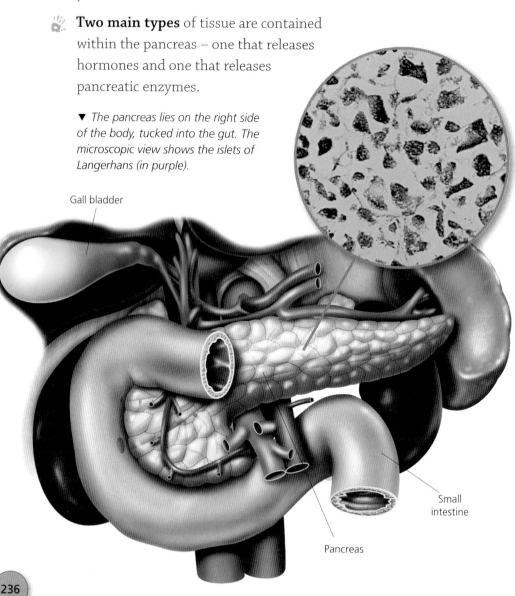

Gall bladder

Small intestine

Pancreas

- **The main type** of tissue consists of thousands of nests of hormone glands called the islets of Langerhans.

- **The islets of Langerhans** release two important hormones: insulin and glucagons.

- **The second type** of tissue is called exocrine tissue and secretes (releases) pancreatic enzymes such as amylase and lipase into the intestine to help digest food.

- **Amylase breaks down** carbohydrates into simple sugars such as maltose, lactose and sucrose.

- **Lipase breaks apart** fat molecules so that they can be absorbed more easily.

- **The pancreatic enzymes** run into the intestine via a pipe called the pancreatic duct, which joins on to the bile duct. This duct also carries bile.

- **The pancreatic enzymes** only start working when they meet other kinds of enzyme in the intestine.

- **The pancreas** also secretes the body's own antacid, sodium bicarbonate, to settle an upset stomach.

DID YOU KNOW?
The pancreas is less than 20 cm long but produces one of the body's most important hormones – insulin.

237

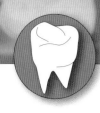

The gall bladder

The gall bladder is a small hollow bag that lies behind the liver and is about 8 cm long.

It is connected to the common bile duct by the cystic duct. The common bile duct connects the liver to the small intestine.

The gall bladder stores a substance called bile, which is made in the liver from waste products.

Bile is a bitter yellow or blue-green liquid that helps to digest fats.

The gall bladder can store about 50 ml of bile.

Bile is released into the small intestine when we eat and helps in the digestion of fats.

Bile contains a fatty material called cholesterol. If there is too much cholesterol in the bile it may start to turn solid and form lumps called gallstones.

Gall bladder

▶ The gall bladder lies just behind the liver and in front of the stomach. It stores bile, a greenish liquid.

- **Gallstones** can reach the size of a golf ball.

- **Some people** with gallstones have their gall bladder removed. You do not need a gall bladder to live.

DID YOU KNOW?

People who have had their gall bladder removed may have to go on a very low fat diet as they cannot digest fats properly.

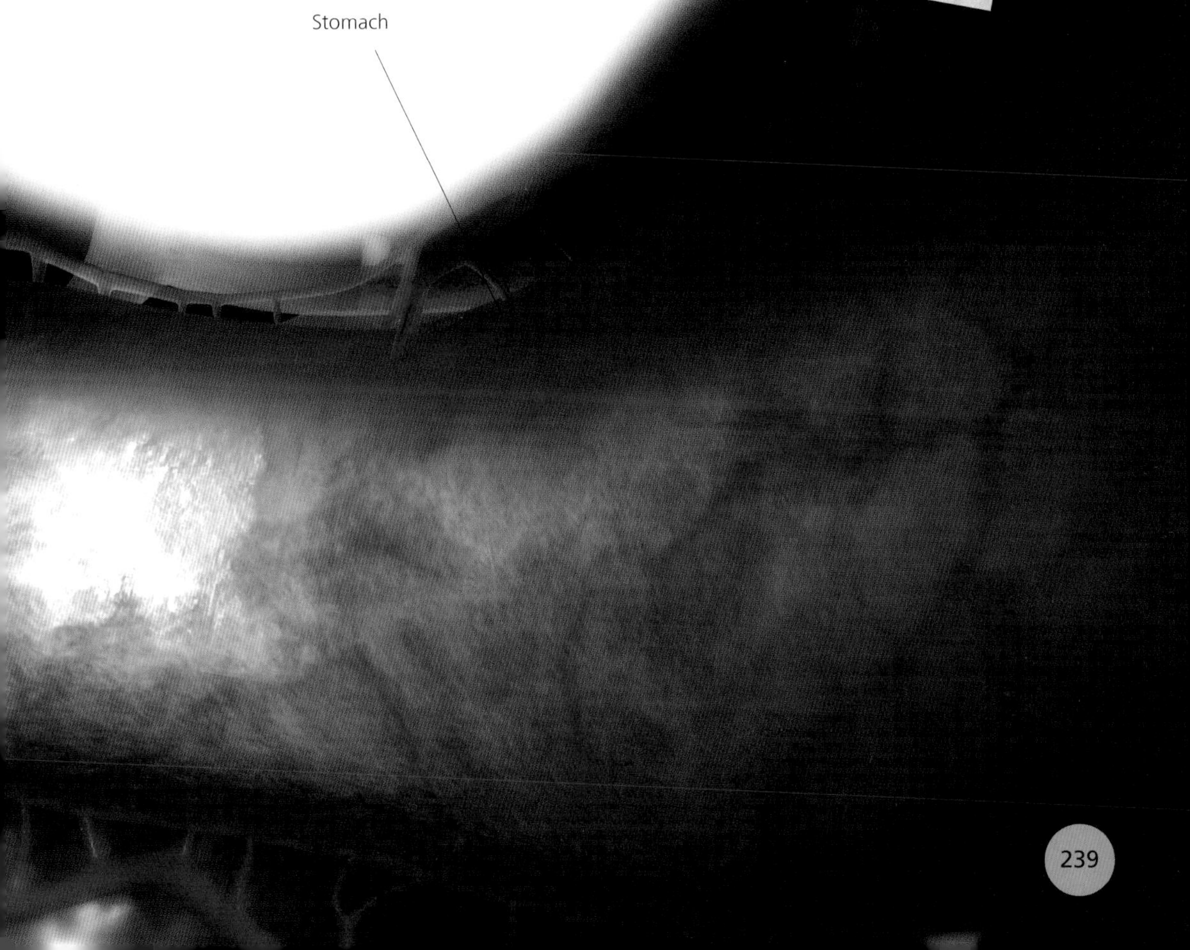

Stomach

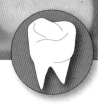

Small intestine

- **Once food** has been broken down into liquid chyme by the stomach it enters the small intestine.

- **Your small intestine** is a 6-m-long tube that is about 2.5 cm wide.

- **It is divided** into three sections, the duodenum, the jejunum and the ileum.

- **The small intestine** is lined with protective mucus to prevent it digesting itself.

- **The lining** also consists of thousands of folds and tiny projections called villi.

- **The villi** give the small intestine a huge surface area. If you could flatten them all out, your small intestine would cover the whole of a tennis court.

- **The first part** of the small intestine, the duodenum, mixes the chyme with enzymes and bile to break it down into molecules small enough to be absorbed.

- **The middle part** of the small intestine, the jejunum, is where food is absorbed. Small molecules such as glucose pass across the villi into the bloodstream, where they can be transported around the body.

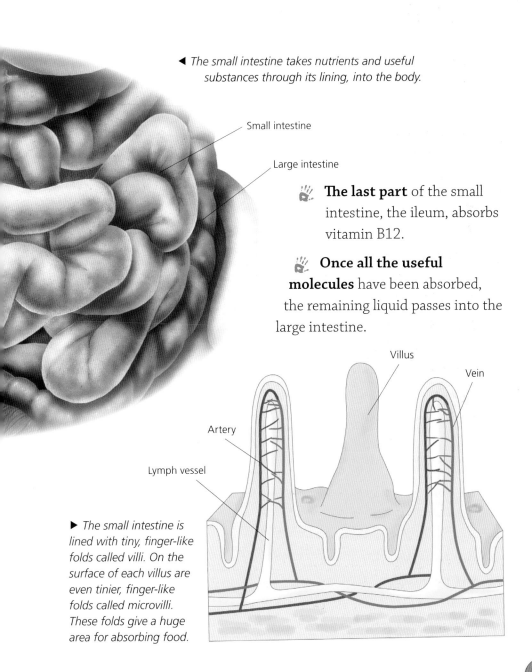

◄ *The small intestine takes nutrients and useful substances through its lining, into the body.*

Small intestine

Large intestine

The last part of the small intestine, the ileum, absorbs vitamin B12.

Once all the useful molecules have been absorbed, the remaining liquid passes into the large intestine.

Villus

Vein

Artery

Lymph vessel

▶ *The small intestine is lined with tiny, finger-like folds called villi. On the surface of each villus are even tinier, finger-like folds called microvilli. These folds give a huge area for absorbing food.*

241

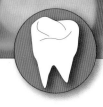

Large intestine

- **The first part** of the large intestine is called the cecum. The appendix is attached to the cecum.

- **A small tube** about 10 cm in length, the appendix sometimes gets infected and has to be removed. It has no function in humans.

- **The main part** of the large intestine is the colon, which is almost as long as you are tall.

- **Although it is** much wider than the small intestine, the large intestine has a smaller surface area.

- **Undigested food** in the form of semi-liquid chyme is converted into solid waste by the colon, which absorbs excess water.

- **The colon soaks up** 1.5 litres of water every day.

- **Sodium and chlorine** are also absorbed by the walls of the colon. Bicarbonate and potassium are also removed.

- **Billions of bacteria** live inside the colon and help turn the chyme into faeces. These bacteria are harmless as long as they do not spread to the rest of the body.

- **Bacteria in the colon** make vitamins K and B – as well as smelly gases such as methane and hydrogen sulphide.

- **The muscles** of the colon break the waste food down into segments ready for excretion.

▶ *This photograph shows the lumpy lining of the large intestine. The small purple worm-like objects are 'friendly' bacteria.*

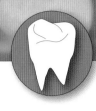

Excretion

- **Digestive excretion** is the way your body gets rid of food that it cannot digest.

- **Undigested food** is prepared for excretion in your large intestine or bowel.

- **Once all the useful molecules** and water have been absorbed, the waste that is left leaves the large intestine and collects in your rectum.

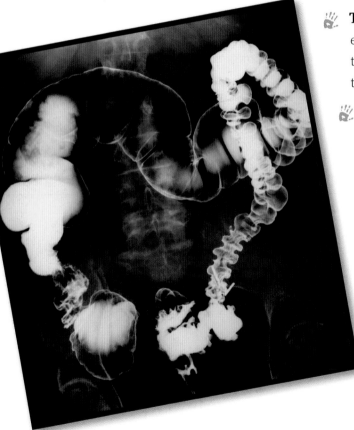

- **This triggers** nerve endings in the rectum that make you want to go to the toilet (defecate).

- **We can control** when we defecate. When we decide to go to the toilet the waste is pushed out through our anus.

- **The anus** is a ring of muscle that relaxes to let out the waste.

◀ This is an X-ray of the colon. Patients drink a liquid called barium to enable their doctor to see the colon more clearly and check it is in working order.

▲ To work well, your bowel needs plenty of fibre – indigestible plant fibres found in food such as beans.

If we decide not to go to the toilet, the waste returns to the large intestine where more water may be absorbed, drying out the waste even more.

Fibre is essential to keep your gut working properly. Fibre is not absorbed so bulks out the waste matter.

About two-thirds of the waste we produce is water.

Up to half of the waste material is friendly bacteria that are found in the gut.

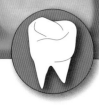

Urinary system

- **The urinary system** removes waste products from the blood and from the body.

- **The kidneys** filter the blood to produce urine. This runs down the ureters to collect in the bladder. Urine leaves the body through the urethra.

- **The urinary system** produces about 0.5–2 litres of urine every day.

- **The kidneys** are a pair of bean-shaped organs inside the small of the back.

- **You can survive** with only one kidney.

- **Kidneys were** once thought to be where our conscience, or feelings of right and wrong, were kept.

- **The ureters** are thin tubes that are about 25 cm long. One leads from each kidney to the bladder.

- **The urethra** is a tube that leads from the bladder to the outside of the body.

- **It is longer** in boys and men than in girls and women as it passes through the penis.

▶ *The urinary system consists of a pair of kidneys connected to the bladder and a tube (the urethra) to the outside of the body.*

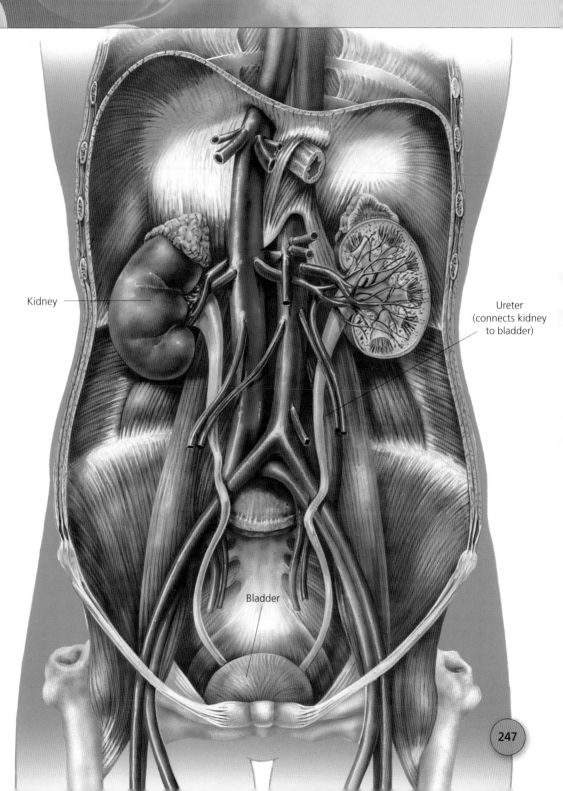

Kidney

Ureter
(connects kidney
to bladder)

Bladder

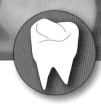

The kidneys

The kidneys are the body's water control and blood-cleaning plants. They are high-speed filters that draw off water and important substances from the blood. They let unwanted water and waste substances go.

About 1.3 litres of blood are filtered by the kidneys every minute.

All the body's blood flows through the kidneys every ten minutes, so blood is filtered 150 times a day.

The kidneys manage to recycle or save every re-useable substance from the blood. They take 85 litres of water and other blood substances from every 1000 litres of blood, but only let out 0.6 litres as urine.

The kidneys save nearly all the amino acids and glucose from the blood and 70 percent of the salt.

Blood entering each kidney is filtered through a million or more filtration units called nephrons.

Each nephron is an incredibly intricate network of little pipes called convoluted tubules, wrapped around countless tiny capillaries. Useful blood substances are filtered into the tubules, then re-absorbed back into the blood in the capillaries.

Blood enters each nephron through a little cup called the Bowman's capsule via a bundle of capillaries.

The kidneys also produce hormones, including one that helps to keep blood pressure normal.

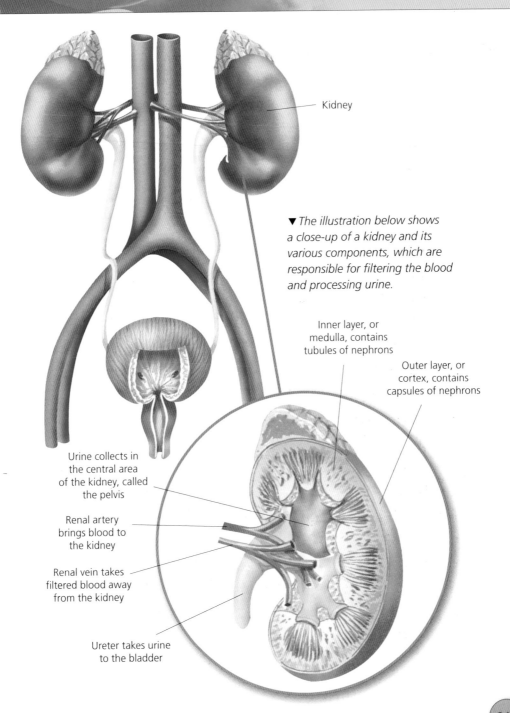

Kidney

▼ The illustration below shows a close-up of a kidney and its various components, which are responsible for filtering the blood and processing urine.

Inner layer, or medulla, contains tubules of nephrons

Outer layer, or cortex, contains capsules of nephrons

Urine collects in the central area of the kidney, called the pelvis

Renal artery brings blood to the kidney

Renal vein takes filtered blood away from the kidney

Ureter takes urine to the bladder

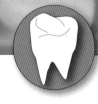

The bladder

- **The bladder** is a hollow, muscular organ that sits deep within the pelvis.

- **It acts as a collection bag** for the urine produced by the kidneys.

- **Urine flows down** the two ureters into the bladder, where it collects until released.

DID YOU KNOW?

Animal bladders have been used to make balls and even musical instruments.

- **The wall of the bladder** is made of smooth muscle and is very folded.

- **As the bladder fills** with urine the folds gradually smooth out so that the bladder can stretch.

- **The bladder** normally holds up to about 600 ml of urine but can stretch to hold up to twice this amount if necessary.

- **As the bladder stretches** it sends nerve signals to the spinal cord and the brain. These tell us we need to empty our bladders (urinate).

- **We start to feel** we need to urinate when the bladder is a quarter full.

- **If we decide** to urinate, we relax the muscle at the base of the bladder and urine passes out through the urethra.

- **At birth**, urination is automatic when the bladder if full. As we grow we learn to control the muscle at the base of the bladder so that we can control when we urinate.

▼ *This highly magnified photograph shows the folded lining of the bladder, which flattens out and stretches as the bladder fills with urine.*

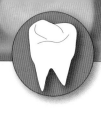

Urine

- **Urine** is one of your body's ways of getting rid of waste.

- **Your kidneys** produce urine, filtering it from your blood.

- **Urine runs from each kidney** down a long tube called the ureter, to a bag called the bladder.

- **Your bladder fills up** with urine over several hours. When it is full, you feel the need to urinate.

- **Urine is mostly water**, but there are substances dissolved in it. These include urea, various salts, creatinine, ammonia and blood wastes.

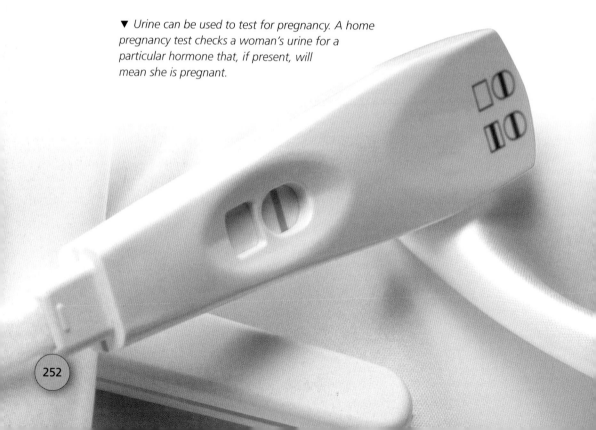

▼ Urine can be used to test for pregnancy. A home pregnancy test checks a woman's urine for a particular hormone that, if present, will mean she is pregnant.

- **Urea** is a substance that is left after the breakdown of amino acids.

- **Urine gets its smell** from substances such as ammonia.

- **Urine gets its colour** from a yellowish blood waste called urochrome. Urochrome is left after proteins are broken down.

- **If you sweat a lot** – perhaps during a fever – your kidneys will let less water go and your urine will be stronger in colour.

- **In some people**, eating beetroot makes their urine go red.

▶ Doctors use urine dipsticks to check urine for different substances, such as glucose or bacteria. This can help identify various illnesses.

253

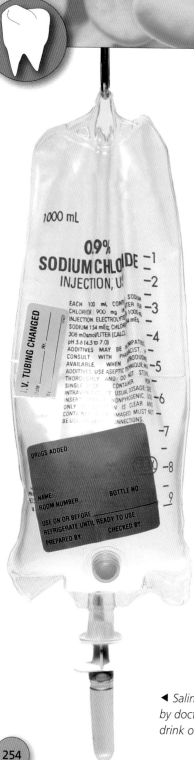

Fluid balance

Your body balances the amount of water leaving the body to match the amount of water entering the body.

We take in water in our food and drink.

We lose water in urine, faeces, sweat and through moisture in the air that we breathe out.

We drink more if we are thirsty. When the amount of water in the body is low, the brain sends a signal to encourage us to drink.

We also become thirsty if the concentration of certain salts in our body is too high. You will probably feel thirsty after eating a lot of salty food.

The amount of water lost in the urine is controlled by several hormones.

The two main hormones that control fluid balance are aldosterone, which is produced by the adrenal glands that lie just above the kidneys, and anti-diuretic hormone, which is produced by the pituitary gland in the brain.

◀ Saline is a solution of water and salt that is used by doctors to replace fluids in people who cannot drink or have become severely dehydrated.

If there is not enough water in the body, hormones are produced that tell the kidneys to take more water from the urine.

If there is too much water in the body, your kidneys will save less water and you will produce more urine.

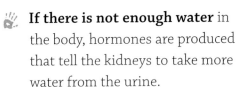

▶ *It is important to replace fluid as it is lost, especially if you have been exercising and sweating.*

255

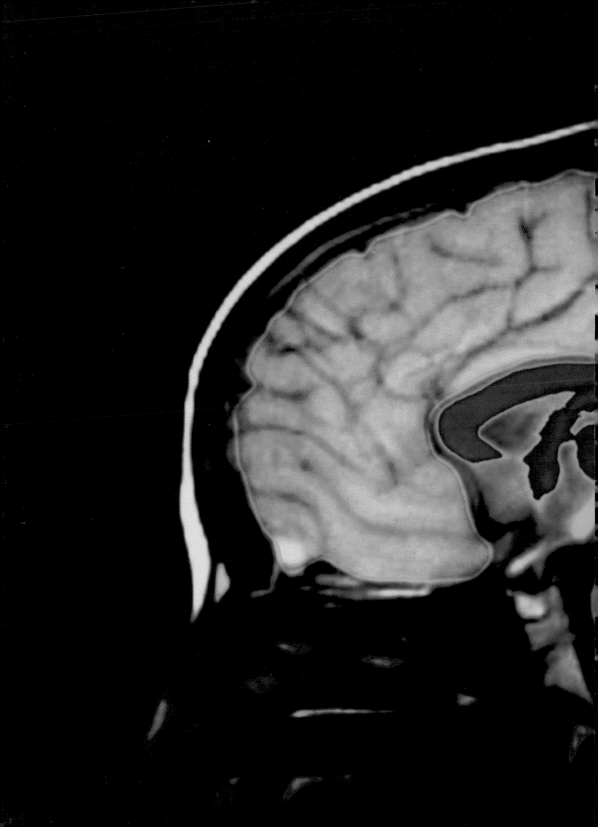

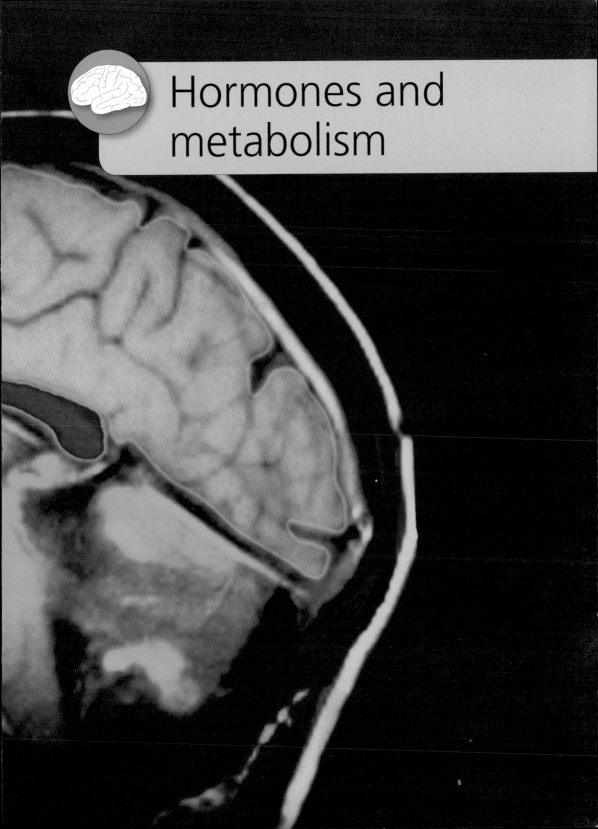

Hormones and metabolism

Hormones

Hormones are the body's chemical messengers, released from stores at times to trigger certain reactions in different parts of the body.

Most hormones are endocrine hormones that are spread around your body in your bloodstream.

Each hormone is a molecule with a certain shape that creates a certain effect on target cells.

Hormones are controlled by feedback systems. This means they are only released when their store gets the right trigger – which may be a chemical in the blood or another hormone.

Major hormone sources include the pituitary gland just below the brain, the thyroid gland, the adrenal glands, the pancreas, a woman's ovaries and a man's testes.

Some hormones only work on certain cells in the body. Others work throughout the body.

Endorphins and enkephalins block or relieve pain.

Oestrogen and progesterone are female sex hormones that control a woman's monthly cycle.

Testosterone is a male sex hormone that controls the workings of a man's sex organs.

The word hormone means 'to excite'.

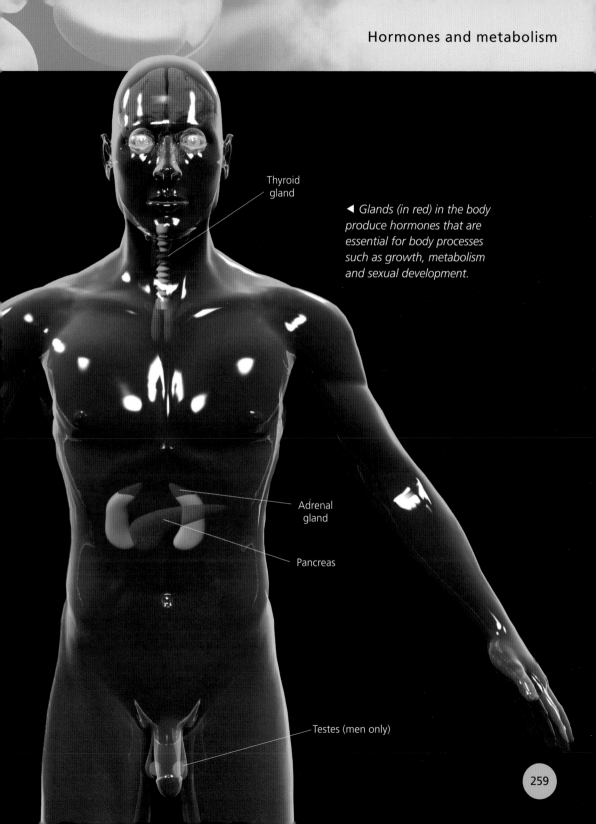

Thyroid gland

◀ *Glands (in red) in the body produce hormones that are essential for body processes such as growth, metabolism and sexual development.*

Adrenal gland

Pancreas

Testes (men only)

Hormonal feedback

It is important that hormone levels are kept just right in the body. If levels become too high or too low they can make us ill.

Levels of hormones in the body are controlled by feedback.

A hormone makes something happen. When it happens, the cells that make that hormone stop producing the hormone.

The hormone levels now fall, meaning the thing it made happen stops. The cells now start producing that hormone again.

This type of feedback is called negative feedback because the event reduces the production of the hormone and hormone levels are kept stable.

Occasionally, an event stimulates cells to produce more of a hormone. The hormone encourages the event and more and more hormone is produced. This is called positive feedback.

Positive feedback occurs in labour when high levels of the hormone oxytocin are needed for birth.

Sometimes more than one hormone controls the same thing. The level of glucose in the blood is controlled by the hormones insulin and glucagon.

Some hormones influence another gland to produce or stop producing hormones.

The pituitary gland influences many of the glands in the body and is sometimes called the master gland.

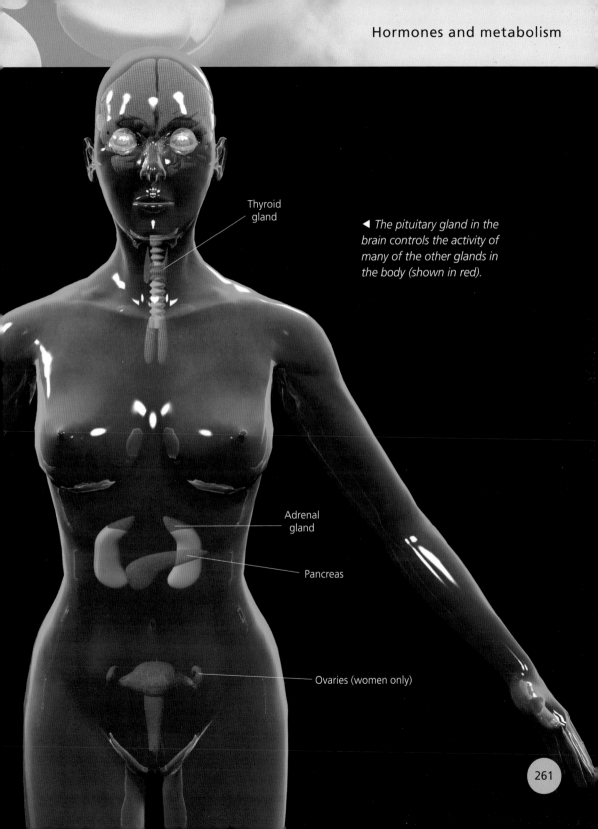

Thyroid gland

Adrenal gland

Pancreas

Ovaries (women only)

◄ *The pituitary gland in the brain controls the activity of many of the other glands in the body (shown in red).*

The pituitary gland

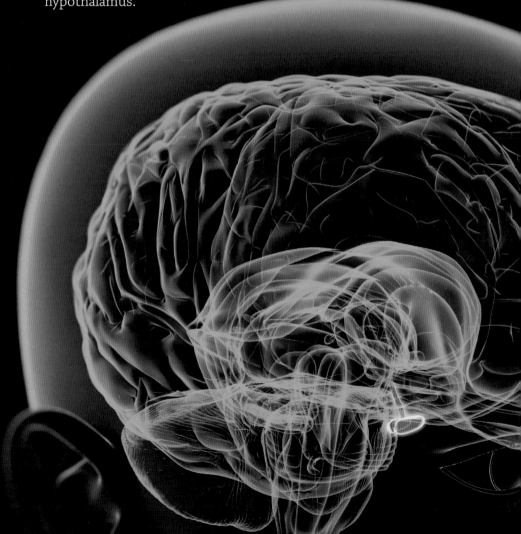

- **The pituitary gland** lies at the base of the brain and is linked to the part of the brain called the hypothalamus.

- **It produces** many important hormones, some of which act on other glands to make them produce hormones.

- **The production** of pituitary gland hormones is controlled by the hypothalamus.

Growth hormone encourages growth in children and teenagers, makes bones stronger and helps build muscles.

ACTH, or adrenocorticotrophic hormone, stimulates the adrenal glands to produce other hormones.

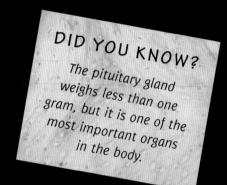

DID YOU KNOW?
The pituitary gland weighs less than one gram, but it is one of the most important organs in the body.

Thyroid-stimulating hormone makes the thyroid gland produce thyroid hormones.

Anti-diuretic hormone acts on the kidneys to reduce the amount of water in the urine.

Follicle-stimulating hormone and luteinizing hormone are involved in reproduction in both men and women. They also affect the production of sex hormones.

Oxytocin encourages labour and makes the breasts release milk when breastfeeding a baby.

Prolactin is produced during and after pregnancy and helps the breasts produce milk for breastfeeding.

◀ The red, pea-sized object at the base of the brain is the pituitary gland, which produces many hormones that act on other glands throughout the body.

The thyroid gland

- **The thyroid** is a small gland about the size of two joined cherries. It is situated at the front of your neck, just below the larynx.

- **The thyroid secretes** (releases) three important hormones – tri-iodothyronine (T3), thyroxine (T4) and calcitonin.

- **The thyroid hormones** affect how energetic you are by controlling your metabolic rate. Your metabolic rate is the rate at which your body cells use glucose.

- **T3 and T4** control metabolic rate by circulating into the blood and stimulating cells to convert more glucose.

- **If the thyroid** sends out too little T3 and T4, you get cold and tired, your skin gets dry and you put on weight.

Thyroid gland

◀ The thyroid gland lies in front of your windpipe and produces hormones that help to control energy levels in your body.

▲ *The thyroid is part of your energy control system and tells your body cells to work faster or slower when you need them to.*

The amount of T3 and T4 sent out by the thyroid depends on how much thyroid-stimulating hormone is sent to it from the pituitary gland.

If the levels of T3 and T4 in the blood drop, the pituitary gland sends out extra thyroid-stimulating hormone to tell the thyroid to produce more.

There are four parathyroid glands at the back of the thyroid. These produce parathyroid hormone, which helps control the amount of calcium in the body.

The adrenal glands

You have two adrenal glands – one just above each kidney. Each gland is divided into two parts.

The outer layer of the adrenal gland is called the cortex and produces corticosteroid hormones.

These corticosteroid hormones include cortisol, aldosterone and sex hormones.

Cortisol increases the level of glucose in the body and increases blood pressure, helping the body react the stress.

Adrenal gland

Kidney

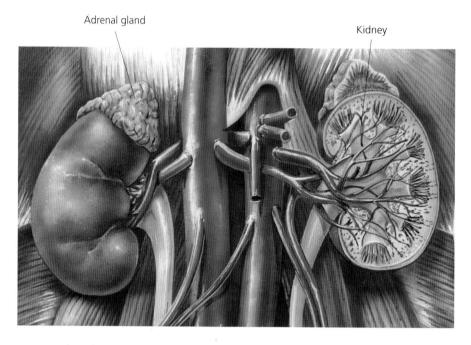

▲ *The adrenal glands sit on the top of each kidney and produce several hormones that help you react to events around you.*

Aldosterone helps the kidneys regulate the levels of sodium and potassium in the body.

The sex hormones include testosterone, which stimulates the development of the male reproductive system.

The production of corticosteroid hormones is controlled by a hormone produced by the pituitary gland.

The inner layer of the adrenal glands is called the medulla and it produces adrenaline and noradrenaline.

Adrenaline and noradrenaline get your body ready for action by increasing your heart and breathing rates and the blood flow to your muscles. This is called the 'fight or flight' response.

Adrenaline and noradrenaline are produced when you are threatened or under stress. You may notice the flight or flight response if you have to do something stressful at school, such as making a speech.

▼ *Adrenaline boosts your heartbeat and breathing during exciting or stressful moments.*

Pancreatic hormones

- **The pancreas secretes** enzymes that aid digestion. It also releases hormones that regulate blood sugar levels.

- **These hormones** are called insulin and glucagon.

- **Both are released** from clusters of cells in the pancreas called the islets of Langerhans.

- **Insulin lowers levels of glucose** in the blood by encouraging cells to take up glucose from the bloodstream, storing it as fat or as glycogen in the liver and muscle.

- **Glucagon raises levels of glucose** in the blood by encouraging the liver to convert glycogen back into glucose and release it into the bloodstream.

▼ People with diabetes need to test their blood sugar levels regularly to make sure they are at normal levels.

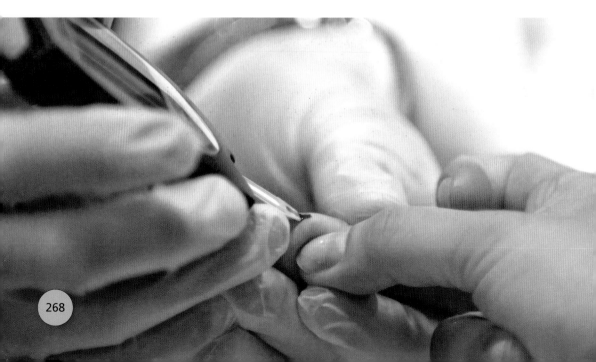

▲ *When we eat sugary food, hormones are released by the pancreas to help keep our blood sugar levels regular.*

Insulin and glucagons balance each other out so that your blood sugar levels are always stable.

Diabetics suffer from the condition diabetes. Some diabetics produce little or no insulin in their pancreas. Others have become resistant to insulin so that their body no longer reacts as it should.

This means that their blood sugar levels are often too high and cells cannot get the energy they need.

Some diabetics are able to control their blood sugar levels by being very careful about what they eat. However many have to control their blood glucose by injecting insulin.

269

Sex hormones

The sexual development of girls and boys depends on the sex hormones.

Sex hormones control the development of primary and secondary sexual characteristics, and regulate all sex-related processes such as sperm and egg production.

Primary sexual characteristics are the development of the major sexual organs, in particular the genitals.

Secondary sexual characteristics are other differences between the sexes, such as men's beards.

- **There are three** main types of sex hormone – androgens, oestrogen and progesterone.

- **Androgens** are male hormones such as testosterone. They make a boy's body develop features such as a beard, deepen his voice and make his penis grow.

DID YOU KNOW?

Boys produce some female sex hormones and girls produce some male sex hormones, but they usually have no effect.

- **Oestrogen** is the female hormone made mainly in the ovaries. It not only makes a girl's sexual organs develop, but also controls her monthly menstrual cycle.

- **Progesterone** is the female hormone that prepares a girl's uterus (womb) for pregnancy every month.

- **Some contraceptive pills** have oestrogen in them to prevent the ovaries releasing their egg cells.

◀ Sex hormones are necessary for normal sexual development in both boys and girls.

271

Male reproductive system

- **The male reproductive system** consists of the penis, scrotum and the two testes (singular, testis).

- **A boy's or man's reproductive system** is where his body creates the sperm cells that combine with a female egg cell to create a new human life.

- **The testes and scrotum** hang outside the body where it is cooler, because this improves sperm production.

- **Sperm cells** look like microscopically tiny tadpoles. They are made in the testes, which are inside the scrotum.

- **At 15**, a boy's testes can make 200 million sperm a day.

- **Sperm leave the testes** via the epididymis – a thin, coiled tube, about 6 m long.

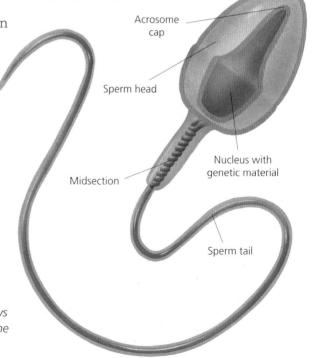

Acrosome cap

Sperm head

Midsection

Nucleus with genetic material

Sperm tail

▶ A mature sperm cell consists of a head, where the genetic information is stored, a midsection and a tadpole-like tail, which allows it to swim rapidly towards the female egg cell.

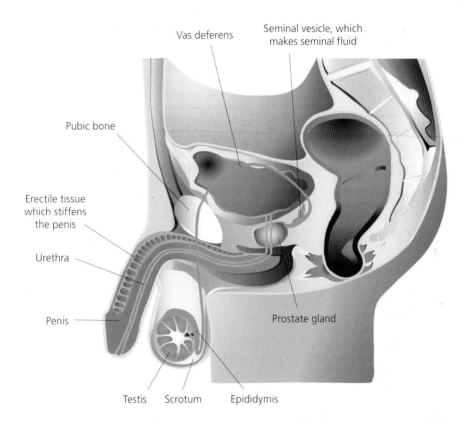

Vas deferens

Seminal vesicle, which makes seminal fluid

Pubic bone

Erectile tissue which stiffens the penis

Urethra

Penis

Prostate gland

Testis   Scrotum   Epididymis

▲ *This is a side view of the inside of the male reproductive organs.*

- **The epididymis** connects to another tube called the vas deferens.

- **Glands called seminal vesicles** lie alongside the vas deferens and add fluids and nutrients to the sperm.

- **The male reproductive system** also produces sex hormones that are needed for the production of sperm and for a boy to develop at puberty.

- **The male sex hormone** testosterone also stimulates bone and muscle growth.

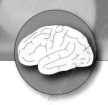

Female reproductive system

- **The female reproductive system** consists of the uterus (womb) fallopian tubes, ovaries, cervix and vagina.

- **A woman's reproductive system** is where her body stores, releases and nurtures the egg cells (ova – singular, ovum) that create a new human life when joined with a male sperm cell.

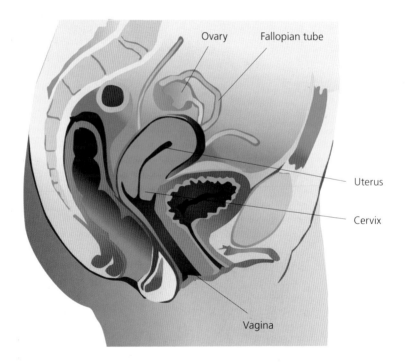

Ovary Fallopian tube

Uterus

Cervix

Vagina

▲ *This is a side view of the inside of a female reproductive system, showing the two ovaries and fallopian tubes, which join to the uterus.*

- **All the egg cells** are stored from birth in the ovaries – two egg-shaped glands inside the pelvic region. Each egg is stored in a tiny sac called a follicle.

- **Baby girls** are born with around 150,000 egg cells that will gradually mature from puberty onwards.

DID YOU KNOW?

Girls are born with all the eggs they will ever produce, but boys produce new sperm throughout their lives.

- **Eggs are gradually released** from the ovaries until menopause, which usually occurs when a woman is between 45 and 55 years of age.

- **The ovaries** sit just near the end of the fallopian tubes. Eggs travel down these tubes to the uterus.

- **The uterus** is a hollow muscular organ that can stretch to fit a baby as it grows in the womb.

- **The entrance** to the uterus is called the cervix. This is usually held closed but opens during labour to let the baby be born.

- **The canal** from the uterus to the outside of the body is called the vagina. It has muscular walls that can stretch during labour.

- **The female reproductive system** also produces sex hormones that are needed for the menstrual cycle and for a girl to develop at puberty. At menopause, the levels of these sex hormones fall.

The menstrual cycle

- **The menstrual cycle** is the way in which a woman's body prepares for pregnancy.

- **It takes place** about every four weeks between puberty and menopause, when hormone levels suddenly drop.

- **Eggs in the ovaries** are stored in follicles. A monthly menstrual cycle starts when follicle-stimulating hormone (FSH) is sent by the pituitary gland in the brain to spur one of the follicles to grow.

- **As the follicle grows**, it releases the sex hormone oestrogen. Oestrogen makes the lining of the uterus (womb) thicken.

- **Halfway through** the menstrual cycle, luteinizing hormone from the pituitary gland encourages the follicle to rupture, and the egg is released.

- **The empty egg** follicle starts to produce progesterone, which also thickens the lining of the uterus.

- **One egg cell** is released every menstrual cycle by one of the ovaries.

- **The egg travels down** the fallopian tubes to the uterus.

- **If the egg is not fertilized**, it is shed with the womb lining in a flow of blood from the vagina. This shedding is called a menstrual period.

- **Menstrual periods** usually occur about every 28 days and last between three and seven days, but vary from woman to woman.

> **DID YOU KNOW?**
> If a group of women live together for a long time, it is thought that their menstrual cycles become synchronised.

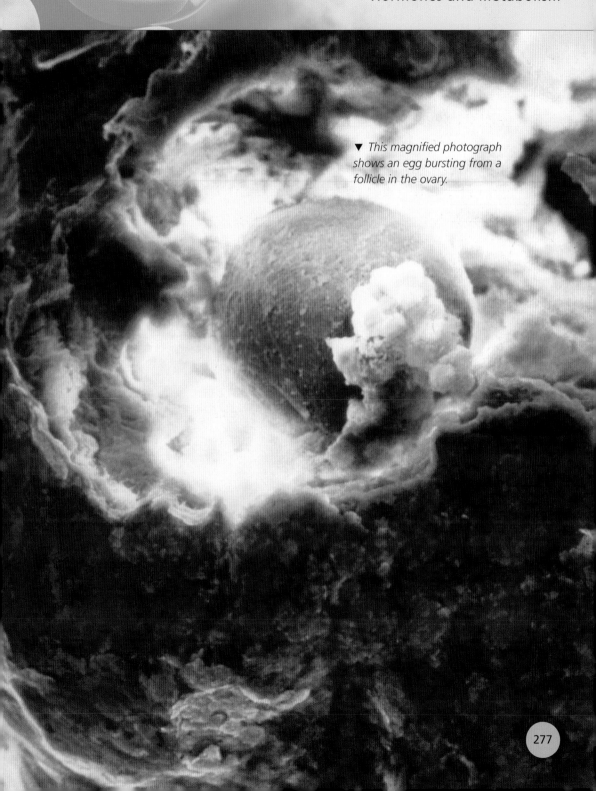

▼ *This magnified photograph shows an egg bursting from a follicle in the ovary.*

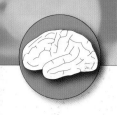

Breasts

🖐 **The breasts** are a mixture of gland tissue and fat, with connective tissue to hold them in shape.

🖐 **They attach** to the main muscle on the chest wall and are held in place by ligaments.

🖐 **Breasts develop** in girls at puberty, usually between the ages of about 11 and 14.

🖐 **The main function** of the breast is to provide milk for newborn babies.

🖐 **During pregnancy**, hormones make a woman's breasts grow and milk glands increase in number and become able to produce milk.

🖐 **Breasts can produce** about one litre of milk a day after a baby is born.

Milk producing glands

◄ Breasts consist of a mixture of fat, connective tissue and glands that produce milk, arranged in four quadrants.

Solid lump in breast

Breastfeeding is best for a baby because breast milk contains natural antibodies that help to protect the baby against infection.

Breasts can become painful just before and during a menstrual period. This is because of changes in hormone levels.

Breasts can change shape and size, especially if a woman gains or loses a lot of weight.

Breast cancer is one of the most common causes of death from cancer in women.

▶ *An X-ray of the breast is called a mammogram. This X-ray shows a solid area, which may be caused by a lump of connective tissue or by cancer.*

279

Reproduction

Reproduction occurs when a developed egg meets a sperm cell during sexual intercourse.

When an egg is ripe, it slides down a duct called a fallopian tube.

If a man and woman have sexual intercourse, the penis is stimulated. Sperm are driven into a tube called the vas deferens and mix with a liquid called seminal fluid to make semen.

Semen shoots through the urethra (the tube inside the penis through which males urinate) and is ejaculated into the female's vagina.

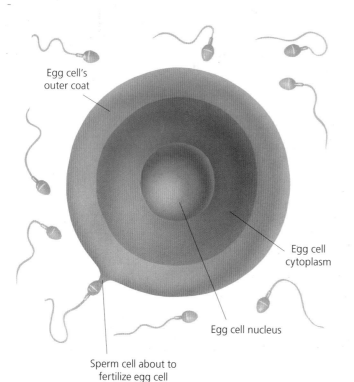

Egg cell's outer coat

Egg cell cytoplasm

Egg cell nucleus

Sperm cell about to fertilize egg cell

◄ *The female egg cell passes along the woman's fallopian tube. At fertilization, tiny sperm cells swarm around the egg until one sperm manages to push its head on to the surface of the egg. The sperm head and egg membrane join, and fertilization takes place.*

▶ *Reproduction relies on a complex series of events that must be timed exactly. Even then, there is only a chance that a baby will be created.*

The sperm from the man's penis may swim up the woman's vagina, enter her womb and fertilize the egg in the fallopian tube.

Although millions of sperm cells are usually released, only one is needed to fertilize the egg.

If the egg is fertilized, the womb lining goes on thickening ready for pregnancy, and the egg begins to develop.

The egg implants into the thick lining of the womb and carries on developing. It is now an embryo or tiny baby.

It takes up to a week for the fertilized egg to implant into the womb. By this time it consists of hundreds of cells.

Rarely, two eggs may be released at the same time and each may be fertilized by a sperm cell. If both implant into the womb, twins develop.

Pregnancy

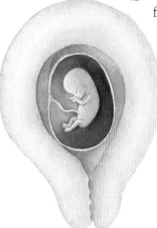

2 months

5 months

▪ **Pregnancy begins** when a woman's ovum (egg cell) is fertilized by a man's sperm cell. Usually this happens after sexual intercourse, but it can begin in a laboratory.

▪ **When a woman** becomes pregnant her monthly menstrual periods stop. Tests on her urine show whether she is pregnant.

▪ **During pregnancy**, the fertilized egg divides again and again to grow rapidly – first to an embryo (the first eight weeks), and then to a foetus (from eight weeks until birth).

▪ **Unlike an embryo**, a foetus has grown legs and arms, as well as internal organs such as a heart.

▪ **Pregnancy lasts** nine months, and the time is divided into three trimesters (periods of about 12 weeks).

▪ **The foetus** lies cushioned in its mother's uterus (womb) in a bag of fluid called the amniotic sac.

3 months

9 months

- **The mother's blood** passes food and oxygen to the foetus via the placenta, also known as the afterbirth.

- **The umbilical cord** runs between the foetus and the placenta, carrying blood between them.

- **During pregnancy** a woman gains 30 percent more blood, and her heart rate goes up.

- **By the end** of the pregnancy the foetus will usually be lying upside down with its head in the pelvis ready to be born.

◀▶ *These are the various stages of development of an embryo and then foetus inside the mother's womb. After fertilization, the egg cell divides and develops into an embryo. After eight weeks, the embryo is called a foetus.*

7 months

Birth

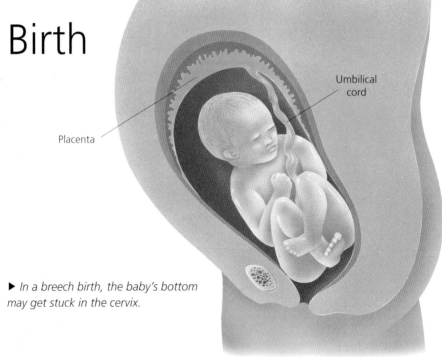

Placenta

Umbilical cord

▶ *In a breech birth, the baby's bottom may get stuck in the cervix.*

Babies are usually born 38–42 weeks after the mother becomes pregnant.

A few days or weeks before a baby is born, it usually turns in the uterus (womb) so its head is pointing down towards the mother's birth canal (her cervix and vagina).

Birth begins as the mother goes into labour – when the womb muscles begin a rhythm of contracting (tightening) and relaxing in order to push the baby out through the birth canal.

There are three stages of labour. In the first, the womb muscles begin to contract or squeeze, bursting the bag of fluid around the baby. This is called breaking the waters.

In the second stage of labour, the baby is pushed out through the birth canal, usually head first.

In the third stage of labour, the placenta, which passed oxygen and nutrients from the mother's blood, is shed and comes out through the birth canal.

DID YOU KNOW?
The youngest baby to be born and survive was only 21 weeks old.

The umbilical cord is the baby's lifeline to its mother. It is cut after birth.

A premature baby is one born before it is fully developed.

A miscarriage is when an embryo or foetus is 'born' before it has developed sufficiently to survive independently.

A Caesarian section is an operation that happens when a baby cannot be born through the birth canal and emerges from the womb through a surgical cut made in the mother's belly.

▼ Babies that weigh below 2.4 kg are known as premature, and are nursed in special care units.

Babies

- **Newborn babies** usually weigh 3–4 kg and are about 50 cm in length.

- **A baby's head** is three-quarters of the size it will be as an adult – and a quarter of its total body height.

- **The bones** of a baby's skeleton are fairly soft, to allow for growth. They harden over time.

- **There are two gaps** called fontanelles between the bones of a baby's skull, where there is only membrane (a 'skin' of thin tissue), not bone. The gaps close and the bones join together by about 18 months.

- **Babies have a gland** called the thymus gland in the centre of their chest. It is important in providing immunity but gradually shrinks after you reach puberty.

- **A baby** has a very developed sense of taste, with taste buds all over the inside of its mouth.

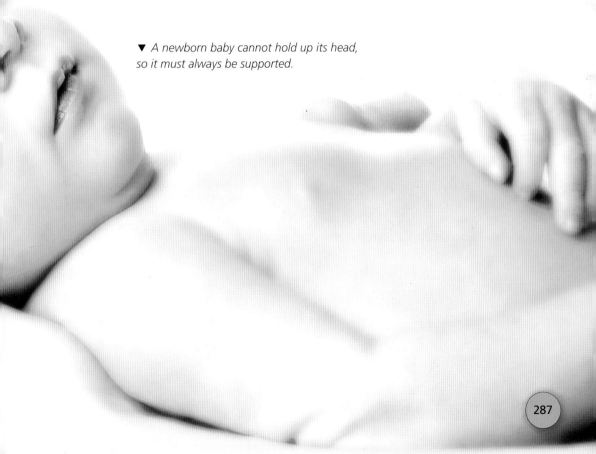

- **Babies have** a much stronger sense of smell than adults – perhaps to help them find their mothers.

- **Their eyesight** is poor to begin with and their eyelids are usually puffy.

- **A baby is born** with primitive reflexes (things it does automatically) such as grasping or sucking a finger.

- **A baby seems to learn** to control its body in stages, starting first with its head, then moving on to its arms and legs.

▼ *A newborn baby cannot hold up its head, so it must always be supported.*

Growth

🖐 **Growth is controlled** by hormones, especially growth hormone, which is produced by the pituitary gland.

🖐 **Your body proportions** change as you grow. A baby's legs only make up about one-quarter of its length, but by the time we are grown up our legs make up almost half of our height.

🖐 **A baby's body weight** usually triples in the first year of its life.

🖐 **By the time** you are two your head is almost the same size as it will be when you are fully grown.

🖐 **Your brain** will be nearly fully grown by the time you are six.

🖐 **The end of long bones**, such as the arm and leg bones are made of cartilage in children. As we grow this cartilage gradually grows to make the bones longer.

▶ *Your final height depends largely on the height of your parents, but a good diet and a healthy childhood will also affect how tall you will be.*

3 years old

 **By the time** we are fully grown the cartilage has been replaced by bone.

 **Baby boys** grow faster than baby girls during the first seven months.

After this, boys and girls grow at roughly the same rate until they reach puberty.

Your eventual height is mainly determined by your genes, but a good diet and good health also make a difference.

10 years old

6 years old

Childhood milestones

As we grow we learn basic skills such as walking and talking. These are called developmental milestones.

Babies usually start to smile at around four to six weeks.

By six to ten months, we are crawling and pulling ourselves upright.

Toddlers can start walking at any time from nine to 18 months. By the age of two they will be able to throw and kick a ball.

▶ Toddlers start to grasp objects at about eight months and will be able to build a tower from around 18 months onwards.

▶ *Children usually start to draw between the ages of one and two years old.*

 **Although babies** are born with a grasping reflex, it takes at least six months to learn how to pick something up just using our fingers and thumbs.

 **At 12 months** onwards we start to scribble, and by the age of three we can draw a straight line.

 **We usually say** our first word at around 12–14 months old and start to put words together between 14 months and two years.

 **We can talk** in sentences by three-and-a-half years old and learn to read at between five and six years old.

 **Between eight and 12 months** we learn to eat with our fingers and between 18 months and two years we learn to eat with a knife and fork.

 **By the time we are five years old** we have learnt all the basic skills we need in life, and can talk, walk, run, play, eat, dress and make friends.

291

Puberty in boys

Puberty is the time of life when boys mature sexually. It is also a time of rapid growth.

The age of puberty varies, but on average it is between 11 and 15 years for boys. The exact age depends on your genes, general health and weight.

Puberty is started by two hormones produced by the pituitary gland – follicle stimulating hormone and luteinizing hormone.

These hormones encourage the testes to produce the sex hormone testosterone.

Testosterone causes physical changes and a desire for sexual intercourse.

During puberty in a boy, the testes grow and hair sprouts on his face, under his arms and around his genitals. Hair may also grow on the chest.

◄ The voice deepens at puberty in boys. This is sometimes erratic, causing the voice to 'break' and make odd noises.

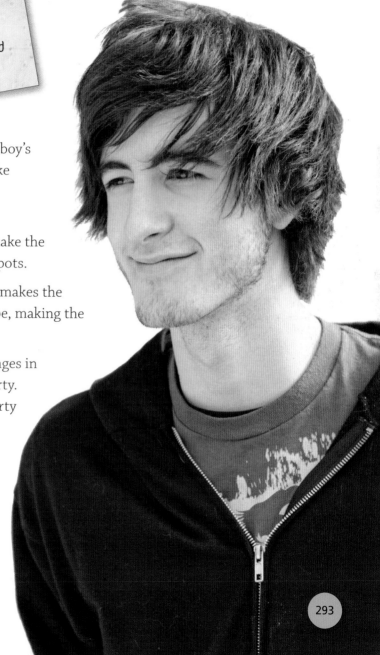

DID YOU KNOW?

Hormones can make you feel angry or sad, but this is normal and temporary.

- **Inside his body**, a boy's testes begin to make sperm.

- **Higher levels** of testosterone can make the skin oily, causing spots.

- **Testosterone** also makes the larynx change shape, making the voice deeper.

- **The body** also changes in shape during puberty. By the end of puberty most males have heavier bones and twice as much muscle.

▶ *Facial hair is one of the signs of puberty in boys.*

Puberty in girls

- **At puberty**, girls mature sexually and grow suddenly.

- **The age of puberty** varies hugely depending on your genes, weight and general health, but on average it is between ten and 13 years for girls.

- **Two hormones** produced by the pituitary gland – follicle-stimulating hormone and luteinizing hormone – start puberty.

- **These hormones stimulate** the ovaries to produce the sex hormones oestrogen and progesterone.

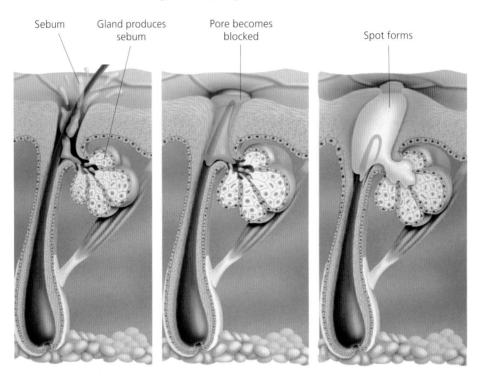

Sebum   Gland produces   Pore becomes   Spot forms
                    sebum   blocked

▲ *During puberty, glands in the skin produce extra sebum, a type of oil, that can block pores, causing spots.*

▲ *Washing your face regularly with a cleanser and warm water will help to prevent spots.*

- **Oestrogen and progesterone** spur the development of a girl's sexual organs and control her monthly menstrual cycle.

- **During puberty**, a girl will develop breasts and grow hair under her arms and around her genitals.

- **The uterus and ovaries** will become bigger.

- **Increased levels** of sex hormones also make the skin oily, causing spots.

- **A girl's body** also changes shape during puberty. The hips widen and body fat increases, especially around the hips, buttocks and thighs.

- **A year or so after puberty** begins, a girl has her menarche (the first menstrual period). When her periods come regularly, she will be able to have a baby.

Ageing

- **Most people live** for between 60 and 100 years, although a few live even longer than this.

- **The longest** officially confirmed age is that of a French woman Jeanne Calment, who died in 1997, aged 122 years and 164 days.

- **Life expectancy** is how long statistics suggest you are likely to live.

- **On average in Europe**, men can expect to live about 75 years and women about 80. However, because health is improving generally, people are now living longer.

- **As adults grow older**, their bodies begin to deteriorate (fail). Senses such as hearing, sight and taste weaken.

- **Hair goes grey** as pigment (colour) cells stop working.

- **Muscles weaken** as fibres die.

- **Bones become more brittle** as they lose calcium. Cartilage shrinks between joints, causing stiffness.

◄ *People in Japan have a long life expectancy. This is probably due to a combination of factors including a healthy diet and certain social customs, which tend to favour the elderly.*

Skin wrinkles as the rubbery elastin and collagen fibres that support it sag. Exposure to sunlight speeds this up, which is why the face and hands get wrinkles first.

Circulation and breathing weaken. Blood vessels may become stiff and clogged, forcing the heart to work harder and raising blood pressure.

> **DID YOU KNOW?**
> In the UK, there are more people aged over 60 than there are aged under 16.

▼ Changes in health care mean more and more people than ever before are keeping fit and healthy into old age.

Metabolism

Body cells are constantly repairing themselves or creating new cells, or substances are constantly being broken down or built up into new substances.

Thousands of these chemical reactions take place in the body every day to keep us alive and healthy. This is metabolism.

There are two types of metabolism – anabolism and catabolism.

In anabolism, complex substances are made from simple ones to build or repair cells. In catabolism, simple substances are broken down to provide energy.

We get energy from food and this energy is used by the cells in the body to keep us healthy and alive.

The basal metabolic rate (BMR) is the amount of energy you need to keep your body going.

Even when you are asleep or doing nothing your body needs energy to keep working. Your heart still beats, you still need to breathe and your temperature needs to be kept normal.

Your BMR decreases with age as you need less energy to keep going as you get older. Exercise increases BMR.

Girls usually have a lower BMR than boys, but women who are pregnant or breastfeeding need more energy and so will have higher BMRs than other women.

◀ People with a physical job, such as fire fighters, need more energy than people who work at a desk all day.

299

The hypothalamus

The hypothalamus is a tiny area of the brain that controls the glands in the body and metabolism.

It helps to regulate sleep, hunger, thirst, the body's temperature, blood pressure and fluid balance.

Nerve signals are constantly being sent to and from the hypothalamus to make sure our body is at the right temperature, and our blood pressure and heart rate are correct.

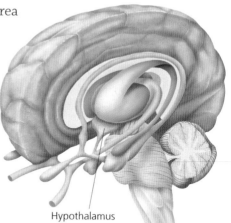

Hypothalamus

▲ *The hypothalamus is a complex area of the brain with a number of important functions.*

The hypothalamus also releases hormones called releasing hormones that act on the pituitary gland.

These hormones encourage the pituitary gland to release hormones that affect growth and reproduction.

The hypothalamus controls the circadian cycle. This is our internal body clock.

DID YOU KNOW?

The word circadian comes from the Latin words 'circa', meaning around, and 'diem', meaning day.

- **Your body clock** is set to a 24-hour cycle.

- **The cycle** is connected to daylight and tells us when we should be alert, eating and sleeping.

- **If you fly around the world** to a very different time zone you will get jet lag. Your internal body clock is still set on the time at home and your body rhythms are upset.

- **The hypothalamus** also controls hunger and thirst.

▼ *When we travel across time zones we get 'jet lag' because our internal body clock needs a few days to adjust to the different time zone.*

Temperature

- **The inside** of your body stays at a constant temperature of around 37°C (98°F), rising a few degrees only when you are ill.

- **Your body** creates heat by burning food in its cells, especially the 'energy sugar' glucose.

- **Even when you are resting**, your body generates so much heat that you are comfortable only when the air is slightly cooler than you are.

- **When you are working hard**, your muscles can generate as much heat as a 2 kW heater (a typical room heater).

▶ The body's temperature can be easily monitored using a digital thermometer.

- **Your body** loses heat as you breathe in cool air and breathe out warm air. Your body also loses heat by giving it off from your skin.

- **The body's temperature control** is the tiny hypothalamus in the lower front of the brain.

- **Temperature sensors** in the skin, in the body's core, and in the blood tell the hypothalamus how hot or cold your body is.

If it is too hot, the hypothalamus sends signals to your skin telling it to sweat more. Signals also tell blood vessels in the skin to widen – this increases the blood flow, increasing the heat loss from your blood.

If it is too cold, the hypothalamus sends signals to the skin to cut back skin blood flow, as well as signals to tell the muscles to generate heat by shivering.

If it is too cold, the hypothalamus may also stimulate the thyroid gland to send out hormones to make your cells burn energy faster and so make more heat.

▲ On a hot day, the skin becomes flushed as blood vessels widen to try to lose heat. Drinking something cold can help to cool us down.

Health and disease

- **Health is partly determined** by your genes. Some diseases run in families and you are more likely to get them no matter what you do.

- **Other diseases** are caused by an unhealthy lifestyle. If you eat well, exercise and look after yourself you are more likely to live a long and healthy life.

- **You should eat** a good balance of foods. Try to eat plenty of fruit and vegetables every day and only eat fatty food occasionally.

- **Regular exercise** is important to keep your bones strong and your muscles healthy.

- **Exercise also helps** to keep your heart healthy and keeps you flexible.

- **If you want** to keep healthy you should not smoke cigarettes, as the tobacco in cigarettes damages lungs and blood vessels as well as other parts of the body.

- **You should also** not drink too much alcohol. Too much alcohol damages the liver and brain.

- **Illness occurs** when your body does not function normally. An illness may be caused by an injury, infection or disease.

- **Regular checkups** by your doctor will spot signs of disease early.

- **You should also** make sure you have any vaccinations that your GPs suggests.

TOP 10 CAUSES OF DEATH	CONTRIBUTING FACTORS
HEART ATTACK	An unhealthy diet and lack of exercise increase the risk of a heart attack
STROKE	A fatty diet and stress increase the risk of brain damage because the blood supply is interrupted
CHEST INFECTION	In undeveloped countries chest infections can be fatal because of a lack of medicine
LUNG DISEASE	Breathing problems caused by smoking cigarettes can be avoided by not smoking
DIARRHOEA	Infected water and food is common in poor countries. Gut infections can kill without treatment
HIV/AIDS	The majority of HIV infections are acquired through unprotected sex
TUBERCULOSIS	Developed countries can prevent tuberculosis with vaccines, but these are rare in undeveloped countries
LUNG CANCER	This is usually caused by smoking cigarettes
ROAD TRAFFIC ACCIDENTS	Poor driving is a killer in many countries
PREMATURE BIRTHS	Many countries do not have good enough health care for babies that are born too early

Diet

Your diet is what you eat. A good diet includes the correct amount of proteins, carbohydrates, fats, vitamins, minerals, fibre and water.

Most of the food you eat is fuel for the body, provided mostly by carbohydrates and fats.

Carbohydrates are foods made from kinds of sugar, such as glucose and starch. These are found in foods such as bread, rice, potatoes and sweet things.

Fats are greasy foods that will not dissolve in water. Some, such as the fats in meat and cheese, are solid. Some, such as cooking oil, are liquid.

Fats are not usually burned up straight away, but are stored around your body until they are needed.

Proteins are needed to build and repair cells. They are made from special chemicals called amino acids.

Fibre or roughage is supplied by cellulose from plant cell walls. Your body cannot digest fibre, but needs it to keep the bowel muscles exercised.

Many ready-made foods now come with food labels on them so that you can see how much carbohydrate, fat and protein they contain.

People in different countries have different sorts of diets. Japanese people eat more fish and rice than people in the UK.

◄ It is important to eat a healthy, balanced diet with plenty of fruit and vegetables, fish and lean meat, fibre and some fat.

The Mediterranean diet, which is eaten by people in areas such as Italy and Greece, contains plenty of fruit, vegetables, fish and olive oil and is particularly healthy.

Carbohydrates

- **Your body's main source** of energy is carbohydrates in food. They are plentiful in sweet things and in starchy food such as bread, cakes and potatoes.

- **Carbohydrates are burned** by the body in order to keep it warm and to provide energy for growth and muscle movement, as well as to maintain basic body processes.

- **Carbohydrates are among the most common** of organic (life) substances – plants, for instance, make carbohydrates by taking energy from sunlight.

- **Chemical substances** called sugars are also carbohydrates. Sucrose (the sugar in sugar lumps and caster sugar) is just one of these sugars.

- **Simple carbohydrates** such as glucose, fructose (the sweetness in fruit) and sucrose are sweet and soluble (they will dissolve in water).

- **Complex carbohydrates** (or polysaccharides) such as starch are made when molecules of simple carbohydrates join together.

- **A third type** of carbohydrate is cellulose.

- **The carbohydrates you eat** are turned into glucose for your body to use at once, or stored in the liver as the complex sugar glycogen (body starch).

- **The average adult** needs 2000–3000 Calories a day.

- **A Calorie** is the heat needed to warm one litre of water by 1°C.

▶ Bread and other wheat products, rice and potatoes are all full of starch, a complex carbohydrate that gives us a steady supply of energy.

Glucose

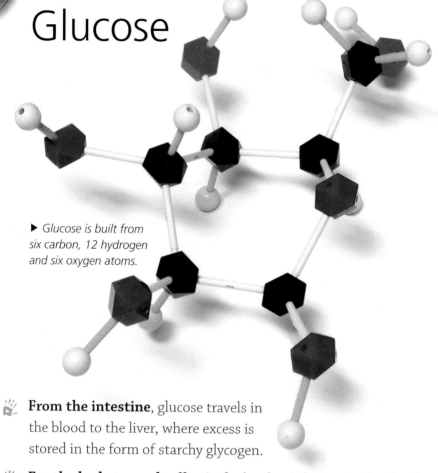

▶ *Glucose is built from six carbon, 12 hydrogen and six oxygen atoms.*

- **From the intestine**, glucose travels in the blood to the liver, where excess is stored in the form of starchy glycogen.

- **For the body to work effectively**, levels of glucose in the blood (called blood sugar) must always be correct.

- **Glucose is the body's energy chemical**, used as the fuel in all cell activity.

- **Glucose is a kind of sugar** made by plants as they take energy from sunlight. It is commonly found in many fruits and fruit juices, along with fructose.

- **The body gets its glucose** from carbohydrates in food, broken down in stages in the intestine.

- **Blood sugar levels** are controlled by two hormones, glucagon and insulin, sent out by the pancreas.

- **When blood sugar is low**, the pancreas sends out glucagon and this makes the liver change more glycogen to glucose.

- **When blood sugar is high**, the pancreas sends out insulin and this makes the liver store more glucose as glycogen.

- **Inside cells**, glucose may be burned for energy, stored as glycogen, or used to make triglyceride fats.

▼ *A blood glucose monitor checks that a person's blood sugar is at a healthy level.*

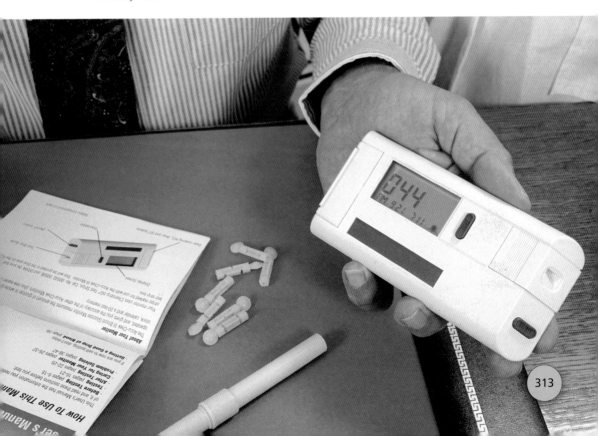

Proteins

- **Proteins are needed** for growth and repair.

- **They are made** from simple substances called amino acids.

- **Proteins are broken down** in the body into amino acids. These are then used to make different proteins within the body.

- **There are 20** different amino acids. Your body can make 11 of them. The other nine are called essential acids and they come from food.

DID YOU KNOW?

Most plants can make 20 amino acids, but humans can only make 11.

◀ Meat, fish and dairy products such as eggs and cheese are our most common sources of protein.

▶ Vegetarians do not eat meat or fish, so must be careful to eat plenty of other sources of protein, such as chickpeas.

Foods that are high in protein include meat, fish, eggs, milk, cheese, nuts, lentils and beans.

A correctly balanced vegetarian diet can provide all the essential amino acids.

About one-sixth of a healthy diet should consist of protein.

People who have an allergy to wheat are allergic to gluten, the protein in wheat.

Some people are allergic to the proteins in peanuts or seafood, or to casein, the protein in milk.

◀ Nuts, such as these almonds, are good sources of protein and contain vitamins and minerals too.

315

Fats

▼ *Fat cells are numerous under the skin, providing your body with a store of energy and a layer of insulation to keep you warm.*

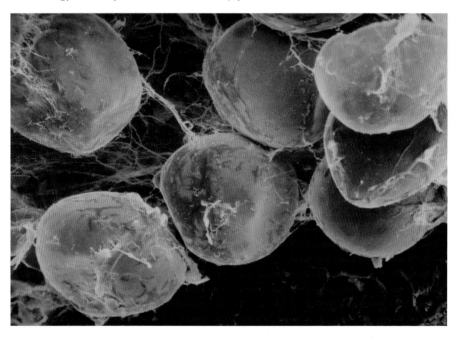

Fats are an important source of energy. Together with carbohydrates and proteins, they make up your body's three main components of foods.

While carbohydrates are generally used for energy immediately, your body often stores fat to use for energy in times of shortage.

Weight for weight, fats contain twice as much energy as carbohydrates.

Fats are important organic (life) substances, found in almost every living thing. They are made from substances called fatty acids and glycerol.

- **Food fats** are greasy vegetable or animal fats that will not dissolve in water.

- **Most vegetable fats** such as corn oil and olive oil are liquid, although some nut fats are solid.

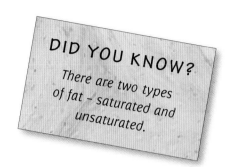

DID YOU KNOW?
There are two types of fat – saturated and unsaturated.

- **Most animal fats**, as in meat, milk and cheese, are solid. Milk is mainly water with some solid animal fats. Most solid fats melt when warmed.

- **Fats called triglycerides** are stored around the body as adipose tissue (body fat). These act as energy stores and also insulate the body against the cold.

- **Fats called phospholipids** are used to build body cells.

- **In your stomach**, bile from your liver and enzymes from your pancreas break fats down into fatty acids and glycerol. These are absorbed into your body's lymphatic system or enter the blood.

▶ *Cheese contains saturated fat, which is linked to high levels of the substance cholesterol in the blood and may increase the risk of a heart attack.*

Vitamins

- **Vitamins are special substances** the body needs to help maintain chemical processes inside cells.

- **There are at least** 15 known vitamins. A lack of any vitamin in the diet can cause certain illnesses.

- **The first vitamins** discovered were given letter names such as B. Later discoveries were given chemical names, such as E vitamins, which are known as tocopherols.

- **Some vitamins** such as A, D, E and K dissolve in fat and are found in animal fats and vegetable oils. They may be stored in the body for months.

- **Vitamin C** is found in fruit such as oranges, tomatoes and fresh green vegetables.

▶ Citrus fruit, such as oranges, lemons and limes, and green vegetables are full of vitamins, which is why they are so important in our diet.

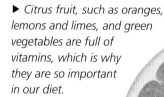

DID YOU KNOW?

Lack of vitamin A ruins night vision because it is needed for the retina at the back of the eye to work properly.

- **Before the 18th century**, sailors on long voyages used to suffer from the disease scurvy, caused by a lack of vitamin C in their diet.

- **There are several** B vitamins. These dissolve in water and are found in green leaves, fruits and cereal grains. Many are also in meat and fish. They are used daily.

- **Vitamins D and K** are the only ones made inside the body. Vitamin K is made by bacteria in the gut.

- **Vitamin D** is made in the skin when we are out in the sun; it is essential for bone growth in children.

319

Minerals

- **Minerals are substances** needed by your body to keep it healthy.

- **You need** about 20 different minerals. Most minerals are simple chemicals, such as calcium.

- **You only need** tiny amounts of each mineral every day but without them you will become ill.

- **Your body** can store some minerals but needs a regular supply of others in your food.

▶ *Many toothpastes have the mineral fluoride added to them to help strengthen teeth and prevent tooth decay.*

◀ Spinach is a good source of iron, which may explain why the cartoon character Popeye the sailor eats it to give himself super strength!

- **A healthy balanced diet** that includes plenty of fruit and vegetables should supply all the minerals that your body needs.

- **Iron can be found** in meat, eggs, and leafy green vegetables. You need iron to help make red blood cells.

- **Calcium helps** build strong bones and teeth. It is found in dairy products such as milk and cheese and fish with bones, such as sardines.

- **Healthy bones** also need magnesium, which is found in nuts, seafood and cocoa.

- **One of the hormones** produced by the thyroid gland contains iodine, which is found in red meat, nuts and leafy green vegetables.

- **You also need minerals** such as selenium for normal heart and liver function, and zinc for growth and energy.

321

Water

- **Your body** is mainly made of water – more than 60 percent.

- **You can survive for weeks** without food, but no more than a few days without water.

- **You gain water** by drinking and eating, and as a by-product of cell activity.

- **You lose water** by sweating and breathing, and in your urine and faeces.

- **The average person takes** in 2.5 litres of water a day – 1.4 litres in drink and 0.8 litres in food. Body cells add 0.3 litres, bringing the total water intake to 2.5 litres.

- **The average person loses** 1.5 litres of water every day in urine, 0.5 litres in sweat, 0.3 litres as vapour in the breath, and 0.2 litres in faeces.

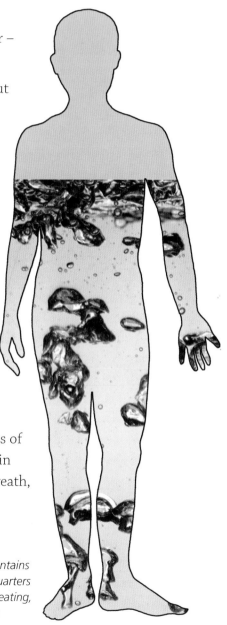

▶ *Your body is mostly water. Even bone contains one-fifth water, while your brain is three-quarters water. You take it in through drinking and eating, and lose it by urinating, sweating and even breathing.*

- **The water balance** in the body is controlled mainly by the kidneys and adrenal glands.

- **The amount of water** the kidneys let out as urine depends on the amount of salt there is in the blood.

- **If you drink a lot**, the saltiness of the blood is diluted (watered down). To restore the balance, the kidneys let out a lot of water as urine.

▶ If you sweat a lot during heavy exercise, you need to make up for all the water you have lost by drinking. Your kidneys make sure that if you drink too much, you lose water as urine.

- **If you drink little** or sweat a lot, the blood becomes more salty, so the kidneys restore the balance by holding on to more water.

323

Body salts

Body salts are not simply sodium chloride – the salt some people sprinkle on food – they are an important group of chemicals that play a vital role in your body.

Examples of components in body salts include potassium, sodium, manganese, chloride, carbonate and phosphate.

Body salts are important in maintaining the balance of water in the body, and on the inside and the outside of body cells.

The body's thirst centre is the hypothalamus. It monitors salt levels in the blood and sends signals telling the kidneys to keep water or to let it go.

You gain salt from the food you eat.

You can lose salt if you sweat heavily. This can make muscles cramp, which is why people take salt tablets in the desert or drink a weak salt solution.

Too much salt in food may result in high blood pressure in certain people.

When dissolved in water, the chemical elements that salt is made from split into ions – atoms or groups of atoms with either a positive or a negative electrical charge.

The balance of water and salt inside and outside of body cells often depends on a balance of potassium ions entering the cell and sodium ions leaving it.

▼ Athletes often drink special sports drinks to make up for the loss of salt caused by sweating.

Fibre

- **Fibre is material in food** that the body cannot break down.

- **Partly digested food** in the gut is given bulk by fibre, making it easier for the muscles in the gut to move the food along.

- **Fibre also** softens partly digested food, making it easier to excrete.

- **Fibre generally** passes out of the body undigested.

- **There are two types** of fibre – soluble fibre, which dissolves in water, and insoluble fibre, which does not dissolve.

- **Soluble fibre** is found in oats, some fruits and vegetables and beans.

▼ Beans, bananas, seeds and nuts are all good source of fibre.

▶ *Peanuts contain a surprising amount of fibre, as well as healthy fats and protein.*

 Insoluble fibre is found in whole grains, wheat, nuts, seeds and some vegetables.

 Foods that contain fibre often help to fill you up so that you are less hungry.

 People who eat foods containing plenty of fibre are less likely to get some diseases of the large intestine, including cancer.

 Some types of fibre, especially soluble fibre, lower levels of fat in the blood and help to prevent heart disease.

327

Exercise

Exercise is any activity that keeps you fit and healthy. Some people do exercise by playing a sport or going to the gym. Others take walks or do something around the house such as gardening.

People exercise because they enjoy it, to keep fit or to lose weight.

When you exercise, your muscles have to work much harder than normal, so need much more oxygen and glucose (a kind of sugar) from the blood.

To boost oxygen, your heart beats twice as fast and pumps twice as much blood, and your lungs take in ten times more air with each breath.

To boost glucose, adrenalin triggers your liver to release its store of glucose.

If oxygen delivery to muscles lags, the muscles fill up with lactic acid, affecting your body for hours afterwards and sometimes causing painful cramp.

◄ Yoga is an excellent exercise for building up flexibility, strength and balance without putting too much stress on the body.

▲ *Walking is great exercise as well as a good way to spend time with family and friends.*

The fitter you are, the quicker your body returns to normal after exercise.

It is always important to wear the right equipment, such as football boots for playing football, and to start slowly to get your muscles warmed up.

Regular exercise multiplies muscle fibres and strengthens tendons. It can help reduce weight when it is combined with a controlled diet.

329

Types of exercise

Regular exercise is important to improve your strength, endurance (stamina or staying power) and flexibility (suppleness).

Strength is how strong your muscles are. A weightlifter is very strong.

Stamina helps you to exercise for a long time without becoming tired. A marathon runner has lots of stamina.

Suppleness is how flexible you are. A gymnast is very supple.

Different types of exercise help to develop strength, stamina and suppleness. Some exercises are good for developing one and some are good for developing all three.

Walking and running are good for developing stamina.

Sports such as football and swimming are good for developing strength, stamina and suppleness.

◄ Cycling is one of the best all round exercises there is – it builds up stamina and strength as well as being good for suppleness and balance.

▲ Team sports such as basketball are good aerobic exercises and great fun too.

DID YOU KNOW?

When you exercise hard, your body burns up energy 20 times as fast as normal.

- **Aerobic exercise** is exercise that is long and hard enough for the oxygen supply to the muscles to rise enough to match the rapid burning of glucose.

- **Regular aerobic exercise** strengthens your heart and builds up your body's ability to supply extra oxygen through your lungs to your muscles.

- **In anaerobic exercise**, muscles are used hard for short periods of time. The oxygen supply to the muscles cannot keep up and they have to use other forms of energy.

331

Fitness

- **The word fitness refers** to how much and what kind of physical activity you can do without getting tired or strained.

- **Fitness depends** on your strength, flexibility (suppleness) and endurance (stamina).

- **One key to fitness** is cardiovascular fitness – that is, how well your heart and lungs respond to the extra demands of exercise.

- **One measure** of cardiovascular fitness is how quickly your pulse rate returns to normal after exercise – the fitter you are, the quicker it returns.

◀ Skiing is one of the most demanding of all sports, and top skiers need to be extremely fit to cope with the extra strain on their bodies.

▲ *Many people keep fit by attending exercise classes.*

Another measure of cardiovascular fitness is how slowly your heart beats during exercise – the fitter you are, the slower it beats.

Being fit improves your physical performance. It can often protect against illness and even slow down the effects of ageing.

Cardiovascular fitness reduces the chances of getting heart disease.

Fitness tests involve comparing such things as height, weight and body fat, and measuring blood pressure and pulse rate before and after exercise.

DID YOU KNOW?

Children and teenagers should get at least one hour of exercise every day.

Types of disease

A **disease** is something that upsets the normal working of any living thing. It can be acute (sudden, but short-lived), chronic (long-lasting), malignant (spreading) or benign (not spreading).

Some diseases are classified by the body part they affect (such as heart disease), or by the body activity they affect (such as respiratory, or breathing, disease).

Heart disease is the most common cause of death in the USA, Europe and also Australia.

Some diseases are classified by their cause. These include the diseases caused by the staphylococcus bacteria – pneumonia is one such disease.

▲ *There are millions of different types of viruses, such as the adenovirus (shown here). Many viruses can cause serious diseases in humans.*

Contagious diseases are caused by germs such as bacteria and viruses. They include the common cold, polio, flu and measles. Their spread can be controlled by good sanitation and hygiene, and also by vaccination programmes.

Non-contagious diseases may be inherited or they may be caused by such things as eating harmful substances, poor nutrition or hygiene, or being injured.

DID YOU KNOW?

The most common disease in the world is tooth decay – so remember to brush your teeth!

Non-contagious diseases may also be caused by body cells acting wrongly and attacking the body's own tissues. This type of disease is called an autoimmune disease.

Degenerative diseases occur in older people as the body's tissues start to get older and either do not function normally or gradually disappear.

Endemic diseases are diseases that occur in a particular area of the world, such as sleeping sickness in Africa.

Diseases can be either contagious (passed on by contact) or non-contagious.

▼ *This microscopic picture shows a cancer cell.*

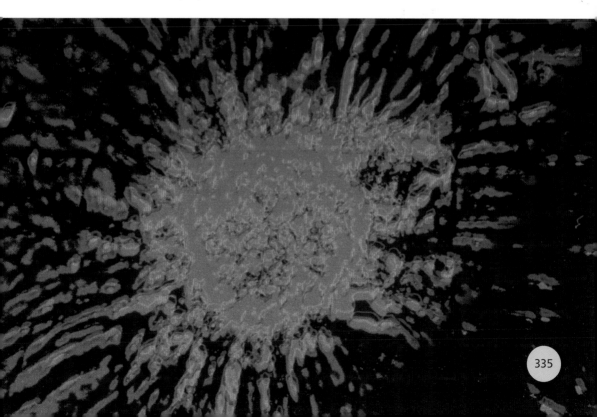

Defence

- **The human body** has several defences to prevent disease affecting it.

- **Our first defence** is the skin. The skin acts as a physical barrier to germs and helps to prevent injury.

- **The skin also produces** sweat and oils that help to keep the skin moisturized and prevent germs from growing.

- **Tears keep our eyes moist** and help wash away dust and dirt. They also contain an antibacterial agent to help destroy germs.

- **Saliva in the mouth** helps to kill bacteria that cause tooth decay and gum disease.

- **Mucus in the lining of the airways** helps to trap dust and germs.

- **Stomach acid** is strong enough to kill most germs that may be eaten or taken in with drink.

- **Good bacteria** in the gut prevent harmful bacteria from growing.

- **Helpful bacteria** that live in a woman's vagina help to keep it slightly acidic. This stops harmful bacteria from growing.

- **The main defence** against disease once germs have entered the body is the body's immune system.

▶ *The gut normally contains good bacteria (shown here in pink) that help to boost the immune system and prevent the growth of disease-causing bacteria.*

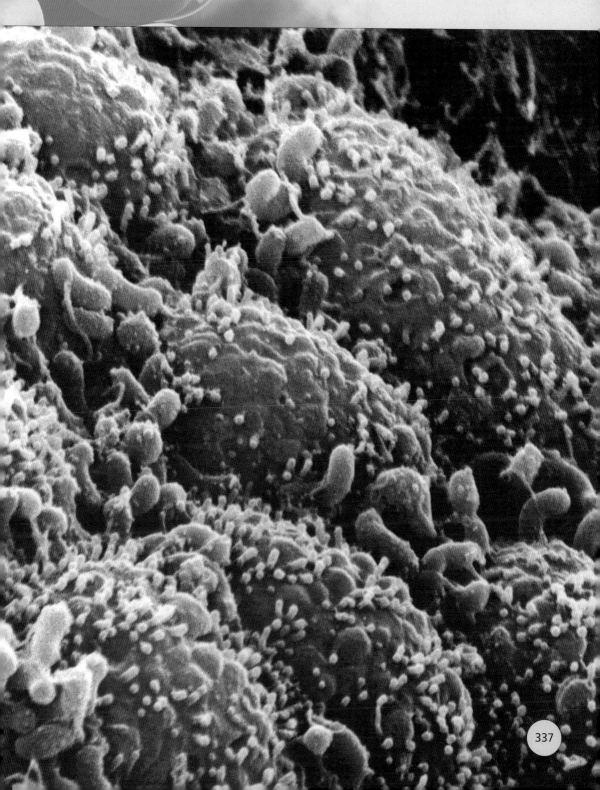

Germs

- **Germs are microscopic organisms** that enter your body and cause harm.

- **The scientific word** for germ is 'pathogen'.

- **When germs** begin to multiply inside your body, you are suffering from an infectious disease.

- **An infection that spreads** throughout your body (flu or measles, for example) is called a systemic infection.

- **An infection that affects** only a small area (such as dirt in a cut) is called a localized infection.

▼ *Once germs such as Anthrax (blue) or E. coli (purple) bacteria enter the body, they multiply rapidly, causing disease and making us feel unwell.*

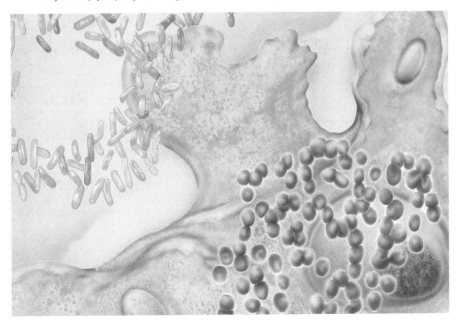

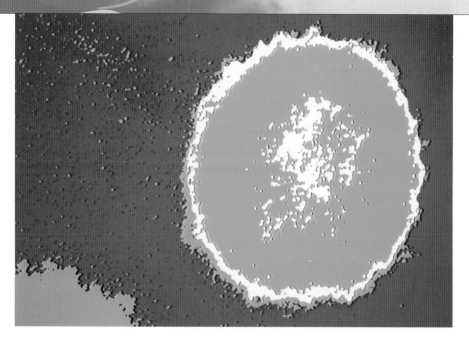

▲ *The disease AIDS (Acquired Immune Deficiency Syndrome) is caused by a virus called HIV (Human Immunodeficiency Virus). This virus gets inside vital cells of the body's immune system and weakens its ability to fight against other infections.*

It is often the reaction of your body's immune system to the germ that makes you feel ill.

There are several types of germ, including bacteria, viruses, worms and fungi.

Germs may enter the body through an injury, such as a cut or a scrape.

Many germs, such as the ones that cause colds, are breathed in.

Some germs can be spread just by being near someone who has an infection. Others can only cause an infection if blood from one person mixes with another.

DID YOU KNOW?

Germs vary in size from microscopic viruses to worms that can grow to several metres long.

Bacteria

- **Bacteria** are single-celled organisms. They are found almost everywhere in huge numbers, and multiply rapidly.

- **There are thousands** of different types of bacteria but most are harmless. Some even do us good.

DID YOU KNOW?

Bacteria can live anywhere, even in regions where there are no living animals or plants.

- **Bacteria can be divided** into three groups – cocci are round cells, spirilla are coil-shaped, and bacilli are rod-shaped.

- **Bacteria usually cause disease** by producing harmful chemicals called toxins. The toxins enter cells in the body and destroy them.

- **Some types of bacteria** do not produce toxins but enter body cells instead.

- **Once the bacteria** are in the cells they multiply until they burst the cell. All the new bacteria then find new cells to enter.

- **Antibiotics** are used to treat bacterial infections. These kill the bacteria in the body or stop then multiplying so that the body has a chance to destroy them.

- **Bacteria commonly cause infections** that affect the airways and lungs. Tuberculosis is caused by bacteria.

- **Bacteria also cause diseases** such as tetanus and typhoid. Bacteria that enter the blood stream can cause blood poisoning.

- **The 'Black Death'** that killed millions of people in Europe in the 1340s was actually a bacterial infection called the bubonic plague.

▼ These rod-shaped bacteria have hairs so they can stick to other cells, and tail-like projections to help them move.

Viruses

▼ *Once a virus has entered a body cell, it replicates and then leaves the cell to infect more cells.*

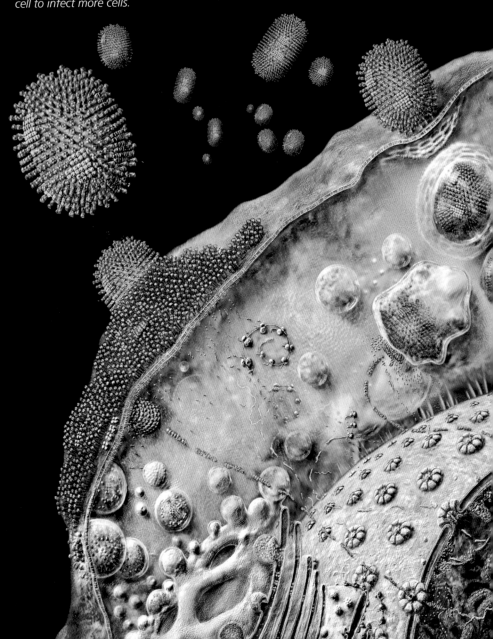

Millions of viruses can fit inside a single cell. They are the smallest living organisms in the world.

Viruses can only live and multiply by taking over other cells – they cannot survive on their own.

They consist of genetic material surrounded by a protective coat.

Viruses cause disease by entering body cells. Once inside a cell they reproduce and leave the cell to go on and infect more cells.

Common diseases such as colds, flu, mumps, measles and chickenpox are all caused by viruses.

Viruses also cause severe infections such as AIDS and fevers associated with bleeding.

Viral infections can be prevented by vaccinations.

An epidemic occurs if many more people than usual get a viral infection. A pandemic occurs if the epidemic affects people around the world.

In 1918 the flu virus infected about a third of the world's population and it is thought that about 50 million people died.

Doctors worry that this might happen again with a different type of flu virus.

DID YOU KNOW?

There are over 200 types of virus that can cause a common cold.

Fungi, protozoa and parasites

- **Parasites are animals** such as worms that may live in or on your body, feeding on it and making you ill.

- **There are two types** of worms that can infect humans – roundworms and flatworms.

- **Worms usually** infect people who eat contaminated food. They usually live in the gut.

- **Tapeworms** can grow to over 10 m long in the gut.

- **Fungi** and tiny organisms called protozoa can also cause illness.

- **Fungi form spores** that may cause disease if you breathe them in. These spores can stay in your body for many years before you become ill.

- **Protozoal infections** are often transmitted by eating or drinking food or water that has been infected, or by insect bites.

- **Malaria** is a serious disease caused by protozoa.

- **Food poisoning** in tropical countries is often caused by infection with a protozoa.

- **Most infections** with fungi, protozoa and worms can be easily treated with drugs.

▶ *Worms can be either flat (flatworms) or round (roundworms). Tapeworms can grow to several metres in length, but pinworms are tiny.*

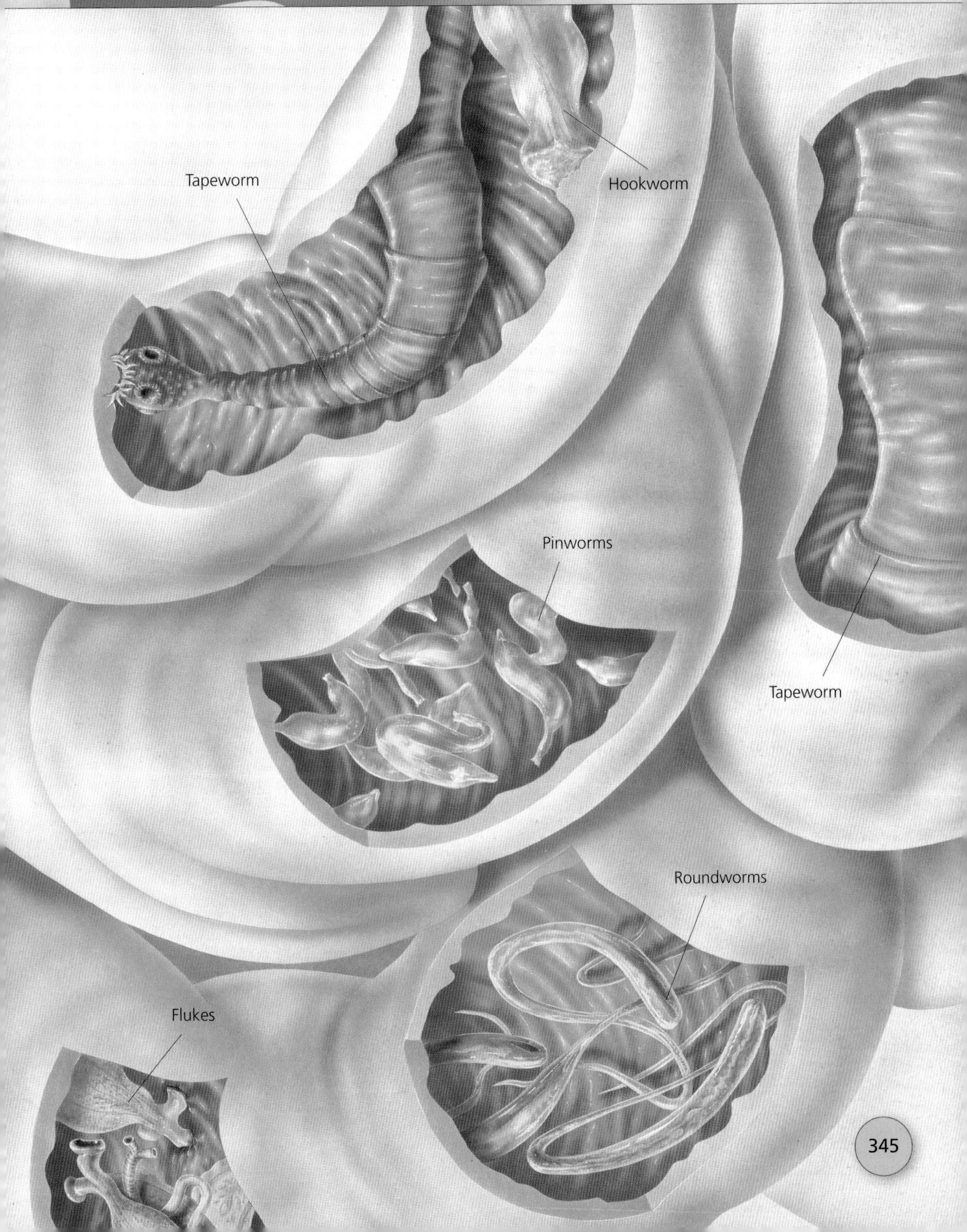

Tapeworm

Hookworm

Pinworms

Tapeworm

Roundworms

Flukes

Diagnosis

- **Diagnosis** is when a doctor works out what a patient is suffering from – the illness and perhaps its cause.

- **The history** is the patient's own account of their illness. This provides the doctor with a lot of clues.

The prognosis is the doctor's assessment of how the illness will develop in the future.

Symptoms are changes that the patient or others notice and report.

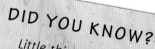

DID YOU KNOW?
Little things, like the colour and shape of your nails, can help your doctor make a diagnosis.

Signs are changes the doctor detects on examination and maybe after tests.

After taking a history the doctor may carry out a physical examination, looking at the patient's body for symptoms such as swelling and tenderness.

A stethoscope is a set of ear tubes that allows the doctor to listen to body sounds, such as breathing and the heart beating.

With certain symptoms, a doctor may order laboratory tests of blood and urine samples. Devices such as ultrasounds and X-rays may also be used to take special pictures.

Doctors nowadays may use computers to help them make a diagnosis.

◀ When a doctor examines a patient, she is looking for clues that will help her to make a diagnosis.

Tests

- **A doctor** may order tests to help him or her find out why you are not feeling well.

- **Tests may also** be done regularly to make sure you are healthy, even if you do not feel ill.

- **Tests may look** at types of cells or levels of chemicals.

- **Blood is usually taken** from a blood vessel in the crook of the elbow and may be tested to look at blood cells or to measure chemicals in the blood.

- **Blood tests** are a good way of seeing if there is anything wrong with your body. For example, they can tell whether you have an infection, if your liver, kidneys, immune system and glands are working normally, or whether your sugar levels are normal.

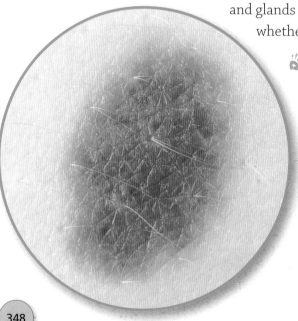

- **Urine may also** be tested for infection, sugar levels and to see if your kidneys are working normally.

◀ *A mole that changes colour or shape may need to be removed to test for a form of skin cancer.*

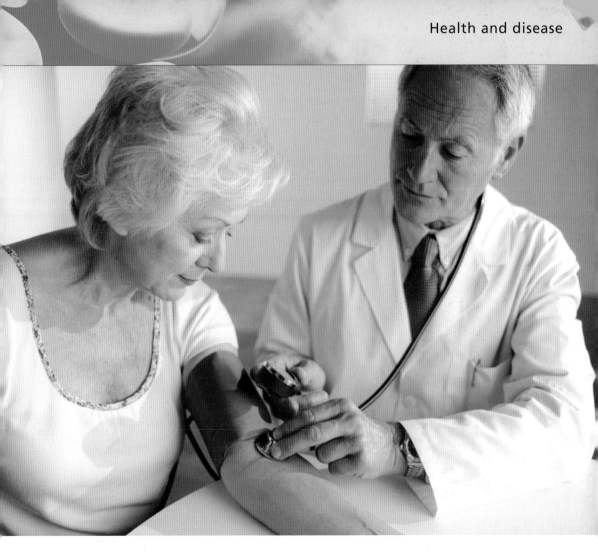

▲ *Blood pressure measurements will give this doctor an idea of whether his patient is likely to develop heart or circulation problems.*

- **A sample** of faeces can be tested for infections in the gut or to see if your gut healthy.

- **Sometimes a piece of tissue** may need to be tested to look for abnormal cells.

- **Tissue is usually taken** during a small operation.

Microscopes

- **Optical microscopes** use lenses and light to magnify things (make them look bigger). By combining two or more lenses, they can magnify specimens up to 2000 times and reveal individual blood cells.

- **To magnify** things more, scientists use electron microscopes – microscopes that fire beams of tiny charged particles called electrons.

- **Electrons have wavelengths** 100,000 times smaller than light and so can give huge magnifications.

- **Scanning electron microscopes** (SEMs) are able to magnify things up to 100,000 times.

- **SEMs show** such things as the structures inside body cells.

- **Transmission electron microscopes** (TEMs) magnify even more than SEMs – up to five million times.

- **TEMs** can reveal the individual molecules in a cell.

- **SEM specimens** (things studied) must be coated in a special substance such as gold. They give a three-dimensional view.

- **Optical microscope specimens** are thinly sliced and placed between two glass slides. They give a cross-sectional view.

- **Microscopes** help to identify germs.

▶ *Microscopes have several lenses that can produce different magnifications. The lenses bend the light shining through the object.*

X-rays

X-rays are a form of electromagnetic radiation, as are radio waves, microwaves, visible light and ultraviolet. They all travel as waves, but have different wavelengths.

X-ray waves are much shorter and more energetic than visible light waves. X-rays are invisible because their waves are too short for our eyes to see.

▼ It is important to keep absolutely still while an X-ray is being taken so that a clear image is obtained.

- **X-rays are made** when negatively charged particles called electrons are fired at a heavy plate made of the metal tungsten. The plate bounces back X-rays.

DID YOU KNOW?
Doctors have been using X-rays to help diagnose illness since the end of the 19th century.

- **Even though** they are invisible to our eyes, X-rays register on photographic film.

- **X-rays** are so energetic that they pass through some body tissues like a light through a net curtain.

- **To make** a photograph, X-rays are shone through the body. The X-rays pass through some tissues and turn the film black, but are blocked by others, leaving white shadows on the film.

- **Each kind** of tissue lets X-rays through differently. Bones are dense and contain calcium, so they block X-rays and show up white on film. Skin, fat, muscle and blood let X-rays through and show up black on film.

- **X-ray radiation** is dangerous in high doses, so the beam is encased in lead, and the radiographer who takes the X-ray picture stands behind a screen.

- **X-rays** are very good at showing up bone defects. So if you break a bone, it will probably be X-rayed.

- **Sometimes a substance** called a contrast medium is used to show up parts of the body more clearly. Contrast medium shows up white on the film.

Ultrasound

Ultrasound uses sound waves that are too high for us to hear to produce pictures of the inside of the body.

The sound waves travel through the body and bounce off our organs, like sonar from a submarine.

Ultrasound scans use a device that sends ultrasound waves through the body and picks up the echoes as they bounce back off objects.

By measuring the echoes the scanner can tell how deep in the body the object is, what shape it is and whether it is solid or filled with air.

A computer converts all this information into a picture.

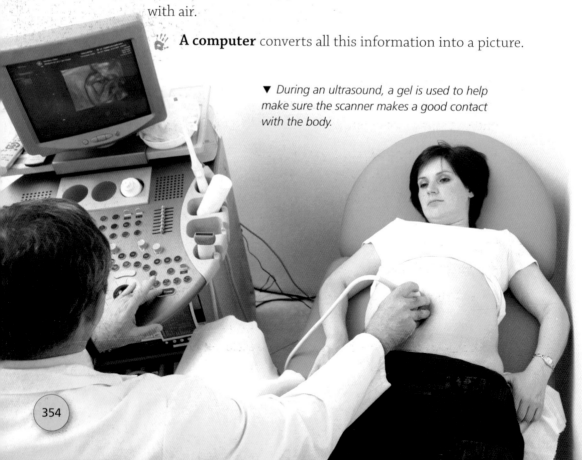

▼ *During an ultrasound, a gel is used to help make sure the scanner makes a good contact with the body.*

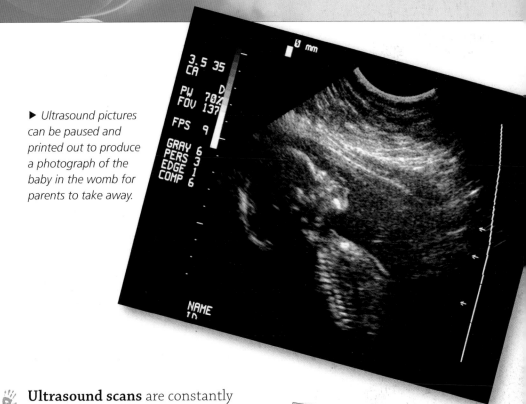

▶ Ultrasound pictures can be paused and printed out to produce a photograph of the baby in the womb for parents to take away.

Ultrasound scans are constantly updated through the scanning device and can show movement.

Ultrasound is completely safe and is used to look at a baby in the womb to make sure it is growing normally and is healthy.

Ultrasound is also often used to look at the heart and the heartbeat.

Any of the organs in the body can be examined using ultrasound.

Because ultrasound shows movement it is also often used to look at the blood flow through blood vessels, especially those in the leg and the neck.

DID YOU KNOW?

3D animated ultrasound scans can now be produced, producing a '4D' effect.

Scans

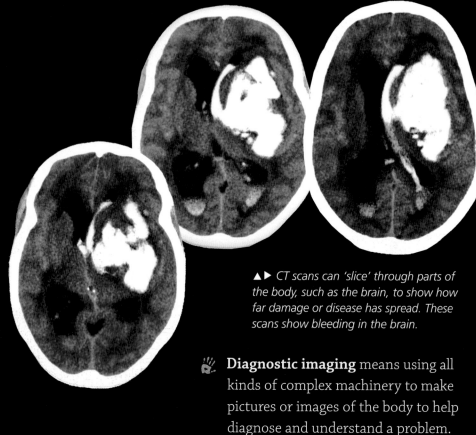

▲▶ CT scans can 'slice' through parts of the body, such as the brain, to show how far damage or disease has spread. These scans show bleeding in the brain.

- **Diagnostic imaging** means using all kinds of complex machinery to make pictures or images of the body to help diagnose and understand a problem.

- **Many imaging techniques** are called scans, because they involve scanning a beam around the patient, to and fro in lines or waves.

- **CT scans** rotate an X-ray beam around the patient while moving him or her slowly forward. This gives a set of pictures showing different slices of the patient's body.

- **CT stands for** computerized tomography.

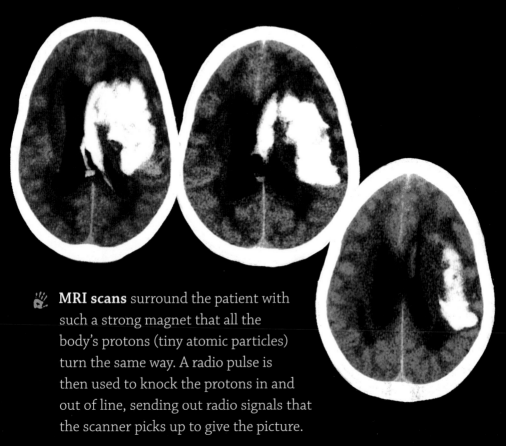

🤚 **MRI scans** surround the patient with such a strong magnet that all the body's protons (tiny atomic particles) turn the same way. A radio pulse is then used to knock the protons in and out of line, sending out radio signals that the scanner picks up to give the picture.

🤚 **MRI stands for** magnetic resonance imaging.

🤚 **PET scans** involve injecting the patient with a mildly radioactive substance, which flows around with the blood and can be detected because it emits (gives out) particles called positrons.

🤚 **PET stands for** positron emission tomography.

🤚 **PET scans** are good for seeing how the brain and heart are functioning.

Drugs

Antibiotic drugs are used to treat bacterial infections such as tuberculosis (TB) or tetanus. They were once grown as moulds (fungi) but are now made artificially.

DID YOU KNOW?
In future, more drugs may be made in animals with altered genes. Insulin is already made in the pancreas of pigs.

Penicillin was the first antibiotic drug, discovered in a mould in 1928 by Alexander Fleming (1881–1955).

Analgesic drugs such as aspirin relieve pain, working mainly by stopping the body making prostaglandin, the chemical that sends pain signals to the brain.

▼ Thousands of different drugs are today used to treat illness.

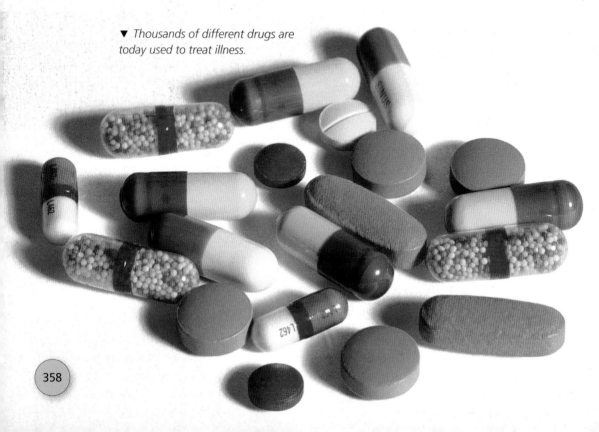

- **Tranquillizers are drugs** that calm. Minor tranquillizers are drugs such as prozac, used to relieve anxiety.

- **Major tranquillizers** are used to treat mental illnesses such as schizophrenia.

- **Psychoactive drugs** change your mood. Many psychoactive drugs, such as heroin, are dangerous and illegal.

- **Stimulants are drugs** that boost the release of the nerve transmitter noradrenaline, making you more lively and awake. They include the caffeine in coffee.

▲ *Alexander Fleming was a British bacteriologist. His discovery in 1928 of the life-saving antibiotic, penicillin, opened a new era for medicine.*

- **Narcotics, such as morphine**, are powerful painkillers that mimic the body's own natural painkiller, endorphin.

- **Depressants are drugs** such as alcohol, which do not depress you, but instead slow down the nervous system.

359

Operations

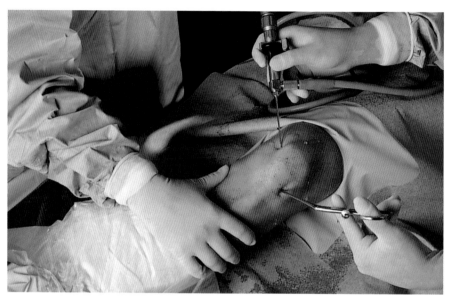

▲ *Many operations are now performed using instruments that allow surgeons to see inside the body without making large cuts.*

A surgical operation is when a doctor cuts or opens up a patient's body to repair or remove a diseased or injured body part.

An anaesthetic is a drug or gas that either sends a patient completely to sleep (a general anaesthetic), or numbs part of the body (a local anaesthetic).

Minor operations are usually done with just a local anaesthetic.

Major operations such as transplants are done under a general anaesthetic.

Major surgery is performed by a team of people in a specially equipped room called an operating theatre.

- **The surgical team** is headed by the surgeon. There is also an anaesthetist to make sure the patient stays asleep, as well as surgical assistants and nurses.

- **The operating theatre** must be kept very clean to prevent an infection entering the patient's body during the operation.

- **In microsurgery**, a microscope is used to help the surgeon work on very small body parts such as nerves or blood vessels.

- **In laser surgery**, the surgeon cuts with a laser beam instead of a scalpel, and the laser seals blood vessels as it cuts. It is used for delicate operations such as eye surgery.

- **An endoscope** is a tube-like instrument with a camera at one end. It can be inserted into the patient's body during an operation to allow surgeons to look more closely at body parts.

▼ *In some operations, laser beams are used instead of a standard surgical knife. They allow more control and precision and reduce the risk of damage or bleeding.*

Transplants

▼ *A heart-lung machine is vital during a heart transplant as it keeps the blood circulating around the body and through the brain, keeping the body alive.*

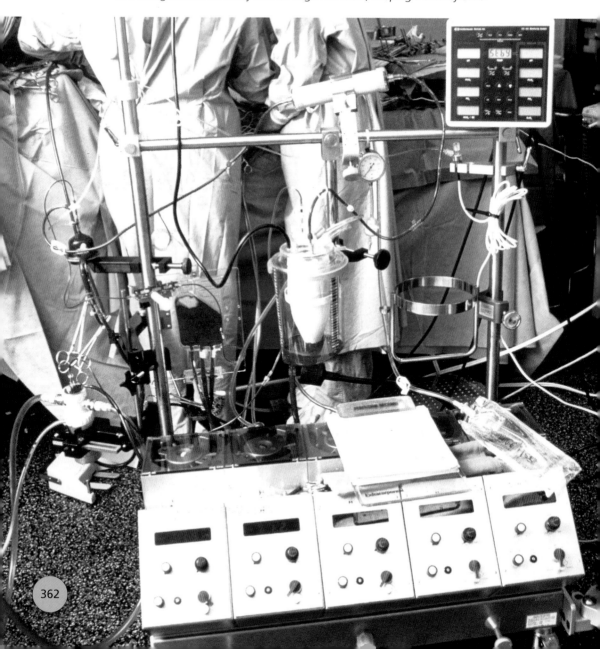

- **More and more body parts** can now be replaced, either by transplants (parts taken from other people or animals) or by implants (artificial parts).

- **Common transplants include**: the kidney, the cornea of the eye, the heart, the lung, the liver and the pancreas.

DID YOU KNOW?
Sometimes the original heart is not removed but just connected to the donor heart, giving the patient a 'double heart'.

- **Some transplant organs** (such as the heart, lungs and liver) are taken from someone who has died.

- **Other transplants** (such as the kidney) may be taken from living donors.

- **After the transplant organ** is taken from the donor, it is washed in an oxygenated liquid and cooled to preserve it.

- **One problem with transplants** is that the body's immune system identifies the transplant as foreign and attacks it. This is called rejection.

- **To cut down** the chance of rejection, patients may be given drugs such as cyclosporin to suppress their immune system.

- **Heart transplant operations** last four hours.

- **During a heart transplant**, the patient is connected to a heart-lung machine that takes over the heart's normal functions.

Therapies

- **Therapies** are used to help someone live a normal life. They can be used by themselves or with drugs or surgery.

- **Physiotherapy** (or physical therapy) is usually used to make muscles and joints stronger.

- **Some physiotherapists** work with people who have sport injuries or who have just had an operation, helping them get fit again.

- **Other physiotherapists** work with elderly people or people who have been ill for a long time, helping them get well enough to live comfortably.

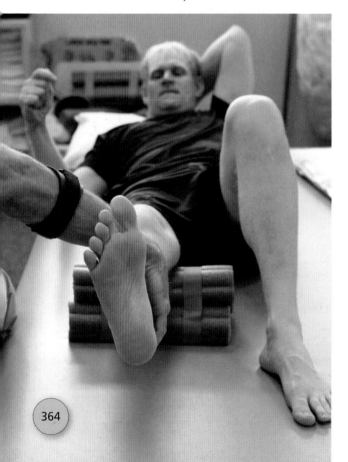

- **People who have difficulty breathing** properly may have a specific form of physiotherapy to help clear their lungs.

- **Speech therapists** help children and people who have difficulty speaking learn to speak and communicate.

◄ *Physiotherapy is used to help a patient recover strength in muscles and joints after an injury or illness.*

▲ *During speech therapy, a child may be encouraged to form sounds while seeing how his or her lips move in a mirror.*

Occupational therapists help people cope with everyday activities.

Psychological therapies are used to help treat people with mental health problems, such as depression.

Many psychological therapies involve talking about your feelings to a therapist.

The therapist helps you to understand why you feel the way you do and how to change the way you feel.

365

Complementary therapies

- **A complementary therapy** is a traditional treatment that is used as well as normal treatment to help to cure an illness or injury.

- **Many complementary therapies** have been used for hundreds of years.

- **Some complementary therapies** have been shown to work by scientific studies; others appear to work but there is no scientific evidence to prove it.

- **Two therapies** that are commonly used and have been shown to work are chiropractic and acupuncture.

▼ Traditional acupuncture has been practised in China for thousands of years and is often used to treat pain in muscles and joints.

- **Chiropractic is usually used** to treat back and neck pain and many doctors will suggest chiropractic treatment for someone who has had back pain for a long time.

- **The chiropractor** moves or manipulates the bones of the backbone and other joints.

- **Acupuncture** is a traditional Chinese treatment.

- **During acupuncture** very fine needles are pushed into the skin to ease pain and help cure illnesses.

- **Other complementary therapies** that are commonly used but have not been proved to work include homeopathy, which uses tiny quantities of substances to treat illnesses and reflexology, which uses pressure on areas of the feet.

- **Complementary therapies** do not replace normal treatment.

▶ *Reflexology uses pressure points on the foot to treat illnesses throughout the body.*

367

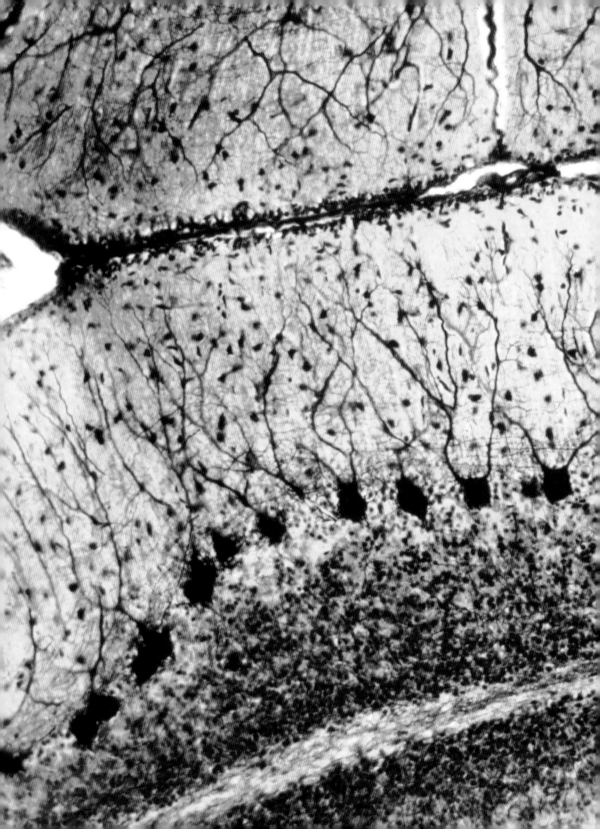

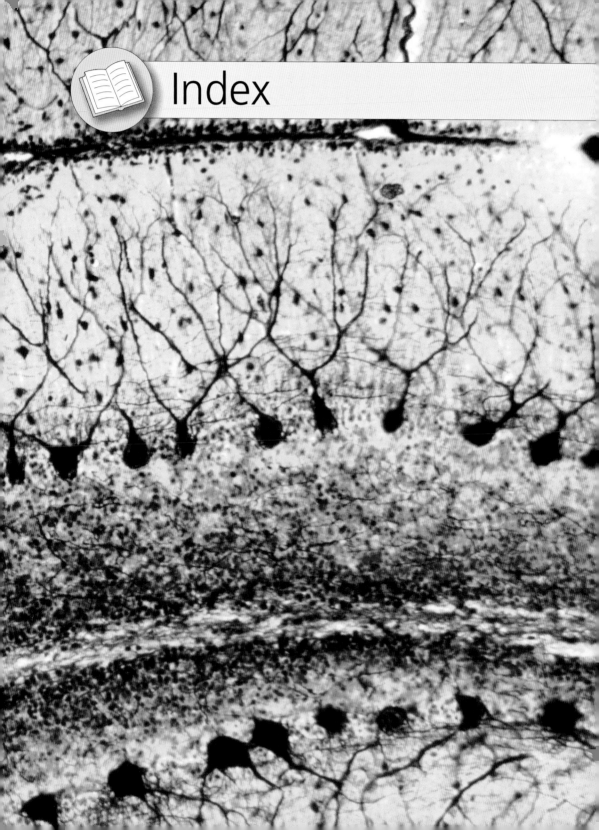

Index

Page numbers in **bold** refer to main subject entries. Page numbers in *italics* refer to illustrations.

A

abdomen *225*
accessory nerves 104
acetylcholine 108
Achilles tendon 75
acquired immune deficiency syndrome (AIDS) 307, *339*
acquired immunity 186
ACTH (adrenocorticotrophic hormone) 263
actin 80
active immunization 192
acupuncture *366*, 367
acute inflammation 189
adenoids *182*, 195, 197
adipose tissue 317
adrenal glands 258, *261*, 263, **266–267**
adrenaline 267, 328
aerobic exercise 331
ageing 50, **296–297**
agoraphobia 147
AIDS 307, *339*
airways 200, *201*, **202–203**
  bacteria 340

airways (*cont.*)
  breathing **206–207**, 208–209
  coughing 210, *211*
  mucus 183, 203, 336
alcohol 235, 306, 359
aldosterone 254, 266, 267
alimentary canal *see* gut
allergies 187, **190–191**, 315
alpha waves, sleep 150
alveoli 204–205, *208*
amino acids 31, 227, 248, 253, 314–315
ammonia 252, 253
amniotic sac 282
amylase *228*, 229, 237
anabolism 299
anaerobic exercise 331
anaesthetics 113, 360
analgesic drugs 358
anaphylactic reaction 191
anatomy **16–17**
androgens 271
  see also testosterone
animal fats 317
ankle 88
antacids 237
anterior anatomy 17
antibiotics 340, 358
antibodies *182*, **186–187**, 190, 192

anti-diuretic hormone 254, 263
antigens 186
anus 220, *221*, 224, *225*, 244
aorta *155*, *156*, 158, *159*
appendicular skeleton 47
appendix *225*, 242
appetite **222–223**
arachnophobia 147
arm *77*, *80–81*, **82–83**
arrhythmia 163
arteries 154, *155–156*, 157, **166–167**
  heart disease 164–165
  pulse 162
  veins and 170, 171
  wrist 82
arterioles 154, *155*, 166
arthritis 189
artificial body parts 71, 73, *159*, 363
ascending pathways 101
ATP (adenosine triphosphate) 81
atria of heart 157, *160–161*
autoimmune diseases 187, 189, 335
autonomic nervous system (ANS) 92, 93
axial skeleton 47
axons 106

polydactyly 85
polysaccharides 310,
    311
pons, brain 150
positive feedback,
    hormones 260
positron emission
    tomography (PET)
    357
posterior anatomy 17
potassium 324
pregnancy *252*,
    282–283
premature babies 285
premolars 216
pressure sensors 112,
    114, *115*
primary sexual
    characteristics 270
progesterone 258, 271,
    276, 294–295
prognosis 347
prolactin 263
proprioceptors 126,
    134, 138, 139
proteins 31, 186, 227,
    235, 308, **314–315**
    see also enzymes
protozoa **344**
psychoactive drugs 359
psychological therapies
    365
puberty 273, 275, 276,
    278
    boys **292–293**
    girls **294–295**

pubic symphysis 67
pulmonary arteries *156*,
    166
pulmonary circulation
    154
pulmonary valve 158
pulmonary veins *156*,
    170
pulse **162–163**,
    332–333
    see also heartbeat

Q

quadriplegia 101

R

radius 82
Rapid Eye Movement
    (REM) sleep 151
recessive genes 37
rectum *225*, 244
red blood cells 22, 154,
    155, 168, 174, *175*,
    178
red bone marrow 52,
    53
reflexes **136–137**, 287,
    291
reflexology 367
rejection of transplants
    363
releasing hormones 300
reproductive system 14,
    62, 63, **272–275**,
    280–281
    see also sex hormones

respiratory system
    14–15
    see also airways; lungs
retina *116*, 117, 118,
    119, 121
Rhesus factors 176
ribs *60*, **60–61**, 200,
    206
rods of eye 118
roughage *see* fibre
Ruffini's endings 114
running 330

S

saccule 126
sacrum 59, 62
saddle joints 68, *69*
saline *254*
saliva 224, *225, 228*,
    230, 336
salts 254, 320, 323,
    324–325
sartorius muscle 76
saturated fat *317*
scanning electron
    microscopes (SEMs)
    350
scans **356–357**
scent molecules 129,
    130–131
sciatic nerve *86*, 102,
    103
sclera *116*, 117
scrotum 272, *273*
scurvy 319
sebaceous glands *182*

Acknowledgements

Cover illustration Alex Pang
All other artwork from the Miles Kelly Artwork Bank

The publishers would like to thank the following sources for the use of their photographs:

Dreamstime.com 24 Shippee; 38 Spanishalex; 41 Olga_sweet; 50 Danny666;
51 Scrappinstacy; 67 Rognar; 71 Mitchellgunn; 87 Razvanjp; 89 Choreograph;
101 Tupungato; 111 Fragles; 113 Banannaanna; 118 Aeolos; 127 Jabiru;
131 Rebeccapicard; 134 Kojoku; 136 Velkol; 147 K.walkow; 148 Diademimages;
149 Nruboc; 151 Achilles; 163 Ronibgood; 165 Khz; 172 Stratum; 202 Eraxion;
207 Tobkatrina; 209 Ligio; 218 Photoeuphoria; 219 Digitalpress; 253 Stratum; 264;
267 Barsik; 268 Jorgeantonio; 273 Jelen80; 274 Jelen80; 279 Doctorkan; 281 Alangh;
286 Kati1313; 288 Assignments; 289 Matka wariatka; 292 Keeweeboy; 312 Cb34inc;
318-319 Egal; 320 Kati1313; 325 Rachaelr; 328 Rognar; 329 Pro777; 331 Afagundes;
332 Tass; 333 Monkeybusinessimages; 352 Hanhanpeggy; 354 nyul; 367 Nataq

Fotolia.com (Bars)V. Yakobchuk; 12-13 Yuri Arcurs; 15 Sebastian Kaulitzki; 17;
28 Yuri Arcurs; 49 Olga Lyubkina; 69 chrisharvey; 85 Andy Dean; 110 Andreas Meyer;
120 Le Do; 139 Kiam Soon Jong; 138 Alexander Yakovlev; 245 Andrew Bruce; 300 Ronen;
311 Tein; 314 Celso Pupo; 318-319 Elena Schweitzer

iStockphoto.com 19 Chris Dascher; 36 Seb Chandler; 47 technotr; 63 Raycat;
62 weicheltfilm; 93 annedde; 112 Maica; 130 deepspacedave; 132 ZoneCreative;
145 ZoneCreative; 146 arlindo71; 162 nyul; 168 Enjoylife2; 193 AvailableLight;
228 hartcreations; 229 Caziopeia; 254 robeo; 270 track5; 289 bonniej; 290 Bennewitz;
291 khilagan; 293 wbritten; 297 bloodstone; 298 shaunl; 323 Jason_V; 327 DNY59;
326 YinYang; 346 Fotosmurf03; 348 zlisjak; 349 peepo; 351 dgrilla; 364 Bryngelzon;
366 Yuri_Arcurs

Science Photo Library 25 Medical RF.com; 26 Zephyr; 33 Eye of Science;
35 Look at Sciences; 66 Paul Rapson; 99 Peter Gardiner; 109 Thomas Deerinck, NCMIR;
115 Anatomical Travelogue; 125 Kairos, Latin Stock; 135 David Mack; 140 Sovereign, ISM;
159 Zephyr; 178 Medical RF.com; 187 BSIP, Laurent; 188 Russell Kightley;
191 Gavin Kingcome; 194 Medical RF.com; 211 John Bavosi; 226 John Daugherty;
236 Jacopin; 239 Medical RF.com; 242 Professors P. Motta & F. Carpino/University
'La Sapienza', Rome; 250 Steve Gschmeissner; 259 Christian Darkin; 261 Christian Darkin;
262 Roger Harris; 277 Professors P.M. Motta & J. Van Blerkom; 278 Callot;
294 BSIP, JACOPIN; 303 Edward Kinsman; 337 Biomedical Imaging Unit, Southhampton
General Hospital; 341 Hybrid Medical Animation; 342 Russell Kightley; 356-357 Zephyr;
359 Science Source; 362 Alexander Tsiaras; 365 Colin Cuthbert

All other photographs are from:
Corel, digitalSTOCK, Image State, PhotoAlto, PhotoDisc

Every effort has been made to acknowledge the source and copyright holder of each
picture. Miles Kelly Publishing apologises for any unintentional errors or omissions.

The
I Ching
Made Easy

Be Your Own Psychic Adviser
Using the World's Oldest Oracle

Roderic Sorrell and
Amy Max Sorrell

HarperSanFrancisco
A Division of HarperCollinsPublishers

Illustrations based on original drawings by Amy and Rod Sorrell.
Set in Guardi and Shannon.

FIRST HarperCollins EDITION PUBLISHED IN 1994

ORIGINALLY PUBLISHED BY BIO-CHING PUBLISHING,
BOX 1172, BISBEE, AZ 85603. 1-800-982-0732

Library of Congress Cataloging-in-Publication Data
Sorrell, Roderic.
    The I ching made easy : be your own psychic adviser using the world's oldest oracle / by Roderic Sorrell and Amy Max Sorrell.
        p.   cm.
    ISBN 0–06–251073–8 (pbk. : alk. paper)
    International Standard Book Number: 0-9632726-0-8
    1. I ching.   2. Divination—China.   I. Sorrell, Amy Max.
II. I ching. English. Selections. 1994.   III. Title.
PL2464.Z7S66 1994
133.3'3—dc20   93–51017
                                                                  CIP

96 97 98 ❖ RRD(C) 10 9 8 7 6 5 4 3 2

This edition is printed on acid-free paper that meets the American National Standards Institute Z39.48 Standard.

Everything has now changed—
except for our way of thinking.

Albert Einstein

We dedicate all the good and virtue we accumulate.
That, by the universal power of truth,
everyone everywhere without exception
may be freed from negative karmic fruits—
such as war and violence, disease, starvation,
nature's disasters and the fear of weapons.
Instead, may they make their lives of use,
be pure in action and intention,
be filled with peace and great compassion.

H. E. Tai Situ Pa, Rinpoche

ACKNOWLEDGMENTS

We would like to thank all our friends and teachers who have loved and supported us in this endeavor, from our first edition to this one. Pioneers all. Independent thinkers. We needed and appreciated your courage.

Our special thanks to the following people:

Our first readers: Joe Barros and Greg Ford. They were willing to read our manuscript and to honestly tell us what they thought. Friends indeed.

Our dedicated volunteers: Lavell Evans, Chuck Rowden, Angie Chassie, Sondra Hartley, and Margaret Hartnett.

Happy days to have such friends. Writing is a lonely game, even when two people are working together. These friends were our joy, and possibly the salvation of our rather dubious sanity.

Our first sale: Kate Taylor. Katie bought *The I Ching Made Easy* while we were still writing it. What trust and love.

Our first talk-radio hosts: John Libynski and Willard Shoecraft, the producer and the host of KIKO Radio in Miami, Arizona, for our first interviews on the air; giving readings with the *I Ching,* talking story, and getting our feet wet.

Our authors' representative: Keith Korman, Raines and Raines. We thought we were a total success just to have a literary agent. Recognition at last. Someone besides us has faith in the book. Keith said, "Wait until we sell the book before you get too excited." Thanks, Keith.

Our editor: Amy Hertz at HarperSanFrancisco. She discovered us in the mailbag, and here we are. Thank you and your staff for seeing our dream, believing in it, and giving us a new one.

Charlie Levenson, our friend and son—for everything, for always.

Mahalo.

The foreword to a work of nonfiction is customarily written by a learned person, familiar with the subject of the text at hand—an expert in his or her field.

When it comes to the *I Ching,* or Chinese *Book of Changes,* I am the furthest thing from an expert. Until I was invited to read an early draft of *The I Ching Made Easy,* I had never *finished* reading a book on the subject. Please note the stress on the word *finished.* I began at least three—but they were too esoteric for me to complete.

I've always been intrigued by the *I Ching,* but found most interpretations on the subject overly complicated. Rod and Amy have written about a complex subject and made it simple enough for anyone, even an idiot like myself, to understand and appreciate.

It is easy for the expert to make a client feel undermined and ignorant, something we all have experienced at one time or another at the hands of lawyers, doctors, and even our friendly neighborhood auto mechanic. They behave like high priests or shamans, forcing us into the role of ignorant disciple or supplicant. I can easily imagine a seancelike ritual of coin-throwing by robed and hooded monks, illuminated only by candlelight.

Amy and Rod have provided the means for anyone to understand and use the *I Ching* for themselves. No magic candles. No theater. No special coins dug from rare ore and smelted by a secret clan in deepest China.

Rod recently suggested in an interview that a successful *I Ching* reading could easily be done at a kitchen table, with only five pennies and a dime (and, I would hope, this book close at hand). Perhaps they should have titled their book *The Fifteen-Cent I Ching.*

The *I Ching* is based on the principle of meaningful coincidences, or the synchronicity of the universe. This is the proposition that all elements exist in a giant arena and in some way communicate their overall plan and direction to each other.

The ability to tap into this synchronistic scheme is available to anyone. It doesn't require any special training, chants, smoke, or mirrors. All you need is the willingness to throw six coins and the means to interpret the results. *The I Ching Made Easy* makes it possible for ordinary people to use the *I Ching* for sorting through the difficult questions that fill their lives.

"Should I take this job offer or hold out for a better one?" "Would marrying (or proposing to or divorcing or making love with) this person be the right thing to do?" "Should we buy a house or rent one?"

When important everyday questions such as these are asked of the *I Ching,* there is a tendency to hope that the answer will be a simple yes or no. Although this does occur, not every response will lend itself without question to one obvious answer. Sometimes there will have to be more discussion, and perhaps you will need to ask another question.

Amy and Rod have included throughout their text stories of how the *I Ching* has responded to questions they have asked. I found these stories

invaluable in gaining additional insight into the readings that I did.

That this book gave me the confidence to use the *I Ching* at all is the greatest compliment I can give. After reading just "The Instant *I Ching*" at the beginning of this book, I was confident enough to ask a question, throw the coins, and interpret the response.

But then, what guarantees are there that anything will turn out as promised? The fact is, there are no guarantees. There are also no promises, except that human beings will make decisions and live with them. Life will, more often than not, go on.

I believe that it is frequently better to make a decision, any decision, than to be paralyzed with fear and dread. *The I Ching Made Easy* gives you the confidence to make a decision and act on it.

This wonderful tool has never been so within our reach. The authors have opened up an ornate puzzle box and revealed its contents to all of us—let's use and enjoy it.

Charles Loren Levenson
Aloha, Oregon, 1994

We have been throwing the coins together and asking questions for ourselves and our friends for more than twenty years. *The I Ching Made Easy* is a result of those years of collaboration and exploration.

Friends have brought to us the most important and difficult decisions in their lives: affairs of the heart, affairs of the world, obstructions on the path of personal development. We usually talked ourselves into a circle of confusion, and then we tossed the coins and consulted the *I Ching*. One answer to life's dilemmas is as good as any other.

Because we had many translations of the book, we were thought to know quite a bit about the *I Ching*. Not so. If anything, we were often confounded by the multitude of contradictions in the various translations.

In each reading with a friend, the person would always ask us to tell them what it really meant, and to put it into our own words. "I don't get it! How does 'the fox gets its tail wet' relate to this question about my relationship with Joe?" How indeed?

Over the years we've continued to put the *I Ching*'s answers into our own words, and this book is the result. It is our understanding of the meaning of life and how to live it.

Thank you to all our friends who, through the years, have shared with us intimate and revealing aspects of their lives, and who have found some enlightenment and help in the responses from the universe. Thank you for your awareness of the vast scope of possibilities in this world, and for your courage in exploring them with us. We have included many of our personal adventures and those of our friends to illustrate how the *I Ching* relates to ordinary life and brings new perspectives to its complexities.

We are continuing to research this fascinating world of synchronistic interplay. Please feel free to share your

I Ching "real-life adventures" with us. Your experiences will help us all to further our understanding of the *I Ching*.

If you wish to receive a free copy of our newsletter, "Kiss the Sky," give us a call at 1–800–982–0732, or drop us a line at P.O. Box 1172, Bisbee, AZ 85603.

We've had a wonderful time working together on this book. Thank you for sharing it with us.

Amy and Rod

Everything flows and nothing stays the same.
Heraclitus, the Greek philosopher

By means of the easy and simple we grasp the laws of the whole world.
Confucius (551–479 B.C.), *Ta Chuan,*
or Great Treatise on the *I Ching*

The word *I* (pronounced "ee") in Chinese means change. Change is one of the basic principles of the universe, the one thing that you can rely on. The word *Ching* means book or classic. *I Ching* translates as the *Book of Changes,* and is one of the few books that has survived from the beginnings of Chinese history. It is thought to be the oldest method of divination in the world. The first people to use the *I Ching* were shamans, magicians, priests, and soothsayers, sometime between 1000 and 500 B.C.—before the births of Buddha, Christ, and Mohammed— and it has been in continuous use ever since.

Life is about changing from one condition to another. We all know that nothing stays the same. When we fall in love, we want that feeling to last forever, but it never does. It transforms into something else. When we are suffering and sick, we welcome change, hoping that our lives will improve.

Often we fear change because it represents the unknown. Most of the time, we just wish we could figure out what to do.

In the pages of the *I Ching* we find the sixty-four types of changes— from "youthful folly" to "ambition" to "abundance"—that cover all of life's transitions. According to Confucius, author of *Ta Chuan,* the Great Treatise on the *I Ching:*

> *The changes, what do they do? The changes disclose things, complete affairs, and encompass all ways on earth—this and nothing else. For this reason the holy sages used them to penetrate all wills on earth and to determine all fields of action on earth, and to settle all doubts on earth.*

For thousands of years wise people have used the *I Ching* to understand the nature of the influences in any situation, and to act correctly without doubt or hesitation. Fortunately, you don't have to be a sage or seer to use the *I Ching*. We *all* have intuitive abilities, even if we haven't yet learned to use them. The process of using the *I Ching* can be the key that unlocks the inner door to these abilities, and allows us to have new and deeper insights into life's inevitable questions.

Our word divination comes from the Latin *divus,* meaning divine or sacred. The Chinese believed that to consult the *I Ching* was to communicate with the spiritual forces of the universe. In the West, however, we tend to disbelieve what we can't prove, and our usual cause-and-effect view of the world explains most things satisfactorily: It rains, and the trees get wet. We forgot to put gas in the car this morning, and now we have to call the tow truck. Yet many things happen that we can't explain. You think of your friend, and she suddenly calls on the phone. You need money for the bus, and look down to find just what you need on the sidewalk.

The *I Ching* works on the basis of what we now call *synchronicity,* the inexplicable coincidences of life. Carl Jung, the renowned twentieth-century European philosopher and psychologist, coined this word from *syn,* "together," and *chronos,* "time": together in time. According to Jung, "Synchronicity takes the coincidence of events in space and time as meaning something more than mere chance, namely, a peculiar interdependence of objective events among themselves as well as with the subjective (psychic) states of the observer or observers."

Using the *I Ching* is synchronicity in action. All possible existing conditions are represented in the *I Ching* in the sixty-four images of life. In the act of tossing the coins we open ourselves to accepting what the universe has to offer. We ask the question and the wisdom of the universe responds through the coins. It is the gift of the *I Ching* to interpret the meaning of the pattern revealed by the coins.

We are all in this universe together. We abide by the same natural laws. Our sharing of space and time means that we are "in synch" and flowing along together. All of the conscious, living elements of the universe, including animals, plants, insects, microbes, you and I, are linked both in the actual, physical, material universe and in the psychic, spiritual, emotional, unseen universes of our hearts and minds. We all exist together within the living ocean of consciousness.

Imagine a vast orchestra playing in the heavens. Listen to the music of the spheres, and dance. Look around you: The dance floor is full of people. The band and the dancers are a single, flowing, rhythmic being. The cells of our bodies vibrate to the music. Our gestures fall naturally into the rhythm. Whether we are aware of it or not, we all move as a single entity. Everything is alive and dances. This is synchronicity.

Jung once wrote, "If a handful of matches is thrown to the floor, they form the pattern characteristic of that moment." The chance fall of the coins we use in casting the *I Ching* is not random and meaningless. It represents the reality of that moment in time.

THE TAO: UNDERSTANDING YIN AND YANG

Albert Einstein wrote, "There is no logical way to the discovery of these elemental laws. There is only the way of intuition, which is helped by a feeling for the order lying behind appearance." The most basic way to describe the universe is to say simply that it *is*. The Chinese call this totality the Tao. But saying that the universe "just is" isn't enough. We need to define the differences in this "is-ness" in order to understand the world around us. The Chinese call these differences yin and yang.

For a start, we need to differentiate she from he, inside from outside, black from white; and at the same time, we can never keep them completely separate. There is always a continuous movement between the two, like day moving into night and night back into day. Ultimately, absolutes are unobtainable. Within the black, there is always some white, and within the white, there is always some black. This is the nature of yin and yang.

Yin is receptive: relaxed, open, flexible. Yin is the time before making a decision, when all is still in the realm of possibility and discovery. It is a state of fluidity, spacious and vast; an ocean of primal chaos. Physically, yin is responsive, pliable, the energy flowing freely. Emotionally, yin is generous, open-hearted, pleasing. Intellectually, yin is broad-minded and interested in new ideas.

Extreme yin tends to be passive and vague. Physically, it is flaccid and weak. Emotionally, it is anxious and vulnerable. Intellectually, it is indecisive and uncertain.

Yang is active: excited, projecting, decisive. Yang is the time when a decision has been made, the actuality; the Big Bang exploding our universe into existence. Physically, yang is strong and firm. Emotionally, yang is confident and certain. Intellectually, yang is enterprising and creative.

Extreme yang tends to be dominating and rigid. Physically, it is tense and tight. Emotionally, it is bossy and aggressive. Intellectually, it is prejudiced and inflexible.

Extremes will eventually turn to their opposite, as with the continuous motion of a pendulum. When we

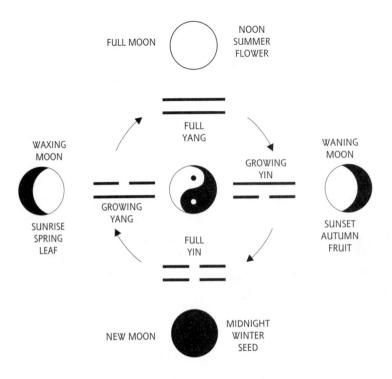

FULL MOON

NOON
SUMMER
FLOWER

WAXING
MOON

FULL
YANG

GROWING
YIN

WANING
MOON

GROWING
YANG

FULL
YIN

SUNRISE
SPRING
LEAF

SUNSET
AUTUMN
FRUIT

NEW MOON

MIDNIGHT
WINTER
SEED

WINTER, SUMMER, SPRING, AND FALL

understand this universal law, our lives flow with greater ease and tranquillity.

THE INTERPLAY OF YIN AND YANG: WINTER, SUMMER, SPRING, AND FALL

Describing things in terms of yin and yang is like painting the world in black and white, sacrificing the detail and shading. To paint in the varying shades of gray, we need to show a mixture of yin and yang.

Just as the year moves through four seasons, the alternating rhythmic flows of yin and yang move through four phases. After yin has reached its limit in the dead of winter, yang enters from below in the beginning of spring. The energy rises from the earth to the sky, just as a plant grows toward the light. Then, in summer, the yang energy moves up to fill both positions. After the full yang days of summer have peaked, the yin energy of fall enters with the beginning of decay and decline.

Everything—from sexual orgasm, to the rise and fall of civilizations, to the way a thought rises and falls away in the mind—follows this rhythm:

The moon moves through four phases—new moon, waxing moon, full moon, and waning moon, and back to the new moon again.

Plant life moves through four phases—from the potential in the seed, to the growing of leaves, the fullness of the flower, the sweet fruit, and back to the seed, the essence of the whole plant.

An entire lifetime moves in this way—conception to birth and early childhood; youth to physical peak; declining physical powers; sickness, old age, and death.

Harmony is the rhythmic interplay of yin and yang: the ability to change from yin to yang and back again with the grace and agility of a dancer. Up and down, left and right, heads and tails, breathing in and breathing out, yin and yang cannot be separated. Like the tides and the seasons, they are changing and moving all the time.

We are not always comfortable with the ebb and flow of energies inside us, or those that encircle and punctuate our lives. We learn early in life not to follow our natural inclinations to surge and recover. We may restrict ourselves unnaturally, or permit ourselves extremes of indulgence. Eventually, however, we fall ill: mentally, physically, or both. Our good health depends on following the ebb and flow of our natural rhythms, enjoying healthy pleasures. When we are tired, we sleep. When we are hungry, we eat. When we feel the pulse and flow in the tide of events, we will swim with the tide and not against it.

The surfer, for example, is constantly shifting the balance, tensing and relaxing moment to moment, seeking that elusive midpoint that means riding the wave to shore. Beneath the surfer, the wave, a vast and powerful force, is itself moved by the power of the moon and planets, which in turn are moved by the still vaster forces of the galaxies.

Finding that point of balance and harmony, the surfer rides on the crest of tension and relaxation and becomes, for a moment, one with the forces of the cosmos. This is the true spiritual experience of any endeavor. When we use the *I Ching,* we discover more about our position on the wave of life. Are we rising or falling? In motion or at rest? About to lose it or in balance? When we increase our sensitivity to the forces in our lives, we reach a higher awareness and discover harmony and balance.

One particular theme frequently recurs in the *I Ching*: "crossing the river." When we understand this theme, we can begin to understand the nature of change.

In ancient times crossing the river was a perilous undertaking. The rivers were wild and untamed by dams and levees. Bridges were few and far between. Strange tribes lived on the unseen far shore; during the crossing you were at a disadvantage and liable to be attacked. Most people never left their village even once in their lives.

When a group of people undertook a journey, many of the villagers accompanied the travelers to the river that separated their territory from strange and alien lands. This was the point of no return, where the uncertain could choose to stay behind and those who were brave enough for the adventure could join the group. Once the river was crossed, there was no turning back.

Crossing the river, then, symbolizes our journey into the unknown. In life we cross many rivers: our first day of school, leaving home and earning a living, getting married. Every night we cross the waters into the world of our dreams, and every morning we come back. Any crisis, insight, or change is a river to cross, and all these crossings transform us.

The *I Ching* is the form, and within that form lie all the possibilities. Let it be the boat that carries you across the river of transformation. Good luck on your journey!

PART ONE

UNDERSTANDING THE I CHING

The origins of the *I Ching* are grounded in the myth of Nu Kua and Fu Hsi, the first sacred couple. Nu Kua (pronounced Noo Gwa) is the Great Mother. Fu-Hsi (pronounced Foo Tsee) is her offspring, twin, and consort, her equal and excellent partner. In the beginning Nu Kua was responsible for the human arts of counting, writing, making calendars, keeping the history of the tribe, and developing social relations. Fu Hsi was responsible for the men: the hunters, warriors, and defenders of the tribe. When men began to dominate all aspects of Chinese society, those gifts developed by the women were attributed to the men. Inevitably, the honor of having invented the symbols of the *I Ching* passed from Nu Kua to Fu Hsi, China's first emperor.

This great philosophy and divinatory device that we have inherited today was largely concerned with kings and wars, clothed and encrusted with the commentaries of millennia. Our aim is to make the *I Ching* meaningful to today's readers without losing any of its ancient essence. We tread the narrow path between trivializing the subtle wisdom and clouding it in obscure and meaningless jargon.

In the 1950s the *I Ching* was translated into English by Richard Wilhelm and Cary Baynes, with a Foreword by Carl Jung. Jung defined our current vision of the *I Ching*, reviving many ancient ideas from our world history and integrating them with the newest concepts in physics, which sees our universe as one single, seamless, undivided, interactive event: a continuous unfolding.

Since the first English translation, there have been numerous other translations and commentaries, and now the philosophy of the *I Ching* has become an integral part of Western culture. Many of them, however, fail to clearly explain the basic elements of the *I Ching*'s language: the Eight Trigrams, the Sixty-Four Hexagrams, and the six lines. You can begin asking the *I Ching* questions immediately, without any knowledge of how the hexagrams are constructed. If you'd like to have a deeper understanding of the hexagrams, the next three chapters will give you a good overview.

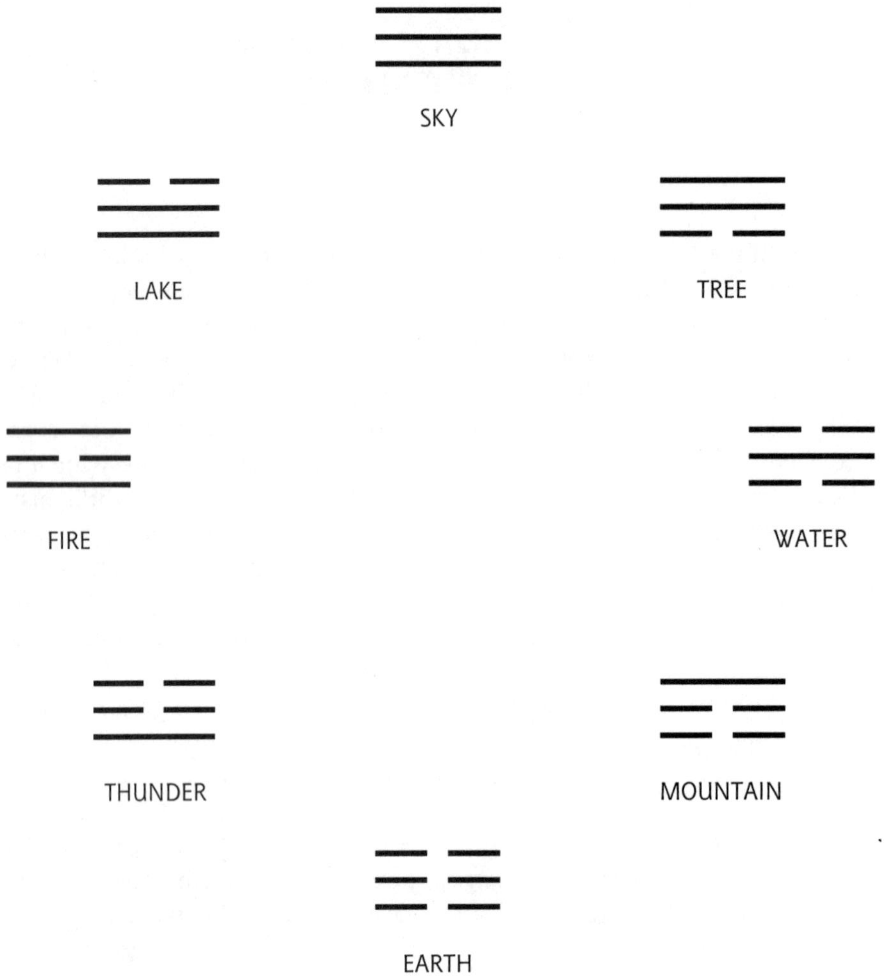

SKY

LAKE

TREE

FIRE

WATER

THUNDER

MOUNTAIN

EARTH

THE EIGHT TRIGRAMS

CHAPTER ONE

Explaining the Trigrams

*When in early antiquity Fu Hsi ruled the world,
he looked upward and contemplated the images in the heavens;
he looked downward and contemplated the patterns on earth. He contemplated
the markings on birds and beasts and their adaptations to the regions.
He proceeded directly from himself and indirectly from objects.*

*Thus he invented the eight symbols in order to enter into
connection with the powers and the light of the gods and goddesses,
and to understand the condition of all beings.*

Confucius, *Ta Chuan,*
or Great Treatise on the *I Ching*

The Eight Trigrams are the basis of the Sixty-Four Hexagrams of the *I Ching*. A trigram is made up of three lines. Each line is either yin (broken) or yang (solid).

—— ——   ——————

YIN   YANG

The Eight Trigrams (numbered zero through seven) are formed from all the various possible combinations of yin and yang. Each trigram represents one of the living forces of the universe. Fu Hsi saw these eight symbols as a means of entering into communion with the living powers of our world and of understanding the human condition.

These symbols represent the different qualities of the outer and inner worlds. He saw then what we are rediscovering now—that all the parts are necessary to the whole.

0 The Earth. Generous, supportive, and forever giving.
1 The Thunder. Wild, shocking, and exciting.
2 The River. Calm one moment, a torrent the next.
3 The Lake. Fruitful, where animals drink and plants grow.
4 The Mountain. Steady and grounded.
5 The Sun and Fire. Brilliant, illuminating, and burning.

6 The Trees and Wind. Gentle, yet penetrating every nook and cranny.

7 The Sky. Vast as the canopy of celestial power.

Everything we know is comprised of these elements. Our bones are the mountains, our blood is the river. Our passions burn with the sun, and our imagination flies on the wings of the wind.

These are the universal and spiritual qualities that unite the natural forces with the human world. The outer world and the inner realms of heart and mind are one.

THE QUALITIES OF THE EIGHT TRIGRAMS

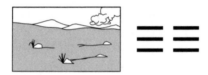

EARTH, PLAINS, MEADOW, GROUND

Accepting / Receptive / Relaxing
Maternal, long-suffering, devoted, tranquil, yielding, humble, careful, frugal, oppressed, peaceful labor

Zero is the number of Mother Earth; like the circle, empty and complete. The ground of our being. The great storehouse. The unsung heroes, self-sacrifice, the masses. The untended fields and wild lands.

The color is deep black. The primordial open field. The black hole.

Spaciousness. Before the beginning, when everything is possible and nothing is realized.

The animal is the cow. Drink my milk, eat my flesh, tan my hide; look into my soft brown eyes and remember me.

Imagine: You are resting comfortably in a vast meadow that leads into the plains beyond. The land is wild and untouched. You are feeling peaceful, relaxed, and open.

THUNDER, AIR, ELECTRICITY, LIGHTNING

Stimulating / Arousing / Exciting
Energetic, decisive, inspired, vital, vehement, rushed, erratic, volatile

One is the number of thunder and lightning. Caught by surprise; that bright and sudden state of mind, in the here and now. Everything is fresh and new.

The color is vibrant red. Action and passion.

The animal is the eagle, ready to surprise an unwary mouse.

Imagine: Without warning, a flash of lightning strikes the ground at your feet, followed by a crack of thunder. Your body quivers and tingles with exhilaration. You are aroused and stirred into creative action.

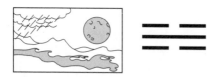

WATER, RIVER, RAIN, MOON

Independent / Separate / Self-reliant

Tenacious, diligent, relentless, enduring, lonely, melancholic, secretive, hardworking, resolute

Two is the number of the river and the pit. Double, double, toil and trouble. Penetrating the heart of darkness. Sexual lunacy, secret affairs. Rebel without a cause. Blood, sweat, and tears. The depth of character to endure hard times.

The color is a moody blue. A midnight quality; dark and watery depths.

The animal is the fox or coyote. The tricksters of Native American legend.

Imagine: It begins to rain, washing everything fresh and clean. The rain collects and becomes a rushing river. Listen to the sounds. Despite the difficulty, you cross the river without being swept away. You can overcome all odds. You are feeling confident and self-reliant.

LAKE, METAL, CAVE, VALLEY

Expressive / Malleable / Tolerant

Joyous, delighted, evocative, lusty, indulgent, obsessive

Three is the number of the cave and lake. The womb of joy. Invoking mystery. Unfulfilled desire. Sorceresses and witches. Lust and litigation. Arguments.

The color is golden yellow. Gold and precious substances.

The animal is the monkey. Lively and chattering.

Imagine: You are by a lake teeming with wildlife; an abundance and variety of birds, plants, and animals display the inventiveness of nature. Your heart is uplifted. You feel enthusiastic and articulate.

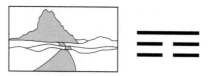

MOUNTAIN, ROCK, HILL

Grounded / Stable / Firm

Restrained, sincere, still, lazy, miserly, stubborn, unchanging, maintaining

Four is the number of the mountains and peaks. Steady, stable, and reliable. The mountain gathers its greatness with the accumulation of small stones, thus hoarding, guarding, and keeping. Retreat, attainment, and completion. Monks and priests.

The color is rich purple. Earthy mountain tones of sunset.

The animal is the dog. Loyal and trustworthy.

Imagine: Feel the steadiness of the mountain beneath you. Take a path winding up the mountain. Your pace becomes steady and regular. You are removed from the noise of the world. In time, you reach the top. You feel calm, grounded, and peaceful.

FIRE, SUN, HEARTH

Reliance / Cooperation / Joining

Brilliant, perceptive, beautiful, enthusiastic, fierce, violent, grasping, clinging, attached, dependent

Five is the number of the fire and the sun. Bright in the sky. Flamboyant and ferocious. Engaging in love and war. The warrior and the movie star, sparkling in the light.

The color is fiery orange. Burning.

The animal is the peacock. Bright and colorful; the eye of the sky in its tail feathers.

Imagine: The sun is high in the sky, and you feel its warmth. The sun bathes everything in a brilliant and beautiful glow. You are joined with everything in the shining light.

TREE, WIND, WOOD

Permeating / Penetrating / Insightful

Flexible, flowing, searching, indecisive, confused

Six is the number of the wind and the trees. The roots penetrate the rock, and the branches reach into the wind. The wind blows to distant places. A calm and even breeze, or gusty and uncertain.

The color is living green. Vegetation of every variety.

The animal is the unicorn. Purity and perfection.

Imagine: You are in a forest. The trees wave and bend with the wind. You sense the roots reaching into the earth below. You travel with the winds of space. You possess deep insight and intuition.

SKY, LIGHT, HEAVENS

Creating / Challenging / Powerful

Potent, expansive, decisive, arrogant, proud

Seven is the number of the heavens and the skies. Creative, active, moving, confrontational. Honorable rulers and wise sages.

The color is brilliant white. Blinding noonday light.

The animal is the dragon. Sky dweller.

Imagine: The power of the universe is flowing through you. Feel the awesome force of the stars and galaxies in the vast expanse of the sky.

CHAPTER TWO

Explaining the Hexagrams

When the Eight Trigrams are placed in pairs, one on top of the other, the resulting combinations are the sixty-four different six-lined images called hexagrams. These hexagrams describe the conditions and attitudes we encounter throughout our lives.

The Chinese gave each hexagram a name and a description, adding stories and proverbs to illustrate their meaning. The reality of these symbols is rooted in our experience of life, in the things around us, and in our own feelings.

We now have a greater complexity. Not just black and white, or shades of gray, but a rainbow of infinite colors. From yin and yang, through the four seasons, to the Eight Trigrams, and now to the Sixty-Four Hexagrams.

In the *I Ching* we have sixty-four descriptions of life and of mind. Are we ordinarily capable of coming up with sixty-four solutions to a problem? When we ask a question of the *I Ching*, it responds with an appropriate answer, the meaning inherent in that moment of time.

UNDERSTANDING THE HEXAGRAMS AS COMPLEMENTARY PAIRS

The Sixty-Four Hexagrams are arranged in complementary pairs. We can understand a hexagram more clearly when we contrast it with its opposite. These descriptions give you a general idea of their meaning.

1 ䷀ LEADS THE WAY	2 ䷁ GOES WITH THE FLOW
3 PLANS AHEAD	4 BEGINNER'S LUCK
5 WAITING FOR OPPORTUNITY	6 MAKING DEMANDS
7 THE LONE WARRIOR	8 WE STAND TOGETHER
9 ALERT TO THE SIGNS	10 TAKING RISKS
11 RIGHT ACTION	12 STOPPED AND BLOCKED
13 SHARES WITH FRIENDS	14 OWNS IT ALL
15 MODESTLY LOW-KEY	16 INSPIRED TO ACT
17 DOING WHAT YOU WANT	18 DOING WHAT YOU MUST
19 DOES IT NOW	20 THINKS IT THROUGH
21 MAKING THE EFFORT	22 FUN AND CELEBRATION
23 TOPPLES AND FALLS	24 RETURNS TO THE WAY
25 ACTS NATURALLY	26 TAKES CONTROL
27 FINDS NOURISHMENT	28 ESCAPES THE PRESSURE
29 ALONE AND IN TROUBLE	30 MUTUAL SUPPORT
31 GIVE AND TAKE	32 SEEING IT THROUGH
33 WITHDRAWS INTO RETREAT	34 BREAKING FREE
35 THE WINNER	36 OUT IN THE COLD
37 FAMILY TIES	38 DOING YOUR OWN THING
39 STUMBLES AND FALLS	40 OUT OF DANGER
41 SMALL IS BEAUTIFUL	42 GROWTH AND INCREASE

43	䷪	MAKING IT PERFECT	44	䷫	DISTURBING INFLUENCE
45	䷬	GETTING IT TOGETHER	46	䷭	MOVING ON UP
47	䷮	RUNNING ON EMPTY	48	䷯	PLENTIFUL RESOURCES
49	䷰	OUT WITH THE OLD	50	䷱	IN WITH THE NEW
51	䷲	SHOCKS US ALL	52	䷳	COOL, CALM, AND COLLECTED
53	䷴	STEADY PROGRESS	54	䷵	FOOLS RUSH IN
55	䷶	REAPS THE HARVEST	56	䷷	ON THE ROAD
57	䷸	BENDS IN THE WIND	58	䷹	STAND UP FOR YOURSELF
59	䷺	RIDES THE WAVE	60	䷻	DEFINES THE LIMITS
61	䷼	SPEAKS FROM THE HEART	62	䷽	JUST GETTING BY
63	䷾	THIS PERFECT DAY	64	䷿	IT'S NOT OVER YET

UNDERSTANDING THE UPPER AND LOWER TRIGRAMS

The lower or inner trigram (the bottom three lines) describes the internal aspect of the situation—the hidden, unconscious, submissive, or developing part; the time of preparation, childhood, learning, and adventure.

The upper or outer trigram (the top three lines) describes the external aspect of the situation—the visible, conscious, dominant, or developed part; the time of career, maturity, and retirement. For example:

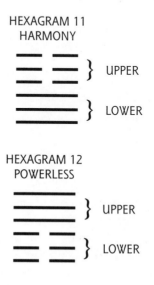

HEXAGRAM 11
HARMONY

} UPPER

} LOWER

HEXAGRAM 12
POWERLESS

} UPPER

} LOWER

A group or society can be divided into those who follow orders and those who give the orders. Those who follow orders are represented by the lower trigram. Those who give the orders are represented by the upper trigram. As an example, let's look at Hexagrams 11 and 12.

Hexagram 11 describes a balanced situation, where ordinary people have power and representation (shown by yang lines in the lower trigram), and the rulers are responsive to this (shown by the yin lines in the upper trigram).

Hexagram 12 describes a stagnant situation, where the rulers have all the power, represented by the three yang lines. Ordinary people have little chance of making their influence felt. This is an unproductive condition, such as a repressive dictatorship or unresponsive management.

The hexagrams can also be interpreted psychologically. Hexagram 11 describes a person in touch with and responsive to his or her feelings. Hexagram 12, on the other hand, describes someone who represses and denies his or her feelings.

UNDERSTANDING THE SIX LINES

At the heart of the *I Ching* are the lines and their meaning. The six lines of the hexagram are numbered from one to six, reading from the bottom and working up, as in the floors of a building. Each line in the hexagram has a par-

ticular meaning, according to its position in the design.

The yin-yang symbols used in this example represent Hexagram 63, called "This Perfect Day."

When you consult the *I Ching,* one of the lines will be indicated as having special significance. This is called the moving or active line, and it reveals your position in the given circumstance.

The way you interpret the response depends on the nature of your question. It's up to you to make the necessary link between the hexagram and your question to the oracle. The following suggestions are keys you can use to unlock the meaning of the *I Ching.*

You can understand the lines in a number of ways. For example, they can be seen as the stages of a lifetime:

Line 6 Old age and death
Line 5 Maturity and achievement
Line 4 Middle age and career
Line 3 Youth and adventure
Line 2 Childhood and learning
Line 1 Birth and infancy

You can also understand the lines as the natural progression of events from the conception of a project to its conclusion:

Line 6 Moving on. When you have gone as high as you can go, it is time to hand over the reins of power and move on to something new.

Line 5 Making it to the top. You've reached your goal. You are now in charge. You're the boss. A sense of achievement. Avoid self-indulgence and plan for the future.

Line 4 Establishing a practice and routine. Things are running normally. You have made the transition. The job is yours, the plane is flying, the book is in the stores, and now it is a matter of gradual, steady progress.

Line 3 Being original and outgoing. This is the graduate making the move from practice to the real world. The amateur becoming the professional. You launch your product/idea/self, working toward your big break.

Line 2 From a beginner to an apprentice. You have expertise in your area and you continue to improve your skills.

Line 1 In the beginning, the beginner. First impressions. Initial intention or decision. Getting a bright idea. Find out if this is what you really want to do, because it's a commitment.

The lines can also represent the search for the Holy Grail—the cup used by Christ at the Last Supper, and the holy object of prolonged quest by medieval knights. We are all seeking something in life. Call it happiness, success, fame, wisdom, or enlightenment. Otherwise, what would keep us going?

Line 6 Returning home. You return to tell your story and move on to the next adventure.

Line 5 Finding the grail. You reach your destination.

Line 4 Progress to the goal. Life on the road.

Line 3 Crossing the river. Committed to the journey. No turning back.

Line 2 Preparing for the quest. Finding out what you need. Getting all your stuff together.

Line 1 Called to the quest. The inspiration to embark on a journey.

You can also understand the six lines as three pairs of lines:

• The bottom two lines are called the lines of earth. They deal with the physical forces, the body and physical sensations, influences from subconscious realms.

• The middle two lines are called the lines of humanity. They deal with social values, the heart and feelings, influences from the worldly realm.

• The top two lines are called the lines of heaven. They deal with cosmic forces, the mind and ideas, influences from higher realms.

In the example above, Hexagram 20, called "Contemplation, Perspective, Observation," the two yang lines at the top indicate that thoughts and ideas are dominant.

CHAPTER THREE

How to Use the I Ching

*When I toss a coin, that coin is linked to
everything else in the universe.*

C. G. Jung

When we can't seem to solve a problem, it is often because we are stuck in the rut of our own habitual thinking and approach to problems. Sometimes we only need one new idea to jog our minds into a fresh insight. The *I Ching* will give us that new idea for the asking. Ready? Dive in!

HOW TO DO AN
I CHING READING

The *I Ching* is a meditative device for learning to trust and develop your own judgment and intuition. Approach the *I Ching* with an open and sincere mind.

Asking the Question

Before you begin a reading, make sure you have a calm space in both your mind and environment. Put aside the pressures and worries of life for this moment. Be wholehearted in posing the question, in laying out the coins, and in reading the answer. Developing

a personal ritual that encourages this state of mind is helpful.

Ideally, your question should be clear. Writing down the question can help clarify it for you. When you have it firmly in mind, throw the coins.

Occasionally, you may compulsively ask question after question about the same problem, until no answer makes any sense. You may be trying to force a particular answer, or you may be tense, hurried, or tired. You may feel confused and uncertain about the situation you are asking about. Either bring the situation you are worried about into focus, or leave the question for another time.

Throwing the Coins

1. Begin with six coins—five of one kind and one of another, all of a similar size (for example, five pennies and a dime). The odd coin will have a special significance in your reading.

2. Contemplate the question you

would like to ask the *I Ching*, and define it clearly in your mind. When you feel ready, write it down.

3. With a sincere attitude and an open mind, hold the coins, relax, and take some slow, deep breaths. Now shake the coins and drop them on a hard surface.

4. Push the coins into a vertical column, keeping them in roughly the same order in which they fall, as shown in the illustration. You now have a random assortment of heads and tails that composes the hexagram that is the answer to your question. The tails represent yin, or a broken line; the heads represent yang, or a solid line (see the diagram below).

5. Use the chart of hexagrams on the inside back cover to find the number of your hexagram. On the left side of the chart, locate the three lines that correspond to your *bottom three coins.* Along the top of the chart, locate the three lines that correspond to your *top*

three coins. The intersection of these two sets of lines will give you the number of your hexagram.

6. Find your hexagram in the book and read the commentary to learn about your general situation.

7. Now look at the six lines. The position of the odd coin in your reading indicates the specific line of advice that applies to your question.

8. Write down the *I Ching's* response next to your question.

A point of interest when you begin to interpret the hexagrams in this book: below the titles for each hexagram are two key phrases. The first phrase that accompanies the illustration, as in Hexagram 1, "Leads the way," is in our own words. The phrase below it, "Strong and untiring," is from the original Chinese. Also, the bolded phrase for *each line* of the hexagram, such as "Dragon swims underwater" for line 1 of Hexagram 1, is

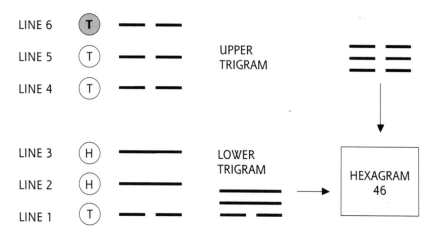

from the Chinese; underneath that is our interpretation of the line.

Example of an I Ching *Reading*

Many years ago we asked the oracle how we should approach it.

Q What is our relationship to the *I Ching*? Please advise correct conduct.

A We received Hexagram 20, "Observation," with line 4 moving.

HEADS ⭕	━━━━━━	LINE 6
HEADS ⭕	━━━━━━	LINE 5
TAILS ⚫	━━ ━━	LINE 4
TAILS ⭕	━━ ━━	LINE 3
TAILS ⭕	━━ ━━	LINE 2
TAILS ⭕	━━ ━━	LINE 1

Hexagram 20 is about preparing one's mind for a ritual. It speaks of being observant and open.

Line 4 tells the story of being invited to visit the king. One sees the richness and beauty of the kingdom, and is pleased to be a part of it. We interpreted this to mean that we should approach the *I Ching* and the riches it has to offer with openness, flexibility, respect, and attentiveness.

If you approach the *I Ching* in this way, the answer will speak to you personally. Bells will ring. And don't forget that many questions, especially questions that involve other people, have two sides. Remember that, depending on how your question is phrased, the *I Ching*'s advice may apply either to you or to the other person. Finally, let the *I Ching* stimulate your intuitive knowingness in the spirit of play. That's all there is to it. Good luck and good fortune!

PART TWO

THE HEXAGRAMS

1

CAUSE

POWER

CREATIVITY

Leads the way

Strong and untiring

SKY

SKY

Sky over the sky. All yang lines demonstrate that creative power is manifest everywhere.

The lines tell the story of the dragon's rise from the depths to the skies.

Intention without reservation. Yin is not present here as a softening factor. You are in a powerful position. All systems go!

LINE 6   Dragon flies too high

You will regret going beyond the limits. Delusions of grandeur. Let it all go and return to a simple life. Withdraw and prepare to re-create yourself.

LINE 5   Dragon flies in the sky

You are a leader of distinction. Winning and triumphant. Select good advisers to help you. An opportunity to successfully accomplish a great ambition.

LINE 4   Dragon leaps into a deep pool

You are in the right position to advance. You may be hesitant, as you are moving into unknown territory. This results in your moving back and forth between one level and the next.

LINE 3   Active all day, worried all night

You are in transition between one thing and another. This is a difficult and anxious time. Ceaseless activity is needed if you are to bring affairs to a successful conclusion.

LINE 2   Dragon appears in the field

Come out into the open. Be available to all people. Seek wisdom and advice from those who know. Learning and gaining information.

LINE 1   Dragon swims underwater

Now is not the time to act. Wait until the time is right to come forth. A temporary seclusion in which you prepare yourself for an exciting adventure.

REAL-LIFE ADVENTURES

Breaking the Rules

We had been together every day for ten years. As in the myth of the ancient tantric couple who spent their lives as one inside one large cloak, we were a loving and tight twosome. We met many extraordinary people, but we had never met anyone who could become part of—rather than blow apart—that most secret, intimate relationship that we shared.

Much to our surprise, however, we suddenly had to consider such an exceptional person. This was to be an intimate encounter that would change our lives. But who wants change when everything is just fine the way it is?

And what about those rules society lives by? The ones that insist we go two by two, not three by three? It's not easy to love openly in this way, and loving in the closet was not our style. The feelings between the three of us already existed. Now what should we do with them? Would this relationship be a blessing or a nightmare?

Q What should we do about this momentous encounter in love?

A We received Hexagram 1, with line 2 moving.

Hexagram 1 means the situation is charged with powerful forces and influences. That was an understatement. It was life on a roller coaster.

Line 2 suggests coming into the open, coming forth. This is a creative and powerful possibility. Go with it and enjoy it. Live, learn, and love. Did we or didn't we follow the advice from the good book? Yes, we did! Stay tuned for more adventures with the irrepressible threesome (see Hexagrams 16 and 23).

Jimmy Carter for President

On October 27, 1976, a few days before the presidential election, we wondered how candidate Jimmy Carter would fare.

Q What are Jimmy Carter's chances for becoming president of the United States?

A We received Hexagram 1, with line 5 moving.

Hexagram 1 indicates a position of great power, such as the U.S. presidency.

Line 5 is the line of achievement and success.

Our interpretation was that he would become the president. He did win the election that year.

George Bush for President

In 1979 George Bush was one of many candidates for president or vice president in the coming convention. We thought him a man to be reckoned with, and we asked:

Q Will George Bush be nominated at the Republican convention?

A We received Hexagram 1, with line 5 moving.

This is the same combination we got for our question about Jimmy Carter. Wow! The chances of any combination appearing twice are 64 times 64 to 1, or 4,096 to 1.

Bush was nominated as vice president, and eight years later he became president.

2

RELAXING

FOLLOWING

RESPONSIVE

Playing along

Docile as a mare

EARTH

EARTH

Earth over the earth. The earth is receptive,
generous, and unselfish. Here, these qualities
are doubled and strengthened.

All yin lines: an acquiescent mood. This is the
unmoving center of your being, doing
nothing and being everything.

The center of the wheel. The center of the cyclone.
The unmoving mover of it all.

With quietness and docility, the yin
mare carries the yang rider.

Go with the flow, and contribute to the motion.

LINE 6   Dragons fighting in the wild

Things have gone as far as they can go. It is time for the imbalances to be corrected. The pendulum, having swung as far as it can in one direction, now makes the return. The end and the beginning.

LINE 5   Embroidered yellow dress

You may be put in charge of something that you do not own yourself. This is very fortunate if you accept the fact that you are the second-in-command and remain loyal. Danger if you try to take it all.

LINE 4   A sack tied up

Keep silent. Be wary of taking on new responsibilities. Your words and actions will be exposed to critical scrutiny. Cash in on available profits. It's in the bag.

LINE 3   Hidden brilliance

Work in the background and faithfully bring things to completion. This is neither the time nor the place to claim the credit for yourself. You may be a confidential adviser.

LINE 2   Dutiful and correct

You are in the right place at the right time. Let your actions be straightforward and uncontrived. By effortlessly responding to circumstances, your actions are correct.

LINE 1   Frost now, ice later

What you see now is an indication of what is to come. Good things can be planned for in your future. Nip a bad situation in the bud.

REAL-LIFE ADVENTURES

Playing Along

In 1983 an entrepreneurial friend of ours in California was offered the job of rescuing a failing business. He normally runs his own businesses, but in this instance he was willing to be employed by another, as the offer appeared to be an excellent one.

Q What is your advice for this offer?

A We received Hexagram 2, with line 5 moving.

Hexagram 2 means service, to go along with, or to work for another.
Line 5 means success in the service of another.
The venture did turn out to be successful, and our friend was well rewarded for rescuing the ailing company.
Because we knew this man, and his history of being his own boss, we included in our interpretation of this reading the possibility that even though the venture would be successful, he might not be personally fulfilled, as it was not in his character to be Number Two. Eventually, he did become his own boss again. It showed us that circumstances and individual character must always be taken into account.

Second-in-Command

In 1986 we were in England, working and studying with the charismatic and gifted therapist and herbalist Vicki Wall. We were considering creating a partnership with her—making a commitment.

Q Will this partnership be advantageous for us?

A We received Hexagram 2, with line 1 moving.

Hexagram 2 means working for another. We realized that this partnership would demand some sacrifice on our part; being second-in-command to someone else's project.

Line 1 means that we are in the formative stage of things; nothing has been decided yet, but the decisions made now will have long-term consequences.

The text advises analyzing the situation very carefully. The subtle signs and indicators that you see now will become the dominant forces of the future.

We studied the situation and saw that there were likely to be political conflicts with others in working with this healer, as disagreements and power struggles were already going on.

We had taken that path once too often. As a result of these insights, we decided not to pursue that partnership.

Frost Now, Ice Later

The next two stories are connected in two ways: First, they have the same hexagram reading and the same line. Second, the stories represent both ends of our family spectrum, our parents and our grandchildren.

The first is about going to see our parents, one of whom seemed to be seriously ailing. As our parents age, the ending of life, rather than the living of it, seems to come up a lot. Any illness or mishap could be the last one. We are always waiting for disaster. There is no misery like worry.

Q Is now the time to visit our parents?

A We received Hexagram 2, with line 1 moving.

Hexagram 2 has to do with going with the flow, being unselfish and responsive. When we visit our parents, we are guests in someone else's house, and thus in someone else's zone of power. This is a passive situation over which we have little control.

Line 1 means that something is happening. Our fears are premature, but justified. The seeds have been sown.

The need to see our mother was strong, and although we recognized in the advice that there was no imminent disaster, we decided to go and see her anyway.

The second story is about visiting our children and grandchildren. We had been trying to visit them for a long time, but physical distance was a great obstacle. This was not an imperative situation, but a growing and disturbing one. The little people become big ones in a blink. Where are we going with our lives when we can't find the time to see the ones we love?

Q Is now the time for us to visit our kids?

A We received Hexagram 2, with line 1 moving.

Again, the feeling is correct, but the time is not. We would be better off waiting. We were comfortable with the advice and didn't make the journey immediately. When we did see them, the timing was perfect.

3

PLANNING

ORGANIZING

PROBLEM SOLVING

Plan ahead

Difficulty at the beginning

WATER

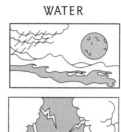

THUNDER

Water over thunder. Thunder means action and
water means danger. Moving into danger.

Make careful preparations before setting out.
You may have unexpected delays that cannot be
planned for, but need to be handled when they arise.
This will ensure eventual success.

Get your act together before you make your move.
If you have already made your move, make
more adjustments before carrying on.

LINE 6   On a horse at a standstill, tears of blood flow

You are stuck in the middle of a situation that you did not prepare for ahead of time. If you are willing to see it through, you will overcome the difficulties.

LINE 5   Difficulty in distributing the fat meat

Difficulties and delays in receiving rewards or benefits. Be content with small returns. Only minor issues will be resolved successfully. Handle a large problem piece by piece.

LINE 4   Horse and chariot waiting to move

You are ready to move. Your next step is to find those whom you wish to join and wait for them to invite you in.

LINE 3   Hunting without a guide, lost in the forest

You may feel weak and lonely and yet be keen to move ahead. Without guidance through the forest of life, you will get lost.

LINE 2   After ten years she agrees to marry

Resist being pressured into a partnership until you are ready. Do not seek immediate solutions. You have the power to refuse and wait. That is the way the weaker partner controls the stronger.

LINE 1   Delays, stay where you are

A strong person in an uncertain position. When you know what you want, you will find what you need. Ask people to help you.

REAL-LIFE ADVENTURES

A Guide in the Forest

Our friend Diane was in her early teens. Her parents were in the process of a divorce, and she would have to change her residence and her parental guardian. Diane wanted to know which of three people to live with: her mother, her father, or her aunt.

She didn't know how to choose the right person. She felt love for all of them, but circumstances were forcing her into making a choice.

Q Which member of my family should I live with?

A Diane received Hexagram 3, with line 3 moving.

Hexagram 3 is about making plans, preparing for the future.

Line 3 indicates the need for a guide in the forest of life. A guide is a guru or teacher, or a trusted friend—one who has been there before, who has already traveled the road with some success.

Line 3 is the point of coming into the world; this also mirrors the age of the questioner—fifteen years old.

This situation could be looked at as a unique opportunity to plan her future.

The *I Ching* response gave Diane an important truth against which to measure her choices. She chose to live with her aunt, a single woman, whose courage and joy in life she had always admired.

Finding Help

Our friend José had a severe cerebral stroke at the age of forty-four. On top of that, he had no medical insurance. He needed government assistance for his survival, as he was now severely disabled, with paralysis of the left side of his body. His thought processes remained intact, however, and he had this question to ask of the *I Ching*.

Q How difficult will it be to obtain the government assistance I need?

A José received Hexagram 3, with line 5 moving.

Hexagram 3 is about getting out of trouble, planning ahead. Getting out of trouble was certainly relevant. José could do none of the work of getting benefits for himself, as he was disabled verbally as well as physically. José's mate had to do endless research and talk to many government people to find out what was possible, what was available, and what red tape they needed to cut through to receive their benefits.

Line 5 says that there is difficulty in getting to the fat: that is, getting to the benefits. You will succeed in small ways, but will not get everything you want in the big issues. It won't be handed to you on a platter. You'll have to fight for whatever scraps you do get. A story for our time.

José received every test known to humankind, and some continuing physical therapy. All of the major help, such as making his house safe for his return, and the daily healing sessions, came from his community of friends. The government subsidies were all minimal, and he and his mate had to fight for them with determination.

4

LEARNING

BEGINNER

UNKNOWING

Beginner's luck

*The student must seek
out the teacher*

MOUNTAIN

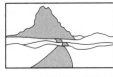

WATER

Water under the mountain. The water represents the restless youth, and the mountains are the heights of wisdom to be attained.

The story is of a student coming to the sage for counsel. The sage has three pieces of advice. The sage knows that if the first piece of advice is ignored, more advice will be of no benefit.

This is also the picture of a young sprout buried under the earth in darkness, ignorant of the world outside yet pushing up to the light.

Part of taking your place in the world depends on having "beginner's mind": keeping your perspective innocent and fresh. How much do you need to know in order to survive?

Be willing to learn.

LINE 6   Do not be a robber, prevent robberies

A superior teacher imparts understanding and frees the student's mind. An inferior teacher instills violence and passes on prejudices.

LINE 5   A fortunate young sprout

You have beginner's luck. You have no doubts about your own abilities. Devoted and gentle, warmhearted and honest, you are able to accept advice.

LINE 4   Entangled in folly

You are out of touch with reality. In your ignorance you have taken on too much. If you obstinately refuse to take advice, life will teach you a lesson.

LINE 3   Throwing yourself away for the money

In your ignorance and enthusiasm you may lose control and throw yourself away on the first offer that comes along. Resist the temptation of a quick profit.

LINE 2   Set up house and start a family

You do have something to offer at this stage, and it is enough to start with. Be tolerant of those taking on new responsibilities for the first time.

LINE 1   The new plant breaks through the earth

Understanding frees the mind from confusion. Clarify what is not understood as soon as it occurs. Ignorance means deliberately ignoring.

A REAL-LIFE ADVENTURE

Risky Business

We found this most interesting: Rod and Amy, with the same question in mind, each did their own reading and received the same hexagram.

We had recently completed designing a computer program that combined biorhythms with daily advice from the *I Ching*. We called our new creation Bio-Ching.

We had been doing the Bio-Ching by hand for our friends for twenty years, researching its validity. With the ease of computerization, we saw the possibility of providing this service to a broader public. This was an investment question about beginning a new business.

Q What is the current status of the Bio-Ching project?
Should we invest our money in this?

A Rod received Hexagram 4, with line 1 moving.

A Amy received Hexagram 4, with line 2 moving.

Hexagram 4 is about coming into the world.

Line 1 is the beginning of the beginning. Many uncertainties and unknowns. This reflected Rod's hesitation to come forth at this stage. He could see all the work that still needed doing on the computer program, and the effort and money required to promote the product.

Line 2 indicates that you can and should go with what you've got. Amy felt ready to start promoting the Bio-Ching, and line 2 reflected her attitude.

The readings told us that there was more work to be done and, at the same time, to go with it. Mixed messages? What to do? Our solution was to complete this book and go on to promote *The I Ching Made Easy* and the Bio-Ching simultaneously. A happy compromise. The best partnerships are bonded with them.

WAITING

PAUSING

ANTICIPATION

Timing is everything

It is favorable to cross a great river

WATER

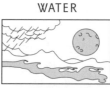

SKY

Water over the sky. The yang strength of the sky confronts the dangerous aspect of water.

The rain has made the river impassable. Wait for the waters to subside and pick your window of opportunity for a safe crossing.

Is it time to go boldly forth where no one has gone before? Practice patience, and you will know when to make your move.

LINE 6   Respecting three uninvited guests

Welcome an unexpected influence in your life. You may not know it, but you need a change, and this is it. Accept what comes your way.

LINE 5   Waited on with food and wine

Having crossed the river successfully, you can rest up and enjoy yourself. The danger may not be entirely over, but you have done all that you can to ensure a successful outcome.

LINE 4   Bloodied, forced from your hole

You may be injured in some way and hiding out. Being encouraged to come out into the open will end the conflict. You will come to no harm. You may have to end the waiting and make a decision.

LINE 3   Stuck in the mud

Impatient to cross the river, you moved before you should have, and now you are stuck in the mud part way across. Predators stalk their prey at watering places, waiting for a moment like this.

LINE 2   Drenched on the riverbank

Close to danger, but not in danger. Like being on a dry riverbank and getting soaked by an unusually large wave. Like being criticized, and passing it off. Hold your ground, the wave will pass.

LINE 1   Out in the rain

You have the strength and talent to handle a dangerous situation. Now is not the time for you to move, as the danger is still far away. Be patient. Stay in out of the rain for now.

A REAL-LIFE ADVENTURE

Changing Lifestyles

One day we were suddenly forced to make a decision about our living situation. Should we continue living privately as a couple, or should we live in a spiritual community? We lived in a condo on the beach in Maui—a permanent holiday—and we loved the privacy of our life together. Who could ask for anything more? Our dog, Moki, having waited patiently through the quarantine period of four months, finally joined us. And guess what? The condo we were renting did not accept pets. So, with no warning, we were forced to move.

That same day—coincidentally or synchronistically—we were offered a space in a meditation community with our new friend, a Tibetan teacher. This would change the direction of our lives: from beach bunnies to recluses. What should we do?

Q Should we make this move to live with the Tibetan lama or continue living on our own? Are we meditators or ordinary people?

A We received Hexagram 5, with line 6 moving.

Hexagram 5 is about taking the plunge into a new venture.

Line 6 says that external influences are encouraging you to make that change.

The influences were the lama and our profound desire to make the spiritual connection with the Buddhist teachings. Honoring these guests meant accepting the lama's kind invitation.

We felt we were being forced out of our little place in the sun and shown a new path, a new possibility. We took the opportunity and our lives were altered. Sometimes there is no resisting fate.

6

CONFLICT
DISSENSION
CONFRONTATION

Stating your case

Meet your adversary halfway

SKY

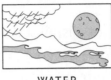

WATER

Sky over the water. Water, which represents demands and disagreements, confronting the sky, which represents authority.

The story is of someone coming to the duke's court with a complaint. You're not in a powerful enough position to necessarily have things go your way.

Be willing to compromise. Mediate.

LINE 6   Awarded a leather sash, it is recalled thrice that day

By demanding satisfaction in a dispute or pushing your advantage unfairly, you may win. But gains won by force soon dissolve into loss.

LINE 5   Disputes settled, supreme good fortune

Your grievances are valid. You now have an opportunity to settle disagreements in a just and fair manner, so that genuine friendship can develop.

LINE 4   Complaint dismissed

An impulsive action has led you to make a complaint that has been rejected. Forget your grievance and get on with life. Accept that things might not always go your way.

LINE 3   Living off your inheritance

You are in an insecure position and feel menaced. Maintain your independence and live within your means. Rely on strategies that have worked for you before.

LINE 2   Withdraw to your home town

You are no match for this conflict. You have taken on someone stronger than you. Back out of it while you can. Retreat to a place in which you feel safe.

LINE 1   Not pressing your demands

A misunderstanding can be avoided by backing off. You are not in a strong enough position to press your demands. You may suffer some criticism for this, but it will turn out well.

A REAL-LIFE ADVENTURE

Get with the Program

In 1987 we were living on one of the Hawaiian islands, and deeply involved as meditators with our Tibetan Buddhist teacher. As engrossing and enlightening as the discipline was, we had many disagreements with the political and hierarchical views of the group, and virtually no power of any kind to create changes. It was a very frustrating situation for us.

We were hosting His Eminence Tai Situ Pa, Rinpoche, a renowned Tibetan teacher and our good friend, for a one-week retreat. Very happy days.

During this retreat we put a question to the *I Ching* concerning our future with Tibetan Buddhism. We were no longer certain that the teachings of the Buddha could continue to outweigh the sexist, chauvinist, authoritarian views that had been cast in concrete by some of the current Tibetan lineages.

Q What is the nature of our future with this group?

A We received Hexagram 6, with line 6 moving.

Hexagram 6 deals with bringing complaints and resolving disagreements.

Line 6 has a nagging quality. You've nagged until you've gotten what you wanted. Resentment has definitely set in.

We had pushed our power and good luck to the limit here. We had the great honor and delight of working closely with a favorite teacher, but virtually nothing had changed, or would be likely to change, with regard to our relationship to the group. There can come a time when the student must leave the teacher—especially if the student becomes critical!

As a member of any authoritarian system that insists on its version of the truth, you are in no position to change the system. Go along or get out. This is not an uncommon attitude, but it is not a basic truth of Buddhism. Buddha taught self-reliance. We felt that our opinions counted for little, and that we were unable to make even the smallest changes in the basic attitudes of the group. We left our teachers and the Hawaiian Islands shortly after this reading. We have worked with many teachers since that time, but have declined to join another group.

7

HONOR

LOYALTY

INTEGRITY

The way of the warrior

*Advance with courage
and discipline*

EARTH

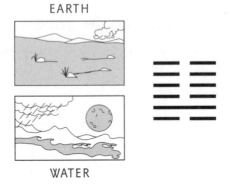

WATER

Earth over the water. The dangerous energy of water is controlled by the willing nature of the earth or the meadow. The utilizing of a powerful force.

In ancient China each soldier carried on his back the flag of the side he was fighting for. It was either sewn onto the back of his jacket or flying on a short pole attached to his backpack. Each and every soldier was a standardbearer defending the flag with his honor and his life.

Personal responsibility and integrity even when not in a position of authority.

Great things will be accomplished. With self-discipline, it is possible to see and correct one's faults.

LINE 6 Establish settlements

Mission accomplished. Reward those who have served well. Employ only the most competent, so that the gains made are maintained and not lost.

LINE 5 Bagging the game

You now have the opportunity to take decisive action. Give each person the task best suited to them. Always know what is going on. Stop when you reach a reasonable goal.

LINE 4 Camp far from the enemy

This is not the time to move forward. A strategic retreat is needed to stay away from trouble. An adjustment or detour is taken in order to preserve the overall plan.

LINE 3 Corpses in the wagon

Disorder and failure due to incompetent and conflicting leadership and poorly delegated authority. Find a competent leader who can bring order. Are you the one, or would you opt for getting out?

LINE 2 A triple promotion

You are rewarded for your dedication and service. Granted three wishes. A responsible leader equal to the demands of an important mission.

LINE 1 An army must set out in proper order

At the beginning of things, it is wise to have a plan. Marshal your resources, think it through, and exercise discipline. Take charge of your own destiny.

A REAL-LIFE ADVENTURE

Loyalty and Authority

This is a story about being appointed to a position of authority by the person in control, without being voted in by the other members of the group. This happened in a university, but it could just as easily have happened in any group situation. Susanne felt she was capable of taking on the responsibility, but she wanted the agreement of her peers. Her purpose was to study and learn, not to play power politics.

Q Is it correct for me to accept this position?

A Susanne received Hexagram 7, with line 3 moving.

Hexagram 7 deals with personal integrity. Who you are with yourself, and how that relates to the common good.

Line 3 indicates conflict, and whether to handle it or have nothing to do with it.

There were many potential conflicts, as in any group. The basic one here was the individual versus the authority, the eternal conflict between the I and the We. If Susanne accepted the position, would she be violating her integrity? Perpetual food for discord. But could she pass up the opportunity for some of that great personal power?

She chose to continue to be a student, and not become embroiled in the internal politics of the group. She refused the appointment. This was her way of maintaining integrity and avoiding conflict.

8

TEAMWORK
AGREEMENT
FRIENDSHIP

Together we stand,
divided we fall

Are your friends trustworthy
and dependable?

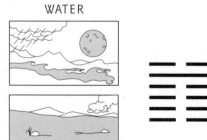

WATER

EARTH

Water over the earth. The earth represents a
group of people getting together to face the danger
represented by water. Belonging to a group or having friends
is the best protection in times of trouble.

In the Chou Dynasty, a group of five families would
get together and live cooperatively, sharing the different
duties and helping one another. Those who hesitate, the
latecomers, are not completely trusted or welcome.

Security is found in sharing responsibilities with others.
Choose your friends carefully, and demand more than partial
involvement. Are you in, or are you out?

LINE 6   No head for cooperation

An unqualified person is in charge, and others lack confidence in their leadership. When we get off on the wrong foot, it is difficult to create a trusting atmosphere.

LINE 5   Allow some of the game to escape

The way to have friends is by allowing them to be with you of their own free will. No bribery or coercion is necessary.

LINE 4   Friends on the outside

Giving or getting support from those outside the group. Turn your attention to newcomers and strangers, those beyond your immediate circle.

LINE 3   Close to the wrong people

Be careful of lending your support to unscrupulous people. Your judgment may have been warped by flattery. Keeping bad company.

LINE 2   Friendship from the inside

You are either one of the in-group, or have an inside connection. Self-reliance and self-esteem.

LINE 1   A plain cup, overflowing with sincerity

When you meet others for the first time, you may feel lonely and insecure. With simple, pure-hearted sincerity, you will attract others to you.

REAL-LIFE ADVENTURES

Choosing a Qualified Partner

We did a reading concerning the placing of our capital with an investment counselor/broker, who promised tremendous returns for us in the bond market.

Even though he came highly recommended, the idea of giving him complete control without clearly understanding what he was going to do with our money made us very nervous.

We were novices in this field of money investment, and we needed some hand-holding. This man was not a good teacher, and he was not keeping us informed. When good communication is absent in any relationship, trust dissolves in direct proportion. We don't function happily or well in ignorance. This guy could be the wizard of Wall Street, but if he treats us like idiots, how can we trust him?

Q Is this the correct action for us to take with our investment capital?

A We received Hexagram 8, line 6 moving.

Hexagram 8 is concerned with the alliance of powers. In this case it was our money and the investment counselor's alleged talent.

Line 6 indicated our lack of confidence in the management of this group.

We decided not to go along with this man. We felt his organization was a group without a head, as his head didn't impress us.

Interestingly, the bottom dropped out of the bond market less than two weeks later. We would have lost two-thirds of our investment overnight if we had gone with this firm. Good luck? Karma? Perhaps it was getting some help from our friends—in this case, the *I Ching*.

Ross Perot for President?

This next story involves the same hexagram as above with the same line moving.

Q How will Ross Perot do in the 1992 presidential election?

A We received Hexagram 8, with line 6 moving.

One of our descriptions of Hexagram 8 says that those who join late will lose out. Perot was in and then he was out and then he was in again. Too little too late. He lost out.

Line 6 indicates again the sense of no head for leadership.

INTERFERENCE

INTUITION

TAKING PRECAUTIONS

Pay attention to your premonitions

Clouds are gathering, waiting for rain

TREE

SKY

The wind in the sky. Touching and sensing distant things. Your creative power is manifesting in subtle and far-reaching ways.

The forecaster reads the signs in the sky and knows what is going to happen. Overlooking the smallest warning sign that something is wrong may hold you back. This may lead to feelings of doubt, uncertainty, and indecision.

As with a puzzle, collect all the pieces together before beginning. You have the sensitivity to know what is going on.

LINE 6   The rain comes, the rain goes

You have weathered the storm. For the moment all is well. Use this time to build up your energy and resources. Your troubles are not over yet.

LINE 5   Sharing wealth with the neighbors

Do not be a user, nor permit yourself to be used. Relationships should be beneficial to all. Mutual trust forms the basis of binding obligations, especially where money is involved.

LINE 4   Sincere speech avoids bloodshed

You have the calmness and sincerity needed to dispel anxiety and the threat of conflict. A forceful approach is not appropriate at this time.

LINE 3   Wheels fall off the cart, husband and wife argue

Getting into arguments and blame whenever anything goes wrong. Stop, before it gets out of hand. Your happiness depends on it.

LINE 2   Persuaded to the right path

Being set straight. Convinced or convincing another to return to the right way. Two people may cooperate to overcome a mutual obstruction.

LINE 1   Returning to the right path

Turn your back on unhealthy company and return to earlier and better days and ways. In your heart you know what is right.

A REAL-LIFE ADVENTURE

Greed Is God

A visiting Buddhist teacher from Nepal, traveling with his American wife and one-year-old son, is giving "a wealth empowerment" at the home of a major patron in Hawaii. Wealth is the capacity to create and embrace good fortune. An empowerment is a blessing and a transmission of a particular aspect of the Buddha.

The teacher has no means of support. He and his family are so impoverished that his wife cannot afford new underwear. And he's going to teach us how to get rich? He's going to introduce us to the Buddha of wealth? What's wrong with this picture? Okay, we'll suspend our disbelief. Our spiritual materialism is ravenous and needs to be fed.

We arrive at the house a half-hour early, after a long and tiring journey across the island. The gate is barred, we hear a King Kong–sized dog growling behind it, and there is a note pinned to the gate telling us to return in three hours. They're not ready. What? Wait a minute!

We take off to a nearby cafe for some breakfast and a consultation with the *I Ching*.

Q What is going on here? Do we really feel that this is the person from whom to receive a blessing of wealth?

A We received Hexagram 9, with line 5 moving.

Hexagram 9 is the power of the mind. The energy to penetrate, and to see the subtle signs that the universe is always showing us. Also restraint and obstacles; doubt and indecision.

In this instance we have literally seen a sign on the gate that says, "Go home and come back later." An impediment to our progress, surely. And whose power of mind is being referred to here? The bestower of the precious empowerment, who is already many hours late and holding? Or clever us, who just made a cross-country trek for promises of money and power?

Line 5 speaks of sharing the wealth. We went to the empowerment with fifty silver dollars to share with our friends. Our generosity was seriously impaired by the rudeness we encountered, not to mention Cujo at the gate.

Inherent in sharing and generosity is the willingness to give and to receive. It felt like we were trying to use the teacher and the empowerment as a kind of get-rich-quick scheme, and the teacher seemed to be using us in a similar way.

Despite our confusion (and the *I Ching's* response), we were willing to play the game, and we returned to receive the ancient teaching. The party was still not ready to roll after a three-hour wait. This was taking longer to start than a rock concert, and was a lot less exciting.

We were again told to wait outside. End of our willingness to persevere. We finally recognized how unethical and uneasy the situation had become for everyone, and we left. Just in the nick of time.

10

COURAGE

DAREDEVIL

TAKING RISKS

Storm the gates of heaven

Treading on the tiger's tail but the tiger does not bite

SKY

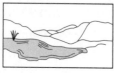

LAKE

Sky over the lake. The self-expression of the lake comes forth to confront the power of the sky. The courage to take on a force greater than yourself.

In southern China there is a small leopard cat, much weaker in strength than a tiger. It will suddenly jump onto the back of the tiger, get hold of the tiger's tail, and use its sharp claws to vigorously scratch the tiger's anus. The only solution for the tiger is to roll on the ground, at which time the small leopard cat flees rapidly.

This means that you can take a risk and get away with it, if you are careful—and small.

LINE 6 Watch your step

If you feel insecure, look back at what you have been doing to see where you are now. If it feels right, carry on with confidence.

LINE 5 Sensitive feet

Tread carefully. Sensitive feet in delicate shoes are unsuitable for heavy treks. When you venture forth, be ready for trouble. Practice patience, and bide your time.

LINE 4 Steps on tiger's tail, wary then lucky

Taking a risk may be scary, but you will get away with it. You are now strong enough to take it on, if you remain aware of the dangers.

LINE 3 Treads on tiger's tail, eaten alive

You are pushing your luck, and biting off more than you can chew. This is not the time to risk it all. You may think that you can do more than you are actually capable of.

LINE 2 Walking a level, easy road

Be honest and open in your dealings, and things will go your way. Be calm and quiet, blend in with the crowd. Be undisturbed by thoughts of loss or gain.

LINE 1 Wearing plain shoes

When in a low position, it is best to keep it simple and you will be safe. Live within your means.

REAL-LIFE ADVENTURES

Taking Risks

A friend asked if she and her son should enter into partnership with an owner of a retail store. Neither she nor her son knew this potential partner very well, but they did know that he was chronically ill and a recovering alcoholic—not altogether the perfect choice as an active and presumably senior partner. What's more, the business was on the skids, and neither she nor her son had any experience in retailing. The son was also dealing with an alcohol problem, and this was an expensive and complicated solution to help get him straight.

Q Please advise on the future of this undertaking.

A Our friend received Hexagram 10, with line 5 moving.

Hexagram 10 examines risk-taking. It also indicates caution and awareness.

Line 5 says that you are unprepared and possibly incapable in some way. Both the questioner and her son were without experience in the running of a retail business, and this particular business was already failing. So much for unprepared and incapable.

We advised against taking this risk. However, she went ahead with it and subsequently lost $20,000. Her son went on, finally, to a rehabilitation center. Unfortunately, the desire to use this business venture as the solution to the real problem (the son's alcoholism) obscured the actual situation.

Keep It Simple

We had an idea for a hand-held computer that displays your daily biorhythms along with *I Ching* advice. Designing a prototype would be a new field for us, and we had been warned by other inventors that it could turn out to be expensive. Great idea—but would we get in deeper than we wanted?

Q Should we get a prototype designed for the Bio-Ching?

A We received Hexagram 10, with line 1 moving.

Hexagram 10 is a response to the elements of risk taking that are involved.

Line 1 says that safe equals simple. That's pretty clear. If there are no complexities (we interpreted that to mean no big expenses) involved, then take the risk. Line 1 also indicates the beginning of something. It was just that; purely in the idea stage.

Eaten Alive

We were beginning as investors in the commodity and futures market, the most volatile win all–lose all game in the financial casino. With nothing more than a chart and the *I Ching* for advice, in a matter of weeks—with an investment of only a few hundred dollars—we made a profit of six thousand dollars in gold and silver futures. Beginner's luck? Easy money!

We then decided we needed an expert. Why? Who knows? Combining mountains of advice from our new broker, we also consulted the *I Ching* on all investments. Unfortunately, we didn't always take the advice we received from the *I Ching*. Sometimes we wanted a particular outcome to an event, and we ignored advice indicating unwanted alternatives. Human nature?

The brokers, in their collective wisdom, were advising us to bet on T-bonds. We bowed to their greater expertise and our own wishful thinking, and took the bet, despite the advice of the *I Ching* that follows.

Q Will T-bond futures advance or collapse before the end of August?

A We received Hexagram 10, with line 3 moving.

Hexagram 10 has to do with taking risks, storming the gates of heaven. An apt description of this most risky of investments, the futures market.

Line 3 describes the gamble as that of treading on a tiger's tail and being eaten alive, and this is exactly what happened. We lost nearly eight hundred dollars. The one piece of advice we should have listened to, we ignored.

So there you have it: Ignore the coins at your peril!

11

PEACE

HARMONY

BENEVOLENCE

*The right place at
the right time*

*Small offerings,
big returns*

EARTH

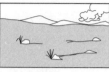

SKY

Earth over the sky. The sky intermingles with the earth. A very fortunate condition. It is heaven on earth.

This hexagram is called Tai, which means great or exalted in Chinese. Mount Tai is the sacred mountain in eastern China. With this quality of greatness or nobility, one has the inner power to do the right thing.

Confidence and certainty in your
actions brings success.

LINE 6   Castle walls crumble into the moat

Eventually the defensive walls will crumble back into the moat. What has been built up will return to its original condition. Defenses may no longer be necessary in a time of peace. The end of an era.

LINE 5   The father gives his daughter in marriage

Give generously and receive generously. Delegate positions of responsibility to others. If you are asking about marriage or a union of some kind, it will work out well.

LINE 4   Not boasting of wealth to your neighbor

You may need to ask others for support and backing. Do this in the spirit of sincerity and friendship. A conspicuous display of wealth will only cause envy.

LINE 3   No plain without a hill, no going without coming

Nothing lasts forever. Downhill follows uphill. You have the strength to ride the changes and maintain your peace of mind. The pendulum swings both ways.

LINE 2   Hang on to a hollow gourd, you will not be swept away

You need a life jacket of some kind to survive a difficult transition. Something or someone to rely on. At times like this, it is important to distinguish between the helpful and the harmful.

LINE 1   Connected at the roots

Your attention is focused outside of yourself. The energy you project inspires others of like mind to join you. You make connections, and use them well.

REAL-LIFE ADVENTURES

Doing the Right Thing

Halloween, 1991, at our home in Bisbee, Arizona. This is a big party night in Bisbee, with street dancing and general mayhem for all, but we felt a need to commune with nature. We wanted to leave the party atmosphere, and spend some solitary time in our mountain retreat.

On the spur of the moment, two party friends—a couple we barely knew—invited themselves to come up to our cabin with us for Halloween weekend. We responded yes, with the idiot generosity of the surprised. It might be great, but on second thought we had our doubts. Time to ask the oracle for advice.

Q Please advise on going to the mountains with our new friends.

A We received Hexagram 11, with line 3 moving.

Hexagram 11 expresses harmony, and a willingness to do the right thing; to make it happen.

We wanted to have a harmonious few days, but we suspected that their idea of harmony was different from ours. We envisioned a silent walkabout for ourselves, and we figured them for an orgy of delight.

Could we make it work in a primitive cabin? We didn't want to miss out on a good party; on the other hand, what about that quiet walk in the woods?

Line 3 says be realistic. Don't bank on everything being perfect.

We interpreted this to mean that our fears were valid. It would not be a peaceful time for us. It would be a social interaction: demanding, and not relaxing. We opted for our walk in the woods, rather than a walk on the wild side.

This hexagram as a whole is one of acting with courage, and trusting your own knowingness. We wanted to be in the natural world of the forest, and our friends wanted to party.

Overcoming the social impulse and saying no is very difficult for us, and it's also embarrassing—especially after we had already said yes! But sometimes it's necessary for our survival.

Love and Marriage

Our friend Amanda asked a romantic question. Her boyfriend was promising marriage, but he was not delivering the goods. Not surprisingly, doubts and fears had arisen in her mind.

Q My boyfriend—can I trust him?

A Amanda received Hexagram 11, with line 5 moving.

Hexagram 11 means everything will go right. Big returns. Generally a very positive hexagram.

Line 5 tells the story of a king giving his daughter in marriage. As the actual issue in question here was the matter of trust in his promises of marriage, this couldn't have been a better reading. Amanda's wedding is set for later this year.

A Brief Encounter

This story is about forming a creative partnership. We had been filming a t'ai chi video, and had made a connection with a talented and experienced editor. Great! We really wanted his help, but we had some doubts. This project was very much our baby, and we were doing every job, with delusions of power and the Orson Wells complex (we can do it better, so we'll do it ourselves). This editor had strong opinions about everything, and we were wary of his overpowering influence.

Q What about working with Willie on the video project?

A We received Hexagram 11, with line 6 moving.

The hexagram describes a good working relationship.

Line 6, as the top line of the hexagram, indicates the end of these favorable circumstances. It will soon fall apart. We had a few very creative evenings and did some excellent work. Then, as we had feared, Willie had his own vision of the film and was overriding us at every turn. We weren't able to find our comfort level together. Over and out.

12

STOPPED

POWERLESS

OBSTRUCTED

Out of touch

Blocked, this can't go on

SKY

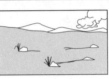

EARTH

Sky over the earth. The sky and the earth
appear to be in their rightful places, but they are
stagnant and not interacting.

The Chinese name for this hexagram is
"wicked, evil, clogged, or stopped."

Untrustworthy and small-minded people are in charge.
In this situation there is little that you can do.

Only small wins are possible.

LINE 6   Stagnation overcome

All obstructions are defeated. Happy days are here again. Having kept the faith during hard times, you prosper when things go your way.

LINE 5   At one with your fate

By not resisting your fate, you become one with it. Doubts and fears no longer have the power to hold you back. The end of bad times. Secure your position.

LINE 4   Given authority, and blessed friends

Despite your nervousness in an uncertain situation, you find the support you need. You have great potential. Things are getting easier.

LINE 3   An offering wrapped in palm leaves

You are at a disadvantage and may be trying too hard to please. Are you pretending to be who you are not? Can you comfortably be yourself?

LINE 2   Lowly people must make humble offerings

In times of stress, we sometimes have to flatter unworthy people. Separate yourself from these people whenever possible.

LINE 1   Pull weeds by the root

At the beginning, you have the opportunity to handle an obstruction before it has taken root. If you do not have the strength to overcome it, distance yourself from it. Ask friends to help with this.

A REAL-LIFE ADVENTURE

Don't Panic

We were vacationing with friends on their yacht in Vancouver, Canada, dreaming of *Lifestyles of the Rich and Famous*. At the same time, we were carrying on a long-distance negotiation on a project in England. We'd never attempted doing business at such a distance, and we did not feel totally in control of the situation.

Late one night we got a call from our attorney, who was handling the transaction in England, saying that the buyer had suddenly added an extra condition.

We did not know what was up. If this deal fell through, we would have to start all over again. We could not afford to make any mistakes.

Q Is this new condition to our advantage or not?

A We received Hexagram 12, with line 5 moving.

Hexagram 12 means something has come up and is in the way. There is a stop here of some kind.

Line 5 says not to act on your fears and run from the situation. Line 5 generally signifies a strong position. This is a minor stoppage, do not be put off by it.

We agreed to the new conditions imposed by the buyer, and yes, the deal went through. All was well. Miracles do still happen!

There are times when you know when to go and when not to go. At other times, you need an angle, a hint, a word of advice.

This was a situation in which we really didn't have a clue as to how to respond, and depended on the *I Ching* for advice as to which way to go.

13

COMPANIONSHIP

SHARING

COOPERATION

*All for one and
one for all*

*Out in the open
with friends*

SKY

FIRE

Fire under the sky. Friends gathering around
a fire under the open sky.

Cooperation, harmony, and synergy. Teamwork.

This hexagram describes people who are alike
and share things with each other.

When like-minded people are united by a common
purpose, great things will be achieved.

LINE 6   With others in open lands

You are in unfamiliar territory with new people. Be open and friendly. The end of one thing and the beginning of another.

LINE 5   Tears, then laughter

The trouble you feared will probably happen. You will survive the danger and be with your friends again.

LINE 4   Climbing the wall and not attacking

Take the high ground. Make your stand from a secure position. If you do this, no force or aggression will be necessary.

LINE 3   Looking for friends with weapons hidden

Some people seek friendship, while keeping their aggressive intentions hidden. Friends should openly join in of their own free will. If you don't play favorites, you can be trusted by all.

LINE 2   Trouble with friends in the temple

You may be taking up with whoever happens to be around, or only with those who flatter you. Family squabbles, in-fighting, and favoritism. Choose your friends carefully and avoid trouble.

LINE 1   Meeting friends over the gate

Getting together with others in informal surroundings. Open your doors and open your heart to all people equally. No need for secrecy. On first meeting people, see the best in them, without prejudice.

A REAL-LIFE ADVENTURE

Green Harvest

The spiritual community we had joined in Hawaii owned a great deal of land, with some fifty acres opening out into wild land and jungle. We found out that it was being used for growing *pakalolo* (Hawaiian for crazy smoke or marijuana).

We were in a situation where the government "green harvest"—the helicopters that patrolled the island at harvest time—were circling over the temple, where we were involved in a month-long silent retreat. The helicopters were definitely not conducive to higher states of awareness. If the plants were discovered, it could mean legal problems for all the members of the spiritual community, even though we were not active participants.

Q What is the situation, and where are we in it?
What to do, what to do?

A We received Hexagram 13, with line 5 moving.

Hexagram 13 means that you are linked in with a group dynamic—in karmic union, so to speak. A marriage of sorts. For better or for worse?

Line 5 says you are not paranoid. Your fears are justified. The situation will be a cause of upset. Tears, then laughter. Expect trouble, and expect to survive.

After our initial nervousness on first discovering the situation, we calmed down and got on with our meditation practice.

On the final day of the retreat, we heard the helicopters hovering over the temple again. They landed, unloaded armed police, and took all the plants they could find. Trouble, as expected, but no further action was taken and we did survive.

PROSPERITY

AFFLUENCE

POSSESSIONS

Having it all

Great wealth is a blessing

FIRE

SKY

Fire in the sky. The sun at noon, giving the idea of the peak of richness and success.

The yin line, in the fifth place, possesses all the other yang lines; like a king at ease in his palace.

The Chinese description of this hexagram is being whole, complete, or fully grown.

When you have good fortune, it is your responsibility to do right by it. Those who have fulfilled themselves and have something to spare, be it money or love, are capable of generosity.

Wealth and endowments make great achievements possible.

LINE 6   With heaven's help, do anything

The benefits you receive, your talents and good fortune, are a gift of the universe. Give thanks for them and use them well. Eventually, your undertakings are blessed with good fortune.

LINE 5   Mutual trust, good fortune

The power of leadership is in encouraging others to willingly give the best of themselves. Your sincerity will make it safe for others to be open and honest. Your greatest asset is self-discipline.

LINE 4   Not boasting averts harm

You may have good fortune but feel no need to boast about it. In this way you avoid resentment from others. No pretenses are needed. Be yourself.

LINE 3   Only a great person can make such an offering

Share your good fortune with others. It takes a generous person to make such a gesture. Using good fortune for personal gain will not work in the long run.

LINE 2   Unharmed in a big carriage

You have the balance and wisdom to put your talents to good use. You are being helped on your way and are traveling in style.

LINE 1   Doing no harm keeps harm from you

Give others no cause to resent your good fortune. Kindness from you invites kindness to you. Stay out of trouble and trouble will stay away from you. Protect yourself from harm, without being aggressive.

REAL-LIFE ADVENTURES

Hidden Treasure

Geneva, Switzerland: Rod was on his way to check out the mystery contents of a safety deposit box left to him many years before by his late father. Great possibilities, or nothing at all?

Q What is in store?

A Rod received Hexagram 14, with line 5 moving.

Hexagram 14 implies wealth and good fortune. Hallelujah!

Line 5 is the position of self-mastery, where one uses the good fortune beneficially.

The contents were a terrific surprise: family heirlooms from a past that Rod hadn't even known existed. There were some beautiful Hungarian china and embroidery, as well as one exquisite diamond ring from his grandmother.

New Year's Surprise

October 29, 1980: Prior to the Carter/Reagan U.S. presidential election, President Carter was desperately trying to free American hostages in Iran, a feat that would be a determining factor for him in the upcoming election. So far, so bad.

Q What are the chances of the hostages being released by election day, November 4?

A We received Hexagram 14, with line 6 moving.

Hexagram 14 sure looks good. Having it all!

Line 6 says "eventually blessed by good fortune." Okay. The hostages will be released. *Eventually* is the key word here.

Two months later, less than an hour after Ronald Reagan, having won the election, officially took office, the hostages were released. As predicted by the *I Ching,* and too late to help Jimmy Carter in his re-election bid.

Line 6 often indicates after the end of something, and for Carter it was. Someone couldn't have planned it better!

15

HUMILITY

MODESTY

GENTLENESS

Not seeking praise or avoiding blame

The blessing of modesty is success

EARTH

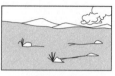

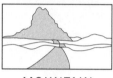

MOUNTAIN

Mountain under the earth. Where there is confidence, there is no need to boast.

The Chinese considered this hexagram to embody the finest human qualities.

This does not mean that you remain inactive. Your activity carries no residue of pride or accomplishment.

Simply do what needs to be done, without looking for any rewards.

LINE 6 Field the army, conquer cities

Use your reputation as a selfless leader to attract others to your cause. Even for those who are more comfortable in the background, there is a time when decisive action is the correct course.

LINE 5 Misfortune from a neighbor, favorable to attack

It is necessary to protect yourself from misfortune. This is a time when you must act. If your cause is just and you do not brag about your success, you will succeed.

LINE 4 Favorable to take action

Modesty cannot be used as an excuse for inaction any longer. Do what needs to be done without losing your quality of humility.

LINE 3 Modest despite achievements

Quietly do your job and carry it through to completion. Your achievements do not alter your humble attitude. Success does not go to your head. Just doing your job.

LINE 2 The expression of peacefulness

You have a reputation for modesty. This quality of unassuming competence is so much a part of you that it is you, and how you are known. This is your natural self-expression.

LINE 1 Modestly modest, cross the big river

Your unassuming self-confidence carries you forward successfully. Difficult undertakings succeed when you simply do what needs to be done.

REAL-LIFE ADVENTURES

End of an Era

August 1991: Gorbachev has disbanded the Communist party in the Soviet Union.

Q Was this the correct move for Gorbachev to make?

A We received Hexagram 15, with line 4 moving.

Hexagram 15 concerns itself with right action—acting from the highest motivation, without thought of personal reward.

Line 4 advises taking action. Modesty doesn't prevent you from acting. Be responsible.

Later on in the same year, the Soviet Union was disbanded by the people, with Gorbachev's help, and soon after that Gorbachev resigned from office.

There was definitely action taken. As to the question of humility and motivation, we can only guess.

Right Action

A college friend in his second year of college had yet to make a career choice. The day of this reading he had laughingly said that maybe he'd go into the field of therapy like us, because there was probably good money in it.

That comment felt insensitive to us. If you want to help people, you help. If you want to make money, do that. This seemed at the root of his confusion. Be a yuppie or be a person of integrity.

Q How do I achieve harmony and balance in my life?

A He received Hexagram 15, with line 5 moving.

Hexagram 15 is about right behavior. About being a good person and acting with humility and modesty.

Line 5 is the chief line of the hexagram. Being a modest person doesn't mean inaction. You do act, but from what motivation?

Find out who you are before you decide what you want to do. Act because it is the right thing to do, not because you will turn a profit.

16

MOTIVATION

INSPIRATION

ENCOURAGEMENT

THUNDER

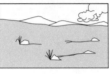

EARTH

*Let's get the show
on the road*

*Appoint helpers, make
your move*

Thunder over the earth. From the stillness of
the earth comes movement and activity. Thunder
generates excitement and anticipation.

Thunder is the music that stirs the planet
and the people into action.

When life feels stale, and you are in a rut, find inspiration
with a new project, or with singing and dancing.

Singing and dancing bring us into harmony with each
other and the cosmos, raising our spirits and energy.

LINE 6   Misguided enthusiasm, change your ways

You have become deluded by your own enthusiasm. You are really in the dark. If you change your ways, you will come to no harm. Wake up from your confused and wasted efforts.

LINE 5   Chronic illness, but no death

Laziness and a difficulty in motivating yourself are not helped by letting others do what you should be doing. This will only weaken you and give others power over you.

LINE 4   The source of inspiration

You are the source of inspiration for others, a guiding light. You have the ability to encourage others to follow your lead.

LINE 3   Looking elsewhere for encouragement

It is better that you rely on your own efforts rather than looking to others to provide for you. You are the only person who can change things. No one else will do it for you.

LINE 2   Steady as a rock, your time has come

Your steadiness and persistence pay off. In not wavering from your principles, good fortune comes to you. Do what needs to be done. Your time has come.

LINE 1   Boasting in public, misfortune

You are expecting more than the situation can give. You may be pretending to be happier than you really are, or boasting of attainments that you are uncertain of. Relax, ease up.

REAL-LIFE ADVENTURES

On the Road Again

Off the road, at home in England, where we had been happily living as a threesome. The perfect couple plus one, so everyone said. The glamour and novelty of our love affair was wearing thin. We still loved one another, but our life together had begun to feel stale and repetitive, laden with emotional problems. Daily life felt like a tread-mill. We recognized the difficulties in sustaining a growing relation-ship among the three of us.

Q What to do? Where to go with our love affair?

A We received Hexagram 16, with line 3 moving.

Hexagram 16 is concerned with relieving inertia in a situation, and getting moving again.

Line 3 indicates that you are indeed getting stale. This condition gradually dawns on you. When you finally feel some urgency, then you make a move.

Get off your butt. Play some music. Have an adventure. To spark things up, the happy threesome took off for India.

Did we blow out of this? You can believe that we did. We were on the road together in Asia and continuing around the planet for over two years. We not only got out of the rut, we flew into the stratosphere.

Back in the Saddle

An equestrian friend was considering having a hip replacement op-eration. At that time, this was a fairly new surgical technique. Our friend was long acquainted with pain and immobility. She had been unable to walk without pain or to ride horses at all for years. Would the operation be a success? Was it worth the risks?

Q Would having a hip replacement operation be beneficial?

A She received Hexagram 16, with line 4 moving.

Hexagram 16 indicates movement arising from stillness. Mobility.

Line 4 expresses breaking out of the ties that bind you. In this instance, a physical immobility of long standing.

The last we heard from our horseback-riding friend, she was back in the saddle again, following two successful hip operations.

17

PURSUIT

AMBITION

THE CHASE

Go for it

The hunt is successful

LAKE

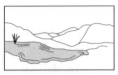

THUNDER

Thunder within the lake. Thunder in the
lower trigram represents action that stimulates
the self-expression of the lake.

The story is of a soldier earning merit by taking captives
for his king. Those were tough times.

Encouraging for taking action and
seeking what you want.

Fulfill your ambitions. Follow your bliss.

LINE 6   Bound with rope, or bound by loyalty

The hunter is now caught, either by the enemy or by bonds of loyalty. One can be captivated by negativity and desires, or be devoted to higher aspirations.

LINE 5   Loyalty is rewarded

Loyal actions are rewarded with success. Truth and goodness shall follow you all the days of your life.

LINE 4   The hunt is over

You have gained everything you need. It would be wise to take a pause. To continue is greedy and would generate envy.

LINE 3   Catch the big one, let the little one go

You are very close to your goal. Give up something of lesser value in order to achieve your objective.

LINE 2   Holding the little one, losing the big one

You still have a way to go. In holding onto something lesser, you lose the possibility of gaining something greater.

LINE 1   Persevere despite a loss, get out and about

You suffer a misfortune from which you recover. A setback may spur you into activity. Ultimately, it works in your favor.

REAL-LIFE ADVENTURES

Having Your Cake and Eating It Too

We were in a quandary. We had a house, a safe refuge with a feeling of security, but we felt trapped financially—rich in land, and poor in dollars; we loved our lifestyle, but we needed to make a radical change.

We had just put our country home in England up for sale, and we received an offer that seemed too low. It was in fact "our bottom line," but dreams die hard. We weren't quite ready to accept the bottom line.

Q Do we take this offer on the sale of our house?

A We received Hexagram 17, with line 2 moving.

Hexagram 17 means actively seeking something. On a hunt. In this case, seeking the one buyer for our property.

Line 2 speaks of goals and choices. As to the goal part, the life we were living was far from our dreams. Selling this house and moving on were only the first parts of that dream of study, travel, and teaching. We were far from our goal. As to the choices, we understood the necessity of letting go of something very dear to our hearts for the greater possibility.

Should we be careful, stay safe, or go for it? A choice had to be made. We could have inquired again of the *I Ching,* if this question of values had been uncertain.

In this instance, we had looked long and hard at the prospect of selling our home, and felt clear as to our interpretation. We went for it. No regrets.

Not Dead Yet

March 30, 1981: President Reagan had just been shot in the left side by a would-be assassin. We had no idea whether he would die, be crippled, or what.

Q What will be the outcome of this attack on the president?

A We received Hexagram 17, with line 1 moving.

This is a very active hexagram. Going for what you want, and having success.

Line 1 indicates that, despite a loss, you will be spurred on to greater activity. And that was the case. Reagan made an amazingly quick recovery. Here's one for the "Gipper"!

18

DECAY

REPAIR

RESPONSIBILITY

Do your duty

Work on what needs fixing

MOUNTAIN

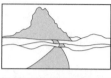

TREE

The tree is under the mountain. The mountain represents an obstacle, a burden to the tree. If it isn't removed, the tree will rot and decay.

The story is of a young man who must temporarily leave his own family because his aging father is ill. He must mind his father's store until he recovers.

Something in your life needs to be repaired. If you are willing to take time off to do it, you will soon return to your original path.

LINE 6   Serve not the mighty, serve a higher purpose

With faultless motivation, you may act in accordance with your most noble aspirations, even when it means breaking some of the rules.

LINE 5   Praised for helping your father

Someone needs your help, and you are praised for giving it. It is worth doing, even though there may be some regrets.

LINE 4   Failing to help your father

You have ignored something until it became a crisis. Overcorrecting now will only make matters worse. Wait till you find the right way to go about it.

LINE 3   Having to help out your father

Impatient and regretful at putting off your own life in order to help someone else. It will work out for the best in the long run.

LINE 2   The son helping his mother, not appropriate

This problem may not be your responsibility. In China it is the daughters who look after their mothers, and the sons who look after their fathers.

LINE 1   The son helping his father, appropriate

You see the need, and set out to handle it right away. Your enthusiasm and energy will see you through, even if you are new to this.

REAL-LIFE ADVENTURES

The Responsibility of Friendship

We felt that we had lost a special closeness with a good friend. How should we deal with this? We also needed to know if our perception was correct. Perhaps it was just too long between letters and visits.

Q What is the true nature of this relationship?

A We received Hexagram 18, with line 2 moving.

Hexagram 18 has to do with handling problems that are distracting you from your main goal.

This happens in relationships all the time. People go out of communication with each other and don't really know why. My fault? Your fault? Does this out-of-communication feeling have nothing to do with me at all? Who knows or remembers?

Line 2 says that there is a problem, and it's not your problem.

When we finally got in touch with our friend, he told us that he had been caught up in a very personal crisis. It was not our relationship that was troubling him at all. His whole life had become a problem for him. We had taken it personally, believing that there was discord between us. Once communication was restored, our friendship was back on the rails.

Needing to Be Needed

We had recently begun practicing and studying with a terrific t'ai chi teacher and comrade since our return to England. We all shared the idea of disseminating this wonderful new art to our friends and neighbors.

We were uncertain about presenting ourselves as teachers. Another martial arts teacher? Big deal. What's more, it would take much time and energy—why get involved? Ego, surely. Right?

Q On starting a practice in t'ai chi at the town hall—please advise correct conduct.

A We received Hexagram 18, with line 1 moving.

Hexagram 18 seemed to refer here to doing what you must. The need was within us to come forth. The duty and responsibility are toward yourself and the expression of your personal needs. After all, the students were not on our doorstep demanding that we teach them.

Line 1 says break out of your personal sense of confinement. When you put yourself on the line and are willing to take responsibility for what you know, the self-doubts drop away.

19

TAKING ACTION

ENCOUNTER

INVOLVEMENT

About to take off

Growing energies will eventually decline

EARTH

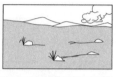

LAKE

Earth over the lake. The expressive energy of the lake moves upward. The earth, or the meadow, represents receptivity. Something is manifesting or breaking into existence. A crisis, a fork in the road, things coming to a head. Something wonderful is about to happen.

The Chinese word for this hexagram means to supervise or control. Also, gaining influence, and decisive leadership.

Take advantage of the good times, remembering to put something aside for a rainy day. Focus your energies.

LINE 6   Sincere and impeccable encounter

You may have already peaked and moved on. From this new perspective, you are free to express your deepest feelings of what is right and true.

LINE 5   Wise leadership

You have the wisdom to look within and find the correct way to handle an important decision. The noble qualities of wisdom, compassion, and action come together in this line.

LINE 4   Perfect handling

People are persuaded by your sincerity and integrity. You are in a position to resolve a crisis in a calm, quiet, and unobtrusive manner.

LINE 3   Reckless moves, bad idea

A complacent and careless attitude in a time of crisis will lead to trouble. Realize your error now and you will avoid calamity.

LINE 2   Being an example for others

Moving out of an old situation into a new one. Opposition will be successfully resolved. You are a positive influence on others.

LINE 1   Friends visit

Coming together with friends. You are an inspiration.

REAL-LIFE ADVENTURES

Beginning Again

After a break of several years, in which we were not practicing as therapists, but rather spent our time quietly in meditation and retreat, we were asked to practice again by a friend needing our help.

This was a young woman, eighteen years old, confused about her identity, and with weight problems. A situation that certainly warranted some counseling.

Q We asked about the advisability of returning to our practice as therapists.

A We received Hexagram 19, with line 6 moving.

Hexagram 19 encourages taking action. The overall sense of the hexagram was telling us to move forward.

Line 6 says to come forth with honesty.

When giving advice, there is an inclination to either demand that others accept your opinion or to say what will please people—rather than straightforwardly saying what you really feel about the situation.

We had ceased to practice as therapists because the conventional methods in which we had been trained were no longer working for us. We had peaked professionally, and instead of going backward, we wanted to begin anew.

This would mean acting honestly and practicing a more holistic approach. This is what we did.

The Raw Energy Needed

Van Nuys, California, 1979: We were visiting Amy's mom and dad. Her father had been complaining for weeks prior to our visit of continuous indigestion. At our insistence, he finally saw his doctor and was diagnosed as having had a series of heart attacks. He was rushed to the hospital.

Q What will be the immediate outcome for Dad?

A We received Hexagram 19, with line 5 moving.

Hexagram 19 says that the energy is there. Good!

Line 5 is a generally favorable position. You are in a position of power. Good, again.

Dad did pull through and is with us today.

HarperSanFrancisco?

We were immersed in our marketing campaign for the first edition of *The I Ching Made Easy* when we were discovered in the unsolicited manuscript pile at HarperSanFrancisco's editorial offices. An unsolicited manuscript hits the big time? It can happen. A little like winning the lottery.

Q Will we sign a contract of partnership with HarperSanFrancisco?

A We received Hexagram 19, with line 5 moving.

Hexagram 19 describes success about to happen, the fork in the road, the turning point that opens up a new vista. Something long imagined comes into real existence.

Line 5 is immensely favorable. A position of authority and delegating responsibility. This is certainly a good omen for making a deal. If you are reading this book now, you know the agreement was a success.

20

CONTEMPLATION

PERSPECTIVE

OBSERVATION

Thinking it through

Wash your hands before making the offering

TREE

EARTH

A tree on the open plains. The tree is also the wind, which blows over the earth searching far and wide and spreading its influence. To see and be seen.

She purifies herself and says a prayer before making her offering. Instead of going ahead automatically, she pauses, creating an alert and observing mind.

Pause, prepare, and collect yourself before doing something of importance. Find a new and fresh perspective. Stop, look, and listen.

LINE 6   Observing others, flawless

You are in a position to observe and form an intelligent opinion on the condition of others, without becoming involved.

LINE 5   Observing oneself, flawless

You have sufficient clarity of mind to evaluate your own actions. Your value is measured by the effect you have on those around you.

LINE 4   The guest observes the kingdom

You've been invited to participate in a venture. Judge the value of this in the way you are treated, and in the atmosphere of your new surroundings.

LINE 3   Observing the ups and downs of life

Carefully look at your past in order to make the best choices for the future. Emphasize and utilize your best traits.

LINE 2   Peering out from behind a curtain

Fear and unfamiliarity are the reasons for your nonparticipation. This is all right. On the other hand, if you are involved, act with courage.

LINE 1   A child's-eye view

It is correct for a child to have an innocent and simple view of the world. For an adult, this may manifest as prejudice, narrow-mindedness, and ignorance.

A REAL-LIFE ADVENTURE

Charlie's Story

In 1981 Amy's son, Charlie, was a young man at the beginning of his career as a filmmaker. One of his first film projects was to do a biography of his father, who is a sculptor.

Q How should I approach this task?

A He received Hexagram 20, with line 4 moving.

Hexagram 20 says get your head straight before going ahead.

Stop and consider all the possibilities.

Charlie, as director/producer/writer of this film, was confident he could fulfill his end. But he hadn't considered his father's attitude toward the project. Would the father be able to have the son in charge?

Finding a new perspective was the specific advice in this hexagram that took Charlie's attention. He assumed that agreement to work together meant cooperation and respect. He was taking things at face value. In fact, the project was not entirely harmonious.

Line 4 indicates a need to carefully check out the new scene.

This advice described perfectly all the elements in Charlie's situation as well. Now he was grown up and was returning to his father with fresh credentials. No longer as a child, but as an independent person.

He went to see his father with this advice in mind, and we think it helped him through the difficult transition from child to man in this relationship with his father. As it turned out, the transition was more difficult for the father to make than for the son.

21

EFFORT

DETERMINATION

MAKING IT GO RIGHT

Let justice be done

Biting through obstructions

FIRE

THUNDER

Fire over thunder. The thunder and fire
are like thunder and lightning in a storm. Shocking
and invigorating at the same time.

Intention without reservation is needed to
overcome the obstacles in your path.

The theme the Chinese gave this hexagram is a
person chewing through an obstruction with intense
determination. The lines describe a person chewing through
different kinds of dried meat or beef jerky.

Now is the time to confront the situation
squarely, without avoiding it. This may well require
discipline and corrective measures.

LINE 6 Wearing a heavy yoke that covers the ears

You have gone too far and are deaf to the advice of others. A prisoner of your own arrogant, heedless ignorance. You have ears that do not hear.

LINE 5 Biting into choice dried meat, find gold, be careful

Your determined action has gotten you a valuable prize. If you become too attached to it, it will be your downfall. Swallowing gold was once thought to be fatal.

LINE 4 Biting into bony gristle, finds an arrowhead

You are determined to get to the heart of a tough and long-standing matter. By energetically attacking the problem, you come up a winner.

LINE 3 Biting into dried meat, finds poison

Confronting the bitter experiences of the past enables you to progress. You may feel ashamed of something you have done. This is your chance to put it right.

LINE 2 Biting so deep as to lose your nose

You are impatient and obsessive. You are too close to the situation to see it clearly.

LINE 1 Shackles on the feet prevent error

Early on, you are restrained from making a wrong move. A word of caution is all that is needed for you to mend your ways.

REAL-LIFE ADVENTURES

Facing the Music

We often do *I Ching* birthday readings for the year ahead. Our friend Darrell asked for a reading for his year ahead.

Q What will 1990 bring for me?

A He received Hexagram 21, with line 5 moving.

Hexagram 21 is about coming clean, making amends, putting things right.

Darrell was involved in a five-year relationship, apparently blissfully content, when he met a new woman and fell passionately in love with her. He had told his long-time mate nothing, and for the last six months had been involved in lies and deception.

Line 5 indicates that you've bitten into the plum pudding and found a gold prize. This has to be handled correctly or it will poison you. Darrell's need for self-discovery and change was so urgent that he had betrayed his mate and best friend.

Now he has to bite the bullet and open his heart to her. Tell his mate all and come clean.

This needs to be done in order to continue in this relationship and begin a new one. Darrell revealed all to her, and she couldn't forgive him the deceit and promptly threw him out. He began his next relationship on this note.

Running After an Illusion

Rod met The Celebrity, a famous actress, in a glamorous circumstance, and they were mutually attracted. Would this be meaningful, or the relationship from hell?

Q What is the potential for this relationship?

A Rod received Hexagram 21, with line 2 moving.

Hexagram 21 asks you to confront the situation head-on without avoiding it. This is not an easy task when you are starstruck. Is it glamour or the real thing?

Line 2 indicates a loss of perspective. You're so close to it that you can't see what you're looking at. This reading offered just enough space for him to take a break and take a look.

The actress's facade dissipated when the crowds thinned, and the woman finally emerged as herself. A whole new person. Biting through can mean biting through the illusions in your own mind.

Was the celebrity pre-Amy? Did they or didn't they? No, she wasn't, and no, they didn't.

22

BEAUTY

CELEBRATION

ACCEPTANCE

The life of the party

Adornment is blessed

MOUNTAIN

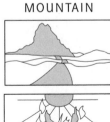

FIRE

Mountain over the fire. The fire represents the desire to join or be part of, and the mountain represents something stable or established.

The lines describe a suitor going to meet his prospective bride. He is looking his best, and though his gifts are small, he is accepted.

Make the most of what you have and who you are. When we seek the best in each other, that is what we find.

LINE 6   Dressed in plain white

Sometimes the finest display is plain and simple. Excessive adornment hides the essential nature of things. Beauty is truth, and truth is beauty.

LINE 5   Though the roll of silk offered is small, it is decorated with garden scenes

Though your gifts may not be the grandest, they are beautiful and offered with the best of intentions. Modest gifts given with good intentions are always well received.

LINE 4   Halted on a white horse; he comes not to rob, but to marry

If you feel awkward in new circumstances, declare your peaceful intentions, and you will be accepted and trusted by others.

LINE 3   The adornments glisten with dew.

Be willing to get involved and face difficulties if you wish to change things. When you look and feel your best, you will attract the favorable attention of others.

LINE 2   Trimming your beard

Looking good helps you feel good. Improve yourself by copying the righteous actions of others. Imitation is the sincerest form of flattery. Fit in by adapting to the behavior of others. Beware of vanity.

LINE 1   With feet adorned, leave the carriage and walk

Be willing to be seen for who you really are. Rely on your own opinions rather than the views of others. Time to stand on your own two beautiful feet. Simple people prefer to walk.

REAL-LIFE ADVENTURES

Coming in Out of the Cold

Interesting synchronicity. Two people, one from Great Britain (Rod) and a lama from Nepal, wished to immigrate to the United States. Each had very different individual circumstances, and both received Hexagram 22.

Q How will the immigration cycles work out?

A They both received Hexagram 22; Rod with line 3 moving, and our friend from Nepal with line 4 moving.

Hexagram 22 has to do with being accepted.

In the instance where line 3 was the moving line, there were innumerable difficulties. From the United Kingdom, Rod began his transition from illegal alien to legal alien. Former spouses had to be located and served with papers. Various marriages and divorces needed documentation, which couldn't be found. Years passed, and finally success.

In the instance where line 4 was the moving line, the questioner was a Tibetan refugee from Nepal who was seeking political asylum in the United States. He was immediately accepted upon declaring his intentions and providing the proper credentials.

Stand on Your Own Two Feet

Mollie was at a catastrophically low point in her spiritual routine. All her childhood beliefs had begun to feel unreal and hypocritical. She felt herself to be at a dead end, facing the sense of emptiness in a life, without a belief system. Searching for new ideas or beliefs felt to her like going from one trap to another.

Q My spiritual life feels empty. Please advise.

A Mollie received Hexagram 22, with line 1 moving.

Hexagram 22 says to lighten up.

It is said that when Confucius received this hexagram, he was irritated at being told he was taking himself too seriously.

Line 1 says that the way to be part of things is to be yourself. Things have gotten too formal and stuffy. Break out of routines and expectations. Don't be afraid to be different.

"Leaving the carriage" refers to the formal spiritual systems, the teachings of your past, and the views of others. Be willing to make your own discoveries. That is such a hard thing to do, but sometimes necessary. As Krishnamurti said, "Truth is a pathless land."

23

FALLING DOWN

DISINTEGRATION

SEPARATION

The ground drops away from under your feet

Splitting apart

MOUNTAIN

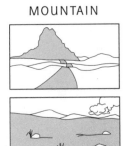

EARTH

Mountain over the earth. The mountain that rises too high above the earth is about to topple. The nightmarish aspect of having a safe refuge destroyed.

A person on a bed is having first the bed, and then himself or herself hacked away. Not a pretty picture.

A stable situation is eroding and deteriorating. Things have run their course and the breaking point has been reached.

Nowhere to go, and no way out. Maintain your generous nature through these difficult times.

LINE 6   A big fruit remains, uneaten

This is a beginning and an end. The seed exists for renewal. Those who hold to eternal truths will survive. Those who are attached to the superficial will be destroyed.

LINE 5   Fish on a line, like a lady-in-waiting

You are no longer in control of the situation or in charge of your destiny. Concede the victory, be a good loser, and you will be protected from the worst of the decay.

LINE 4   The mattress splits

This is a highly unstable position. The slightest deviation will put you into sudden and unexpected danger. You are not immune to misfortune. You are close to disaster.

LINE 3   Cut down to size, blameless

This is the time to break away from bad company and join with honest friends. Choices and distinctions have to be made that may separate you from some of your associates.

LINE 2   The frame of the bed is split

The framework of your life is deteriorating. This is a situation that needs attention and handling. Those you rely on may not be fulfilling their obligations.

LINE 1   The legs of the bed are split

The beginning of a destabilizing influence. What you rely on is eroding. Fix it now. You may have to handle a lack of discipline or wavering intentions in yourself or others.

REAL-LIFE ADVENTURES

Splitting Apart

We were an intimate threesome (the same infamous threesome in the first story of Hexagram 1). We had been traveling together on a pilgrimage in the East for more than a year, through India, Sri Lanka, and Nepal. We traveled in very primitive parts of our planet, together every minute of every day, in circumstances that consistently left a lot to be desired. "Four Star" was in another universe. Indoor plumbing represented the height of luxury on this journey.

The going was getting rougher and rougher. Our practice of patience with one another was wearing thin. We were breaking apart as friends, with great resistance from all concerned.

Q Should we continue our adventure together to the next port of call?

A We received Hexagram 23, with line 6 moving.

Hexagram 23 describes a situation of disintegration. The last glimmer of light is being eroded or attacked, as in the winter solstice, the shortest day of the year. It didn't take a genius or great intuition to read the handwriting on the wall. The final breaking up of our friendship.

Line 6 says the biggest fruit is left uneaten. After everything splits apart, the best of all of us remains. There is never a total destruction. We went our separate ways shortly after doing this reading. Our companion went to a cave in the Himalayas, and we continued the journey together. Our next port of call? Maui. Party on!

Fix It Fast

In 1990 Amy went for her yearly gynecological checkup, feeling fine—and the doctor diagnosed an ovarian cyst. This was considered an extremely serious problem, and surgery was indicated. Thirty days until the next exam, and if the cyst was still there (which was what the medicos assured Amy would be the case), bingo—instant hysterectomy.

Q Please advise on this condition.

A Amy received Hexagram 23, with line 1 moving.

Hexagram 23 is not a happy response to the question. There *is* an existing condition that needs immediate attention.

Line 1 is hopeful because it indicates the beginning of a situation. Correction may still be possible. Fix it now or it will worsen.

In response to the *I Ching* image of erosion and destabilization, Amy was forced to confront both the psychological and physical influences in her life, and change what could be changed.

This included her own attitudes, abusive people, toxins in the body, diet, and exercise. In short, why does the body break down and what can we do to heal ourselves?

Amy went into retreat for those thirty days, with an intense healing regimen, laughingly referred to by us as "the blitz technique." It's thoroughly unscientific, as you include every possible device at your disposal and never know what exactly did the trick.

No matter. Happy endings. The healing occurred. In thirty days the cyst was no more and the medicos had retreated, saying it was probably not there in the first place. Oh, really?

24

RETURN

RENEWAL

REBIRTH

Coming home

Safe return, friends visit

EARTH

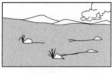

THUNDER

Thunder under the earth represents the
first stirring of spring energy following the sleep
of winter. Coming back to life.

A person returning home after a journey, or
coming back on track after making a detour.

This is a new beginning for you.
Your chance to begin again.

LINE 6   Missed the return

You have caught the tail end of something. Too little and too late. This is only a short-lived affair, a brief encounter. A small obstacle to be overcome before you reach your destination.

LINE 5   Sincere return

By examining your motives, you are able to return to the right path. Holding on to past mistakes is not helpful.

LINE 4   Starting out with others, returning alone

Part company with someone who is leading you astray. This may mean traveling alone.

LINE 3   Repeatedly returning

There is no avoiding this situation. You will be faced with this lesson again and again until you get it right. Perseverance is the key to overcoming these dangers.

LINE 2   A good return

You will return order to your life by correcting any mistakes in your associations. Treat those you depend on with honesty and consideration. Respect good advice.

LINE 1   Returning from a short distance

Returning to your original purpose is easy, as you've only made a brief detour. Errors are quickly seen and soon corrected. Nothing has been lost.

REAL-LIFE ADVENTURES

Death, Emptiness, and Crisis

Rod and Amy in Cambria, California. Living our life by the sea. We were meditating, fasting, writing, walking the dogs. Sounds idyllic, but judging from the question, maybe not. Or maybe just a bad hair day? Only three words in our notes to describe the feelings of this question.

Q Death, emptiness, crisis.

A We received Hexagram 24, with line 3 moving.

Hexagram 24 is returning to the correct or true path. To do that, the errors that led you off the path must be seen and corrected.

Line 3 says that you will be repeatedly faced with these feelings until you handle them decisively. "Repeated returning" means that you're trying a lot of different things and not committing to any one thing. No staying power.

And yet you do keep trying to find some measure of stability. The good part is your continued willingness to give it another go.

Like it or not, these feelings of death and emptiness do arise and cannot be ignored. With the right attitude, these desperate hours offer the opportunity for renewal, however painful the confrontation might be.

Chance for a Rebirth?

For many years we had a healing center in England, but this part of our lives seemed to be coming to an end. We wanted to move on—from England, from that lifestyle, and toward new horizons. It was at this time that we became friends with a blessed spiritual teacher.

We hoped that he might be the inspiration we needed to keep our center open and create a renewal of purpose.

Q Will this teacher be a renewal for us?

A We received Hexagram 24, with line 6 moving.

Hexagram 24 is a return of energy.

Line 6 says you missed the boat.

The immense process of change had already begun for us. This was too little, too late. Our friend, Lama Ganga, died only one year after we threw the coins. His time with us on earth was limited, and it was our time to move on. It was a profound experience, but another path had already been embarked upon for all of us. We were fortunate to have had the opportunity of friendship with this dear man, however brief.

25

UNEXPECTED

SPONTANEOUS

OPENNESS

Act naturally

*Expect nothing,
be as you are*

SKY

THUNDER

Thunder in the sky. Movement represented
by thunder, acts under the inspiring influence of the sky.

"The natural" acts spontaneously in response to
the forces of the universe in a genuine and uncontrived
manner. There is wholehearted sincerity without
deceit. Acting without seeking reward.

The Chinese would say that their actions were
sanctioned by the will of heaven.

Your judgment is not clouded by expectation
or ambition. Be open to inspiration and
unexpected good fortune.

LINE 6   Traveling without a plan invites disaster

The time has passed when you can rely on the inspiration of the moment. Instead of just blundering ahead, stop for a while and develop a plan.

LINE 5   Use no medicine when nothing is wrong

An unexpected misfortune will pass of its own accord. Doing anything will only aggravate the condition. You may be taking on someone else's troubles.

LINE 4   Carry on, no harm will come to you

You are in a time of transition, and may feel isolated and helpless. Everything will be all right if you trust your own judgment and act accordingly.

LINE 3   The traveler takes the ox; his gain, and the farmer's loss

One person's gain is another's loss. Unexpected good or bad luck. Attachment to loss and gain. The attempt to ensure against losses and guarantee gains is impossible. Take what comes.

LINE 2   Reaping without sowing

Involve yourself fully in the action at hand. Let the results take care of themselves. Take advantage of opportunities that are open to you right here and now. Allow it to happen naturally.

LINE 1   Go forward, expecting nothing

If at the very beginning your intentions are pure, then all the actions that follow will be righteous. Act without expectation or hope of reward, and you will succeed.

REAL-LIFE ADVENTURES

Police Story

We are friends with Maxwell, who is homeless and lives out of his van. He is mixed up in the street life, and who knows what else? He asks to use our address for his mail and for some official purposes—we didn't ask what. This is a dubious favor but we like him, so we say sure.

Then the police call, asking after Max. They are vague about why they want to speak with him. This puts us in a bind: Do we stick to the story that he is living at our address, do we rat on him, or do we say we never heard of him? Self-preservation or loyalty to a dubious friend? We told them the truth. That he was using the address but not living with us, and no, we didn't know where he was living.

Just being in contact with the police seemed to generate feelings of fear and guilt. We felt paranoid and nervous. And what had we done? Nothing, other than let a homeless friend use our address.

Q What has happened with Max, and what is our involvement?

A We received Hexagram 25, with line 5 moving.

Hexagram 25 says don't worry, and don't invent explanations.

Line 5 told us that the trouble was not our fault and that it would pass of its own accord. We shouldn't try to change the situation.

The situation did handle itself. Max did whatever needed to be done, and we were out of it. No action on our part was ever needed. There is no misery like worry.

Taking Control

Rod's immigration cycle seemed to be stagnating in a lengthy morass of endless paperwork. He hadn't been actively pushing the process along, but was going with the flow, however turgid. What's the rush? He had allowed things to take their own course, responding to events, rather than forcefully determining them. Expect nothing—and nothing was pretty much what he got.

After a year of nonaction, discontent began to arise. Instead of going with the flow, Rod said, "Come on, let's get a move on. This has been going on for too long, with no results."

Q What is the situation with my immigration status?

A Rod received Hexagram 25, with line 6 moving.

Hexagram 25 is about acting in an unpremeditated way. Acting naturally. That's what he had been doing, but it was no longer working for him.

Line 6 is the end of spontaneity. Now you need to take control of the situation, and develop a plan of action. Line 6 often shows the limit or end of a condition.

Rod did develop an alternate plan of action, which put him more in control of the situation. Any idea that you are really in control when dealing with immigration authorities is only a virtual reality at best.

26

CONTROL

HARNESSING POWER

TAKING THE REINS

Take the bull by the horns

*Eating without sowing,
cross the river*

MOUNTAIN

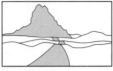

SKY

Mountain over the sky. The energy
of the sky is held fast and controlled by the
stability of the mountain.

This hexagram requires that you be bold
and exert your control.

You are involved with powerful energies.

Stay in charge. Take care of business.

LINE 6 Walking the sky road

Events reach a climax and then reverse. When you have brought everything together and under your control, there is an ease and effortlessness to your actions.

LINE 5 Tying up a castrated pig

You are able to turn harmful actions to good by discovering the source of the error and correcting it. The use of brute force will not work as well as understanding the problem.

LINE 4 Cover the horns of a young bull

It is easy to direct the course of a powerful force in its early stages. Correct bad habits before they control you, and establish beneficial ones.

LINE 3 Practice chariot riding and self-defense daily

The way ahead is open, and you are keen to advance. In your eagerness to move ahead you may become careless. Perfect those abilities you need.

LINE 2 The axle falls off the carriage

In racing forward, you lost your balance and everything fell apart. This is not your fault. Fix it up, and then you can carry on.

LINE 1 Danger is at hand, desist

You are not strong enough yet to rush ahead. Back off and avoid trouble. A powerful friend may advise you to slow down in order to avoid misfortune.

REAL-LIFE ADVENTURES

Taking the Reins

Debbie-Lee came to us for advice in Palm Springs. She was a rape victim, and was clearly unhinged by the violation she had suffered. She had been assaulted more than two years before, and was not yet fully healed mentally.

She had been advised poorly by alleged professionals that she should have made a recovery by now, and it was inferred that she was being self-indulgent. When we met Debbie-Lee, she was suffering from extreme loss of self-esteem.

Q I've been told that I should get on with my life, but I still feel abused and afraid.

A Debbie-Lee received Hexagram 26, with line 2 moving.

Hexagram 26 is about taking charge of your life.

In line 2, the original Chinese text talks about the "axle falling off the cart." When this has happened, everything has to stop until you fix it.

Debbie-Lee's life had fallen apart and she felt it needed to be put together again. Sometimes you have to take time out from regular life and fix what needs to be fixed. We would have no doubt about this if our car wasn't running, but what about when it's our minds? She was able to use the picture of the cart as a simple focus for the work ahead. Whatever works.

The I Ching Made Easy

Close to the completion of the writing of this book, we needed some moral support. We thought we were close to the end. Actually, it was nine months until birthing time. And that was the first edition.

This is the second. Where does it end?

Q Please advise as to *The I Ching Made Easy*.

A We received Hexagram 26, with line 3 moving.

Hexagram 26 indicates the action of controlling a powerful situation.

Line 3 says work at it. You are going to have to work at it on a daily basis. If you do, you will have success.

The reading indicated for us the potential and value of what we were engaged in, and also the need for continual attention to and time for the project. In retrospect, this provided us with the impetus to carry on until we reached completion.

27

FEEDBACK

FULFILLMENT

NOURISHMENT

You are what you eat

*Those who see you feed
your face want some too*

MOUNTAIN

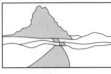

THUNDER

Mountain over thunder. Mountain represents
solid matter, like food. Thunder represents action,
as in chewing and digesting.

The Chinese called this hexagram "cheeks"
or "jaws," and by extension, the act of nourishment.
The upper trigram is the upper jaw, which is fixed. The
lower trigram is the lower jaw, which moves.

The idea that you are what you eat also
refers to the company you keep.

Distinguish between need and greed,
self-development and self-indulgence.

LINE 6　Being the source of nourishment is both dangerous and lucky

You are the source of nourishment. Either your wisdom feeds others, or you are a sacrificial lamb. Once the fulfillment has taken place, you will be free to move on to something new.

LINE 5　Forsaking established ways

Even though you are in charge, accept the influences of those you admire. You may need to act in an unorthodox way. Make no dramatic moves.

LINE 4　Filling your face, the tiger gazes past you

It is now valid to satisfy your needs and wants. The tiger indicates the intensity of your passion. You are able to sidestep the dangers of greed and desire.

LINE 3　A slap in the face

Eating junk food fails to gratify, so you are driven to eat again. Greed has led you to this. Break the habit. What will bring you lasting satisfaction?

LINE 2　If you eat until you choke, you'll get a slap on the back

You are being greedy and causing yourself harm. This is the line of "shop till you drop." Don't you know when enough is enough?

LINE 1　Disregarding your turtle soup, you watch me eat

You have everything you need, and yet you look at what others have with greed and envy. You may be discarding spiritual nourishment for worldly greed.

REAL-LIFE ADVENTURES

Permission to Shop

This is a yearly reading for Amy, done on our move to Bisbee, Arizona, after two years of being on the road. We had just purchased a hundred-year-old house/shack, laughingly described as a "fixer-upper." We're talking intense renovation. We fondly referred to our new domicile as "rubble without a cause."

We looked forward to collecting all our stuff in one place and satisfying our nesting desires and inclinations.

Q What is Amy's yearly reading for 1988?

A Amy received Hexagram 27, with line 4 moving.

Hexagram 27 has to do with satisfying your desires. Finally, a reading we can love.

Line 4 says that you can indulge your desires safely. A rare line indeed. How nice. What great good fortune. Permission to shop.

It was the year to renovate, decorate, and create a stable environment. All the things you can't do when your life is one of continual travel.

Just a Quickie

We had just rented an exceptional apartment on the ocean at Laguna Beach. It seemed great good luck, although it was only a month-to-month agreement.

Q We are both feeling quite nervous and there is a feeling of some big change just around the corner.

A We received Hexagram 27, with line 6 moving.

Hexagram 27 is about being nourished and the company you keep.

Line 6 is the end of nourishment. We nourished our landlords with rent, and we were in turn nourished by our oceanside environment, but this was to be a very brief sojourn in Laguna.

The missing piece of information as to why we could only have this great apartment on a month-to-month basis finally came to light. Our landlords had neglected to fill us in on a few important details.

The male half of the twosome who owned the apartment we were renting was awaiting sentencing on a child abuse charge. He had already been found guilty, and if sentenced to a jail term (which is what did happen), they would have to sell their house to get money for appeals and lawyers.

The Book-Signing from Hell

We did this reading during a book-signing, which indicates how much attention we were getting. We were feeling like we would have done better across the street at the Jiffy Lube garage. We were in our strongest phase in the marketing of our book, and defeating the competition meant using every available device.

Q What is happening here? Are we invisible?

A We received Hexagram 27, with line 3 moving.

Hexagram 27 says you are who or what you eat. Why are you doing a book-signing in a discount supermarket in a Tucson summer heat wave (that's 125° Fahrenheit in the shade)? What is at work here? Desperation or greed?

Line 3 is the junk food line. Food that does not nourish just leads to more desire for more nourishment. The Chinese advise not doing this again for ten years (book-signings in supermarkets?). We agree. It was an inappropriate source of nourishment. People were coming in with cartons of old books to sell or exchange in a store as big as some small towns. Poor psychic nourishment for these two nervous authors.

28

PRESSURE

TENSION

TRANSCENDENCE

I've had all I can take

The roof beam sags

LAKE

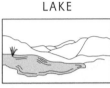

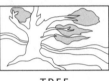

TREE

The tree is under the lake. It has been
overwhelmed with water and is drowning.

The four yang lines in the middle are too heavy
and are going to break out of the structure.

Picture a building with so many extra rooms, furniture,
and decorations that the columns and beams supporting it
are sagging under the weight. It might collapse at any moment.
The whole situation has become too weighty. You don't have
the energy to carry on this way. Something fundamental
has to change, and then you can start afresh.

Free yourself from any burdens and move on.
Prepare to stand alone.

LINE 6 In over your head

You are getting in too deep and overextending yourself. Going beyond what is reasonable leads to disaster. Good intentions may have turned to delusions of grandeur.

LINE 5 Withered willow makes flowers, old wife gets young man

A cosmetic fix that does not handle the underlying situation. A burst of useless glory. You may be taking on something past its prime. It will not last long.

LINE 4 Roof beam is strengthened

You have the strength and support to take the pressure. You may have successfully made a difficult transition from an excessive or uncomfortable situation. Do not add to the burden.

LINE 3 Roof beam sags to breaking point

You cannot take the pressure. This is unfortunate for you. Look for some help.

LINE 2 Withered willow sprouts shoots, old man gets young wife

An unusual but productive union of two extremes; strength balanced with gentleness. A new lease on life. A balancing act.

LINE 1 Spread white rushes under the offering

Carefully prepare a soft place on which to gently put a heavy load. In dealing with powerful forces, be exceedingly deferential and pliant.

A REAL-LIFE ADVENTURE

Taking the Pressure

Since the beginning of our mutual discovery of meditation, we had a personal dream of doing a retreat from the world, going on a walk-about like the aboriginals, or becoming *babas*—holy people, like the Hindus in India.

The Hindus believe that when their families are grown, they are free to let go of worldly goods and affairs and search out their spiritual truths. In India full-time holy men are made—not born. They just go out there on the streets and practice until they get it right. Just for the guys. No women becoming holy women. Plenty of females in their pantheon of goddesses and gods, but not in real life.

Here in the West, however, hitting the road with only a back-pack, prepared to beg for sustenance, is equated with homelessness, indigence, vagrancy, and so on. We have no word for *babas* here, and no place for them. Deep retreat and leaving the world is not as possible for us.

Four years had passed since we had decided to do a long retreat. We traveled the planet searching for a retreat location and finally found an appropriate situation, only to spend the next year and a half making it habitable. This had better be a powerful goal.

When we finally had all our necessities set up, however, we had no inclination to do the type of retreat we had envisioned several years before. Instead, we became involved in writing the book you are now reading, and making our meditation a part of ordinary life.

Still, we wondered what the other path would have been like. We fixed the house so that we could do a retreat in it, but that is not what we are doing.

Q What is happening with our spiritual practice?

A We received Hexagram 28, with line 4 moving.

Hexagram 28 is about dealing with the burden of responsibility. The image is of the "roof beam" straining to bear a heavy weight. Giving yourself too hard a time. Ease up. You need to proceed easily, without becoming too intense.

Line 4 says that you are capable of bearing the burden. There does seem to be a division or separateness here of having to live one lifestyle or the other; a spiritual life or a worldly one. Surely they co-exist somewhere?

We still find it difficult to create a space for our meditation practices in our worldly lives, and often need to "get away" from our daily routine and head for the hills.

Recently, we had to give up the opportunity to go on retreat with His Holiness the Dalai Lama, who was giving a teaching on compassion and patience. He was only an hour away from our home—it was the chance of a lifetime. Instead, it was family crisis time; our ill and aging parents needed our close attention for several weeks. Could we say that our parents had to fend for themselves so that we could learn all about compassion and patience? Get over yourself!

The spiritual practice is life, and life is the spiritual practice.

29

ABYSS

CRISIS

PITFALL

WATER

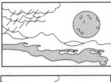

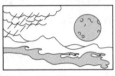

WATER

Dark night of the soul

*Trust your heart and you
will get through*

Water over water. Water signifies toiling alone in dangerous
circumstances. Double water is double trouble.

The Chinese for this hexagram is a pit, booby trap,
or hole. Danger and crisis. Primeval chaos.

Pits were used to confine prisoners in ancient China.
The pits were often filled in and the prisoner buried alive.
So much for the good old days.

You will succeed by maintaining an unshakable and abiding
trust in your own deepest instinct of what is right.

LINE 6   Tied up in a prison hedged by thorns

Trying to get out of trouble just got you in deeper and deeper. You could not help yourself. This is not a good situation. There is no escape, but you will survive.

LINE 5   The earth runs out before the pit fills in

Your troubles come to an end just before they completely overwhelm and destroy you. You will not be buried, but it will be close.

LINE 4   Wine and grain lowered down by rope

Help comes to you in your hour of need. In the end you come to no harm. Economize in a time of crisis. A small and sincere gesture will suffice.

LINE 3   Falling into the pit, doing nothing

There is nothing you can do about your dangerous condition; therefore do nothing. You have been living with danger for so long that you have become accustomed to it.

LINE 2   Surrounded by pits, small gains

You are safe for the moment, but surrounded by danger. Cautiously seek to improve your situation by going around obstacles you cannot overcome.

LINE 1   Falling into the pit, misfortune

You have fallen into a dangerous place; a pit within a pit. Unfamiliarity may have led you to overestimate your ability, resulting in a careless repetition of errors.

A REAL-LIFE ADVENTURE

Do Not Pass "Go"—Go Directly to Jail

In Hawaii, in the 1980s, we were head residents at a retreat center. The main house was only approachable by carved steps zigzagging up the mountain through an immense guava forest. Those who made it up that hill to the center were ready for the welcome of a cup of green tea and an open ear. Everyone had a story to tell.

Two days before Christmas, Nick made his way up the mountain. A therapist, he had become addicted to prescription drugs. When his doctor refused to prescribe more drugs for him, in the madness of his addiction, he forged his own prescriptions. He had been caught, tried, and found guilty. He was about to receive his sentence.

Q Am I going to go to jail?

A Nick received Hexagram 29, with line 6 moving.

Hexagram 29 means you are in trouble. It seemed inevitable that Nick would have to pay his dues.

Line 6 indicated with certainty that he did have to go to jail, and he did.

The "date hedges" referred to in line 6, which had brutal thorns, were used as a barbed wire fence in ancient China, to keep in prisoners, cattle, and so on.

The sentence was much shorter than he had feared it might have been. We kept in touch with him. The term in jail did not handle his addiction, however, and so the madness continues.

30

NURTURE

RELIANCE

SHINING

Mutual support

Raising cattle is good

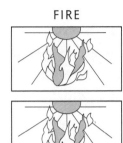

FIRE

FIRE

Fire within the fire. Fire represents our intimate connection with each other, and thus our dependence on each other.

Fire depends on fuel for its existence. The fuel is represented by the yin lines and the fire by the yang lines in the hexagram.

In order to shine out, be brilliant and flamboyant, the fire must cling closely to its source of energy.

Plants and trees depend on the sun and soil. What do you depend on for your strength? When you know what this is and nurture it, you will shine in your brilliance.

LINE 6 March forth and capture enemies

This is your chance to root out the source of destructive influences once and for all. It is not necessary to engage in wholesale correction when you have isolated the source of the problem.

LINE 5 It is good to cry

Grief and regret for past errors demonstrates your genuine concern. You will do your best, despite your limited ability to help. You may have lost, or gone beyond, your support system.

LINE 4 Fire flares up, burns, dies away, and is soon gone

A temporary burst of enthusiasm with no long-term commitment or foundation will not last long. A flash in the pan. You may tend to jump from one thing to the next.

LINE 3 As the sun sets, beat the drum or sigh with grief

Everything comes to an end sometime. You can either accept this with good humor, or be miserable and depressed. What you have been relying on may no longer be working for you.

LINE 2 A golden glow, very lucky

Your environment is supportive and favorable. You tread a balanced path, free of extreme actions. You see things clearly and in proper perspective.

LINE 1 Wearing golden shoes

You are joining in something for the first time. First steps tend to be awkward and impulsive; be sensitive and willing to adapt. You may have a meaningful encounter with a remarkable person.

REAL-LIFE ADVENTURES

Gorbachev—Remember Him?

In February 1982 we asked the *I Ching* about Premier Gorbachev and how he was doing in reforming the system in Russia.

Q Is Gorbachev a hero, or a Don Quixote chasing windmills?

A We received Hexagram 30, with line 3 moving.

Hexagram 30 says you burn bright as long as you have a support system.

This seemed to mean the support of the people and a system that people believed to be working.

Line 3 says change or succumb. The situation is in a decline. Use what remaining energy and power you still can access to establish a new system.

In these uncertain times, what can you depend on? The Communist system had failed. Gorbachev could either drum up enthusiasm for something new, or go down with the ship. He would need tremendous determination and the support of the people to make it go right.

He did persist through tremendous adversity, and then he was retired. Now, the USSR is no more. The people still have bread lines and no potatoes for the coming winter. What else is new?

Mutual Support

Amy in Maui. A renowned woman teacher was coming to Maui to do a weekend workshop—one of the many New Age workshops of the month. Only women were being invited to participate.

Amy had adverse feelings on one-sex encounter groups. What did gender have to do with one's spiritual life? Of course, the rarity of a woman teaching anything was too good to miss. A dilemma?

Q Please advise on doing this workshop.

A Amy received Hexagram 30, with line 1 moving.

Hexagram 30 is 100 percent affirmative as to group encounter and therapy. Interdependence. No question. Do the weekend. It will be beneficial.

Line 1 speaks of meeting a remarkable person. A precious possibility. All the participants that weekend were remarkable.

With a little help from Amy and friends, the retreat ultimately did include two men with the thirteen women, so that hurdle was leapt over with ease.

31

INFLUENCE

INCISIVE

SENSITIVITY

Give and take

It is good to marry

LAKE

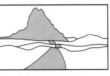

MOUNTAIN

The lake over the mountain. The mountain forces the warm air up, which then cools and forms clouds. Rain falls from the clouds feeding the lake. The lake in turn feeds its moisture to the mountain so that plants and trees can grow.

Lovers are sensitive to each others' every subtle change of mood, and respond accordingly. Each is sensitive to the needs of the other.

Affecting others and, in turn, a willingness to be touched or transformed by them.

Use penetrating and decisive action in making your influence felt and in getting your point across.

LINE 6 Using your mouth

You have the gift of persuasive communication. Use this influence for the good of all people. Resist the temptation to flatter others for selfish ends. Be aware of mindless and cruel talk.

LINE 5 A pain in the neck

Stand firm on your principles and beliefs. Do not let others push you around, even if this results in the end of an involvement. With no regrets, decisively keep your eye on the prize.

LINE 4 Friends respond to your concerns

You are in the midst of activity and confusion. Remain focused on and sensitive to the major issue. Your feeling for others will inspire them to come to your aid.

LINE 3 Taking a step, grabbed by the heels

You have the desire to move forward without clearly knowing what you want. Circumstances may hold you back. Learn to walk before you run.

LINE 2 Restless calves

Resist the impulse to rush forward. You have become involved too soon. You may feel that you have been pushed into something before you are ready. You may move when invited to do so.

LINE 1 Wiggling your toes

When people wiggle their toes they are impatient to get going and have their attention elsewhere. Do not be too hasty in responding at this early stage. This may be just the beginning of big plans.

A REAL-LIFE ADVENTURE

Motormouth

A mutual friend introduced us to a Big-Time (self-professed) New Age Guru, proficient in the ways of crystals and creative channeling and similar current esoterica. She was telling us she could "do things for us," like a Hollywood pitch: "I can get you in the movies, baby. Fame and fortune will be yours." Pushing buttons that we didn't know we had. Is she for real or having us on? Too much praise makes one wonder. Are we really that terrific?

Q About this person. Who is she? Please advise.

A We received Hexagram 31, with line 6 moving.

Hexagram 31 has to do with the way we influence one another and how we respond to that influence.

Line 6 in the ancient text speaks of both the value and the danger in using your mouth. In this case insufficient substance backing up the talk. Be aware and beware.

Little epilogue: Nothing came of her offers to us, but we know, now that our friendship has strengthened with time, that her intentions are good. She was simply promising more than she could deliver, rather than being deceptive.

32

PURPOSEFUL

CONSTANT

PERSISTENT

THUNDER

Seeing it through

Continuing is blessed,
keep to your course

TREE

Thunder over the tree. The tree or wind is a
subtle and unwavering permeation. Thunder is action. Together
they represent the idea of perseverance.

This hexagram describes a marriage, in which the
qualities of flexibility and adaptability are required. You
move like partners circling a dance floor.

Keep your goal in mind as you persist through all the
inevitable obstacles. You will find your way.

LINE 6 Always agitated, not good

All that is constant is your agitation of mind. Being rushed and impatient leaves you open to attack and misfortune. Relax and calm your restless heart.

LINE 5 Loyal obedience, good for followers, bad for leaders

If you are in charge, accept the responsibility by being aggressive and adaptable. If you are not in charge, it is right that you loyally follow the decisions of those who lead. Which are you?

LINE 4 Gets nothing on the hunt

You are going about something all wrong. You may be impatient to progress, but first you need to know what you want and where to find it.

LINE 3 Not keeping your place

If you fulfill your current obligations you will be trusted. You may be tempted to act beyond your means in order to be somewhere else. You may also be plagued by indecision and dissatisfaction.

LINE 2 No more regrets

By letting go of the past and any regrets, you are free to concentrate on the future. Circumstances may not allow the full expression of your talents. Do nothing radical; be calm and adaptable.

LINE 1 Impatiently persistent, not good

You are determined to make a long-term commitment before you know where you are going. Demanding too much. Adapt to what is going on now.

REAL-LIFE ADVENTURES

Brian's Story

Our friend Brian had a business contract to fulfill in Taos, New Mexico, and at the same time he felt a strong need to move on. He understood his ethical obligation to complete his part of the agreement, but at the same time he wanted to begin his new life. Follow that dream.

Q What to do?

A Brian received Hexagram 32, with line 3 moving.

Hexagram 32 is concerned with persistence.

Line 3 indicates that because he is unhappy with his obligation, he is acting in a confused manner and this will get him into trouble.

He's sitting on the proverbial fence. He can't make a move with any degree of certainty. Therefore he should not make any move. He should continue with his present course, as best he can, until he knows what he wants.

He followed the oracle's advice, waited, and thought things through. He concluded, eventually, that although he wanted to explore new avenues in his life, he would move on only when he had completed his obligations.

Being There

Somewhere in Bisbee: We had just completed the renovation of our temple/guest house and were ready to open our doors to our friends and begin morning meditation sessions.

We were eager to do this, but we had doubts. Would we get any response? Should we bother? So much responsibility. Too much? Are we up to it? Being there every morning. What's in it for us?

Q Meditation mornings. What does the future hold?

A We received Hexagram 32, with line 5 moving.

Hexagram 32 indicated that the only future there is for this practice is if we make the future happen through our own efforts.

Line 5 again reiterates the idea of persistence and the assumption of personal responsibility. If you're going to do it, then do it. If not, then don't worry about it. If you are a leader, then lead. If you're a follower, follow.

Interesting response. We compromised somewhat here. Instead of seven mornings each week, we resolved that we were capable of making the effort three times a week.

We persisted with the practice, even on those cold winter mornings when only one or two people made it up the mountain. Our friends confirmed that our always being there, even if they were not able to, was a source of inspiration.

33

RETREAT

WITHDRAWAL

SANCTUARY

SKY

Safe in seclusion

*Little pig, stay where
you are*

MOUNTAIN

Sky over mountain. The strength of the sky has
retreated to the top of the mountain to concentrate on
developing its power. Seclusion is appropriate.

The different aspects of withdrawing from the world,
either by choice or by force of circumstances.

The piglet is either penned up and fattened
for the feast or running for its life.

Now is the time for you to avoid the distractions of
the social world. In conflict or stress, walk away and find a safe
place in which to regain your strength.

Focus on the matter at hand.
Find out who you really are.

LINE 6   Little pig, fat and happy

Having done your best and succeeded, you may now withdraw from the struggle of life and retire in comfort.

LINE 5   Little pig is rewarded for seeing it through

What you set out to do, you accomplished. Congratulations. Now quit while you are ahead. The ability to leave when the party is over is an excellent one.

LINE 4   Only a great person can offer a little pig

Withdrawing from entanglements to concentrate on a specific goal is not as easy as it may seem. If you're going to do it, be prepared to do whatever it takes.

LINE 3   Little pig is tied up

Though you may not want to, you need to withdraw from a situation that you thought was safe, but is no longer. Return to your home base and concentrate on what is most important.

LINE 2   Bound with yellow ox hide, no one can undo it

You have a calm and steadfast determination; an unshakable trust in a great ideal or person you admire. This bond should be a comfort and not confine you.

LINE 1   Piglet turns tail

Retreat from danger as soon as you become aware of it. You are not in a position to cope with it. Leave nothing exposed for others to attack.

A REAL-LIFE ADVENTURE

The Desperate Hours

Early on in our relationship with each other, we planned our first retreat together. We were seeking to quiet our restless minds and wake up from the dream. When we met, we had both been meditating for years, and now we would have a partner for a week-long retreat of fasting (from food, speech, and sex) and meditation.

High up on a distant misty mountainside, in the remote backcountry of the island of Maui, there was a small meditation hut, isolated from the busy world below us.

Off to the mountaintop alone. Here comes one of the great tests of any relationship: Will we still be speaking to each other after a week of nothing but us?

Q Before we go on retreat, what is your advice?

A We received Hexagram 33, with line 4 moving.

Hexagram 33 has to do with going into retreat. A perfect response to this question.

Line 4 indicates that you are in a situation that you may not be up to. This was the case.

We made many agreements for that retreat: In order to eliminate distractions, we would fast from food, speech, sex, and using perfume or ornaments. We had no obligations to the other, other than the support of our presence. One by one, we broke all of these agreements in the course of a single day.

Our motivation was strong, but the task was too great. We had bitten off more than we could chew. We felt that we were merely going through the motions, and that our hearts were not really in it.

If we had paid more attention to the reading, we would never have set ourselves up for such a fall. Or would we have? Human nature persists in failing to or refusing to—read the signs.

Vows are not taken lightly in any tradition. When we next saw our meditation teacher, we expressed our devastation at not having kept our vows. "It's all in the motivation," she told us. "If you began with sincerity, there is no loss, and no failure."

34

BIG AND STRONG

OPPORTUNITY

BREAKING FREE

Going over the wall

*Great strength
correctly applied*

THUNDER

SKY

Thunder over the sky. The tremendous energy of the sky moves
into the action of thunder and frees itself of restraints.

A charging ram is breaking out of its enclosure.
The four yang lines are the ram's body, and
the two yin lines are its horns.

As a powerful person you have an
extraordinary sense of purpose. Enough to break out
of your confinement and shake things up.

Be sure that what you're doing is the right thing.

LINE 6   Horns stuck in the fence

Using brute force is unpopular and will only get you stuck. Relax. The situation will improve on its own. Be gentle and you will achieve the results you seek.

LINE 5   Letting the ram go free

If someone wants to break free, let them go without regret. Let others have their own way. You can easily let go of your stubborn nature. There is no need for you to force the issue.

LINE 4   A ram butts the fence and breaks free

Your window of opportunity has appeared. You have the strength, and the barriers are weak. Use your power wisely, and keep it under control.

LINE 3   A ram butts the fence and gets its horns stuck

Throwing your weight around will do you no good. You only get more entangled. You have the option to refrain from using force to get your way.

LINE 2   Loyal and persevering

Even if you are at a disadvantage, continue to be loyal and persevering, and you may break free of restricting circumstances. Accept help in doing this. Power balanced with self-mastery.

LINE 1   Fidgety feet, bad luck to go ahead

Impatient, but unprepared to start a venture. You are not strong enough yet to make that break for freedom. If you start now, you will soon wear out. Bide your time.

REAL-LIFE ADVENTURES

Let Him Go

Our friend Luanne was involved in an intimate relationship. Her lover had just met another woman and seemed to be getting involved with her. Luanne wanted to know whether this was going to be a breakup for her and her lover.

Q Is this the end of the affair?

A Luanne received Hexagram 34, with line 4 moving.

Hexagram 34 talks about getting away from a confining situation.
Line 4 speaks of the ram breaking free.
Clearly, this is a window of opportunity for someone. This could be seen as a window for either of them, but in that this has a feeling of escape, it doesn't bode well for a furthering of their love affair. Luanne's fears that her lover was about to leave her proved to be justified.

Across a Crowded Room

Sam had a strong affinity for the *I Ching,* and used it often and anywhere. When questions arose in his life, he asked advice on the spot. Why wait?
One night he was at a party, and he noticed his girlfriend staring across the room at another man. Was this love at first sight for her? She appeared transfixed—struck by Cupid's arrow. Or was this just one of those party flirtations? In jealous confusion, he found a quiet corner and threw the coins.

Q Is this love, lust, or what? Should I be worried?

A Sam received Hexagram 34, with line 5 moving.

Hexagram 34 is about breaking free.

This is the very incident we all fear: Our partner will fall in love with someone else. Sam saw the end of their relationship and the beginning of her new relationship. She was breaking free.

Line 5 says let it go. If it's yours, it will come back to you.

35

SUCCESS

WINNING

POPULARITY

Everybody loves a winner

*The king sees you three
times in one day*

FIRE

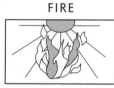

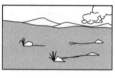

EARTH

Sun over the earth. Triumph and success.
A sunny day.

The story is of the Marquis of Kang being
awarded territory and horses by King Wu. If the King
sees you three times in one day, you are in favor.

You're the tops. The favorite.

Make the best of it. Nothing lasts forever.

LINE 6   Advancing spears at the ready, suitable for taking a city

Aggressive action is sometimes necessary, especially if you waited too long to correct something. When you have achieved your goal, resume a more peaceful way of doing things.

LINE 5   What was lost is regained

Though you may not be able to see the outcome clearly, don't worry about loss or gain. Just do what your heart tells you is right, and you will succeed. Something lost will be restored.

LINE 4   Advancing like a squirrel, danger

This is not the time or the place for major gains. You may be tempted to get something that is not rightly yours in an underhand way. Act in an open and straightforward manner, or not at all.

LINE 3   Everyone approves of you, no doubts

Doubts disappear. You have earned the trust of people and they approve your decisions. You have a flexible nature and a firm will.

LINE 2   Help from your grandmother

It saddens you that jealous colleagues make progress difficult. Do not worry. Your talents will be noticed by an enlightened leader, and you will receive help. Patience will get you there.

LINE 1   Your proposals are rejected

You are not in a sufficiently powerful position to single-handedly get all of what you want. Wins are mixed with losses. Keep working at it and your time will come. Rebuffed at first, success later.

REAL-LIFE ADVENTURES

Winning and Losing

Sri Lanka, 1982: Amy was addicted to tobacco. She wanted to quit, but was finding it very difficult to do so.

Q Wanting to stop smoking and not making it happen. Will I ever win at this?

A Amy received Hexagram 35, with line 2 moving.

Hexagram 35 has to do with being a winner.

Line 2 indicates that you may not make it on your own, unless you get help. Help was on its way.

Amazingly, a book put out by the American Cancer Society, recommending a twenty-one-day plan that involved breaking down addictive and stress-related habits of the body and mind, happened to find its way into Amy's hotel bedside table. Like magic.

Finding this book in a remote watering hole in Sri Lanka was a welcome synchronicity. It was also an intrinsic key to unlocking the habit patterns and breaking the addiction.

Neighbor from Hell

For years we had comfortably shared a common stairway to our house with one other family. Then, all of a sudden, our next-door neighbor began a descent into some sort of mental breakdown.

He took it into his head that we shouldn't be using his stairway, and became continuously abusive. Instant neighbor from hell. As it was our only access, this could be a real problem. It's not possible to reason with insanity. This person is not playing by the rules. Social niceties aren't working. Should we call for reinforcements, and who would that be?

Q How should we approach this situation?

A We received Hexagram 35, with line 5 moving.

Okay, we're winners. This is going to work itself out. The sun over the earth is a good image for bringing things into the light of day.

Line 5 advises us to press on and resolution will occur. Assert your rights. No regrets, worries, or self-doubt. This is corruption and must be faced head-on.

We did just that. We continued to approach this man with good humor and a winning attitude. He was not going to draw us into his web of madness. Oh, no? Read on. (See Hexagram 44 for part 2 of this story.)

There were no overnight rewards. Resolution of this problem took years. There is the appearance in these stories that a situation occurs, the oracle is consulted, the advice is taken, and the situation resolves itself. Not so. Life is not always a neat thirty-minute TV sitcom.

And the Winner Is

A perfect winning story.

Q U.S. presidential election, 1980: How will Ronald Reagan do?

A We received Hexagram 35, with line 3 moving.

Hexagram 35 is a winner. Synchronistically, this hexagram has come up often in response to political election questions.

Line 3 says that everybody likes you. No doubt about it. And guess what? Reagan won the presidency by a landslide. Any questions?

DAMAGED

REJECTION

INVALIDATION

A light in the darkness

Persevering in adversity

EARTH

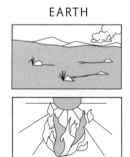

FIRE

The fire is buried under the earth. Not a happy
place to be. All is in darkness.

The Chinese tell the story of Prince Chi being put in jail
for criticizing the behavior of his unworthy king. In order to
survive he had to pretend to be mad. Don't we all?

Feeling alone in your viewpoint. Under attack and unable
to speak out. Eventually doubting your own reality.

Even in the darkest hour, hold onto your integrity.
It might be all that you have.

LINE 6   Rises to the sky, then falls to earth

Pride comes before a fall. Your motives are good, but you may have attempted too much. Now that you have been brought down to earth, you can take the more modest route to success.

LINE 5   A light in the darkness

You are closely involved with the wrong people. The best you can do is refuse to participate in the injustice. Keep your inner light bright and stay hidden. The light can be obscured, but not extinguished.

LINE 4   Penetrating the heart of darkness

You are aware of a bad situation because you are close to the heart of it. Fortunately you remain uncorrupted by it, and so you can escape unharmed. Discovering secret plans.

LINE 3   Capturing the rebel chief

You have the power to confront what is wrong and set it right. Though you correct the major error, it will be a while before everything returns to normal. The reign of darkness is ending.

LINE 2   Wounded in the left leg, rescued with a strong horse

You suffer an injury, but find a means of rescue. You are able to protect yourself from attack and can withdraw to safety. Harmed but not hindered.

LINE 1   Damaged in flight, not eating for three days

You alone notice the signs of decay, and decide to swiftly withdraw from trouble. Those who fail to see this might think that you are strange and criticize you for leaving.

A REAL-LIFE ADVENTURE

The Battered Wife

When we lived in England we were way ahead of our time—doing counseling by telephone before the 900-number craze hit in the United States. In fact, it was here that we began our "Instant *I Ching*" readings. We kept six coins in a dish by the phone. To give advice to the caller, we would shake the six coins and arrange them in a vertical line. This was the beginning of the coin-throwing method we use in this book.

In this instance it was a woman calling. Her husband was being constantly abusive to her, both physically and mentally. This situation was causing her to feel ashamed and insane. She was so beaten down that she had lost any sense of self-worth. She no longer had any certainty as to the rightness of her own opinions. True brainwashing. The constant stream of invalidation from her husband was causing her to believe that she was the one who was sick and in trouble.

Q Am I the one who is crazy, or is it my husband?

A She received Hexagram 36, with line 5 moving.

Hexagram 36 has to do with the denial of your reality.

Line 5 tells you to maintain your inner light at all costs.

When the caller heard the title of the hexagram, "Invalidation," and the story of Prince Chi, who had to pretend to be insane in order to survive, she burst into tears. She immediately recognized the rightness of her own feelings.

Her intuition was confirmed, and this gave her the courage to survive, without falling into doubt about her own worth. It was many years before she was able to leave this injurious life and make a new one on her own.

A reading is a mirror for the question. It may do no more than confirm our feelings about something and nudge us in the right direction.

At best it will confirm an intuition, so that the truth can be recognized, where previously there had been only a sea of doubt and conflicting realities.

37

HOME

FAMILY

BELONGING

Family ties

*Domestic qualities are
an advantage*

TREE

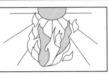

FIRE

Tree or wind over fire. The wind fans the flames
of the fire. This suggests home and hearth.

In Chinese, this hexagram literally means "house people,"
the women, children, and helpers of the household.

The individuals in a family do not work
for pay or for themselves. They each play their
part in contributing to the family.

Join in the social framework that you
support and that supports you.

Find your place in the order of things.
Where do you belong?

LINE 6 Earning respect

You may be on your own. Earn the respect of others by being friendly and helpful. Be sincere and set a good example. Rely on yourself, not on others.

LINE 5 The king is in the castle

With everything in good order and domestic relations harmonious, you have nothing to hide and nothing to fear. The family naturally loves and forgives each other, creating a secure and happy life.

LINE 4 She is the treasure of the house

Even though a person may not be in charge of things, he or she is nevertheless able to increase the wealth or happiness of the family.

LINE 3 Upset at strictness, better than humiliating frivolity

Too much discipline in a group may cause resentment, but if there is no discipline, everything falls into chaos. Agreed-upon rules, consistently enforced, hold the balance.

LINE 2 Stay home, making the meals

Stay within the home or social structure. This is not the time to strike out on your own. At this time your obligations overshadow your personal wishes.

LINE 1 Stay home, lock your doors

Home is where you are safe and can close the doors against a hostile world. Decide who is family and who is not. Who is on the inside and who is on the outside?

REAL-LIFE ADVENTURES

Home, Home on the Range

We were on holiday in Hungary and had an important life decision to make concerning our future. We had just received a small inheritance, and new opportunities were now possible. Travel and study; see the world? Or live a simple life and invest the money in home improvement?

Before we asked our question, we drew a picture of a luxury cruise ship with Hexagram 56, "The Traveler," next to it, to represent life on the road.

We also drew a picture of our home with Hexagram 37 next to it, to symbolize the idea of staying at home.

Q What should we do with this recently received inheritance?

A The reading turned up Hexagram 37, with line 4 moving.

Hexagram 37 is home and hearth, one of the two alternatives we had given ourselves. We don't normally draw illustrations of our questions. An amazing bit of synchronicity.

Line 4 speaks of the need to be conscientious in our roles as homeowners. Treasure the house, or the house is the treasure.

We used our inheritance to renovate our nine-hundred-year-old Benedictine monastery, which really needed some tender loving care, inside and out, and to enjoy the privilege of our years as caretakers of this exceptional estate.

This is a good example of the *I Ching* leading you uncompromisingly to an answer.

Was He Family?

Annie and Steve had been friends for years. They were like family to each other. But when they became business partners and live-in roommates, the intimacy and related stress caused the friendship to go sour and fall apart. Annie was upset and disillusioned.

Q Is there any way to salvage this friendship?

A Annie received Hexagram 37, with line 1 moving.

Hexagram 37 says that this is a family matter. Is he family?

Line 1 advises you to lock your doors. This is decision time. Is he on your side or not? Is he on your side in life, and therefore on your side of the door? Is this friend worthy of being inside your life as family?

Annie felt uncomfortable in Steve's presence, and relieved when he left her space. The question answers itself in your heart.

38

SOLITARY

THE STRANGER

ALIENATED

Hearing a different drummer

Estranged, can do only small things

FIRE

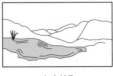

LAKE

Fire over the lake. These two elements are in contradiction.

The Chinese word for this hexagram means "to squint, stare at, be unusual or strange." Also, "eyes that look in different directions."

When you are unhappy with the company you keep, your eyes wander and you feel you don't belong. It may be because you think you look odd or are out of step with others.

When you are in an alienated position, you can only do small things, make small improvements.

Retain your uniqueness and individuality without becoming self-obsessed and antagonistic.

LINE 6   Pigs covered in mud

Being on your own has made you wary. An apparent threat puts you on your guard. Tension and suspicion give way to relief when you see that no harm is meant.

LINE 5   Join in the feast at the ancestral temple

Accept the invitation to join in the feast of life. What harm could come from this? Join in the fun. Overcome the barriers that separate you from your friends.

LINE 4   All alone, you make a good friend

You can overcome your isolation and loneliness. Find people with similar interests, and communicate in truth and sincerity. You will then come to trust each other.

LINE 3   Cart and oxen halted, bad beginning—good end

You are warned away from making a move when you see the trouble others get into when they try the same thing. Doubts hold you back. You may be temporarily separated from a partner.

LINE 2   Secret meetings in an alleyway

Formal relationships with someone may be difficult or strained. If you meet by chance, or in informal, secret, or unusual surroundings, use this opportunity to make a lasting bond.

LINE 1   Your horse returns of its own accord

Your bad fortune is not your fault. Include your antagonist in your world and face your deepest fears. Your troubles will run their course, and what is lost will be restored.

A REAL-LIFE ADVENTURE

Running After Enlightenment, or Hello, Dalai

We were on a meditation retreat in Scotland. By a strange coincidence, we received a letter there from an old friend, then living in Bodh-Gaya, the Buddha's place of enlightenment in India. He invited us to visit him there and attend an initiation being given by His Holiness, the Dalai Lama.

This was a major spiritual event. There were going to be hundreds of thousands of people attending.

"Why don't you come?" he wrote. "It would be a unique opportunity to sit where the Buddha sat to gain his enlightenment, and be with the Dalai Lama in this place of power."

We were already in retreat with a great teacher and were not quite sure of the wisdom of taking off for India at a moment's notice, although we did have an intense spiritual longing to be there.

Q To go or not to go see the Dalai Lama?

A We received Hexagram 38, with line 3 moving.

Hexagram 38 is about doing your own thing.

Line 3 gives the picture of someone being warned or frightened into staying where they are, when they see what is in store for them.

We knew from experience what the conditions would be like in India—very difficult. We decided not to go. Months later we read that fifty people had been trampled to death in their rush to receive the blessing from the Dalai Lama.

And what were we chasing after? We were already in retreat with a great teacher.

39

IMPASSE

BARRIERS

OBSTACLES

Stumbling block

Favorable for retreat, not for advance, visit the wise one

WATER

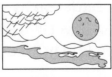

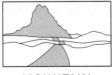

MOUNTAIN

Water over the mountain. The river and the mountain range are formidable barriers that can both protect and hinder.

Halting when faced with danger.
Something stands in your way.

When you stumble, pause and draw back to a safe position. You may need to let go of excess baggage in order to be free to move on.

We find out who we really are when faced with difficulties. Find the inner strength for overcoming obstacles. Stop and look within.

LINE 6   Blocked, return to inner wisdom

You are wise enough to know that some obstacles are best handled by staying put and working on your own thoughts and attitudes. You may be in a position to help others with this advice.

LINE 5   Friends catch you as you fall

Just as you are about to fall, someone rushes forward and catches you. You have friends to help you in your time of need.

LINE 4   Blocked now, advance with help

You are too weak to advance right now. Pause and gather strength through the support of others, and then move on.

LINE 3   Moving is blocked, come back to friends

If you go forward you will come up against obstacles. Return to a secure base where you have friends. Wait for help to come to you.

LINE 2   The servant encounters obstacles on behalf of the king

You are responsible for handling a problem which is not of your own making. If you cannot handle it by yourself, get some help.

LINE 1   Going is blocked, coming back is praised

If you go forward, you will get into trouble because you are weak and without help. You will be admired for having the good sense to stay where you are. Wait for a more favorable time to advance.

A REAL-LIFE ADVENTURE

Waiting by the River

We had arrived in Varanasi, India, having left our traveling companion in New Delhi, many thousands of miles away. He was planning on meeting us in Varanasi sometime in the next week. We had no idea where we would be staying, so we agreed to be on the main steps at the River Ganges every day at noon for ten days, until we met up again. None of us had ever been to this city before, but we had read about the main steps and seen pictures. It seemed the perfect meeting place.

The moment we arrived at the steps, we realized what a crazy idea this was. There were thousands of people there all day, and more than one set of steps leading to the river. Are we in the right place? All these people. Will we find each other again? Panic city. Like waiting to meet someone at the airport. The plane is late and you immediately go into doubt. Am I in the right airport? Is this the right day?

Q No contact with our friend yet. Do we wait, or return to Delhi and look for him?

A We received Hexagram 39, with line 3 moving.

Hexagram 39 advises not moving when faced with obstacles. So much for traveling to Delhi and looking for our missing friend (not one of our best solutions anyway).

Line 3 emphasizes this general theme by saying that you will fall over if you go. You are better off staying where you are. Help will come to you.

We were ecstatic with that, as traveling anywhere in India is not exactly like going to the corner grocery store for a loaf of bread.

The very next day, within minutes of our arrival at what we hoped were the right stairs, there he was, shining out in the crowd.

40

RELIEF

ESCAPE

FREEDOM

The line of least resistance

Get free and return home

THUNDER

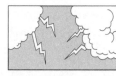

WATER

Thunder over the water. From the thunder above, falls the rain. The thunderstorm breaks, clearing the air of the tension that has built up. Getting out of danger.

If there is something you have to do, then do it quickly. If there is nothing more you have to do, and nowhere else you have to go, then return home.

Forgive yourself and others.
Follow the line of least resistance.

LINE 6 Aim at the hawk high on the wall, a direct hit

Someone not personally involved can act impartially to overcome a stubborn problem. Aim high and release yourself from the last barriers to your freedom. The troubleshooter overthrows the chief troublemaker.

LINE 5 Free yourself, and inspire others

Your determination and understanding have given you freedom. This is an example and an inspiration to others. Opposition to your ideas melts away. Cooperation with others resolves negativity.

LINE 4 Pull out your thumb

You have become involved in something you should pull out of right now. Luckily, you are not too deeply involved, so getting out is easy. If you do it now, you will benefit; if you wait, you may lose.

LINE 3 Carrying baggage on top of a carriage invites attack

By taking on too much you may be pretending to be what you are not and taking shortcuts. This will be unpopular and you may be attacked. Let go of inflated ambitions. Just do what you can.

LINE 2 Bags three foxes, rewarded with a golden arrow

The three foxes are greed, hatred, and ignorance. Eliminate these faults and be richly rewarded. Act now, be precise and single-minded. You may be given a position of responsibility.

LINE 1 If it must be done—do it now, no harm

You can put something right before any real damage is done. Don't delay. Borrow strength and wisdom from those who have it by working with them. Helping and being helped in turn.

REAL-LIFE ADVENTURES

Desperately Seeking Perfection

About ten years into our relationship, we were at a crisis point. This was not a once-in-a-lifetime event, but whenever these feelings arise in our relationship, we feel as though it's the end of our world. Rod had a number of personal doubts about his life and many of his values. How does anyone cope with their own problems and still create a life with another?

Q Is it possible to create a relationship, knowing that we have more than enough problems just dealing with ourselves?

A We received Hexagram 40, with line 6 moving.

Hexagram 40 is about clearing the air.

Line 6 indicates that it is possible to achieve high ideals. You must aim high. What's your alternative? Rejoice—you have no choice! You are the troubleshooter and the troublemaker.

If we each had to be enlightened before we could create a partnership with another, this would be a really lonely planet.

A relationship is not a static image of perfection, but the evolution of two people living and loving together. It is not always perfect, and sometimes, not even close. As Woody Allen says in *Annie Hall,* "A relationship is like a shark, it has to keep moving forward, or it dies. And I think what we have here is a dead shark."

We are both glad to say Rod took the advice. We're still aiming high and rejoicing. No dead sharks for us.

Getting Out While the Going Is Good

This is an investment or a gambling story, depending on your viewpoint. When to get in and when to get out. The *I Ching* advised us when to get into the deal (investing in the French franc), and now we felt it was time to get out, as we had made a nice profit. Our broker was telling us to hold on to the investment, assuring us that there was more profit to be made. Greed is definitely God here. Knowing when to quit, especially if you're winning, is never easy. Time for the oracle.

Q Is it time to take our winnings and run?

A We received Hexagram 40, with line 4 moving.

Hexagram 40 talks about getting out of trouble. Okay. What more did we need to know?

Line 4 says pull out your thumb, and out comes the plum. Do it now. We thought so, and the *I Ching* confirmed. A fast call to our broker, and we were flying. Another brilliant decision by these two new kids on the block.

This story has a postscript. Our broker decided, against our judgment, to wait for a better price, and by the time she finally acted (two days later), about a third of that win was down the tubes. Now means now.

41

LETTING GO

CLEANING OUT

SIMPLE

Getting down to basics

Two bowls of rice
are enough

MOUNTAIN

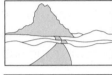

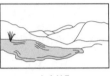

LAKE

Mountain over the lake. The lake
represents enthusiastic self-expression, and
is limited by the mass of the mountain. This is
the path of increase within reduction.

Eliminating the unrewarding activities and people in
your life increases time for what is valuable.

When applied to one's psychological
condition, less becomes more. Take out the trash in
your life, and get more done with less effort.

Economize—emotionally as well as
materially. This is not the time for extravagant
gestures. Small is beautiful.

LINE 6   No longer decrease, increase now

The goal of simplifying your life has been achieved. Now you can develop a more expansive attitude. Share your good fortune with others, and benefit yourself without taking from others.

LINE 5   A gift of many valuable tortoiseshells
cannot be refused

In simplifying your life, you have made room for a wonderful and unexpected opportunity. Take this help from above. This is gaining without seeking gain.

LINE 4   Lessen the feverish haste

Reduce the stress and rush in your life. Cool the feverish pace and things will work themselves out. Improve your habits now and friends will come to your aid.

LINE 3   One gains support, and three move as one

When one person makes a stand, others will join in support. One for all and all for one. To be effective, a group of people must work as one. Letting go of individual needs and desires.

LINE 2   Advance, but not as to war

Be neither stubborn, nor too easy to please. Help others, so long as it does not weaken you. Be responsible for your duties, without looking to take over a higher position.

LINE 1   A small offering is quite acceptable

Give the help that is needed and then quietly leave. Keep it simple. Overextending yourself for others may harm you and create dependencies and obligations.

REAL-LIFE ADVENTURES

Handling Illness

England, 1980: Amy was suffering from chronic gallstones, with painful attacks. An elective operation to remove the offending organ had been suggested by the allopathic surgeons. Unless your life is in danger, British surgeons don't recommend removing the gallbladder, so we had to make a choice between surgery and handling the condition ourselves.

Q Are there any alternatives to an operation?

A We received Hexagram 41, with line 4 moving.

Hexagram 41 indicates the need for simplification.

Line 4 led us to lessen the feverish pace of our lifestyle.

This was an important reading for us—it precipitated an enormous life change. We had been studying old Eastern and new Western techniques of self-healing for years, and here was our opportunity to seriously put them into practice.

We began by slowing down, meditating, changing our diet, and handling stress. Now that the need had arisen, we had our chance to test many possible solutions to a disease, other than surgery. Our own test case.

There was no removal of the gallbladder for the next four very healthy years. When the attacks returned, however, the operation did have to be done. Things have a way of working themselves out, but not always as and when we expect.

Accept the Gift

We met a great spiritual teacher, and we were offered a ritual blessing that would introduce us to her spiritual practices and bring us within the group. There were some strings attached, as with any commitment.

We knew that if we accepted the blessing, we would have a commitment each day to say a prayer, to keep the reality alive. We felt we might be locking ourselves into something, and we weren't sure what it was. We had been working for years to simplify our lives. Why add the complexity of a daily ritual unless we believed it to be valuable? That was the crux of the problem: determining what was valuable.

Q Should we accept this blessing?

A We received Hexagram 41, with line 5 moving.

Hexagram 41 says you make time for what is valuable. You simplify your life because you have chosen one path instead of the confusion of many.

Line 5 says that you cannot refuse a valuable gift. What a glorious and precious opportunity to receive a blessing from a great teacher, who showed us that we create our own oasis within ourselves.

42

BENEFIT

INCREASE

EXPANSION

The more, the better

Go ahead with your plans

TREE

THUNDER

Thunder below the tree or wind. Thunder is action and movement. The tree or wind represents the power to penetrate and permeate everywhere.

Together, they indicate a state of increase and benefit. A time of decrease is followed by a time of increase, as the pendulum swings.

Add what is lacking. This does not mean that you indulge your whims. What you add should be to your benefit.

You now have the energy to undertake something that demands courage and daring, which will renew your self-confidence.

LINE 6 Always expanding invites attack

You have gone as far as you can go. If you carry on like this, you will be exposed to attack. Impulsive greed has warped your mind. Shopping till you drop. Get yourself straight, then help others.

LINE 5 Honesty is the best policy

Virtue is its own reward. Act without thought of gain. You are fortunate to have trustworthy friends and to be someone worthy of the trust of others.

LINE 4 The authority to move the capital city

You can be relied on to undertake an important task. Having proved your worth, you can now rely upon the support of others. Use people of influence to help your cause.

LINE 3 Gain through misfortune, the authority of the jade seal

A time of transition, when you can turn an unfortunate event to your advantage. Your sincerity will see you through. Learning from your losses. Finding help in a time of hardship.

LINE 2 A gift of many valuable tortoiseshells cannot be refused

Persevere in being unselfishly open and helpful. You may be given something of great value. Accept it graciously. An unexpected gift is a blessing.

LINE 1 Do great deeds

At the beginning of a project, energy is high and intentions are unwavering. All opposition can be handled. Make the best use of this time by going ahead. If expert advice is available, use it.

REAL-LIFE ADVENTURES

Death and Diamonds

This situation has to do with our friend Rupert, who wanted to make a diamond sale in Zurich, Switzerland. He had never done anything like this before, and he came to us and the *I Ching* for advice.

Q What can I expect from this diamond sale?

A Rupert received Hexagram 42, with line 3 moving.

Hexagram 42 is generally favorable.

Line 3 indicates that he could act successfully outside of his normal sphere of activity. The unfortunate event in this case was that the diamonds being sold were part of Rupert's inheritance from his recently deceased father. Anything gained would be permeated with his feelings of loss.

On his return from Zurich, Rupert related that this hexagram came to mind when the diamond expert took the diamonds, put them in a tiny bag attached to his belt, and told him that he would have it valued for him by tomorrow. "Trust me," he said. Right.

Rupert was afraid he might never see the goodies again, and at the same time had the inner sense that everything was going his way. Coming up roses. He went for it, and yes—the dealer was honest and the sale was a success.

Healthy Choice

Our friend Rachel was nearing forty and wanted to have a baby, but had discovered that two large benign tumors had formed in her uterus. She called them her "alien baby." In her journey into allopathic medicine, she was told by the first two very respected professionals that she must have a hysterectomy. Not a surprise, and not what she wanted to hear.

With the third doctor (the only woman), she got lucky. Here was a doctor willing to try to save the uterus and remove the tumors. Tricky, and certainly more dangerous than removing everything, but why not? Dreams do come true.

Q How will this operation go?

A We received Hexagram 42, with line 3 moving.

Hexagram 42 has to do with expansion, benefit, increase. Good things happening. A fortunate hexagram.

Line 3 says that an unfortunate event will be to your advantage. You will gain from it in the end. It promises success for the operation and also for becoming pregnant. We know that the operation was performed and was successful. So far, so very good.

43

DETERMINATION

REVELATION

BREAKTHROUGH

The courage of your convictions

Take the matter up at the king's court

LAKE

SKY

Lake over the sky. Clouds in the sky. It is about to rain. Something is about to happen.

The one yin line in the top position is holding back the five yang lines from advancing. On a personal level, there remain doubts or reservations.

An influential person may be against you. This needs to be handled with determination. Now is the time to openly declare your position. Differences are being defined. Lines are being drawn and sides taken.

Take measures either to separate from negative influences or to handle them. Avoid resolving the situation by force. Be open in declaring your intentions.

LINE 6 Without warning

Without warning, evil is removed from power. If you are ashamed of something, put it right. No hiding from the light. Prepare against unexpected disasters.

LINE 5 Dealing with weeds

It is important not to be influenced by weak people or negative ideas. It is also important not to abandon anyone. Do what needs to be done and keep your balance.

LINE 4 Leading a sheep as a sign of surrender

The white flag of surrender. Unless you are willing to be led, your stubbornness will lead you into defeat and you will be forced to make changes anyway. You are only free to follow along.

LINE 3 Struck on the cheek, wet in the rain

It may be annoying to have to put something right, but pride, embarrassment, or impatience should not prevent you making a fair compromise. Otherwise, it is best you go your own way.

LINE 2 Night raids, nothing to fear

There is danger around you. If you are ready, you will have nothing to fear. Forewarned is forearmed. Strength is in being prepared. Like having burglar alarms.

LINE 1 Stumbling forward

Your first move forward is too hasty. You're liable to fall flat on your face. You are being driven by powerful but erratic forces. Wise up. If you are not equal to the task, you will fail to carry it through.

REAL-LIFE ADVENTURES

Fried Green Tomatoes

We had a friend who was farming tomatoes on one of the Hawaiian islands. This was a new way for him to earn a living. Even though there was a shortage of tomatoes in Honolulu at that time, we sensed failure in this project. Neither he nor his partner were doing a single thing to handle the marketing of their crop, and our farming friend had a strong bias against anyone cooking his tomatoes. He believed that cooking tomatoes made them toxic. All this combined to form a picture of negative intentions and ultimate failure.

Q How will our farming friend do with his tomatoes?

A We received Hexagram 43, with line 3 moving.

Hexagram 43 has to do with a blind spot in your thinking, and the need to break through it. A fatal flaw.

Line 3 speaks of making corrections and compromising. Our friend had excessive pride, sufficient to prevent him either seeing or making the needed changes.

The fatal flaws were his inability and unwillingness to judge character, as well as his often stated aversion to doing business. His partner disappeared at a critical point in the distribution process, leaving hundreds of boxes of tomatoes sitting on the dock, rotting in their crates. They never made it to the customers.

Needless to say, he didn't make any money off the venture. He left Hawaii with many regrets, and possibly a little wiser.

The Good Life

Many years ago, we had the notion to start a market garden, be self-sufficient, and barter with the proceeds. Too much TV probably, and we bought into the romantic ideals.

Q Is it a good idea to be self-sufficient and start a market garden?

A We received Hexagram 43, with line 5 moving.

Hexagram 43 is about handling a blind spot in your thinking. Were we romanticizing this?

Line 5 says that you will end up dealing with weeds. You're not thinking straight. Deal with the weeds of your erroneous thinking.

In retrospect, we can see that this was a ridiculous idea. Messing around with plants every now and then does not make you a successful farmer, and planting a couple of acres with carrots was not necessarily going to aid our survival.

Instead, we traveled and made a much better living doing what we did best: counseling some of the shattered and neurotic minds of various city environs.

44

INTRUSIONS

ENCOUNTER

UNDERMINING

A disturbing influence

*The woman is powerful,
do not marry her*

SKY

TREE

Tree under the sky. The tree or wind has the characteristic of being uncertain of its direction. This intrudes upon the energy of the sky as an unexpected and unsettling influence.

This hexagram has strong sexual connotations. The single yin line entering in at the bottom of the hexagram represents a single woman seducing five men (represented by the five yang lines).

Interpreting beyond the sexist thinking of ancient China, we have the idea of a disturbing influence insinuating itself into the normal state of affairs.

Expect the unexpected.

LINE 6   Locking horns; regrettable, but not your fault

You may have to get tough with someone whose aggression and stubbornness have driven you into a corner. When it is over, resume your peaceful ways.

LINE 5   A melon wrapped in leaves, as though from heaven

A slice of sweet melon wrapped in spicy willow leaves, a tasteful presentation. Favorable for a cooperative venture. In time, the fruits of your labor ripen into rich rewards. It may come unexpectedly.

LINE 4   No fish in the basket, misfortune

The cupboard is bare. If you cut yourself off from people and stand apart, then they will have no confidence in you. You may lose their help and assistance.

LINE 3   Staggering from weakness

You are in a weakened condition. This disadvantage may keep you from getting further into trouble. If you are uncertain, decide what it is you really want, and go for it with determination.

LINE 2   One fish remains, do not give it away

You are not obliged to give away what you have, when you have only enough for yourself. Take all necessary steps to protect your assets. All your eggs are in one basket, so watch that basket carefully.

LINE 1   Stopped with a brake of iron

You feel constrained and frustrated, but maybe you are afraid that if you break your bonds and run free, you will go on a wild rampage. Find the balance between restraint and excess.

REAL-LIFE ADVENTURES

Locking Horns

We had been advised previously by the *I Ching* to "practice patience" with our neighbor from hell (see the story in Hexagram 35), who had been trying to stop us from using our mutual staircase for months. He had tried every means short of physical violence: barking dogs at the top of the stairs, horrible looks, and nasty, bitter words. We kept our good humor as best we could by being polite and by trying to keep the peace, but then he became physically abusive.

So much for patience. The situation hadn't improved; it had worsened. We were thinking about taking legal action, an unheard-of solution for us, as communication has almost always worked to solve life's little disputes.

Q What now? Please advise correct conduct.

A We received Hexagram 44, with line 6 moving.

Hexagram 44 is concerned with intrusions and disturbing influences into the normal state of affairs.

Line 6 says that you are in for it. Conflict may be unavoidable. Line 6 also indicates that you've put yourself into an awkward situation. Even if we're not the ones going crazy, craziness is being directed at us. It's time to get tough.

What is our responsibility here? Having exhausted all personal means of handling this dispute, the only alternatives left to us were the courts and the police, and that worked. As soon as we decided to take a stand, the bully backed down.

To Win a War

In 1978 Israel was about to attack southern Lebanon, as it did again in 1993.

Q What is going to happen here?

A We received Hexagram 44, with line 5 moving.

Hexagram 44 describes the intrusion of an unexpected element into a situation. Israel could be construed in this instance as the intrusion of an unexpected element.

Line 5 indicates the ripe fruit falling easily into Israel's lap. The attack was successful, and Israel gained the Golan Heights territory. And the beat goes on.

45

JOINING IN

GATHERING

INTEGRATION

LAKE

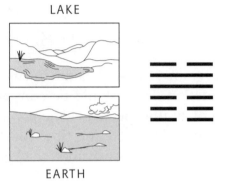

EARTH

Gathering of the clan

*Assemble around the shrine
and make offerings*

The lake resting on the earth. This is a gathering place
for all the water. A place of rest and healing.

This is the process of recovery, as in a
fever. The fever, often thought of as the illness, is
actually the body's process of recovery.

The Chinese word used to describe this hexagram shows
a thicket of trees, a sacred grove, a meeting place.

Integrate scattered energies into a coherent
whole. Recover and nourish the roots of your
being. Get your act together.

LINE 6   Weeping and wailing, not your fault

Your position at the top is no longer secure. You tried to keep it together, but you failed. This is not your fault. One thing has come to an end, and now you should do something else.

LINE 5   Gathering around the leader or going on your own

Even when in a commanding position, not everyone will automatically follow you. It is how you behave that will inspire others to have confidence in you. Despite this, some people will go their own way.

LINE 4   Great good fortune, no blame

Though you are not handling things in the best way, the fact that it turns out well saves you from criticism. Flattery may have distorted your perspective.

LINE 3   Sitting around and complaining

Feeling rejected. Your need for companionship may lead to reckless moves. This is not bad enough to cause offense. It may be time to leave and go find something better.

LINE 2   Guided along, present a small offering with sincerity

A sincere gesture on your part demonstrates your willingness to give of yourself and accept help. Making the effort compensates for your shortcomings. You might receive a gift.

LINE 1   Uncertain about joining in, have no fear

First attempts at making your own decisions are often awkward and confused. Decent people will not laugh at you if you ask for help. When you are clear about what you want, then it will happen.

REAL-LIFE ADVENTURES

Facing the Confusion

We were doing psychic consultations in England. A woman called Marian came to consult with us. She did not want to stay with her husband, and she was too frightened to leave. She was involved in an unhappy marriage, but she hadn't been in the world or on her own for so long that she was terrified of leaving. She saw herself in a no-win situation.

Q Should I stay with my husband?

A Marian received Hexagram 45, with line 1 moving.

Hexagram 45 suggests the need for integration.

Line 1 indicated that her intentions were too scattered. Marian needed to sort out the many conflicting forces in her life. She was not ready to make a practical decision. She needed to figure things out and make preparations before she made her move.

We introduced her to a trusted marriage counselor, and hoped that this *I Ching* reading would be the first step in the integration of her life.

Family in Crisis

Our folks came to visit us, and Mom had a stroke. She was now in our local hospital. It could mean a huge life change for our parents. She is suddenly disabled. Will she need to go into convalescent care? On the fifth day following our dear mother's stroke, we asked about her future and Dad's.

Q Will she die here? Will they manage to make the trip home? When and if they get home, will they be able to manage on their own?

A We received Hexagram 45, with line 5 moving.

We were told what we needed to do next, and were given a glimpse into the future.

The first step was to gather the clan. We have a brother, and he should be here. We were exhausted, scared, and in need of familial support. The crisis served as a focus for bringing everyone together and resolving old differences. As to the glimpse into the future, Mom and Dad survived this latest test and were able to return home and maintain their independent lifestyle. As Dad loves to say, "'The Golden Years?' You've got to be kidding!"

46

ARISING

GROWTH

MOVING UP

Upward mobility

Have no fear, see the wise one

EARTH

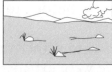

TREE

Tree under the earth. The tree pushes its way up through the earth. The energy is moving upward and outward.

This is not a sudden or aggressive movement, as the tree is a flexible and penetrating force. The earth just needs to be moved aside for the tree to reach the light.

You are favored for a promotion of some sort. Do not be afraid to make a move or see someone influential.

LINE 6 **Rising into the darkness with eyes shut**

You are moving into unknown territory. Stay alert to hidden forces and adapt to your new surroundings. When in the dark, you cannot lose heart halfway.

LINE 5 **Keep on climbing up the ladder**

Move upward in a patient and steady way, like climbing stairs, step by step and stage by stage. Appreciate the enlightened help that you are fortunate to have.

LINE 4 **Climbing the mountain with offerings**

You are moving up and participating with powerful forces. Though not at the center of power, you are invited to participate. Patient step-by-step progress, as in climbing a mountain.

LINE 3 **Taking over an empty city**

Something that comes to you very easily may be of little value or might soon be lost. Check out its real worth before going for it.

LINE 2 **The sincerity of a small offering is blessed**

Consistent and unwavering effort is needed. Close relationships need no more than a sincere gesture to celebrate the beginning of a venture. You will support someone by being loyal and consistent.

LINE 1 **Entrusted with a promotion**

Good fortune at the first stages of promotion, from a low position to a higher one. Welcomed into the group. Good fortune through being obedient and responsive. A meeting of the minds.

A REAL-LIFE ADVENTURE

Unknown Territory

We were living in Palm Springs, a place that combines healing waters with luxury and self-indulgence. A playground for rich conservatives.

Bobby arrived in our lives, a fascinating and unconventional person, even by our standards. He took the meaning of the word *freedom* to new limits, jumping into the Hilton pool fully clothed, or walking down the main street in a loincloth—looking like the reincarnation of Jesus Christ. He was capable of knowing our thoughts before we voiced them and had the courage to confront us with them. He was perceptive, and at the same time, scary and unpredictable. Was he a madman who should be taking his medication, a sorcerer who saw through all our pretensions, or a con artist looking for a mark?

He forced us to question all our safe assumptions, throwing us into a wonderful state of confusion. We became aware of our own inhibitions and of our desire to break free. We found it difficult to maintain our balance.

Q Who is Bobby, and how should we respond to him?

A We received Hexagram 46, with line 6 moving.

Hexagram 46 is about fearlessly developing your potential, and growing.

Line 6 says that you are moving into unknown territory and implies that there is always some danger in doing this. You don't know where you are going to find yourself. Too true in this instance, but we went for it anyway.

You don't always have an itinerary before you take a trip. It's more comfortable if you do, but there's a great adventure to be had in embracing the unknown.

47

DEPLETED

BURNT OUT

EXHAUSTED

Running on empty

*What you say is
not believed*

LAKE

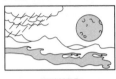

WATER

The water is below the lake. The water
should be in the lake. Instead it has drained
out and the lake is dry.

The Chinese image used to describe this
hexagram shows a tree hemmed in by a box. It is
cut off from light and nourishment. This means to
be weary, tired out, anxious, or in difficulty.

You are at a dead end. There is a sense
of futility and isolation.

This is a great challenge to your character. Hold to your
deepest convictions and you will come through it.

LINE 6　Entangled in vines

Exhausted with being exhausted. You only think that you are trapped. The trap is of your own making and exists in your own doubts and uncertainties. Change your ways. Get over yourself.

LINE 5　Burdened with responsibilities

The exhaustion of responsibilities. Being stuck in a job and not getting what you want. If there is a lack of cooperation, do something to bring people together, and then conditions will improve.

LINE 4　Crawling along in a bronze carriage

Delayed in a traffic jam. You are not getting the support you need. You are unable to do what you really want to do. You will gradually build up your energy and overcome this state of exhaustion.

LINE 3　Stuck under a rock, grasping at thorns

You are between a rock and a hard place. There may be no way out, or insufficient energy with which to get out. Even at home there may be no one to give you comfort.

LINE 2　Exhausted from eating and drinking

Always chasing our desires is exhausting, and ultimately unsatisfying. We may be trapped by favors we have accepted. If you want change, help is on its way. There is success after hardship.

LINE 1　Beaten with sticks and imprisoned for three years

Your desire for advancement is frustrated. You may be feeling hopeless after what is only a minor setback. You need help in getting out of your depression. This could be a valuable learning experience.

A REAL-LIFE ADVENTURE

Entanglements

Our dear friend Katie came to visit us in the United States for a change of scene and some new perspectives. Her partner of twenty years had dumped her by telephone; the ultimate insult. She was left with a tiny place to live in England, and not a lot else. While she was our guest, she met a Mr. Right Enough, and wondered whether to extend her visit here. Going home was going back to a dead-end situation. Where was her life going?

Q Should I extend my visit?

A Katie received Hexagram 47, with line 6 moving.

Hexagram 47 indicates that the energy has drained out of the situation. The situation is that you have been heavily invalidated, made less of, and have no juice. Exhausted and burnt out.

Line 6 says that although there's a feeling of being trapped, extrication is both possible and easy. At first we couldn't understand this answer, as Katie was only too happy to remain here. That was the whole point. Stay and get involved. Finally, we all realized that the answer could refer to what she had left behind in England, rather than this present affair. The *I Ching* was answering the question behind the question.

"Entangled by vines" means that it can be pulled apart with some ease, rather than being entangled by chains, for instance.

Katie took the opportunity to explore her feelings with her new friend, and remained here another two weeks. This was not the answer to her life's problems, and she did return to her native land to finish what was left incomplete. Now she's off to Australia and new beginnings.

48

SOURCE

THE WELL

RESOURCES

Drinking from the well of life

You can move the town but not the well

WATER

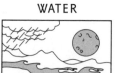

TREE

Water over wood. Wood represents the wooden bucket that is lowered into the well. It brings up the water for all to drink.

The well is the center of village life and well-being. In ancient China, eight families would share a well; their fields surrounded it like spokes radiating from the hub of a wheel.

The cooperative sharing and protecting of mutually held resources.

If you are to benefit from a resource, it must be accessible and in good working order.

LINE 6   The well has been left uncovered

Your resource is made available for all to use. Leaving the cover off the well is a careless act. You may be acting too freely with yourself or your resources. Is this a good thing, or are you giving yourself away?

LINE 5   People drink from the well from which pure water flows

Your resource is of great value. Let it be used and appreciated. Keep good company and be helpful.

LINE 4   The well is repaired

The well has no water in it because the inlets are blocked. Repair and keep clean your lines of communication. Refresh and improve yourself so that your juices flow freely once more.

LINE 3   The well is clear, but no one drinks from it

Your resources are available but remain unused. Talents unrecognized and gone to waste. Opportunities should not be missed. Appreciate what people have to offer.

LINE 2   Shooting fish in a well, the bucket leaks

Your abilities are being misused. You are wasting your talents on unworthy pursuits. Energy is leaking away. Channel your efforts and reach for something worthy.

LINE 1   No one drinks from a muddy well

Your resources have become polluted and unusable. Toxic waste. The dregs of society. There is nothing worth catching at an old watering hole. When things reach bottom there is nowhere else to go but up.

REAL-LIFE ADVENTURES

The Holy Waters of Mother India

We find ourselves in the ancient city of Varanasi (formerly Benares), the oldest and most holy city of India, situated on the sacred Ganges River. Each of us felt deeply drawn to this center of power and ancient teachings.

It is believed that to die in Varanasi is to find liberation from the wheel of suffering. It is also an interesting place to live.

All day, every day, the dead are being cremated on outdoor funeral pyres, if they can afford the wood. If they can't afford the wood, their bodies are simply cast upon the waters of the Ganges, as are the bodies of animals and miscarried babies.

This city, bathed in the smoky light of the burning of the dead, is an easy place to meditate on the nature of our ephemeral and fleeting existence. We felt that we could stay in this remarkable place forever or leave the next day. Moment to moment—ecstasy to horror and back again.

Q What is the nature of our relationship with this holy location?

A We received Hexagram 48, with line 5 moving.

Hexagram 48 is about drinking from the waters of life. This is a place of nourishment and should be treated with a correct measure of respect.

Line 5 told us that we were in the right place at the right time.

The magic of a place such as Varanasi is available to those who are open to it. We did sitting and walking meditations everywhere in the city. We allowed the city to talk to us. We practiced our t'ai chi on the rooftops of ancient palaces, keeping company with the city-dwelling monkeys and parrots. We made love in decrepit rooming houses, with wraithlike junkies silently drifting through the night.

We had come to the well to drink deeply of its influence and see how each of us reacted to these potent waters. It was a tantric rite. We can only advise that being in India is not a vacation. Don't go for the room service, go for the encounter.

Toxic Waste

A couple we knew had been together, split up, gotten back together again, then apart, and so on. Endless games, none of them too happy. One partner was violent and abusive, but the other was still sufficiently addicted to the relationship to need to question the *I Ching* about it. Some questions look obvious in retrospect; but when we are immersed in confusion, nothing is obvious.

Q What is the future of this relationship?

A She received Hexagram 48, with line 1 moving.

Hexagram 48 is about your resources; your sources of energy, inspiration, and love.

Line 1 says you are living next door to, or inside of, a toxic dump. Drink here at your peril. When our friend received this response, the nature of the relationship became crystal clear, and they finally went their separate ways.

49

REFORM

CHANGE

REVOLUTION

*Out with the old, and
in with the new*

*When your day comes,
you will be believed*

LAKE

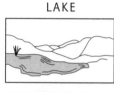

FIRE

Fire below the lake, or metal. The fire melts the metal, transforming it into many shapes, for a multitude of purposes.

The snake shedding its skin is a vivid picture of casting off the old and worn to make way for the new. A metamorphosis. A complete change of form and substance.

For an effective change, five things should be considered:

A real need.

Right timing.

The necessary support.

Unselfish motives.

Avoiding excesses.

LINE 6   The leopard's beautiful spots

Having made a complete and fundamental transformation, you are now ready to consolidate your position. Others will turn to you for your leadership and wisdom, imitating your example.

LINE 5   The tiger's brilliant stripes

You have made extraordinary reforms in the way things are done. You do not need the affirmation of others or of the *I Ching* to know what to do. Others gladly follow your lead.

LINE 4   Confidently change the rules

You are responsible for implementing needed reforms. Trust that it will turn out well, even though there may be some resistance to change.

LINE 3   Only when the change is discussed
three times is it trusted

It is important to discuss the issues and gain a solid base of support before attempting any reforms. When you have sorted things out, you will have the agreement you need.

LINE 2   The day has come to make that change

The day of change has arrived, and you are well placed to assist the revolution. Let others know what is going on, so that they can contribute as well.

LINE 1   Wrapped up tight in yellow oxhide

To make any radical changes, you need sufficient support and personal strength. For now, develop your sense of security. Be like a baby, safely wrapped up in a blanket.

REAL-LIFE ADVENTURES

Make That Change

Change takes many forms. Each hexagram is an image of a specific type of change. This hexagram, "Revolution," has to do with making a radical change. Out with the old and in with the new.

Pablito was about to take a ritual peyote initiation in Death Valley, California. His guide gave him this potent mind-altering drug as a means of shifting him out of his rigid way of thinking, and to deliberately cause a revolution in his mind. After ingesting the peyote, and as the effects of the hallucinogen were beginning to alter his perspective, he consulted the *I Ching* about the journey he was undertaking into the land of mystery.

Q What advice do you have for my journey?

A Pablito received Hexagram 49, with line 5 moving.

Hexagram 49 says that there are five guidelines for making a radical change: a real need, the right timing, the necessary support, unselfish motives, and the avoidance of excesses. If these guidelines are not followed, calamity will result from the misuse of power.

Pablito had prepared properly for the encounter, and this reading confirmed his impeccable intention. This was to be a profoundly spiritual transformation.

The courageous tiger with its brilliant stripes in line 5 was the perfect protector for a journey into the desert.

This was Pablito's one and only experience with peyote—all that was needed.

The West Is the Best

Our friends Keith and Melissa were living in Taos, New Mexico, and considering a move to California. They had journeyed there twice, and were now seeking a new perspective from the *I Ching*.

Q What are the prospects for a move to California?

A Hexagram 49, line 3 moving.

Hexagram 49 is about making radical changes in your life.

Line 3 says discuss it three times before making a final decision. Keith and Melissa took this to mean that making another trip to California would equal three times, and off they went on their third journey to California.

Know before you go. This works well before making radical changes in our lives.

50

ORDER

STRUCTURE

SECURITY

The new order

The cauldron, good fortune and success

FIRE

TREE

Fire rising from wood. The control and use of fire is one of the great developments in civilization.

The Chinese call this hexagram "The Cauldron." It was used in state sacrifices and was thus a symbol of the state and the power of the emperor. The cauldron and the fire together represent the security and safety of the pot cooking on the stove.

Perpetually renew and regulate your vital energy. Create order. Discover new ways of doing things.

LINE 6   The cauldron has a jade carrying rod

Everything you do will be to your advantage. You are firm yet flexible. You have a cool hand in hot situations. Supreme good fortune.

LINE 5   The cauldron has bronze handles

Everything is now in working order. You are open to hearing the truth. Everyone is cooperating to make it work out well. You have a handle on the situation.

**LINE 4   The legs of the cauldron snap,
            spilling the food, making a mess**

Lack of support and carelessness has led to a breakdown and harm has occurred. You may have taken on too much and broken down under the strain.

**LINE 3   The cauldron's handles are too hot to
            touch, the food burns**

Your impatience has spoiled an opportunity. Now it is too hot to touch. When things cool down you will get a handle on the situation and there will be improvement.

LINE 2   The cauldron is filled with food

What you believe in will be realized. You have what you need, and this enables you to be independent. Others may resent your good fortune, but they cannot harm you.

LINE 1   The cauldron tips over, opportunity to clean it out

Turn an unfavorable situation to your advantage by making a clean sweep of things. In unusual circumstances you may need to improvise and make do.

A REAL-LIFE ADVENTURE

Getting into Print

It's 1980: An earlier version of the book that you are now reading—all nine hundred weighty and largely incomprehensible pages—is with the managing editor of a well-known British publishing house. This is another of those "big chance" moments in life.

Q Concerning the future of our book on the *I Ching?*

A We received Hexagram 50, with line 6 moving.

Hexagram 50 represents, in this case, the validity of the new ideas, concepts, and visions in our book. A new system of ideas.

Line 6 means that we should present something in an accessible manner.

The jade handle on the lid of the cauldron works because it does not get too hot to hold. Make it easy to handle and to understand. That was not the book we had at the time. It was obscure, obtuse, and long-winded.

The editor emphasized the value of the original research we had done and suggested a tighter and more coherent version. Her encouragement prevented that vision from dying a premature death.

We were being told that the failure of rejection was not the failure of the idea itself. Be patient. The line indicated the importance of making these ideas more understandable.

When the Chinese sage writes a book, the completed manuscript is put away in a drawer. Nine years later it is taken out and read again. If it is still satisfactory, it is worthy of being published. Not a very fast-track idea, is it?

51

SHOCK

SURPRISE

EXCITEMENT

All shook up

The thunderbolt strikes terror, but not a drop is lost

THUNDER

THUNDER

Thunder and more thunder. Anyone who has been in the midst of a heavy thunderstorm knows what it feels like.

A blinding flash of lightning on a pitch-black night. The shock of coming across something quite unexpected. Scared and then excited. First terror, then laughter.

The germination of a seed in the spring. The stimulation of sexual arousal.

The subtle difference between terror and excitement. Some enjoy the storm and some run from it. What is your thrill level?

LINE 6   Thunderbolt trailing away, strikes his neighbor

A situation that you have failed to handle is fading away. The danger is aimed not at you but at those around you. You are not in a position to act aggressively. Let it pass.

LINE 5   Thunderbolts everywhere, be prepared, no losses

Keep an even mind despite the shocks and confusion and you will suffer no setback to your plans. There are things to be done and great gains to be made. It will all fall into place.

LINE 4   Thunderbolt, fall in the mud

Shock has immobilized you. You have succumbed and are stuck in the mud. You may be stuck in the middle of a project. Frozen at the controls. Bogged down.

LINE 3   Loud thunderbolts shake you up

Being surrounded by shocks can wake you up and get you to do things you didn't think you could do. Act now, with presence of mind.

LINE 2   Dangerous thunderbolts, take to the hills

As with a flood or earthquake warning, you must get out of harm's way. You will regain what you have lost when the threat is over.

LINE 1   After the thunderbolt, laughing with relief

A surprise leaves you shaken, but you learned something of value. After the initial panic, a relief of tension. Sometimes risks must be taken.

REAL-LIFE ADVENTURES

Down and Out in Delhi

New Delhi, India, 1982: We had been traveling in the East for over a year, and it felt like lifetimes. We were more than half nuts by this time; exhausted and constantly on the defensive in this environment. Is it time to go home for a hamburger and the ordinary life, or should we go on to further exotica, disillusion, and despair?

Q What stage are we now at on this journey of discovery in the East?

A We received Hexagram 51, with line 4 moving.

Hexagram 51 says that there are two reactions to surprise and shock. It can have a beneficial effect, as in getting the adrenaline flowing, or collapse you in the mud, quivering in fear.

Line 4 indicated again what we already knew: that the multiple shocks of being constantly with each other and the arduous circumstances of the journey had left us overwhelmed. We were simply exhausted with the adventure. Time to rest up.

Electric Shock

Bisbee, Arizona, 1989: We had nearly reached the end of a major renovation with our hundred-year-old house. We were looking forward to the next step in our lives with both excitement and trepidation. We had found a house to live in, spent time and money to make it habitable, and now we could live our life.

Buying a computer was about writing this book; but we also felt that bringing a computer into our lives and becoming "computer literate" would be like bringing another intimate partner into our marriage: it would be time consuming, demanding, and it wouldn't do the washing up.

Q Is this the appropriate time to finally buy our computer?

A We received Hexagram 51, with line 5 moving.

Hexagram 51 refers to the shock and confusion of renovation. As anyone knows who has been involved in the "delights" of home improvement, the end of dust, disorder, and paying bills is never in sight.

Line 5 strengthened our resolve, telling us that the worst was over.

We took that to mean that the daily level of grime and building aggravation was on a decline, and it would be safe to bring this new addition into our lives.

Also, the computer itself was going to be a shock and surprise. We had arguments we never anticipated about this machine. Jealousy strikes on the home front. How did we settle it? Visitation rights and time-sharing.

52

STILLNESS

TRANQUILLITY

STABILITY

No hurry—no worry

*Passersby do not see you
in your courtyard*

MOUNTAIN

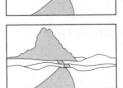

MOUNTAIN

The mountain over the mountain. A range
of mountains is the vision of stillness.

The Chinese image used to describe
this hexagram shows an eye above a person,
meaning to observe or contemplate.

Stillness is a state of alert readiness. Readiness
means that you are aware of what is going on
around you. When it is correct to sit, you sit,
and when it is time to move, you move.

The stillness and calmness of the mountain
inspires the meditative mind.

LINE 6 Perfectly still

Stop when you reach the top. You have persevered and made it to your goal. Go no further, or you will fall off the mountain.

LINE 5 Shut your mouth

You can be a fast talker who does not give anything away, even when under pressure. On the other hand, your big mouth could get you into trouble. Think before you speak.

LINE 4 Keep completely still, avoid harm

Be calm, gentle, and honest. Handle any upsetting situations by relaxing and quieting yourself. If you do this, you will be unaffected by the turmoil around you.

LINE 3 Keeping so still, you give yourself heartburn

Forcefully restraining your natural desires will only create tension. Trying to induce calmness by means of artificial rigidity will give you an anxiety attack. Ease up; give yourself a break.

LINE 2 Keeping your legs still

You want to act, but are advised to hold yourself in check. You may be unable to prevent another from acting foolishly.

LINE 1 Keep your feet still

This is not the time to be swept off your feet or to engage in impulsive actions. Stop now before you make a wrong move. Be happy with where you are now.

A REAL-LIFE ADVENTURE

Trying Too Hard

After many years of meditation with a wonderful Zen guide, Rod approached what was to be his last formal Zen retreat with sadness in his heart. Loss is always behind sadness. Loss comes when something is ended or you fear it is about to end.

A separation had already taken place between Rod and his teacher. The familiar rituals were no longer bringing comfort. They felt stale and empty. He could not even bring himself to talk to the teacher about it.

All life cycles have a beginning, a middle, and an end. The art is in knowing where you are in the cycle: wash, rinse, or spin dry? One of the most difficult things to discern is if something has really ended or if you are quitting just because the going got too tough. Midway into the retreat, Rod consulted the *I Ching*.

Q The retreat appears to be going well, and yet I feel sad. Please advise.

A Rod received Hexagram 52, with line 3 moving.

Hexagram 52 has to do with being still, as in meditation.

Line 3 indicated an inappropriate persistence in this practice. His heart wasn't in it. Heartburn seemed inevitable. Trying too hard. Time to let go.

53

GRADUAL PROGRESS

DEVELOPING

ADVANCE

By the book

Favorable for marriage

TREE

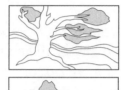

MOUNTAIN

The tree grows slowly on the mountain. The Chinese describe this situation as the formal stages toward marriage: courtship, engagement, and the wedding.

Another picture used to describe this hexagram is the migration of wild geese. Geese are loyal to their mates and regular in their migration patterns. The arriving, nesting, and departing of the geese mark the natural cycles of the year.

Though it may seem to be a long way away, do not abandon your goal. Progress stage-by-stage and you will get what you want.

LINE 6 **The wild goose flies into the clouds, its feathers used in the sacred dance**

You have gone beyond ordinary success, and so may feel distanced from your friends. Your actions serve as an inspiration for others.

LINE 5 **The wild goose finally reaches the summit**

With strength and flexibility you finally reach your goal. It may take longer than you expected. Ultimately, you are invincible. Projects bear fruit. Marriage and children are possible.

LINE 4 **The wild goose manages to perch on a flat tree branch**

You find a safe place to stay a while. The journey isn't over yet. The place you have found is a suitable niche to which you can adapt, but this is not a permanent home.

LINE 3 **The wild goose reaches for the high desert plains**

In your hurry to succeed, you have gone off on your own and lost your way. Projects will not reach completion. Defend your position rather than attacking others. Betrayal by partners is possible.

LINE 2 **The wild goose lands on some dry rocks**

The first step of the journey is successfully completed, and you have found a safe, though temporary, resting place. Share this good fortune with your friends. This is a time to enjoy each others' company.

LINE 1 **The little goose struggles to the shore**

The first steps of any journey are dangerous. You are open to criticism because you are a novice. Be persevering and keep your goal in mind. Call for help if you need it.

A REAL-LIFE ADVENTURE

The Best Meditation—Ever

During the seventh day of a seven-day silent group retreat, Amy was suddenly attacked verbally by Alex, a friend and one of the retreat participants. For no apparent reason he jumped up and began ranting and raving, putting down the teacher and calling Amy a Jewish bitch psychologist. True! but delivered with such vigorous disgust and relish?

Amy restrained herself from either crying or screaming. She completed the retreat prior to asking any question of the *I Ching* or handling the situation.

Q How can I best handle Alex, who has just had this psychotic episode?

A Amy received Hexagram 53, with line 6 moving.

Hexagram 53 speaks of maintaining a balanced and steady progress toward a goal. Good advice, of course, and the opposite of the feelings that had been stirred up in the incident.

Line 6 in the original text talks about a goose flying into the clouds and its feathers being used in a sacred ritual dance. We interpreted this to mean reaching your goal by transcending this world of conflict. An encouraging statement.

Amy normally handles things head-on. The Tibetan lama she was meditating with on this retreat had a leave-it-alone approach. Being in retreat was a helpful circumstance for taking an objective attitude.

Partly from the sheer surprise at being in deep silent meditation one moment, and then looking up to see a dear friend waving his arms around and hurling abuse at her; and partly from the discipline of maintaining the sacred silence and forbearance of the retreat, she made no response and kept her silence. She had managed to maintain control, even though she was seething inside.

Afterward, the lama told Amy that managing to complete the retreat without breaking the silence, and continuing to meditate, was the best meditation she had ever done.

When tempers had cooled (after many months of silence), Amy and Alex resolved the situation peaceably. The art is in being able to be aggressive or tolerant at will. The wisdom is in knowing when.

IMPULSIVE

PASSIONATE

FLAWED

Fools rush in

*Advancing to war
brings misfortune*

THUNDER

LAKE

Thunder over the lake. The lake represents the desire
to break free of restraints and come forth. The thunder represents
a sudden, instinctive rush, as in sexual excitement.

Together they imply a very energetic but
possibly rash and premature display.

You are in danger of taking on too much too soon.
Emotions make you hasty and reckless. However, nothing
ventured, nothing gained.

Having the courage to take risks is what life is about.

LINE 6   **The basket is empty**

You either have something of little or no value, or you are doing something without really meaning it. Empty gestures.

LINE 5   **The bride is more modestly dressed than the bridesmaids**

You have no need to show off or be the big shot. When you have the upper hand, stand back and let others shine.

LINE 4   **Delaying marriage, all in good time**

It will take longer to reach your goal than you expected. Wait until the time is ripe to do something. A delay may be to your advantage.

LINE 3   **Hoping to be a wife, ending up a concubine**

Your expectations are too great to be fulfilled now. Wait for a better opportunity, or you may feel that you sold out for less than you're worth.

LINE 2   **Seeing with one eye, stay in seclusion**

When you cannot see clearly, stay out of sight. You may feel bogged down. An imperfect relationship can be worked out. Concentrate on one thing at a time.

LINE 1   **The younger sister becomes the second wife**

With good connections, advances can be made, even if you are not fully qualified, or are lacking in some way.

REAL-LIFE ADVENTURES

Ignoring the Omen

Hurley, England: We were preparing to take a holiday abroad in Hungary, returning to the home of Rod's father to discover his roots. Our romantic need to take this journey to the theoretical homeland was pretty unreal, as Rod's dad was a Jewish refugee from Budapest who escaped from his native country with only his life and the clothes on his back.

Q What advice for our holiday?

A We received Hexagram 54, with line 2 moving.

Hexagram 54 indicates some sort of disadvantage.

Line 2 expresses that you are not seeing things clearly and are headed for trouble. The line literally advises to stay at home. Don't go. This was a memorable reading, as we felt obligated to take the journey and so ignored the advice.

The trip was full of disasters. If it could go wrong, it did. Frogs raining down from the sky, tires blowing out, no room at the inn—things like that. So much for ignoring the omens.

Selling Blue Sky

Maralee wanted to sell her restaurant, which she had been struggling to keep going for two years. There really wasn't much to sell—a too-short lease, some paltry equipment, and two years of customer goodwill. "Selling blue sky" is the term for selling a business with little or no saleable value.

Maralee had borrowed her starter money and wanted to pay that money back. So she asked for much more money than the cafe was worth, and had waited for a year with no buyer.

Q Selling the business. Will I get my price?

A Maralee received Hexagram 54, with line 6 moving.

Hexagram 54 says you want and need more than you're worth. You are at a disadvantage, and need to come to terms with how things really are.

Line 6 emphasizes this. It describes a situation where nothing is available. Get realistic. The reason there is no buyer is that there is nothing to sell. Sad but true.

PLENTY

HARVEST

ABUNDANCE

*Make hay while the
sun shines*

Be like the noonday sun

THUNDER

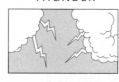

FIRE

Thunder over fire. Fire represents a brilliant
display of acquisitions, and thunder represents uninhibited
action. Together they suggest the peak of glory. Along with
this goes the message of impermanence.

Everything is going your way. This is your moment
of glory, your opportunity to grab the brass ring. You may look
back on this in later years as the best time of your life.

You may not get this chance again. Be decisive.
Make it happen. Go for it.

LINE 6   Peering in at the palace gate, empty for three years

Things are not as good as they seem. Outward grandeur will not cover inner weakness. You may be living beyond your means. In not sharing your good fortune, you have become isolated and conceited.

LINE 5   Your shining inner light wins blessings

You are well received and your gifts and talents are appreciated. You have something to celebrate. You have the support of able helpers.

LINE 4   Heavy curtains cut out all the light

Cut off from the light and in the dark. This is an obstructed and unsuitable position. Confusion and lies abound. You cannot see or be seen. When you understand the confusion, you will see the light.

LINE 3   So many flags darken the sky; a broken right arm

The flags are semaphore or signal flags. You are so bombarded with cross messages that you suffer an injury. It is not too serious, and you will soon recover. You may even be able to turn this to your advantage.

LINE 2   The curtains are so thick that even at noon the lamps must be lit

Extravagant gestures will only obscure and confuse your real intentions. Be open and sincere. No need to hide behind a facade of luxury.

LINE 1   Meeting your partner, good for ten days

Someone of significance is willing to help you. If you take advantage of this generosity, realize that they may want something from you in return.

REAL-LIFE ADVENTURES

Playing the Market

We became interested in playing the investment market. We were especially fascinated with the buying and selling of commodities; like gold and silver, soybeans and coffee. The stuff that makes the world go round, and keeps it awake. This is an interesting and complex way to make some money with your money. A little like going to Vegas or playing the lottery.

For the first few months, we haunted the library and studied all the books we could find on the subject. Then we spoke to all the professionals in the field who would talk to us. There are hundreds of investment counselors or brokers who'll spend hours talking with you. This is their way of hooking you into playing the game, and getting your money.

Then we experimented with paper (practice-pretend) trading, and finally decided on an investment counselor, one out of the multitude with whom we had been speaking. This broker talked and talked, and involved us in many complex deals. With some we made money, and with some we didn't.

We began to get very confused and to feel that we were in way over our incapable heads. Was it a mistake to have gotten into this game? Was it a mistake to have chosen this person as our guide?

Q What to do with this relationship? Keep the game going or get out?

A We received Hexagram 55, with line 3 moving.

Hexagram 55 is about making hay while the sun shines. We surely had been trying to do that, and with some success, until we got confused and lost it.

Line 3 means that you are receiving mixed and crossed messages, causing an injury of some kind. Our injuries were of a mental and financial nature.

We terminated the relationship with this broker when we realized that we needed to make educated decisions, right or wrong, for ourselves. Doing what someone else tells us to do, without fully understanding how the decisions were being made, was not for us.

Over the Hill

In 1976 we were the proud owners of an antique English Rover—the car, not the dog. Mahogany and old leather. What a beauty. Difficult to abandon, even in its old age, with inner parts almost impossible to locate, and consistent breakdowns in the most inconvenient places imaginable.

Q Should we sell the car?

A We received Hexagram 55, with line 6 moving.

Hexagram 55 tells of something that has reached its peak.

Line 6 obviously indicated that we had reached the end of the road, and may be going over the hill.

The sun sets on the old Rover. Fade to black.

56

TRAVELING

TRANSITION

IMPERMANENT

Just passing through

Auspicious for the wanderer

FIRE

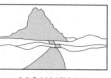

MOUNTAIN

Fire on the mountain. A brush fire flares up,
and moves on elsewhere. This gives the image of
movement, impermanence, and restlessness.

In days gone by, travel was a perilous
undertaking. The traveler understands nonattachment.
The traveler has few friends and is not burdened with
unnecessary possessions or responsibilities. This is
no place for long-term arrangements.

When you are on the road, be polite and cautious.
You are in a vulnerable position. Do not expect
too much. Pay attention to details.

It happens now, or not at all.

LINE 6   The wanderer's nest burns up

In taking your good fortune for granted, you lose it. Laughter at another's misfortune may turn to tears when misfortune strikes you.

LINE 5   The wanderer shoots a pheasant with one arrow

You demonstrate your talents and find a good position. Even though you are a stranger, you are welcomed. Make the most of opportunities offered without being boastful.

LINE 4   The wanderer gains possessions and an ax

You find a place to settle down, and the means to make a living. But in your heart you are not content. You feel out of place. You are not doing what you really want to be doing.

LINE 3   The inn burns down and the wanderer loses the servant

When a quick temper leads to arguments, things may be said that cannot be taken back. Your resting place is no longer safe. You have lost the goodwill of others, and it is best that you leave.

LINE 2   The wanderer finds an inn and a servant

You have found a good place to stay, where the facilities are adequate and the people are friendly. Though this is not your permanent home, you can afford to stay for a while.

LINE 1   Inattentive and petty-minded wanderer

If you know where you are going and are well prepared, you will enjoy a great adventure. An agitated and small-minded attitude, on the other hand, leads to mistakes, ill will, and frustration.

REAL-LIFE ADVENTURES

Staying a While

We were living in our magnificent inherited home in England, "The Refectory." It was out of another era, and way beyond our means of support. The only way we could continue on in this situation was to turn the place around from our private residence to a retreat center for healing.

Our friends in England were supportive of our doing this, but we personally felt that we had too much to learn, and too far to go on our own journey of self-evolvement, to commit ourselves to such a project.

Q Do we open a healing center?

A We received Hexagram 56, with line 2 moving.

Hexagram 56 is about moving on. Nothing lasts forever. Are you getting stuck?

Line 2 says that the traveler has found a comfortable place to stay. Yes, that was true. It was too comfortable, and that made it easy to forget that we were travelers.

We knew that it was impermanent, and yet we became attached. And how! The heart breaks with the realization that we must leave this place of enchantment. We were able to stay for a while longer, but the bottom line is—you are the traveler.

On the Road

The "Rod and Amy Road Show" lands in Hawaii, and as if that's not enough, we finally find two great spiritual guides, after years of wandering and seeking.

Q It feels so good to be here. Is this our permanent place at last?

A We received Hexagram 56, with line 4 moving.

Hexagram 56 says that you are still on the road.

Line 4 says that something is still not right. Your heart is not at ease.

You can rent a place, get a car, and try to settle down, but that feeling of being the traveler won't leave you. It's not yet the right time to put down roots. We remained in Hawaii for four years, always renting, never buying. Forever the wanderers?

57

GENTLE PENETRATION

FLEXIBILITY

PERMEATE

Bending with the wind

Make your intentions known

TREE

TREE

Tree or wind over tree or wind. This hexagram shows a sacred grove in which the trees and their branches bend in response to the wind. In this way they adapt to circumstances and avoid being uprooted.

The Chinese name for this hexagram means to crouch or bow down. By observing quietly and closely, one gains insight.

You are able to move into a subject and examine it in depth, without losing your openness.

With a flexible mind, you have a great advantage.

**LINE 6 Kneeling before the throne,
losing your property and your ax**

Either an excess of flexibility, or greed and ambition, has resulted in your losing all that you have. What is given is taken away.

LINE 5 Bad beginning, good ending

This is a turn for the better, from bad luck to good luck. Be flexible and adaptable and you will come out ahead. All's well that ends well.

LINE 4 Bagging three kinds of game

You may feel you gave up something by being flexible, but you have gained by doing this, and you will reap great rewards. Act with confidence.

LINE 3 Repeatedly kneeling in submission

Because of your stubbornness and uncertainty, you may find yourself forced to submit, against your will, again and again.

LINE 2 Kneeling before the throne, blessed by the shamans

You have been noticed, and it is your ability to adapt to the will of those in power that has gained you a position of influence. Take advantage of professional assistance and suggestions.

LINE 1 When in doubt, be as steady as a warrior

Are you coming or going? Indecision is corrected by developing a firm will and singleness of purpose. When you have a plan and the resources to implement it, then you may advance.

REAL-LIFE ADVENTURES

Stoned Immaculate

Q In 1984 a friend asked what the effects of marijuana would be on his body and mind.

A He received Hexagram 57, with line 4 moving. Hexagram 57 is flexibility of mind, and insight.

The trigram tree or wind, doubled, is an apt description of the marijuana mind. The mind opens and spreads it wings. Moving freely, comfortably forgetful of where it came from or where it is going. Breaking through rigid habits and opening to new horizons. The excess of this flexibility is panic and indecision.

Line 4 indicates that there is much to be gained for the questioner in experiencing this new reality.

Bending or Breaking?

Our client was an entrepreneur who had the opportunity to involve himself financially and as editor-in-chief in the publication of a new glossy magazine. He had some doubts, however, about whether this opportunity was as good as it seemed.

Q What about this magazine opportunity?

A He received Hexagram 57, with line 3 moving.

Hexagram 57 is about adapting to circumstances. What are the circumstances, and how much adaptation is going to be required?

Line 3 indicates that pride is the button here.

He did start this venture. In order to keep it going, he was forced to invest a considerable amount of his own money in it, again and again. He discovered in a short time that he had far less power and control than he had been led to believe would be the case. Eventually, he was forced to abandon the magazine venture, without recouping any of his investment.

On the basis of this reading, we had warned him against taking this on. C'est la vie. Asking for advice is one thing. Taking it is another.

Bowing Before the Throne

How to approach your new editor and publisher: We had received our first telephone call from HarperSanFrancisco, saying our book (which we had sent in unsolicited) was the rage of the office, and they wanted to publish us. We're happy, needless to say, and want to do all the right things and not blow this terrific opportunity to reach a wider audience (and sell out!).

Q How should we approach this partnership with HarperSanFrancisco?

A We received Hexagram 57, with line 2 moving.

Hexagram 57 is about trees bending in the wind. Making your back flexible. Some funny pictures arise here. How low do we bend?

Line 2 says bow before the throne. It will be to your advantage. We told our editor this, and shared a big laugh when she said she wanted to send a copy of this to all her other authors. We continue to be pliant. Putty in her hands. And if you're reading this now . . .

58

SELF-CONFIDENCE

ENCOURAGEMENT

PLEASURE

Straight talk

Speak your mind

LAKE

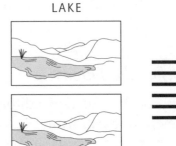

LAKE

Lake over lake. This is a doubled trigram. Friendly interchange. The most important question we need to ask about the universe is, "Is it friendly?"

Joyous self-expression. Come out into the open, and freely express your ideas and feelings. Seek people and influences that are responsive to your openness.

Difficulties are more easily overcome when you are enjoying yourself. Your ingenuity and inventiveness will serve you well.

LINE 6   Encouraged to come forth

This is an opportunity for you to come out into the open and participate. There is also a temptation to be self-indulgent.

LINE 5   Trusting a thief

You are surrounded by people who want to take advantage of you and who may not be telling the truth. Be wary of whom you trust.

LINE 4   Calculating the odds

Be happy with what you are doing now. What you have is good. Worrying and figuring about it will only confuse and agitate you. Complete what you have begun.

LINE 3   A tempting offer

Are you pleasing yourself or doing something in order to please another? There may be some external temptations. Happiness comes from within.

LINE 2   Sincere speech

When you know who you are and what you want, you are free to speak the truth from your heart. Win the confidence of others with sincerity, not flattery.

LINE 1   Natural speech

Come forth and speak your mind in a joyous and spontaneous way. This is the simple and natural expression that comes at the first moment of seeing something beautiful.

REAL-LIFE ADVENTURES

City of Joy

We have just crossed the Death Valley desert and arrived at the oasis of Palm Springs, California. And what an oasis. "Rodeo Drive" in a desert wilderness, or so it appears to us, bathed as we are in two-day-old sweat.

Q This place is gorgeous. Would it be good for us to stay a while? Please?

A We received Hexagram 58, with line 6 moving.

Hexagram 58 means self-expression. The image of two lakes: no scarcity of that element here. Palm Springs is an endless stream of pools and healing waters (chlorinated and natural).

Line 6 means forced to come forth. We did feel that way. It was in our phase of being *real* instead of being *nice*—an identity crisis that had just begun, and continues to this day.

It was a time for us of immense explorations. We met some extraordinary characters and were forced to break out of many rigid boxes of our own construction.

Eventually, we burnt out from too much sun and fun, and it was time to move on.

Time to Move On?

This is about two of our friends, a partnership of two entrepreneurs, running a small cottage industry out of their spare bedroom. Not getting rich, but paying the rent and with plenty of free time.

They were approached to combine their little business with a much larger company. Sell out, you might say. Though what's not to like? More money and better benefits, but hardly any free time. So what? It's the American dream, isn't it?

Still going strong on their current course, they felt torn and indecisive. This was a big decision. One that would definitely influence the course of their working lives together.

The interesting synchronicity here is that they asked two questions, one for each alternative; that is, "Go?" and "Stay?" and received the same hexagram for both questions. The differing lines indicated the difference in position and intent within the same hexagram. Another wondrous bit of synchronicity?

Q Should we stay, just the two of us?

A They received Hexagram 58, with line 3 moving.

Q Should we begin working with others?

A They received Hexagram 58 again, this time with line 4 moving.

Hexagram 58 is to do with fulfilling your own karma, rather than someone else's. Doing your own thing.

Line 3 relates to a tempting or distracting offer. This must be carefully examined.

Line 4 is about calculating the future. Go figure! We can't always dictate what our future will be.

What are your true feelings and motivations? If you are happy, keep doing what you're doing. You're not finished yet.

59

BREAK UP

DISPERSE

SCATTER

Riding the wave

Bring blessings to the temple

TREE

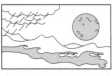

WATER

The tree or wind is over the water. The wind over the water breaks up the rigid ice floes and stirs the water into waves. Once you've broken the ice, the rigidity is gone.

The Chinese word for this hexagram means a flood of water. The flood is frightening at first, but then sweeps you to the high ground.

Wood, wind, and water gives us the image of boats sailing on the water. Travel and trading.

In a situation of dissolving and scattering energies, it is important to remain focused on your original intentions.

Keep your balance in unsettled times. Ride the wave without getting wiped out.

LINE 6   Swept far from your sorrows

Though you have successfully survived a harmful encounter, you may still wish for more pleasant surroundings where you will not be threatened again. Out of harm's way.

LINE 5   Dripping in sweat, you are summoned to the king's palace

The offer of a new experience may make you sweat and tremble. Take the offer if you can keep your cool.

LINE 4   Swept from the herd on to a hilltop

Events sweep you out of a rut and out of the way of danger. Let go of old habits and routines. Do the unusual; change your life.

LINE 3   Swept away by the flood

External events have taken your mind off your own troubles. Help yourself by helping others.

LINE 2   Swept along by the flood

You may not know where the tide of events is leading. Ride the current wave of energy. Seize opportunities as they arise. Someone is by your side and will support you.

LINE 1   Rescued with the aid of a strong horse

With the help of a friend, you can get out of a difficult situation before it gets out of hand. A disintegrating situation can be handled if caught soon enough.

REAL-LIFE ADVENTURES

Truth or Dare?

Not born in the U.S.A., Rod is working on his immigration status. We have been totally honest with our legal counsel and found that we told him too much and worsened our case.

Confusion had arisen over missing divorce papers from twenty years ago, and now Amy would have to get redivorced and remarried to Roddy. It's always good to retake your vows, but for the government? What a lot of fuss over nothing.

Our legal counsel was obligated by law to reveal what he knew to the immigration authorities.

Q How should we handle all the confusion and complexities?

A We received Hexagram 59, with line 2 moving.

Hexagram 59 is concerned with the flow of energies.

Line 2 clearly says ride the current wave of energy. It will lead you to safety.

We decided to keep our current lawyer, tell the truth, and deal with the consequences. The process took almost a year, and now Roddy is a legal resident. Hallelujah! The difficulties that seem to arise when we are honest and open often lead us to consider more devious approaches.

Riding the Wave

Our friend Cathleen feels sad, out of control, and unsure about her life with her mate of fifteen years. Her relationship with him seems to be breaking up.

Q Please advise. What is the true nature of my current situation?

A Cathleen received Hexagram 59, with line 5 moving.

Hexagram 59 confirms her feeling of dissolution and breaking apart.

Line 5 says that you will be swept up to the king's palace. The breakup of the relationship will propel you toward new and demanding possibilities.

Cathleen left the countryside of Ireland for the city of London. She has changed her life and is meeting the challenge.

60

DISCIPLINE

GUIDELINES

LIMITATIONS

Freedom within the form

*Too much restraint
is not beneficial*

WATER

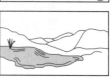

LAKE

The water is over the lake. There should be enough rain to fill the lake, but not so much that it overflows. The valley collects the water and guides it into a single stream.

The tendency to collect, organize, and measure out.

Having discipline or structure in your life is good, as long as the restraints do not create bitterness and resentment. Ease up if this is the case.

LINE 6 Painful restraint

Giving yourself too hard a time leads to exhaustion, bitterness, and resentment. Do not blame yourself. Ease up and take a new direction.

LINE 5 Content with discipline

Self-discipline is the key to your happiness. With discipline and a structure to your life, there is predictable order and progress.

LINE 4 Safe within the boundaries of your life

You are accustomed to leading an orderly life. The discipline and restraints you abide by are a reliable and comforting structure. Keep to your routine.

LINE 3 A regrettable lack of restraint

If you failed to control a situation before it got out of hand, you have no one to blame but yourself. You are responsible for your condition.

LINE 2 In not leaving your house, you miss your chance

If you hold back now, you will miss your opportunity. You may fail to act when it is to your advantage to do so. Fear and doubt. Find an outlet for energies before you become frustrated.

LINE 1 Stay home, and out of danger

If you stay where you are, you will avoid trouble. Wait for a more favorable opportunity. Know what is possible and what is not possible. Control yourself. Know your limits.

REAL-LIFE ADVENTURES

Showing Some Restraint

Passion for a new love, be it a person, place, or thing, is a wonderful emotion. And confusing.

Joanne had met a special man on a trip to Bakersfield and was in love. Of course, there were complications. He was involved with another woman and still living with her.

He said it was an association of habit and convenience and that he already had his bags packed to come and join Joanne, but he could not come right away. He had to earn some money first, and that would take several months. They had only known each other for two days. They had barely kissed.

Perhaps, in her heart, she didn't quite trust him or his story. It is an age-old tale. You can just imagine the doubt and confusion in her mind and heart. She considered returning to Bakersfield to fight for her man.

Q Should I go after him?

A Joanne received Hexagram 60, with line 1 moving.

Hexagram 60 says act with restraint. Chasing her lover to Bakersfield wasn't appropriate here.

Line 1 says by not going out your door, you avoid harm. The advice could not have been clearer.

She followed the advice and did not rush off to Bakersfield to see what was happening. She kept her cool, stayed at home, and maintained trust in him.

By waiting, she preserved her strength and integrity, not to mention some dignity. He had to make the effort, and he did. Happy endings. Miracles never cease to amaze us, do they?

L.A. Story: The Earthquake of 1994

Donna is a jewelry designer in New Jersey. In August 1993, she was invited to participate in a jewelry convention in Los Angeles, which was to take place the following January.

Q Should I go to the convention in Los Angeles in January?

A Donna received Hexagram 60, with line 1 moving.

Hexagram 60 indicates limitations. Donna had no idea what the limitations might be.

Line 1 says stay home and out of danger. Wait for a more favorable opportunity. Okay. Scary, but not specific. Donna uses the *I Ching* for all of her major decisions, professional and personal. So she accepted the advice, without knowing why. What trust. When the "great quake" hit Los Angeles at exactly the time she would have been there, all became clear. This particular reading was so memorable that she had to call and relate it to us. Thank you, Donna.

61

TRUSTING

WHOLEHEARTED

CENTERED

From the heart

*Modest offerings are
well received*

TREE

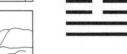

LAKE

The tree is over the lake. The tree shades the lake from the excessive heat of the sun, and the lake provides the tree with moisture. Each cares for and protects the other.

The Chinese word for this hexagram means middle or center. Being in the center means not losing yourself in sights and sounds and forgetting who you are and what you are doing.

An attentive and constant love. Like a mother hen; sitting on her eggs, hatching them, and caring for her chicks. There is a saying on Wall Street: "Put all your eggs in one basket, and then watch that basket very, very carefully."

With sincere and single-minded dedication,
great things can be accomplished.

LINE 6   High-flying chicken

When an arrogant chicken tries to fly too high, it will crash to earth. You have taken on too much. Keep on this way and you will come to grief.

LINE 5   Wholehearted sincerity

You are committed to high ideals, which protect you when you waver. Your integrity and sincerity persuade others to join you.

LINE 4   A lone horse breaks from the herd

Make a break from any negative influences. This may involve leaving the group you are now with. It will be to your advantage, especially if there is something greater to which you aspire.

LINE 3   Beating the drum, then stopping; weeping, then singing

Some activity has captivated your attention. You are dependent upon it for your sense of well-being and wholeness. If the object of your attention is worthy, then you will prosper. If unworthy, you will fail.

LINE 2   A crane calls from the shade, her chick responds

A mother hen, hidden in the shade, calls, and her chick replies. This is a natural response, perfect and complete in itself. Responding to a call from the heart.

LINE 1   Be prepared

Quietly develop your inner stability of mind. Don't let anyone distract you from this. You may be in for a surprise. Someone may betray you. Be prepared.

REAL-LIFE ADVENTURES

Not from the Heart

Tony wanted to involve himself in a get-rich-quick scheme—selling a mail-order self-help book.

He had not read the book he proposed to promote, and had already invested in buying a mailing list.

He was asking the *I Ching* if he should do it, when he had already committed himself to the project. It didn't seem correct to us to ask a question when the questioner was really only willing to accept a response that agreed with his decision. However . . .

Q Should I take on this business venture?

A Tony received Hexagram 61, with line 3 moving.

Hexagram 61 says that you must be wholehearted and honest in order to succeed.

Line 3 indicates that your attention is on something outside of you. If what you have your attention fixed on is beneficial—fine; and if it's not worthy of that fixation?

That seemed fairly obvious to us, in that Tony wanted to promote a book that he had not even bothered to read. His motivation hardly seemed to be "from the heart."

Also, because he was deeply involved financially, he needed a favorable response from the oracle and was unwilling to hear anything else. He'd put all his eggs in a shaky basket and it had to work.

Tony carried on and lost his shirt. Needless to say, there is no substitute for giving 100 percent of yourself.

T'ai Chi

In Chinese this hexagram is called Kung Fu, "centered—sincerity in the middle."

We were about to travel two hundred miles to attend our first weekend workshop in t'ai chi with a renowned Hawaiian master of the art. A long way to go with only a few hours familiarity with the practice.

Q Trip to Laguna for t'ai chi. How will it go?

A We received Hexagram 61, with line 3 moving.

Hexagram 61 is a perfect hexagram to describe t'ai chi; balanced and wholehearted.

Line 3 indicates that this is a powerful connection. This could be a significant force or factor in our lives.

We already felt that t'ai chi was a form of meditation that we had been searching for since we had first begun our explorations into aikido and yoga.

There is the same line in both these real-life adventures, with important differences. In the first instance, there was a vested interest in getting a particular response from the oracle, and a lack of sincerity. In this story, there was a sincere commitment. And in both, a strong link to the object of inquiry. If you're not willing to do whatever it takes, it won't get done.

Sugar Blues

A commodity investment question.

Q Sugar at $11.75. Will it rise above $12.50 in the next two weeks?

A We received Hexagram 61, with line 6 moving.

Hexagram 61 is about integrity. No real clue there.

Line 6 says the crazy chicken will fall flat on his face. This is our type of clue, and definitely not a good omen.

That was the very day sugar peaked. We then went into the "sugar blues" stage of diminishing returns. For the next four months it trended steadily downward from that high point to settle at $9.75.

We took the advice of the *I Ching* and left it alone. We made no bets. Once again, we put our trust in the oracle and were not disappointed.

DETAILS

CAUTION

GETTING BY

THUNDER

Don't push your luck

Fly low, little bird

MOUNTAIN

Thunder over the mountain. Thunder is action and the mountain is stillness. Action is emanating from stillness.

A small bird tries to fly too high. It should stay closer to the ground. Only small moves are possible.

You are not in a position to make major changes to the situation. Pay attention to details. Keep a low profile.

LINE 6 The flying bird is netted

You only know how to advance further and further into trouble. You demonstrate your arrogance by attempting a task beyond your capacity.

LINE 5 Clouds but no rain

There is the promise of rain, but the clouds pass by without any rain falling. You will attain a lesser ambition but not a greater one. Accept what comes your way and be satisfied. Do what is easy.

LINE 4 Be on your guard against a dangerous encounter

The course you are now taking may lead you into trouble. If you do go on, be cautious. It is better that you stay where you are. Be wary of pushing your luck.

LINE 3 Attacked from behind

If you go too far, you are likely to be attacked. Showing off leads to accidents. Stay alert and protect your rear.

LINE 2 Missing the boss, meeting the assistant

If you cannot get through to the boss, be content with seeing the second-in-command. Though you may miss a big opportunity, you will not miss a lesser one. Be content with a limited fulfillment of your goals.

LINE 1 Flying bird meets with bad luck

You are strongly inclined to make a move before you are ready. This, however, will lead to an unfortunate encounter that you are not able to avoid.

REAL-LIFE ADVENTURES

Plucked from Obscurity

A friend was offered an excellent position in her chosen profession. Not the top position, but one close enough to lead her to believe that she could indeed gain the top rung. She appreciated receiving the offer.

Q What will come of this offer?

A She received Hexagram 62, with line 5 moving.

Hexagram 62 says don't expect too much. Don't push your luck.

Line 5 indicates that your dream of number one power will not be realized. You are still the little bird.

A wonderfully self-evident reply. This is a great job, but not *the* job. There is no portent of great things to come. It indicates only small advantages to be gained.

Room with a View

We had been traveling in India for what was beginning to feel like forever when we were offered an extraordinary house, high in the mountains, with an endless view of the Ganges River. What a beauty. Of course, nothing is perfect. There was no toilet (in India, that means the toilet is anywhere outside); there was no kitchen (in India, that also means anywhere outside).

There were three of us traveling together at that time. For the two men, these were not insurmountable problems. For Amy, the four-star princess, this was a lot less than perfect.

Q This remarkable house in Vashisht. Do we stay a while?

A Hexagram 62, line 6 moving.

Hexagram 62 says don't push your luck. This would be pushing it. We were already exhausted, and walking half a mile to the village well for every glass of water seemed an added unnecessary discomfort.

Line 6 says further and further into trouble. Okay. Bad idea. Let's accept this as enough of a warning to move on, which we did.

63

CLIMAX

CULMINATION

ACHIEVEMENT

This perfect day

Good at first, chaos later

WATER

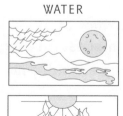

FIRE

Water over fire. The fire rises and warms the water. The water drops down and cools the fire. When the fire and water are in an exact balance, a magical transformation occurs.

A spring morning with the dew on the grass, the warmth of the sun breaking through the mist, and the promise of a wonderful day.

In this hexagram all the lines are in their appropriate places. In perfect balance for a flawless moment, and already changing into something else.

You have made it. You are lucky.

LINE 6   Getting your head wet

Recognize when you are in over your head. Carelessness toward the end of a venture leads to trouble. These difficulties will not be too great and will be over soon.

LINE 5   The sacrifice of an ox is not as blessed as the modest offering

A simple gesture given with sincerity counts for more than a grand and phony display.

LINE 4   Your jacket got soaking wet

Minor setbacks make you doubtful, cautious, and nervous. Take precautions against predictable accidents.

LINE 3   It takes three years to subdue the badlands

It takes a strong and determined person to undertake a difficult task without wearing out. Victory may leave you exhausted. Are you up to it?

LINE 2   She loses her veil; it will be returned within a week

Something lost will be returned, without your having to make any special effort to go after it.

LINE 1   The little fox gets a wet tail

Pull back and put on the brakes at this early stage. Minor difficulties are a warning of what is to come. Prepare for things before they become a problem.

REAL-LIFE ADVENTURES

Taming the Wild Elephant of the Mind

In Nepal: We met Emily, another wanderer in the East. She was considering going off on her own to do a long and solitary retreat. She asked for a reading.

Q Is it auspicious or not to do the work alone?

A Emily received Hexagram 63, with line 3 moving.

Hexagram 63 has a sense of transformation. The birth of something new.

Line 3 describes the time when you finally strike out on your own. "It takes three years to subdue the badlands" is the original Chinese phrase for line 3.

This is an interesting reply, as the journey Emily had in mind was a solitary three-year retreat. A long and arduous task; the confrontation of the wild lands of her own mind.

The only question is, are you up to it? She felt ready to strike out on her own. She remained in Asia for over three years, meditating and studying. She was up to it.

This Is Your Lucky Day

In Kathmandu, Nepal, an angry and confused encounter: everyone talking in different languages, involving hotel owners, taxi drivers, and what seemed like half the street population of Nepal. We both lost our composure, and Rod lost his wallet, which contained all his money and papers. Panic city.

Q What to do? Is there a chance of getting anything returned, or do we have to cancel all the credit cards and get a new passport?

A We received Hexagram 63, with line 2 moving.

Hexagram 63 means this is your lucky day.

Line 2 says that what you have lost will be returned within the week. Well, if this had happened in New York City, it would be a pretty unreal possibility. In Nepal, as luck would have it, that same evening, our taxi driver returned the wallet—intact, and a simple thank you from us was all he wanted.

We've always felt grateful for the honesty and generosity we encountered in that gentle kingdom.

SECOND WIND

NOT THERE YET

UNFINISHED BUSINESS

It's not over till the fat lady sings

The little fox gets its tail wet

FIRE

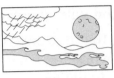

WATER

Fire is above water. The fire blazes up and the water flows down. They are moving away from each other. It will take some effort to bring them together in a positive interaction.

It is winter and the little fox, treading cautiously on the ice, is halfway across the river. The ice cracks and the little fox falls in, getting its bushy tail wet. It will either drown or make it to the far shore.

The wise old fox, on the other hand, listens to the water under the ice. What is the undercurrent? Does the ice sound thin? The wise old fox has the qualities needed to cross the river.

This is the time after the peak, when there is still another river to cross. Though success is not assured, it is certainly possible if you can sustain the effort.

Keep your tail up. It's not over yet.

LINE 6   So drunk that you get your head wet

It is alright to have a drink, but not to become a fall-down drunk. You have an over-inflated picture of yourself. Has success gone to your head?

LINE 5   Pay for the next round of drinks

Be generous in sharing your good fortune. If you win the lottery, it is only right that you buy everyone a round of drinks.

LINE 4   Tame the wild country after three years

To do something that may take three years requires dedication and a willingness to work for what one believes in. Act boldly, with strength and determination, and you will find your rewards.

LINE 3   When you are ready, cross the river

Though you are ready to move forward, you need help in overcoming the obstacles in your path. This may involve a slight pullback and a fresh start in order to succeed.

LINE 2   Braking the wheels

Step on the brakes; surprises lie ahead. Proceed slowly and carefully and you will do well. Take precautions against possible accidents.

LINE 1   A wet tail

The ice cracks under the little fox halfway across the river. Avoid getting involved in something until you know that you can take it to completion. Know your limits.

A REAL-LIFE ADVENTURE

Another River to Cross

Two readings for Amy for her year ahead, 1993, both Hexagram 64.

Q What's in store for me in the year ahead?

A Amy received Hexagram 64, with line 3 moving.

The first reading was done on the Celtic New Year (on October 31, Halloween). The second was done in December, on Amy's birthday. Both readings asked advice for the year to come. Both readings had line 3 moving.

Hexagram 64 says it's not over till the fat lady sings. Changes and more of same. Also, the need to follow through after the high, the win, or the completion. You have to persist and cross the river. There is no stopping midway or you drown.

Line 3 indicates that you may need some help, and help *was* on the way. In that year we completed publication of the first edition of this book, and we began our promotion by sending books all over the planet, hoping to be discovered and prepared not to be. And then . . . ?

We were discovered. And the game begins all over again, and in a new way. Changes. And this time, for a change, welcome ones. Magical. Discovered in the unsolicited manuscript bag by the brilliant editorial staff at HarperSanFrancisco.

P.S. The final and funniest synchronistic interplay with Hexagram 64 is that the HarperSanFrancisco logo is a picture of fire over water, Hexagram 64.

A human being is a part of the whole, called by us "universe," a part limited in time and space. He experiences himself, his thoughts and feelings as something separated from the rest—a kind of optical illusion of his consciousness. This delusion is a kind of prison for us, restricting us to our personal desires and to affection for a few persons nearest to us. Our task must be to free ourselves from this prison by widening our circle of compassion to embrace all living creatures and the whole of nature in its beauty.

Albert Einstein

Our existence is a game. We play our part in the theater of life, playing for fun or playing to win. The universe and everything in it is alive and aware that it is alive. There is passion, humor, and vast intelligence. Every part of this living universe is connected to every other part. All is in constant change, and nothing stays the same. This world we live in is our mutual dream, the dream we share with all of life. This is the I Ching *view.*

Roderic and Amy

Row, row, row your boat,
Gently down the stream,
Merrily, merrily, merrily, merrily,
Life is but a dream.

Popular song

alchemy: The medieval science of transformation; turning lead into gold was an analogy for conscious human spiritual evolution.

Baynes, Cary F.: He rendered Richard Wilhelm's translation of the *I Ching* into English (first published in 1950).

binary: A method of arithmetic using the number two as its base; the *I Ching* and computer logic both use binary arithmetic.

Bio-Ching: A combination of an individual's biorhythms and daily advice from the *I Ching*. Every combination of the three biorhythms has a corresponding hexagram; this enables you to know what hexagram is active for you on any particular day, along with the level of your biorhythmic energies.

biorhythm: *Bio* means life. The rhythmic flow of life energies in the body. The three major biorhythms are the twenty-three-day physical energy cycle, the twenty-eight-day emotional energy cycle, and the thirty-three-day intellectual energy cycle.

Bouvet, Father Joachim: Jesuit missionary in seventeenth-century China who wrote to Leibniz about the *I Ching*; this was the first introduction of the *I Ching* to the West.

Buddha: "Enlightened One"—a name given to those who realize the enlightened mind—usually refers to Siddartha Gautama Sakyamuni (ca. 563–ca. 483 B.C.).

Changes, Book of: The English name for the *I Ching*.

Confucius, or K'ung Fu Tzu (551–479 B.C.): Chinese philosopher and statesman. He retired to his native state of Lu at the age of seventy and spent his time writing commentaries on the classics, including the *I Ching*. He said that if he had another fifty years of life, he would spend it studying the

I Ching. As it was, he wore out three copies.

dharma: Sanskrit for "the truth"; also refers to the teachings of the Buddha.

divination: From the Latin *divus,* from which we get the words "divine" and "divinity." Originally, this was the act of calling on the gods and spirits for help. Today, it denotes paranormal perception, using the synchronistic throw of coins, as in the *I Ching,* or using cards, as in the Tarot.

Einstein, Albert (1879–1955): Mathematical physicist and philosopher, famous for the theory of relativity, his revolutionary theory of the nature of space and time.

Fu Hsi (2953–2838 B.C.): First emperor of the Legendary Period of Chinese history. With his wife Nu Kua, invented knot writing, agriculture, established social relations, and formulated the eight trigrams, the foundation of the *I Ching.*

genetic code: The DNA pattern on which all life-forms are based. The sixty-four nucleotide triplet codons (the "alphabet" of the genetic code) correspond to the sixty-four hexagrams of the *I Ching.*

hexagram: One of the sixty-four "changes" or readings in the *I Ching;* a diagram formed of six yin or yang lines.

I Ching: A Chinese book of divination and wisdom, probably the oldest such book in the world. *I* or *Yi* means, variously, "the changes"; "the chameleon," which changes the color of its skin according to the environment; "the sun and moon," showing the changes between day and night; or "the simple and easy." *Ching* means "book" or "classic."

Jung, Carl Gustav (1875–1961): Swiss philosopher and psychologist. A friend of Richard Wilhelm, he wrote the introduction to his translation of the *I Ching* and coined the word "synchronicity."

karma: Unfinished business from the past returning to be completed. As you sow, so shall you reap. What goes around comes around. Destiny or fate.

lama: A spiritual teacher in the Tibetan Buddhist lineage.

Leibniz, Gottfried Wilhelm von (1646–1716): Mathematician and philosopher, the inventor of binary arithmetic now used in computer technology. He came to know of the *I Ching* through Father Joachim Bouvet.

lines: The individual parts of a trigram or hexagram and the meaning connected with each of them. A line can be a yin line (broken) or a yang line (solid). The six lines in the hexagram are numbered from the bottom up, as in the floors of a building.

moving line: A moving line is one in which the energy is in the process of changing from yin to yang or from yang to yin. In a reading the moving line is the one to pay the most attention to, as it indicates your position in the situation.

synchronicity: A word coined by psychologist C. G. Jung meaning "together in time," from *syn,* meaning "together," and *chronos,* meaning "time." According to Jung, "Synchronicity takes the co-incidence of events in space and time as meaning something more than mere chance, namely, a peculiar interdependence of objective events among themselves as well as with the subjective (psychic) states of the observer or observers."

Ta Chuan: The Great Treatise; commentary on the *I Ching* attributed to Confucius.

T'ai chi ch'uan: Chinese art of rhythmic movement; it is valued as a meditation, a healing practice, and a martial art.

Tai Situ Pa, Rinpoche: The current spiritual leader of one of the four major sects of Tibetan Buddhism.

tantra: The esoteric or secret teachings of Hinduism and Buddhism.

Tao: Literally, the way, gateway, or path; the undifferentiated wholeness that lies behind all things;

the art of living in harmony with life.

three-coin method of divination: More recent than the yarrow stalk method, it came into use about a thousand years ago; it is more complicated than the method described in this book. Though most English translations of the *I Ching* describe the three-coin method, present-day Asian fortunetellers consider it cumbersome.

trigram: A diagram made up of three (*tri*) yin or yang lines. The Eight Trigrams of the *I Ching* can be combined to form the Sixty-Four Hexagrams. In the three lines of a trigram, the lines are called the lower, middle, and upper lines.

Wen, King (1171–1122 B.C.): Imprisoned by Emperor Jou the Terrible in 1132 B.C. for seven years for the crime of criticizing the emperor with a sigh. While in prison Wen was inspired to stack the Eight Trigrams on top of each other to form the Sixty-Four Hexagrams. In a vision he saw the names of the hexagrams and the text that went with them.

Wilhelm, Richard (1873–1930): A philosopher, scholar, and missionary who spent much of his life in China. In 1913, with the aid of Lao Nai-hsuan, a scholar of considerable repute, he began a translation of the *I Ching* into German.

His translation was rendered into English by Cary F. Baynes and published in 1950. He was a close friend of C. G. Jung.

yarrow stalk method of divination: The yarrow stalk method is the oldest way to consult the *I Ching*. It is no longer in current use in Asia, being too lengthy and convoluted. Simpler systems, similar to the one described in this book, are used for everyday questions.

yin and yang: The two primordial qualities. Yin represents the tendency to be relaxed, open, and inflowing; the chaotic aspect of the universe. In readings it is shown as a broken line. Yang represents the tendency to be firm, decisive, and outflowing; the orderly aspect of the universe. In readings it is shown as a solid line.

Zhou, Duke (d. 1094 B.C.): Also known as Tan, Duke of Chou, he was the son of King Wen, later to become King Wu the Valiant. The text that accompanies the lines of the hexagrams in the *I Ching* is attributed to him.

The following books investigate (among other things) the role of synchronicity in the fields of physics and the mind:

Bohm, David. *Wholeness and the Implicate Order.* London: RKP, 1981.

Bohm, David, and F. David Peat. *Science, Order, and Creativity.* New York: Bantam, 1987.

Capra, Fritjof. *The Tao of Physics.* Glasgow: HarperCollins, 1992.

Combs, Allan, and Mark Holland. *Synchronicity, Science, Myth and the Trickster.* New York: Paragon, 1990.

Jung, C. G. *Synchronicity.* Princeton University Press, 1973.

Peat, F. David. *Synchronicity: The Bridge Between Matter and Mind.* New York: Bantam, 1988.

Zukav, Gary. *The Dancing Wu-Li Masters.* New York: Bantam, 1979.

The following books are a constant inspiration to us. These authors play a continuing part in our development:

Aitken, Robert. *Taking the Path of Zen.* San Francisco: North Point Press, 1982.

Collin, Rodney. *The Theory of Celestial Influence.* London: Vincent Stuart, 1958.

Dhargyey, Geshey Ngawang. *Tibetan Tradition of Mental Development.* Dharmasala: Library of Tibetan Works and Archives, 1978.

His Holiness, the Fourteenth Dalai Lama. *Freedom in Exile: The Autobiography of The Dalai Lama.* New York: HarperCollins, 1990.

Hubbard, L. Ron. *The Creation of Human Ability.* Edinburgh: Hubbard College of Scientology, 1967.

McKenna, Terence, and Dennis McKenna. *The Invisible Landscape: Mind Hallucinogens and the I Ching.*

San Francisco: HarperCollins, 1994.

Ornstein, Robert. *The Evolution of Consciousness.* New York: Prentice Hall, 1991.

Sheldrake, Rupert. *The Rebirth of Nature: The Greening of Science and God.* New York: Random Century, 1990.

Tai Situ Pa, Khentin. *Way To Go.* Eskdalemuir: K.D.D.L., n.d.

Talbot, Michael. *The Holographic Universe.* New York: HarperCollins, 1992.

Wilson, Robert Anton. *Quantum Psychology.* Phoenix: New Falcon Publications, 1990.

The following books explore biorhythms:

Gittelson, Bernard. *Bio-Rhythm.* New York: Warner, 1988.

Thommen, George S. *Is This Your Day?* New York: Crown, 1973.

These are some of our favorite books on the I Ching:

Blofeld, John, trans. *I Ching: The Book of Change.* New York: Dutton, 1968.

Cleary, Thomas, trans. *The Buddhist I Ching.* Boston: Shambhala, 1987.

Cleary, Thomas, trans. *The Taoist I Ching.* Boston: Shambhala, 1986.

Green, Jim, trans. and interpreter. *The Chou I.* Makawao: Private publication, n.d.

Lee, Jung Young. *The I Ching and Modern Man.* Secaucus, NJ: University Books, 1975.

Palmer, Martin, Kwok Man Ho, and Joanne O'Brien. *The Fortune Teller's I Ching.* New York: Ballantine, 1986.

Reifler, Sam. *I Ching.* New York: Bantam, 1974.

Schonberger, Martin. *The I Ching and the Genetic Code.* New York: ASI Publishers, 1979.

Siu, R. G. H. *The Portable Dragon.* Cambridge, MA: M.I.T. Press, 1968.

Sung, Z. D. *The Symbols of the Yi King.* New York: Paragon Book Reprint Corp., 1969.

Walker, Barbara G. *The I Ching of the Goddess.* New York: Harper & Row, 1986.

Whincup, Greg, trans. *Rediscovering the I Ching.* New York: Doubleday, 1986.

Wilhelm, Richard. *Lectures on the I Ching.* Bollingen Series 19, 2. Princeton University Press, 1979.

Wilhelm, Richard, and Cary F. Baynes, trans. *The I Ching.* Princeton University Press, 1950.

Wing, R. L., trans. *The I Ching Workbook.* New York: Doubleday, 1979.

Yan, Johnson F. *DNA and the I Ching.* Berkeley: North Atlantic Books, 1991.